THE STATE OF THE PRESIDENCY

THOMAS E. CRONIN

THE STATE
OF THE
PRESIDENCY

LITTLE, BROWN AND COMPANY

BOSTON   TORONTO

CONTENTS

1 The Presidential Condition   1

2 The Cult of the Presidency: A Halo for the Chief   23

3 Prerogatives: Discretion with Constraints   53

4 The Braking of the Presidency   85

5 The Swelling of the Presidency   117

6 Palace Guard Government: Patterns of White House —
Departmental Relations   153

7 The Cabinet in Presidential Government   177

8 The Vice Presidency in Presidential Government   211

9 The Shaping of the Presidency: The Presidential
Job Description — A $200,000. G.S. 118?   237

10 Making the President an Effective Executive:
Separating Possibilities from Panaceas   261

11 Making the Presidency Safe for Democracy   289

Appendix: Selected Information on the Presidency   325

Selected Bibliography   337

Acknowledgments   343

About the Author   345

Index   347

THE STATE OF THE PRESIDENCY

CHAPTER 1

THE PRESIDENTIAL CONDITION

The institution of the American presidency is now the center of great controversy and debate. It has served us well during most of our nearly two hundred years. But the excesses and abuses of presidential power in recent years have aroused an understandable anger in the American people. Even some of our leading candidates for the presidency wonder aloud whether the institution is viable, whether integrity can be sustained by its occupants, and whether as a society we might not have fashioned an institution that tempts its incumbents to abuse the public trust. We run the risk of a confused and increasingly cynical public, disturbed with politics in general, seizing on the arrogance and extravagance of recent presidencies and condemning not only the abuses but also much that is essential in the presidency. We are in danger of a public that seeks retribution against the institution of the presidency.

We need to understand how the presidency works rather than to punish the institution for the acts of a few individuals who temporarily abused its powers. We need to understand especially that vicious cycle of overpromising, underdelivering, and the resulting public disaffection or self-destructive attitude that in turn weakens the legitimacy that alone can permit individuals in a democracy to provide leadership. Our analysis here can only be a beginning, a sorting out of conditions and problems, a tentative perspective in which to place the complexities of democratic presidential leadership. The intent is to demythologize the American presidency for the reader and to help him or her gain a more rigorous appreciation of its promise, performance, and limitations. I trust, too, that we will better appreciate why America so often of late has failed to receive the kind of presidential leadership that so many believe we critically need.

Two questions guided the writing of this book: How can the presidency become a more effective executive and political institution? How can the presidency be made safe for democracy (i.e., more open, more accountable)? A prime paradox of the modern presidency is that it is always too strong, always too weak. A president will always have too much power for the realization of that cherished ideal — government by the people — yet never enough to solve all the problems we expect him to solve. What enhances one president's power to serve the general interest also enhances the capability of an irresponsible president to abuse vast power. Yet too many restrictions can make the presidency unmanageable, and the unmanageability of the office may well contribute to irresponsibility and unaccountability.

We know now that what is good for the presidency is not always good for the nation. A bigger and bigger presidency is not necessarily a better one. A strong presidency is not one that concentrates power in a highly centralized, highly shielded White House. We know too that isolation, secrecy, and resort to surprise weaken rather than strengthen presidential leadership. Sadly, we have learned as well that the office which was long thought only to ennoble the occupant can also be a source of distortion and deception.

The presidency is an underdefined institution. We have never been wholly clear about what we expected of it. The Constitution is vague on the matter. And the public mood toward the office is often ambivalent and fluctuates. There is a need now, perhaps more than ever in the past, to probe exactly what responsibilities must be lodged there, what the presidency can do well, and what could be assigned elsewhere. Is it possible to have a strong and effective presidency that is also leaner, more open, and more democratic than it is presently? What kinds of hierarchical leadership do we need? How much of the needed leadership in the nation should we expect solely from a president? What are the capabilities of the presidency as a planning and executive institution? How can the responsibilities of the presidency be shared more effectively with the cabinet, the vice-presidency, or with responsible and accountable executive office officials?

There is, of course, no foolproof institutional change that would assure presidential accountability. Many of the structural reforms suggested in the wake of Vietnam and Watergate would not have prevented our presidents from escalating that war, or the Watergate affair, the Ellsberg break-in, or the Nixon coverup. And those which would have limited their ability to abuse presidential powers would also have impeded a better person in the proper use of it. Plainly, we need an effective presidency, capable of swift and informed action in case of emergency. We need a president who has the political skills and character to enlist the energies and allegiance of the Congress, the bureaucracy, his party, and the nation not only to see that the laws of the nation are faithfully executed but also to encourage the tremendous forces for good at large in the country. National security and international economic requirements all move in the direction of increasing presidential responsibilities. Congressional regeneration is clearly needed; but no one, not even the most partisan congressionalist, entertains the notion of a return to congressional government. In short, there is little likelihood of lessening the burdens on the presidency.

I believe it is exceedingly important, then, to reassess the purposes, the powers, and the recent performance of the American presidency. What was it intended to do? What do we now expect it to do? What can be done to insure a more effective performance and at the same time to enhance its character as an accountable, responsible, democratic institution? To make the presidency safe for democracy is neither an idle nor a flippant idea. The physical and psychological swelling of the presidency has recast it so that some people think the presidency is inconsistent with cherished democratic ideals. Yet the swelling of the presidential role in national affairs is by no means the same thing as effective leadership. The task of fashioning a presidency that is simultaneously better equipped to lead and closer to the American people must be at the top of the nation's agenda.

A president of the United States is expected to perform three overriding functions: to provide symbolic affirmation of the nation's basic values and aspirations, to recast the nation's policies in line with contemporary needs, and to galvanize the vast machinery of government to carry out his programs and those he has inherited. The slippage or gap between the second and third of these functions and the reasons for it are prime concerns throughout this book.

The 1960s and early 1970s showed repeatedly that good intentions, high-minded promises, and a passion for action don't solve problems. Our recent presidents, John F. Kennedy, Lyndon B. Johnson, and Richard M. Nixon, have all been activist, power-maximizing, and relatively strong incumbents. Gerald Ford's presidency is more difficult to assess at the time of this writing, but most indications suggest that his, too, will lean in this direction. Under the banners of the New Frontier, the Great Society, the New American Revolution, and WIN, these presidents pledged major innovations and social change. Each also generated, however, a grievously large gap between promise and performance. Despite a rash of legislation passed and considerable sums of money spent, the resulting national programs nearly always were inadequate. Presidentially proclaimed wars on inflation, poverty, crime, urban decay, pollution, hunger, cancer, and fuel shortages have had little more than marginal impact.

Why do such substantial disparities develop between expectation and result, especially when so many people view the institution of the presidency as a supremely powerful — sometimes too powerful — instrument for national leadership? Hasn't presidential authority dropped atomic bombs, sent men to the moon, and committed troops to all corners of the world? Haven't White House staffs and advisory networks grown in size and in professional expertise? Haven't presidential powers expanded greatly at the expense of Congress? Who can rival the president's publicity? Who else possesses such an arsenal of authority, resources, and prerogatives with which to fashion a significantly different and better kind of country? Yet, despite all the experts and resources presidents supposedly command, they are unable to accomplish a reasonable proportion of what they promise or even of what they try hard to do.

Our society expects that newly inaugurated presidents should be able to effect most, if not all, of their top-priority intentions, whether through legislation, executive decree, persuasion, appointment, or other forms of presidential leadership. Presidents should be able, at the very least, to see that the laws of the land are faithfully executed, that federal programs bring about changes or preserve the status quo, as intended. Yet the record of the recent past has been disillusioning. Confidence in the credibility of national leaders has been dramatically diminished. Americans are growing callously accustomed to presidential promises that go unfulfilled. The annual unveilings of a president's legislative priorities and programs now have much in common with the Madison Avenue broadsides that advertise each year's "spectacular" new line of automobiles. Perceptive citizens are increasingly sensitive to the performance of both.

Assessing the role of the presidency without reference to the whole of the American governmental system is hazardous. The presidency, on the one hand so centralized and highly personal, is also hydra-headed: it is a center of ever-accumulating roles and obligations, functions, and expectations. Its institutional job description is being rewritten constantly. The office changes from incumbent to incumbent and undergoes substantial alteration even as a single president passes through successive political seasons. As Woodrow Wilson noted, it is much easier to write about a president than to write about the presidency.

Nonetheless, the central concern of this analysis is the manner in which recent presidents have tried to fulfill the responsibilities of national policy leadership, especially in domestic areas. *Public policy* can be thought of as proposed or adopted courses of action; *leadership,* as the capacity to effect desired changes that otherwise would not have occurred. For this analysis, *policy implementation leadership* represents conscious attempts by a president to bring program performance in line with enunciated goals.

To estimate the effectiveness of presidential leadership, an understanding of the factors — both real and imagined — which impede a president's influence over the formulation and implementation of public policy is crucial. Presidential capacity to make the country a significantly better place, from whatever point of view, is more constrained than is generally appreciated. Also, the familiar characterization of the presidency as embodying the broadest public interest should be qualified. Can presidential leadership really be assessed apart from the biases of the observer, or does our opinion of his leadership depend on whether we happen to like the incumbent and what he is trying to accomplish?

Although a president can precipitate the nuclear destruction of a substantial portion of the world, presidential influence over domestic program implementation is relatively fragile. A president is seldom a free agent in his own country. It is misleading to infer from his capacity to command nuclear weapons that he is also vastly powerful in effecting sustained innovations in domestic policy. As one recent president commented on his frustrations in achieving domestic progress: "Power? The only power I've got is nuclear . . . and I can't use that." [1]

A refined and systematic picture is needed of how the presidency operates, of what it can and cannot do, and of the constraints that shape its usual performance. To recognize that we have exaggerated expectations on the office would itself be a significant step forward. But we should, at the same time, attempt a positive reinterpretation of the role of the presidency in contemporary society. The view that presidential governance consists primarily of a confrontation between the character of a president and that of a national problem is a fallacy that grossly overemphasizes presidential personality and style. Seldom is the presidential personality considered in the context of the day-to-day administrative realities of the executive branch; seldom are presidential decisions held under a microscope to sort out the diverse elements of necessity, drift, and miscalculation.

If individual presidents had devoted more time to domestic programs and their implementation, would the great domestic wars have been won? Or is the presidency inherently incapable of providing leadership for changing the behavior of people and institutions? Reappraisals and revisionism are clearly needed. But overreaction to the events of the past ten years or so just as clearly needs to be avoided. It would be unfortunate if a new and skeptical orthodoxy, overgeneralizing about presidential irrelevance and impotence were to replace the old, indulgent, and worshipful orthodoxy that overgeneralized about presidential wisdom and competence.

PRESIDENTIAL PARADOXES

The presidency has existed under a crisis of definition since the end of the nineteenth century when the nation's unification, industrialization, and emergence as an international power indicated to Woodrow Wilson and to like-minded progressives that the nation had changed markedly, but its government had not. Numerous experiments and ad hoc reforms since then have generally effected a strengthened, or at least enlarged, presidential establishment. With the advent of television, nuclear weapons, and an expanded federal role in domestic affairs, the presidency has become, for better or worse, a preeminent focal point for change. But seldom have the consequences of the growing and changing presidency been understood.

As the institution of the presidency has become the center of controversy, some have wanted to curtail its functions and authority because they think the presidency has too much power. Others no longer trust the presidency on a variety of specific issues such as war-making or tax reform. Still others want to tie a president's hands for personal reasons or for the benefit of special interests.

Historically, of course, conservatives have been more averse to increasing presidential power than liberals. Still, conservatives have occasionally wanted to strengthen the president's hand, for instance, in order to subsidize certain industries, strengthen the nation's military posture, promote tougher criminal sanctions, or curb the influence of "the liberal media." Liberals have generally applauded a strong presidency when it has been in the hands of a Roosevelt, Truman, or Kennedy and when regulatory or redistributive social goals were sought. Overall, however, it does seem clear that in much of the debate over the proper limits of presidential power, attitudes are shaped pretty much by which party is at the moment in control of the White House.

Watergate and Nixon's subsequent forced resignation served to unite Americans of disparate ideologies. The view took hold that the checks were not checking and the balances were not balancing. The rule of self-restraint had been badly shattered, perhaps by all branches, but especially by the presidency during the late 1960s and early 1970s. The concentration of information, government by secrecy, and war-making without consultation, and the extensive use of executive privilege, executive agreements, impoundment, reprogramming, and wiretapping angered Congress and upset a substantial portion of the public. Lies, enemy lists, and egregious violation of the rights of privacy and of the judicial process outraged Americans. What was right too often became subordinated to what would look good, as a public relations imperative seized and seemed to bewitch White House occupants.

The presidency is unusually subject to paradoxes and dilemmas. The Constitution and subsequent enlargements of the office have assigned to it so many ill-defined roles that it is impossible to achieve any single or comprehensive definition of presidential powers, duties, and obligations. But, whatever the definition, voters want results — and soon. Too often the general public expects that results can be achieved merely because a president says something; it rarely differentiates between what the president can do as chief executive of domestic programs and as commander-in-chief of a nuclear-powered military service of some 2.3 million personnel. Even General Alexander Haig, Nixon's last White House chief of staff, apparently forgot the difference when he passed on orders to top justice department officers to fire Archibald Cox, the special Watergate prosecutor, in October of 1973. Haig's now-famous exhortation went, in effect, like this: "This is an order from your commander-in-chief." The ability to control a single act of the government is a vastly different phenomenon from the ability to control its total direction.

The American public wants both accountable leadership and excellent performance — a "profile in courage" — which can come about only when a president is independent of conventional thinking. A president is asked to represent the unrepresented and the under-represented, yet he is expected to be responsive to the electoral majority. And no doubt the plutocrats who bankroll candidates with tens of millions of dollars per campaign have still other expectations. Thus, both consensus leadership *and* innovative leadership are sought. When a president does not follow the majority's sentiment, that majority is incensed; but when he goes along with majority sentiment, the minority that disagrees feels that he lacks courage and moral leadership and that he is an unprincipled politician to boot.

Americans want a common man in the White House, yet they also want uncommon leadership. The latter involves talents of a gifted organizer, an expert practitioner of coalition politics, a sophisticated user of expert advisers, and someone who can inspire. Initially Gerald Ford was welcomed as a representative person, even as a common man, at least relative to the more formal, distant, and sometimes arrogant Johnson and Nixon. As dismay and disapproval of Ford's performance in office grew, people readily said that the president was not quite fit for the job, that the office required a more gifted intellect and a better decision-maker. Ford was criticised for his inability to galvanize the confidence of the nation and to raise our hopes. For one of the chief virtues of our more talented leaders — an instinctive tendency to raise people's hopes — turns out to be one of their chief liabilities later on in office. On the surface this ability is an essential ingredient of societal leadership, but the elevation of hopes beyond what is attainable in the short run can lead to severe frustrations. Cynical disillusionment sometimes builds up in those who do not fully appreciate the obstacles to creative leadership, or who have plainly been misled and lied to. We want a president who serves as a custodian of past traditions and certain ritual principles, yet is an innovator, a creative catalyst for change, and even a prime inventor of our dreams for the future.

Today the presidency as an institution defies our inherent societal apprehension of concentration of power. Our political system was founded and designed to diffuse power. But the events of the past fifty years have created a swollen presidential establishment and an irreversible expansion of presidential emergency powers. Nuclear weapons and the possibility of our instant involvement in a nuclear war provide little alternative for the realization of divided power, properly checked and balanced. This is one of the most thorny of presidential paradoxes. For nearly every American recognizes the unavoidable necessity for a strong chief executive ever capable of swift and devastating retaliatory nuclear resources. Yet the more concentrated executive power becomes, the greater will be the temptation on some future occasion to employ it to weaken, if not wipe out, opposing power centers. A president could plunge the nation into war, suspend civil liberties, and take other autocratic actions — all on the pretext of protecting the people. People of all political persuasions, even while they prize a strong, effective presidency, fear its potential for too much focused power and for dictatorship. The impact of these contradictions is difficult to weigh. Doubtless, however, they add to a gnawing unease and deep-seated public ambivalence toward the office and the occupants.

Another of the ironies of the presidential condition is that we yearn for a president who is above politics, who eschews playing politics with an issue. But a president *must* be a politician and the presidency is quite rightly a highly political office. To define a politician as a schemer and an intriguer, a person who primarily seeks office for personal gain, is only one of several possible interpretations. But, more objectively, a politician can and ought to be thought of as a person capable of making the desirable and difficult possible. And, in America, at least, we insist too that he employs democratic means and operates within the Constitution.

There are dishonest people in politics, as in all professions, but too often forgotten is the existence of clean politics — the skillful art of compromise, negotiation, and mediation — and that this is the only way democratic leadership can work. Thus, a president, although he may look more "presidential" when he hovers above the bargaining and pushing and hauling of the political process, abdicates that process to those who would use it as they like and removes himself from the business of America. Our effective presidents have recognized the need for dissent and for personally entering into political controversy. The president who insists on consensus and chooses to stand aloof above the political battles of the day isolates himself from contact with reality. He becomes a ceremonial leader and a poll-taker rather than a decision-making political executive. In effect, he abdicates. We can no more take the politics out of the presidency, as purists would like, than we can take the presidency out of politics.

Although the public prizes boldness and initiative, a shrewd president must avoid trouble and understand what a nation cannot do. If he fails to take decisive action, he is called weak, passive, or worse; if he acts too decisively, he is called unconstitutional and dictatorial. And perhaps the greatest dilemma for a president is that he is asked to use power continuously, even though by doing so he will usually lose popular support and prestige. He is asked to do something, preferably something miraculous, even in excruciating situations when no one can win, no one can be satisfied, and even when there is little he can do except to manipulate statistics. Ironically, such problems as crime in the streets, international fuel shortages, or cancer, which are nearly unresolvable by presidential leadership, have evoked outlandish promises quite out of proportion to presidential ability to effect solutions.

At the heart of these conflicting demands stands the ever-present dilemma that a search for a president is always a search for both a democratic political leader and a talented chief executive. Both roles and both activities are esteemed, though not necessarily at the same time, and the one tends to negate the other — if not in the process of recruiting the candidates, then in the incentives affecting behavior in office. Gifted executives seldom become candidates for the presidency, and those rare presidents who were talented executives often were ill-equipped to handle the representative and political dimensions of leadership. Politicians, on the other hand, seem to be systematically trained to ignore administrative implications. Their incentives subordinate managerial and bureaucratic activities to symbolic or priority-setting ones.

Both the public and presidents cherish the presidency as a locus for symbolic, unifying friendship. In lieu of a national church or a royal family, the White House at times serves as a national shrine. A president is expected to generate hope, confidence, and a sense of national purpose: to "bring us together," to "let us reason together," to remind the people of past greatness and future glories, or to "bring America home again." Even when they do not know precisely what to do, presidents must act as moral leaders or teachers, provide assurance and inspiration to the people, and summon society to ever higher achievement. In this role of political folk hero, a president sustains the people's sense of direction and reaffirms the nation's credibility and legitimacy. One former White House adviser put it this way: a presidency preoccupied with program management and monitoring would be a presidency lacking "the fluidity and the crisis orientation and the flexibility that is important. . . . It is more important to symbolize solutions than it is to achieve them in operations. Getting legislation passed or getting a department to do things is never going to be as important as talking to the people through the media and providing symbolic leadership about new directions." [2]

The historian Bert Cochran offers, in a biography of President Truman, this apt commentary on the presidential condition:

The modern Presidency is not primarily a machine for self-expression. Caught in a swirl of conflicting tides, the President maneuvers and manipulates, grants concessions to this bloc or that bloc, to maintain a social equilibrium, working within the confines of basic laws, institutions, and dispensations. . . .

[A president] is part of an intricate governmental and extragovernmental machinery so that what he is and is not able to do is more dependent on circumstances, contingencies, and interactions than on personal exercises of will and assertions. To think, in these circumstances, that it's possible to say something meaningful about American history and national administrations by grading Presidents, like term papers, is to sink into scholastic fatuity. It is to mistake preference and caprice for analysis. It is to reduce history to a parlor game. It caters to the same craving for the banal that has led our modern Presidents to become pyramid builders in order to help along their passages to immortality.[3]

BECOMING PRESIDENT VERSUS BEING PRESIDENT.

An ability to get elected and even reelected is decidedly different from an ability to govern the nation. Some observers are convinced that what it takes to become president even unfits a person for the executive and administrative side of the job. That is to say, the qualifications for *political man* to win the highest office are quite unrelated to the qualifications of *executive man* needed to govern and to implement major policy changes in office.

The administrative challenge in the presidency is now of mammoth proportions. Even in peacetime the job includes enormous new obligations to oversee the responsiveness of the executive branch and to implement programs. Talented departmental leaders must be recruited. Delegation must be precise, communications instructive and understandable. Who else can better motivate, educate, and inspire federal officials to higher levels of public commitment?

Who else can authoritatively mediate interdepartmental squabbles and tame those bureaucrats who see themselves as the chief constituency of their own departments? Who else is to preside over the critical following-up of programs and to insure that it is done energetically? All this and more is expected of the modern presidency. Robert F. Kennedy wrote about his brother's new insight into these obligations at the time of the Cuban missile crisis in 1962: "The President believed he was President and that, his wishes having been made clear, they would be followed and the missiles removed. He therefore dismissed the matter from his mind. Now he learned that his failure to follow up on this matter had permitted the same obsolete Turkish missiles to become hostages of the Soviet Union." [4]

A president today must preside as well over a highly specialized and swollen bureaucracy of his own, a presidential establishment that comprises dozens of support staffs and advisory councils within the executive office of the president and numbers its staff in the thousands. Moreover, a president must understand complex organizational systems and know how to operate effectively with and through numerous bureaucracies at all levels of government. Further, as Irving Kristol has noted, the independence of the bureaucracy from the White House is likely to be even greater in the near future in part as a result of Watergate:

If power flows to Washington — as it has for more than 50 years now — there are only two places it can comfortably flow to: the presidency and the federal bureaucracy. Indeed, our last three presidents have been openly engaged in a struggle for power, not with Congress, but with the bureaucracy. And one consequence of Watergate, already visible, will be to strengthen the bureaucracy at the expense of the White House. The "independence" of the regulatory agencies, and even of cabinet departments, from "interference" by the White House has suddenly become a sign, not of bureaucratic intransigence, but of political morality at its best.[5]

Meanwhile, management consultants urge that (1) there should be no central operating staff in the White House, (2) the president needs strength and ambition in his departmental administrators, and (3) he must work hard to get fresh thinking but recognize that anyone providing fresh ideas is, almost by definition, critical of the accepted wisdom and will therefore seem obviously disloyal.[6]

Such responsibilities require talents that few recent presidents have brought to the job. In fact, the presidential recruitment process makes good and experienced administrators virtually ineligible. Aside from the vice-presidency, the U. S. Senate has become the major on-deck circle for the presidency. At one point in 1971, 10 percent of the Senate members were candidates for the Democratic nomination in 1972, and the same pattern seems to be holding for the 1976 race. Since Franklin Roosevelt's time, the two major parties have nominated for president one general, two governors, four incumbent or former vice-presidents, and seven former or incumbent U. S. senators. Some observers contend that the vice-presidency is preparation for nothing at all and that being a U. S. senator often isn't much better.

Senators, more easily than governors, gain exposure to national security issues, especially if they are members of one of the several foreign relations or military affairs committees. They can travel abroad more easily than governors, and they gain national exposure from the Washington press corps. They can prepare themselves as specialists on world affairs and minimize their role in sticky problems within their states. In addition, they are seldom held accountable to the public for program failures. Governors, on the other hand, must often raise taxes or preside over controversial battles on welfare, education, or medical expenditures, take the blame for prison riots and how they are put down, and even inform the population that public services face budget reductions. These are not the kinds of actions upon which recent national careers and presidential campaigns have been easily launched. Yet governors, particularly from the large heterogeneous states, doubtless gain the best first-hand apprenticeship as domestic-policy executives.

The style and talents required for senatorial self-advancement and presidential leadership differ markedly. Senators have small staffs, few managerial challenges, little or no opportunity to have individuals of independent stature, or cabinet caliber, working for them. Yet one of the most sensitive aspects of presidential leadership is to strengthen the hand of cabinet officials and at the same time insure that they remain presidential agents. Most senators have had no first-hand experience with administrative leadership, and many of those who have become president have had little interest in bureaucratic administration. Ironically, standard practice in many other countries and in most well-run corporations requires that no one assume the top executive office without having proved throughout his or her career that he or she is capable of administering large departments and major new undertakings.

The modern president cannot manage the whole of government from the White House. He cannot personally oversee all of the routine administrative activities any more than can a corporation president, prime minister, or a pope. Thus the task is to organize monitoring and implementation operations so that they run on behalf of the president, yet without consuming too much of his personal time and energy.

COMPETING AREAS OF NATIONAL POLICY

Several incentives converge to induce a president to concentrate on foreign policy at the expense of domestic policy. With increasing frequency domestic policy has taken a subordinate place to aggregate economic policy as well. President Kennedy, for example, let it be known that he wanted *above all else* to be remembered as a president who not only prevented war but also won the peace. He wanted history to record that he laid the foundations for peace not only in his time but also for generations to come. Although foreign policy responsibilities have been preeminent historically, contemporary presidents have even less choice than many of their predecessors. Foreign policy and national security responsibilities, especially in the nuclear age, cannot be delegated; they are ultimately executive in character and presidential by constitutional tradition or interpretation. Kennedy was fond of saying that the difference between domestic and foreign policy was that between a bill being defeated and the country being wiped out. But aides report that Kennedy became far more engulfed by foreign policy matters than even he liked. After just ten days in the White House, he talked as though he were nearly overwhelmed by the flood of international crises facing the United States:

No man entering upon this office, regardless of his party, regardless of his previous service in Washington, could fail to be staggered upon learning — even in this brief ten-day period — the harsh enormity of the trials through which we must pass in the next four years. Each day the crises multiply. Each day their solutions grow more difficult. Each day we draw nearer the hour of maximum danger, as weapons spread and hostile forces grow stronger. I feel I must inform the Congress that our analyses over the last ten days make it clear that — in each of the principal areas of crisis — the tide of events has been running out and time has not been our friend.[7]

Former White House advisers from each of the three most recent administrations agree that a president spends from one-half to two-thirds of his time on foreign policy or national security deliberations. In some instances this emphasis on foreign policy and national security has occurred by choice, most notably for President Nixon, who said, "I've always thought this country could run itself domestically — without a President; all you need is a competent Cabinet to run the country at home. You need a President for foreign policy; no Secretary of State is really important; the President makes foreign policy." [8] President Johnson, on the other hand, although strongly disposed by his experience toward domestic programs, was unable to prevent his presidency from being consumed by military affairs. And President Ford found out, albeit gradually, that many if not most of our economic troubles were inexorably related to world-wide economic problems.

Presidents devote substantially more of their State of the Union addresses to national security matters than to any other topic. Through a detailed quantitative analysis of these addresses, one scholar found that "this policy is clearly the prime presidential concern ... [and] that greater attention to international affairs results from the experience of being president. Attention to this policy area grows over time ... in a pattern that can be related to the election cycle." Special focus on national security matters "mounts during the first, second and third years, then drops as a president faces re-election. During a president's second term, concern with international involvement grows again . . . substantially higher [in fact] than . . . during the first term." [9] Other scholars persuasively attribute this accentuated attention to more formal presidential powers in the national security area, better sources of information, and the weakness of Congress in this sphere.

In addition, well-organized interest groups are less likely to differ with presidential intentions in foreign policy matters, and vice versa: most special interests want the nation well protected and want to stop the spread of communism and make the world safe for American trade and travel. Former Nixon counsel Leonard Garment pointed to yet another reason when he explained Nixon's preference for foreign policy in this way to Theodore White: "In foreign policy, you get drama, triumph, resolution — crisis and resolution so that in foreign policy Nixon can give the sense of leadership. But in domestic policy, there you have to deal with the whole jungle of human problems." [10]

In any case, it is vastly more "presidential" to be concerned with national security and world peace than with domestic problems. One notion holds that where a president should be involved is where he can make global and dramatic choices. International travels and summit meetings with foreign leaders generate favorable publicity and confer stature on an incumbent, whereas at home he may be criticized as just another time-serving politician. International to-ings and fro-ings are intertwined, of course, with domestic politics; they may even be undertaken to attract news coverage away from unsuccessful or embarrassing domestic initiatives. At home a president may be hamstrung by an opposition-dominated Congress, by a narrow electoral margin, by a hostile press, or by a scandal in his administration; but twelve miles off shore a president virtually is the United States, and few people qualify their loyalty under such circumstances. The purpose of many presidential trips is largely symbolic, but the American people are tolerantly disposed. When the president uses the powers of his office to bring about better chances for peace, it is hard to resent his powers even if he does not succeed. And the president will be rewarded in the opinion polls for trying. Nixon used this strategy, but certainly challenged its acceptable limits, when he claimed, implicitly if not explicitly, that the invasion of Cambodia, secret bombings in Indochina, and the Ellsberg break-in were all necessary for national security reasons — all contributing to the orderly building of a structure of lasting peace. And he got away with this argument — one must remember that it was his lies about tapes, taxes, and Watergate that soured the American people on him.

The second-largest portion of presidential policy time is spent on aggregate economic policy. "Aggregate economics" refers here to monetary and fiscal policy, trade and tariff policy, inflation, unemployment, the stability of the dollar, and the health of the stock market, as opposed to the more explicitly domestic concerns of education, ecology, health, housing, welfare, social justice, and the quality of life. From the beginning of the Nixon administration, the supremacy of economic over domestic policy was clear from the attention paid to it as well as in explicit pronouncements. Typical were the remarks of a presidential press secretary on the occasion of the establishment of the Council on Economic Policy: "Let me simply conclude by saying that President Nixon feels that, with the single exception of national security and defense, he has no higher obligation to the American people than that of providing the leadership to insure a healthy, prosperous economy." [11] Ford's economic summit conference of 1974 was additional evidence of the growing concern for aggregate economic policy.

A president can scarcely hide from the hard, visible quantitative economic indicators: unemployment rates, consumer price indexes, the Gross National Product, interest and mortgage rates, commodity prices, and stock market averages. These figures are available to everyone, and the American people increasingly judge their president on whether he can cope aggressively with recession and inflation, whether he can offer effective economic game plans (preferably without tax increases), and whether he can use the nation's budget as an instrument for insuring a healthy and growing economy.

Since the passage of the landmark Employment Act of 1946, the health and promise of the economy have been among the two or three major issues in presidential politics. The issues of tax reform and income redistribution, irritating and complex though they may be, are always on the agenda of national politics, and a president is held responsible for economic conditions during his term. But a president's statutory responsibilities for maintaining full employment and pursuing stabilization policies often are not matched by political resources or available expertise. In many areas of domestic policy consumers are relatively weak or unorganized, but an uneven performance by the economy will call down on a president immediate pressure from wealthy businessmen, unions, and farmers, and from their large delegations of friends in Congress. Moreover, when the economy enters a period like the 1974 recession-inflation (or "stagflation" as it is called by some), pressures from the voting public become large as well. When the crunch is on, workers want jobs, even if they must come at the expense of the environment. Bread-and-butter pocketbook issues nearly always are more salient to the working class than quality-of-life issues; the latter often are of more concern to the well-educated patrician class, or at least to a portion of it. All of this doubtless encourages or shapes presidential attention to issues and areas of concern.

The factor of measurement also adds to the incentives for preoccupation with international and economic concern. To judge whether an allied nation is being invaded, whether large-scale U. S. corporate interests abroad are being nationalized, or whether unemployment has increased significantly is easier than to discern whether the criminal justice system has been improved, whether civil liberties have been enhanced, or whether poor children are learning or eating better.

So presidents concentrate on those areas in which they feel they can make the greatest impact, in which the approval of interest groups and the public can be most easily rallied. Crises and emergencies are what presidents are for, whereas getting involved in domestic policy is costly both financially and politically. Moreover, a newly elected president soon finds, if he did not know already, that budgets are virtually fixed for the next year-and-a-half, and that in domestic matters he is dependent on Congress, specialized bureaucracies, professions, and state and local officialdom. Is it surprising, then, that the implementation of domestic policy has become the orphan of presidential attention? Is it possible that presidents rationalize that they must concern themselves with foreign and aggregate economic policy as they lose heart with the complicated, hard-to-affect, no-win, no-gain domestic problems?

Recent presidents have increasingly organized and differentiated their staffs and cabinets around these three functional policy areas — foreign, economic, and domestic — but such compartmentalization ignores relations fundamental to the health and security of the nation. What may be differentiated for organizational convenience cannot be completely separated when considering policy and political implications. An exclusively domestic, or foreign, problem is a rarity, and many issues intersect all three areas. Critical problems such as unemployment, inflation, trade, the fuel shortage crisis, drug abuse, or environmental problems — not to mention war — depend on policy integration and planning that cut across these divisions. In addition, the ability of the United States to assist in solving world problems derives in large measure from its ability to solve its own domestic and social problems. Time and again, however, specialized staffs set up in the presidential establishment treat new problems as if they were solely foreign or economic or domestic. A presidency that overspecializes and overcompartmentalizes its staff and its information-gathering apparatus will doubtless be a presidency unable to provide what should be the essential presidential contribution: the capacity to integrate, synthesize, and comprehend diverse policies and their costs, their liabilities, and their effects, not only singly but also in relation to one another.

ON DIRECTING THE DOMESTIC ESTABLISHMENT

Is the presidency strong enough to manage the vast domestic government? The president is surely a most visible national leader in a nation grown increasingly used to organizational hierarchies. Listening to presidents, however, a person begins to feel that their inability to direct the domestic establishment has become almost total. They all complain of frustration and a recurrent sense of powerlessness over domestic programs and labyrinthine departmental bureaucracies.

Kennedy, after two years in office, complained publicly that the nation's problems "are more difficult than I had imagined" and that "there are greater limitations upon our ability to bring about a favorable result than I had imagined." [12] He noted also that although numerous accounts described the allegedly extensive powers of the presidency, the limitations of that office were in his judgment generally underestimated. One of his White House aides put the frustration more bluntly: "Everybody believes in democracy until he gets to the White House and then you begin to believe in dictatorship because it's so hard to get things done. Every time you turn around, people just resist you, and even resist their own job." [13] The same John Kennedy who in many ways inspired the country was moved to quip about a relatively low-priority project, the architectural remodeling of Lafayette Square across from the White House, "Let's stay with it. Hell, this may be the only thing I'll ever really get done." [14]

President Johnson also expressed disappointment over seemingly slow and uncooperative departmental responses. He attempted to ride herd on a multitude of programs by insisting on getting up-to-date figures on various federal and international grant programs, and he routinely required written departmental reports. But eventually he resorted to vesting more and more authority for departmental coordination in the White House staff and the Bureau of the Budget. It was no doubt a dissillusioned President Johnson, tired of continually battling the bureaucracy, and perhaps believing that a significant portion of the programs for which he had fought so hard had been sabotaged by indifferent officials — who solemnly warned the incoming Nixon administration that it should spare no effort in selecting thoroughly loyal people to staff key departmental positions.

President Nixon bemoaned the inefficiency of the federal government and talked of the "nightmares" he inherited and of the increasing crisis of public confidence in operations of the government. The replacement of every original cabinet officer from Nixon's first term was a further expression of frustration. In early 1971 he admitted that "when you come into office one has ideas as to what he can accomplish, and he believes he can accomplish a great deal . . . [but] after he gets in, he finds that what he had hoped, in terms of achieving goals, will not be as great [sic] as the actual performance turns out to be." [15]

Of course, this presidential litany about powerlessness, of inexorably looking like a "loser" in domestic matters, can be in part self-serving: it can be conveniently used to suggest that presidents personally are more or less blameless for not seriously undertaking the painful domestic fights that need to be fought. It remains true, however, that the ability to set priorities and have laws passed is decidedly different from the ability to implement policy in desired directions; and that the ability to halt a policy, as by impounding congressionally appropriated funds or vetoing legislation, is quite different still from the ability to achieve positive innovation. If any lesson of presidential power was demonstrated repeatedly in the 1960s and early 1970s, it was this: the presidency must stay involved well after the bill-signing celebration if its initiatives are not to be derailed or sabotaged in the labyrinth of bureaucratic politics or modern federalism. In fact, presidential impact on the lives of the American people has been marginal. Presidents have been unable to assure real program changes, partly because so many presidentially sponsored programs required manipulating multilevel bureaucratic systems.

National domestic policy has been changing in character. No longer is the federal government merely constructing interstate canals or highways, building veterans' hospitals, or writing social security checks. Federal social programs now try to change how people think and how local institutions behave. Few of the new programs of the 1960s were or are now administered directly from Washington: most are run in concert with a maze of state and local governments, professions, and interest groups. Local leaders and interest groups insist on having discretion over the disbursement of federal funds, especially those for problems of race, poverty, urban decay, and environmental pollution. Reference to distinct presidential policy or Washington guidelines is minimal. Presidential intentions invariably become compromised. As Martha Derthick points out: "[The federal government] gets them to carry out its purposes by offering incentives in the form of aid, which they may accept or not, and by attaching conditions to the aid. To achieve results, federal officials must have enough knowledge of local politics to perceive what incentives are necessary; they must direct the incentives to those holders of local power whose support is required to achieve the federal purpose. In short, they must intervene successfully in local politics." [16]

The administrative side of the presidency is the least glamorous and least envied aspect for presidents and public alike. Presidents too often appear to gain control over the routines and loyalties of the government, only to find themselves later defending the appearances rather than acknowledging the illusions. Franklin Roosevelt came to the White House belittling the managerial tasks of the presidency: "That is the least part of it. It is more than an engineering job, efficient or inefficient. It is preeminently a place for moral leadership." [17] But by 1937, under fire for creating so many new agencies and with Congress threatening to move in, Roosevelt acknowledged that his preoccupation with emergency programs during his first term had caused him to give administration less than the consideration it deserved. He despaired that "the President's task has become impossible for me or any other man. A man in this position will not be able to survive White House service unless it is simplified." [18] After a time a president usually chooses to spend his scarce political capital on new policy initiatives rather than on implemental or management strategies.

A question that arises constantly within the White House is how to organize the executive office to insure that presidential priorities are carried out. The strategy of executive organization most often celebrated in traditional public administration textbooks is that of hierarchy. The assumption is that the president's values should prevail: the White House sets policy and executive branch subordinates obey policy directions and accept budgetary levels as sent down by the White House. To this end, a strong and effective presidency requires a strong cabinet that is responsible for the actual operation of programs and reports directly to the president.

But the federal executive branch does not function as a unidirectional hierarchical system. In the American political system, program goals are not spelled out very clearly, complex problems must be dealt with incrementally, and presidential authority is constantly leaking away. Departmental personnel at bureau or division levels often believe that they know best how to run their own programs. Some cabinet positions are weak; some departments are even celebrated for their deviance from White House goals. Field personnel feel themselves closer to the problems and to the local people and often believe they must adapt federal programs to local conditions. Career professionals in government service do not believe that a president's generalist lieutenants possess the expertise they often, in fact, do. Special interest groups constantly press for separate agencies or departments to represent their areas of concern. And, over time, the White House begins to distrust even its own cabinet.

Presidential leadership has become less a matter of authority flowing downward and more a question of the extent to which loyalty extends upward. The mix of pressures on a typical bureau chief — from Congress, from his department, from his program's constituency, and from politics at his own level — makes it difficult for him to respond solely to White House intentions, even if these are communicated thoroughly and consistently. And frequently they are not. David Brinkley, a veteran observer of White House occupants and Washington politics, rendered the following verdict:

This town is sort of like a great big steamboat that keeps going its own way regardless of which way the wind blows, or how elections go, or how the current goes; it keeps going, and it might move one degree in one direction, but it essentially keeps going the same direction. It goes on grinding out paper, spending money, hiring people, getting bigger and bigger and more troublesome all the time, and nothing seems to affect it. Presidents don't affect it. Every President I've known or know of has complained about the fantastically cumbersome size of this establishment here. As far back as Harry Truman, I was covering the White House and Truman said, "I thought I was the President, but when it comes to these bureaucracies, I can't make 'em do a damn thing." [19]

ON ANALYZING THE PRESIDENCY

The presidency defies any simple methodological analysis. To attempt to assess the presidency and its workings by focusing narrowly on presidential character, on bureaucratic politics, or on the functions of legislative relations, advisory processes, or party leadership would be to recast the presidency unrealistically to suit the explanation. Just as a primary task for a president is to mediate and synthesize various policies and various subpresidencies, so an important task for students of presidential leadership is to integrate a variety of methodological and theoretical approaches.

This book focuses on how well the presidency succeeds in inducing improvements in national programs, in guiding action toward a higher quality of government and a higher quality of life. What discretion and constraints are involved in the making of presidential choices? If the independent variable is what the president intends, then the dependent variable is whether this intention succeeds. Logically, four possibilities exist: a president might want to initiate change toward some stated goal and subsequently (1) succeed or (2) fail; alternatively, he might actively want not to change policy in a certain area and (3) succeed or (4) fail in this. But measurement is not simple: presidential leadership seldom can be accounted a success or failure with finality, controlled experiments are impossible, and data often are complex or inaccessible.

Trying to assess whether a president has accomplished what he had intended is a thorny problem. First, what did he really intend? Hagiographers, but not social scientists, may allow themselves the assumption that their subjects' intentions and actions are identical. It would be surprising if, from time to time, a president, like other politicians, did not act symbolically to conceal his actual intentions. For example, although actually wanting a legislative initiative to fail, he might publicly desire it to succeed — anticipating that the onus for the failure would fall not on him but on Congress or the opposition party. Also, he can exercise substantial power to block the initiatives of others or to defend the status quo against attack. Presidential influence is very readily seen when it is used negatively to deny someone a position or to veto a bill.

In terms of this discussion, the most demanding — and the most illuminating — test of presidential capacity occurs when a president wants to depart boldly from the status quo to promote some timely and innovative redistribution of economic resources, reform, or regulation. Most presidents have said that they ran for this highest of political offices because of the opportunities it would provide to accomplish positive objectives of this kind. On such occasions the formal powers of the presidency need substantial reinforcement from the informal, more personal skills of the individual. And on such occasions one can try to reach some judgment about whether the incumbent has succeeded or failed. Assessing the outcome entails another problem: public policy is a continuous process, being shaped while it is being executed. In a sense, there is no final result. The best that can be done is to state a few basic assumptions that may mitigate the intrusion of these methodological problems — of presidential motive or program outcomes — upon analysis.

Extensive interviews with White House staff and cabinet members who served in the Kennedy, Johnson, and Nixon presidencies have been relied upon in establishing presidential intentions. A total of fifty senior aides were interviewed: twenty-four who served under Kennedy, thirty-six under Johnson, and thirteen under Nixon. Obviously, several aides served under more than one president.[20] Interviews with these White House counselors, which usually lasted three hours but occasionally ran to five and six, ranged over about a dozen major aspects of White House and presidential work. An effort was made to record verbatim responses, and anonymity was promised. In addition, twenty recent cabinet secretaries and a dozen members of the subcabinet were interviewed. These interviews were designed to discuss departmental policy matters as well as to elicit generalizations about cabinet or subcabinet roles and responsibilities. Quotations given in the text without citation (for the sake of preserving anonymity) come from these personal interviews, but the administration and the individual's general role are usually indicated.

Emphasizing the outcomes of policy, it can be argued, forces the conclusion that presidential success is small. It stacks the deck because the tasks of making life less brutish or of making government more responsive are extremely difficult, and gains nearly always are incremental. But to ignore the concrete impact of policy is even less defensible: the measure of policy success must not become the charade of the legislative box score.[21]

No part of this analysis intends to suggest that a president is devoid of influence or that the question of who serves in the office is unimportant; nor should the description of the limits and constraints on the presidency offer the false comfort that presidents are thus kept sufficiently accountable. The politically talented president can discover how to avoid politically fatal costs while making maximum use of available resources. The shrewdest president — or a president at his shrewdest — may use available prerogatives to purchase further political resources quite apart from the attainment of specific national objectives. It is ever possible that some politician engaging endlessly in further acquisition of political authority might even renounce or fail to recognize the ends for which presidential prerogatives and influence are granted.

A society that demands greatness *and* justice from its presidents needs first to understand the dependence of presidential success on a leader's abilities to distinguish what can be done from what cannot. Moreover, cost-free or mistake-proof presidential leadership that seeks major policy innovation as its cardinal aim will remain an illusory goal. But even if substantive presidential leadership very often has only a marginal effect on the overall outcomes of the total governmental process, it is seldom negligible.

NOTES

1. Lyndon B. Johnson, quoted in Hugh Sidey, *A Very Personal Presidency* (Atheneum, 1968), p. 260.
2. Personal interview.

3. Bert Cochran, *Harry Truman and the Crisis Presidency* (Funk and Wagnalls, 1973), pp. 120, 393.
4. Robert F. Kennedy, *Thirteen Days: A Memoir of the Cuban Missile Crisis* (New American Library, 1969), p. 95.
5. Irving Kristol, "The Inexorable Rise of the Executive," *Wall Street Journal,* 20 September 1974, editorial page, p. 12.
6. See, for example, Peter F. Drucker, "How to Make the Presidency Manageable," *Fortune,* November 1974, pp. 146–49.
7. John F. Kennedy, State of the Union Message, 30 January 1961, *Public Papers of the Presidents* (1962), pp. 22–23. (U.S. Government Printing Office.)
8. Richard Nixon, quoted in Theodore White, *The Making of the President 1968* (Atheneum, 1969), p. 147.
9. John H. Kessel, "The Parameters of Presidential Politics" (Paper presented at the 1972 Annual Meeting of the American Political Science Association; processed), pp. 8–9. Washington, D.C., 5–9 September 1972.
10. Leonard Garment, quoted in Theodore H. White, *The Making of the President 1972* (Atheneum, 1973), p. 52.
11. Presidential press secretary Ronald Ziegler, 1 December 1972, *Weekly Compilation of Presidential Documents* (4 December 1972) 8:49:1711–12. (U.S. Government Printing Office.)
12. John F. Kennedy, during a television interview, 17 December 1962, *Public Papers of the Presidents* (1963), p. 889.
13. Personal interview.
14. John F. Kennedy, quoted in Richard Rovere, "Letter from Washington," *New Yorker,* 30 November 1963, p. 53.
15. Richard M. Nixon, during a television interview, 5 January 1971, *Weekly Compilation of Presidential Documents* (11 January 1971) 7:33. Three weeks later in his State of the Union message [address], the president announced his "New American Revolution" program and in the course of the discussion criticized the Washington-based federal establishment some ten or eleven times.
16. Martha Derthick, *New Towns In-Town* (Urban Institute, 1972), p. 84.
17. *New York Times,* 13 November 1932.
18. Franklin D. Roosevelt, quoted by Herbert Emmerich, *Federal Organizations and Administrative Management* (University of Alabama Press, 1971), p. 207.
19. David Brinkley, during a television interview, *Thirty Minutes With . . .* (Public Broadcasting Service), 13 July 1971.
20. These formal interviews have subsequently been supplemented with more than twenty less formal discussions, especially with aides who served in the Nixon–Ford period. And, of course, the Watergate hearings and trials provided countless additional data on the Nixon administration.
21. Case studies of national programs launched by presidents — the Teacher Corps and the so-called "War on Crime," to be published separately — offer specific and detailed illustrations of the character and success of presidential implementation leadership. These case studies, undertaken at the same time as the preparation of this book, informed several aspects of it.

CHAPTER 2

THE CULT OF THE PRESIDENCY

A HALO FOR THE CHIEF

*In a relative but real sense one can say of a President what
Eisenhower's first Secretary of Defense once said of General Motors:
what is good for the country is good for the President, and
vice versa.*

    — *Richard Neustadt,* Presidential Power,
      (John Wiley, 1960), p. 185.

*I am of those who believe that America is the hope of the world,
and for that time given him, the President is the hope of America.*

    — *Daniel P. Moynihan, 21 December 1970
      (White House release, processed), p. 11.*

*Too many of us have misattributed the grandeur and mission of
the United States to the politician who temporarily holds our
nation's highest office. Treated like an exalted being a President
begins to think he is exalted.*

    — *Jack Anderson,*
      (Parade Magazine, *15 December 1974), p. 4.*

Thoughtful Americans have been troubled recently by the apparent expansion of presidential powers, especially in the sense of the assumption of powers for which there seems to be no checks or balances, and the imprudent exercise of existing powers. Since the Vietnam War and the Watergate affair, people have become more skeptical of the once prevailing view that what is good for a president is also good for the nation. But for decades American social scientists have glorified the power-maximizing presidency: the president needs help, the president speaks for no special interest, only the president represents all the people, the presidency is the chief source of progressive and creative initiatives — these statements express the standard textbook wisdom.

Political science textbooks summarize current thinking and guide the work of contemporary researchers. For more than twenty years after the Franklin D. Roosevelt presidency, most textbook treatments of the American presidency seriously inflated and unrealistically interpreted presidential competence and beneficence. If society and our political system were to be led, they suggested, leadership would have to come from the White House. Whatever strengthened the president's hand, strengthened the nation. Introductory American government textbooks and related political writings in the 1950s and 1960s endorsed the activist, purposeful, power-maximizing model of presidential leadership. They often glorified the manipulative leader, and almost all of them exaggerated to some degree past and future presidential performance. Such distortion risked misleading students and leaders alike about the invention and carrying out of creative civic and political responsibilities. Moreover, these writings hardly prepared the nation for the abuses of presidential power witnessed during the late 1960s and early 1970s. Perhaps some of the distorted interpretations of what a president could and should accomplish actually encouraged some of these abuses.

The discussion that follows focuses on dominant themes in orthodox textbook accounts of the presidency which were gathered from a review of about three dozen standard college texts and other treatments of the presidency written in the 1950s and 1960s.[1] The intention is simply to let the reader recognize the tendencies toward inflating the presidency rather than to calculate the degree of exaggeration. The term *textbook presidency,* used here for convenience, applies not only to these formal works, most of them by professors of political science, but also to those similar images of presidential power and personality that were promulgated through the press and the broadcast media by reporters, columnists, and commentators working under the pressure of tight deadlines. The total effect, deliberate or not, was to create almost out of whole cloth a larger-than-life image of the presidency, an evocative iconolatry that has often had grievous consequences.

Doubtless most of these writers and journalists were mirroring the predominant popular views of the times. As will be discussed in more detail later, the extraordinary events of the period — the Great Depression, World War II, the cold war, the development of nuclear weapons — made old conceptions of politics and leadership outmoded, or so most people apparently believed. It is easy today, especially after Vietnam, Watergate, and other unsettling presidential actions, to look back with dismay at the sugar-coated, romanticized depictions of the promise of the presidency. However, until very recently social scientists have expressed surprisingly little concern about the possibility of the abuse of presidential power.

If the excesses and abuses of presidential power in recent years have aroused an understandable anger in many Americans, it should serve to encourage not retribution against the presidency but a rational search for ways to make the presidency safe for democracy, that is, accountable to the American public and able to accomplish what can be realistically expected of it. The promise of the American presidency may have been oversold, overstated, and stretched beyond reality, but denying the importance and the need for effective presidential leadership would be to overstate the case, as well as misleading. The following dissection of the textbook presidency should be viewed, then, primarily as an attempt to reformulate the possibilities for an effective presidency that is also leaner, more open, more democratic and *within* the Constitution.

THE TEXTBOOK PRESIDENCY:
THE 1950s AND 1960s VERSION

Franklin D. Roosevelt personally rescued the nation from the depths of the Great Depression, and the stalwart soldier of freedom, with Harry Truman, brought World War II to a proud conclusion. The courageous Truman personally committed the nation to resist communist aggression around the globe. General Eisenhower pledged that as president he would "go to Korea" to end that war — and he did. John F. Kennedy pledged to put a man on the moon, and, even though it took awhile, this was achieved. These are the prevailing idealized images that most American students read and remember. For convenience, if not always accurately, textbooks give eras or major events such labels as "the Wilson years," "the Hoover depression," "the Roosevelt revolution," "the Eisenhower period," and "the Kennedy Camelot years."

Presidents were expected to perform as purposeful activists who know what they want to accomplish and relish the challenges of the office. The student learned from textbooks that the presidency was "the great engine of democracy," "the American people's one authentic trumpet," and "the central instrument of democracy." With the New Deal presidency in mind, these textbooks portrayed the president instructing the nation as national teacher and guiding the nation as national preacher. Presidents, they said, should expand the role of the federal government to cope with the increasing nationwide demands for social justice and a prosperous economy. The performances of Harding, Coolidge, and Hoover were lumped together as largely similar and rejected as antique. The retiring reluctance of Eisenhower generally elicited a more ambiguous appraisal: after a brief tribute to him as a wonderful man and a heroic military leader, he was categorized as an amateur who lacked both a sense of direction and a progressive, positive conception of the presidential role. What was needed, most texts implied, was a person with the foresight to anticipate the future and the personal strength to unite us, to steel our moral will, to move the country forward and make it governable. The vision, and perhaps the illusion, was that if only Americans could identify and elect the right person, their loftiest aspirations would be fulfilled.

Studies in political socialization stress repeatedly that children's views of authority and government center on an American president, a towering, "glittering mountain peak" of benevolence, power, and wisdom, someone who can win and end wars as well as cure the nation's socioeconomic ills.[2] As children grow older and are exposed to textbooks and discussions of current events, however, it is commonly assumed that the views derived from norms taught in grade school or by parents become more tempered, and that teenagers or young adults become, perhaps, even cynical about political leaders. But introductory high school and college textbooks doubtless reinforce rather than refine youthful expectations about presidential leadership.[3]

Ironically, the Watergate scandals have increased the need to subject textbook wisdom to closer scrutiny, for the new frustration and apathy aroused by Watergate have done much to dash and distort popular expectations of the presidency. While on the one hand aspirations have crashed, on the other hand yearnings, sometimes feverish ones, have been rekindled for new candidates who are above politics and could somehow cleanse the office and elevate its performance to match the textbook portrait of the presidency.

ASCRIPTIONS OF POWER AND VIRTUE. With minor variations college texts of the 1950s and 1960s stressed that the contemporary presidency was growing dramatically larger, gaining significantly more resources and responsibilities. This expansion was often described metaphorically as "wearing more hats." With rare exception texts not only devised and approved but openly celebrated an expansive theory of presidential power. Students read that more authority and discretion in determining policy devolves to the president during war and crises and that because the country was engaged in sustained international conflict and acute domestic problems, presidents were constantly becoming more powerful.[4] One text pointed out, "as the world grows smaller, he will grow bigger." Another exclaimed that the "President . . . bears almost the entire burden of the formulation of national policy and the definition of the national purpose." The following presidential job descriptions have been taken from five of these introductory texts:

The president is the most strategic policy maker in the government. His policy role is paramount in military and foreign affairs.[5]

He [John F. Kennedy] also became the most important and powerful chief executive in the free world. His powers are so vast that they rival those of the Soviet Premier or of any other dictator. He is the chief architect of the nation's public policy; as President, he is one who proposes, requests, supports, demands, and insists that Congress enact most of the major legislation that it does.[6]

The evolution of the Presidency is the story of a frequent and cumulative increase in the role — or, better, the roles — that the President can play and is expected to play in the American political system, and, more recently, in the world. Every "great" President has left the office somewhat altered and enlarged. The Presidency is like a family dwelling that each new generation alters and enlarges. Confronted by some new need, a President adds on a new room, a new wing; what began as a modest dwelling has become a mansion; every President may not use every room, but the rooms are available in case of need.[7]

The President of the United States of America is, without question, the most powerful elected executive in the world. He is at once the chief formulator of public policy as embodied in legislation, leader of a major political party . . . chief architect of American foreign policy. And his power and responsibility are increasing.[8]

If the President is a king, it is equally clear that he is no mere constitutional monarch. For in an era in which many monarchies all over the world have disappeared, and the power of kings has declined, the power of the President has enormously increased . . . through subtle and usually informal changes, attributable mainly to the fact that the President is the literal embodiment of American mass democracy and . . . the symbol of the pervasive egalitarianism which from the beginning has characterized the emergent forces of the American democratic ideal.[9]

To the teenager or young adult, textbook discussions of the extensive resources available to the president cannot help but convey the impression that a president must have just about all the inside information and good advice anyone could want, especially when they point out the vast arrays of experts, strategic support staffs, and intelligence systems. Usually, too, a lengthy listing is included of the National Security Council, the cabinet, the Office of Management and Budget, the Council on Environmental Quality, the Council of Economic Advisers, White House domestic-policy staffs, and countless high-level study commissions. A casual reading of such chapters fosters the conclusion that a contemporary president can both set and shape the directions of public policy and can see to it that these policies *work as intended.*

The conviction that the president knows best, that his advisory and information systems are unparalleled, is readily encouraged by a passage like the following:

The President has not only the authority but the capacity *to act. For example, he has at his command unmatched sources of information. To his desk come facts channeled from the entire world. Diplomatic missions, military observers, undercover agents, personal agents, technical experts gather tons of material which are analyzed by experts in the State Department and elsewhere. Since the President draws on the informed thinking of hundreds of specialists, his pronouncements have a tone of authority.*[10]

To this vast reservoir is added the capacity of the presidency for systematic thinking and planning, similarly described as awesome and superbly suited to the challenges of the day:

Presidential government is a superb planning institution. The President has the attention of the country, the administrative goals, the command of information, and the fiscal resources that are necessary for intelligent planning, and he is gaining the institutional power that will make such planning operational. Better than any other human instrumentality, he can order the relations of his ends and means, alter existing institutions and procedures or create new ones, calculate the consequences of different policies, experiment with various methods, control the timing of action, anticipate the reactions of affected interests, and conciliate them or at least mediate among them.[11]

This same theme is outlined in Theodore White's *The Making of the President 1960,* often used as a supplementary text: "So many and so able are the President's advisers of the permanent services of Defense, State, Treasury, Agriculture, that when crisis happens all necessary information is instantly available, all alternate courses already plotted." [12] Elsewhere, White pays lavish tribute to America's "action-intellectuals," whom he designates as the "new priesthood" of national policy making. These "best and brightest," recruited from prestigious universities and research centers, are credited with being a benign and "propelling influence" upon our government, "shaping our defenses, guiding our foreign policy, redesigning our cities, reorganizing our schools." [13]

Clinton Rossiter's *The American Presidency,* published in 1956 and still widely read, contains one of the most lucid venerations of the American presidency. Rossiter describes the presidency sympathetically as a priceless American invention that not only has worked extremely well but also is a symbol of the continuity and destiny of the American people.

Few nations have solved so simply and yet grandly the problem of finding and maintaining an office or state that embodies their majesty and reflects their character.

There is virtually no limit to what the President can do if he does it for democratic ends and by democratic means.

He is, rather, a kind of magnificent lion who can roam widely and do great deeds so long as he does not try to break loose from his broad reservation.

He reigns, but he also rules; he symbolizes the people, but he also runs their government.[14]

Rossiter, both fully aware of his own biases and seemingly quite convinced that the myth of presidential greatness and grandeur was to be cultivated, writes about the Lincoln legacy:

Lincoln is the supreme myth, the richest symbol in the American experience. He is, as someone has remarked neither irreverently nor sacreligiously, the martyred Christ of democracy's passion play. And who, then, can measure the strength that is given to the President because he holds Lincoln's office, lives in Lincoln's house, and walks in Lincoln's way? The final greatness of the Presidency lies in the truth that it is not just an office of incredible power but a breeding ground of indestructible myth.[15]

Such lavish prose hardly discourages awe and admiration, if not exactly reverence, for the presidency.

Perhaps the most respected specialized treatment of the presidency written in the 1950s or 1960s was Richard Neustadt's *Presidential Power* (1960).[16] Neustadt's insights countered much of the conventional wisdom by stressing the highly political and bureaucratic context in which presidents must operate, the obstacles posed to presidential directives by Washington empire builders, and the scarce resources available to a president who wants to reverse policy directions. Although his analysis found the president's position limited and tenuous, one in which he must grasp for just enough power to get by the next day's problems, Neustadt seemed personally to prefer a more powerful president — one who would guard his options and would impose his will. But implicitly, if not explicitly, his study held on to the hope that a shrewd and manipulative leader could and should be a powerful engine of change. Indeed an aggressive, ambitious politician, determined to get his way and ever-distrustful of the motives of others, seemed to be what was needed.

Neustadt applauded the FDR ideal type and detailed possible strategies that might promote a similar power-maximizing presidential performance. Yet in his often brilliant dissection of the requisites for effective presidential entrepreneurship, there is no skepticism that what is good for a president might not be what is in the best interests of the nation. Rather the imperative for assertive, ambitious leadership overshadows any hint that a president's objectives might be deficient. Thus Neustadt can write: "The men who share in governing this country frequently appear to act as though they were in business for themselves. So in a real though not entire sense, they are and have to be." [17] Protecting the president's options, guarding his reputation, and enhancing his professional image assume near exclusive priority, while discovering ways to improve the quality of policy-formulation or making presidents accountable are generally ignored. Neustadt's *Presidential Power* was, of course, a product of the times. The foremost problem of the presidency at that time was how to help it gain control over the drifting Washington policy apparatus. The problem — so it was perceived by most people at that time, apparently — was how to put a president into the driver's seat, and thereby provide some central direction on the major issues of the day. People generally assumed that whoever became president would use the powers of the office for purposeful ends in the public interest, and always would use democratic means.

On balance, however, Neustadt's portrait did little to temper the image of the president as a potentially powerful, independent architect of U. S. public policy. In many ways his analysis was a period piece; he indicted Dwight Eisenhower for failing to honor the textbook ideal of the power-consuming activist, for an imprecision of purpose that dulled his sense of power and its use, for mistaking generalities for concrete undertakings. But Neustadt's assumptions and emphases, which amount to a resurrection of the New Deal presidential image from the "Eisenhower Reformation," have been criticized for causing him to misread Eisenhower's motives and mislead readers to the conclusion that power and political expertise alone can insure excellent and wise leadership.[18] It also led to the view that if a president lacks a consuming hunger for the office and a penchant for manipulating people, then he or she is unfit for the office. Neustadt, as well as other textbook writers who dwell on the necessity for more power and political influence in the presidency, may also be criticized for failing to see, as events of the recent past suggest, that lack of power was seldom the problem: power has been used arbitrarily or for ignoble ends, and presidents and their advisers have lacked the wisdom to know what to do with the power they already had.

PERSONALIZATION OF THE PRESIDENCY. Post-New Deal textbooks on government emphasize also the importance of personal attributes: "The President's values, his qualities of character and intellect, his capacity for leadership, his political skills, his definition of his own role, and the way he performs it — *these are fundamental determinants* of the working of the American government and of American politics." [19] Emphasizing a president's personality or character or offering psychohistories of past presidents captures the attention of students and adults alike. In studying presidential leadership we should, of course, seek to come up with some clues and rough guidelines to what kind of person can handle the job and also form some idea of what the presidency does to the occupant. But despite the flurry of this type of research, major methodological pitfalls still exist. The links between personal character and presidential policy making are important, but social scientists to date have been unable to predict with any degree of rigor exactly what personal characteristics will produce desirable leadership in public policy.

Some recent research, notably the work of James David Barber, Alexander George, and Erwin Hargrove, has alerted us to the need for a democratic temperament, openness, and the capacity to listen and to the value of a sense of joy in presidents. But stressing desirable personality characteristics may well have a tendency to recreate merely another kind of textbook presidency tradition. We could easily develop a cult of the "activist-positives," to use Barber's phrase. Barber's conclusion that activist, power-conscious, and power-maximizing presidents are not, because of those qualities alone, fit for the office is a very welcome break with the textbook tradition, but not all of his conclusions suggest such a marked departure. He says, for example, "for better or for worse, the Presidency remains the prime focus for our political sentiments and the prime source of guidance and inspiration for national politics. . . . If he is lucky and effective, he can call forth . . . new energies, a new vision, a new way of working to suit a perennially new age." [20] But the institution needs to be secularized, and presidents, regardless of their personality attributes, are not entitled to any more respect than their words and actions earn for them. We cannot be content with the verdict that a happy, healthy president — one who loves life and enjoys his job — is sufficient for the country. "The point is that a President can be a healthy personality and yet have a deficient view of the world" or an undesirable set of values.[21]

Not surprisingly, the personalization of the presidency is also reflected in campaign rhetoric. Presidential candidates proclaim how personally courageous and virtuous a president must be. Nelson Rockefeller recited a litany of necessary qualities in 1968:

The modern Presidency of the United States, as distinct from the traditional concepts of our highest office, is bound up with the survival not only of freedom but of mankind. . . . The President is the unifying force in our lives. . . . The President must possess a wide range of abilities: to lead, to persuade, to inspire trust, to attract men of talent, to unite. These abilities must reflect a wide range of characteristics: courage, vision, integrity, intelligence, sense of responsibility, sense of history, sense of humor, warmth, openness, personality, tenacity, energy, determination, drive, perspicacity, idealism, thirst for information, penchant for fact, presence of conscience, comprehension of people and enjoyment of life — plus all the other, nobler virtues ascribed to George Washington under God.[22]

John Kennedy as a presidential candidate similarly emphasized the crucial personal requisites of a potential president. Certain men, he claimed, could so enjoin the nation's best inclinations that these United States could and would "move forward" — and he promised to be that type of individual. Four years later Lyndon B. Johnson went even farther, asserting that the president of this country must be able to "ignite a fire in the breast of this land, a flaming spirit of adventure that soars beyond the ordinary and the contented, demanding greatness from our society and achievement in our government." [23]

The personalized presidency is as well a central feature of contemporary political journalism. No one does more to embellish this perspective than Theodore White, whose "Making of the President" volumes not only enjoy frequent university use but also serve as textbooks for millions of adults who savor the explanations of an insider. White's concentration on the styles and personalities of the candidates promotes a benevolent, almost liturgical, orientation toward the presidency. His narrative histories have an uncanny knack of creating suspense about the outcome of an election well after it actually took place. The melodramatic style promotes a heightened sense of reverence for the eventual victor akin to that felt for royalty. White first describes the field of seven or eight competing hopefuls, which becomes four or five; eventually the field is narrowed down to two or three national candidates. Finally, one person remains. Clearly, it seems from White's approach, the victor in so drawn-out and thoroughly patriotic a ritual deserves the nation's deepest respect and approval. Moreover, White subtly purifies the victorious candidate. In what must be the classic metamorphosis at the root of the textbook image of the presidency, the individuals who assume the presidency seem to change physically and, it is implied, spiritually. White says about President Kennedy's first days in the White House in 1961: "It was as if there were an echo, here on another level, in the quiet Oval Office, of all the speeches he had made in all the squares and supermarkets of the country. . . . He had won this office and this power by promising such movement to the American people. Now he had to keep the promise. He seemed very little changed in movement or in gracefulness from the candidate — only his eyes had changed — very dark now, very grave, markedly more sunken and lined at the corners than those of the candidate." [24] He writes of Richard Nixon soon after his ascendancy in 1969:

He seemed, as he waved me into the Oval Office, suddenly on first glance a more stocky man than I had known on the campaign rounds. There was a minute of adjustment as he waved me to a sofa in the barren office, poured coffee, put me at ease; then, watching him, I realized that he was not stockier, but, on the contrary, slimmer. What was different was the movement of the body, the sound of the voice, the manner of speaking — for he was calm as I had never seen him before, as if peace had settled on him. In the past Nixon's restless body had been in constant movement as he rose, walked about, hitched a leg over the arm of a chair or gestured sharply with his hands. Now he was in repose, and the repose was in his speech also — more slow, studied, with none of the gear-slippages of name or reference which used to come when he was weary; his hands still moved as he spoke, but the fingers spread gracefully, not punchily or sharply as they used to.[25]

DIMENSIONS OF THE TEXTBOOK EXAGGERATION. To summarize, four propositions can be singled out as the main constructs of the textbook ideal of the presidency. Two accentuate the dimension of omnipotence; two others, a moralistic-benevolence dimension. As a group these constructs do not necessarily describe the orientation of any particular author. Taken together, however, this admixture of values, legend, and hyperbole made up the textbook presidency of the 1950s and 1960s.

Omnipotent-Competent Dimension:

1. The president is *the* strategic catalyst for progress in the American political system and the central figure in the international system as well.
2. Only the president can be the genuine architect of U. S. public policy, and only he, by attacking problems frontally and aggressively and by interpreting his power expansively, can slay the dragons of crisis and be the engine of change to move this nation forward.

Moralistic-Benevolent Dimension:

3. The president must be the nation's personal and moral leader; by symbolizing the past and future greatness of America and radiating inspirational confidence, a president can pull the nation together while directing its people toward fulfillment of the American Dream.
4. If, and only if, the right person is placed in the White House, all will be well; and, somehow, whoever is in the White House is the best person for the job — at least for a year or so.

The significance of the textbook presidency is that the whole is greater than the sum of the parts. It presents a cumulative presidential image, a legacy of past glories and impressive performances — the exalted dignity of Lincoln, the Wilsonian eloquence, the robust vitality of the Roosevelts, the benign smile and lasting popularity of Eisenhower, the inspirational spirit of Kennedy, the legislative wizardry of Lyndon Johnson, the globetrotting of the first-term Nixon — which endows the White House with a singular mystique and almost magical qualities. According to this image, the office of the presidency seems to clothe its occupants in strength and dignity, in might and right, and only men of the caliber of Lincoln, the Roosevelts, or Wilson can seize the chalice of opportunity, create the vision, and rally the American public around that vision. Collectively, this portrait of the presidency can hardly help but stretch the student imagination; literally, it boggles the mind.

ORIGINS OF THE TEXTBOOK PRESIDENCY

The advent of television and the emergence of the United States as a strategic nuclear power combined to make the American presidency a job of far greater

prominence than in Coolidge's day or earlier. Some other mutually reinforcing factors have also contributed to the runaway inflation in the capabilities attributed to presidential leadership:

1. Human and cultural expectations: for example, a need for symbols and
   for the reassurance that heroic individuals still exist
2. Political and electoral-system values: for example, the desire for national
   stability and the loyalty to national institutions
3. Goals of textbook authors: for example, the desire to train citizens and
   celebrate the Roosevelt presidency
4. Research methods: for example, limited access and data
5. Institutional focus of studies: for example, compartmentalism versus comparative and contextual analysis
6. Vast expansion of the role of the federal government.

HUMAN AND CULTURAL EXPECTATIONS. A basic human tendency is to
believe in great personages, to believe that someone, somewhere, can and will
cope with the major crises of the present and future. In the post-New Deal,
post-Franklin Roosevelt era, most Americans have grown accustomed to expecting their president to fill this role. Who, if not the president, is going to
prevent the communists from burying us, pollution from choking us, crime and
conflict from destroying our cities, oil-producing nations from freezing us to
death, and pornography from slipping into our neighborhood bookstores and
theaters? Within the complexity of contemporary political life, the presidency
serves our basic need for a visible national symbol to which we can attach our
hopes. Something akin to presidential cults have emerged in the United States,
just as personality cults, hero worship, reverence for aged leaders, and other
forms of authority worship have flourished in most societies. (Some observers
have suggested to this writer that in many ways we have witnessed the Latin-
Americanization of our chief executive.) Although Americans like to think of
themselves as a nation of hard-headed pragmatists, they have a persistent and
definite tendency to regard notable former presidents as folk heroes.

Certain presidents, especially those who have enlarged the office and enlarged
the place of the nation on the global landscape, are placed on a pedestal rather
than under a microscope. Portraits of Washington, Jefferson, Lincoln, the
Roosevelts, and Kennedy occupy many a classroom wall alongside the American
flag. Even mediocre presidents become, for awhile, national heroes to at least
a sizeable portion of the populace. Many presidents become the prophets of a
secular civil religion as well. Presumably, deification is frowned upon, but
canonization or something like it is not unusual, especially among children in
the early years of schooling.

Is this yearning for the unique or heroic prophet among us a deep-seated religious need? Systematic evidence is lacking. A perceptive philosopher and student of social phenomena, Michael Novak, who has wrestled with this question, concludes that a president's actions

> ... *seep irrepressibly into our hearts. He dwells in us. We cannot keep him out. That is why we wrestle against him, rise up in hatred often, wish to retch — or, alternatively, feel good, feel proud, as though his achievements were ours, his wit the unleashing of power of our own.*
>
> *Hands are stretched toward him over wire fences at airports like hands extended toward medieval sovereigns or ancient prophets. One wonders what mystic participation our presidents convey, what witness from what other world, what form of cure or heightened life. The president arouses waves of "power," "being," "superior reality," as if where he is is history. . . . His office is, in quite modern and sophisticated form, a religion in a secular state. It evokes responses familiar in all the ancient religions of the world. It fills a perennial vacuum at the heart of human expectations.[26]*

To be sure, not everyone would go so far as Novak in this liturgical interpretation of the role of the president. Indeed, despite the fact that Novak's analysis appeared after the Vietnam and Watergate episodes, he writes as though he still believes rather strongly, that — certain tragedies of the presidential promise notwithstanding — presidents, for better or worse, play a crucial psychological role in our lives, even though we like to feel we are rational democrats.

Political scientists have usually not read in such meaning, or at least have not infused their view of the presidency with connotations of a civil religion. As the following passage from one notable social scientist's text illustrates, the typical textbook interpretation merely generalized freely from past performances to a bright, optimistic future: "When Presidents are great heroes elected by a vast and vigorous majority, or when they are forced by a catastrophe and crisis to unexpected greatness, then the Presidency is as powerful as the sun, obscuring all other stars with its own light. But when neither heroic personality nor calamitous circumstance expands its influence, then it is only one star among many almost unnoticeable in a Milky Way. Yet through all this fluctuation one can discern a long-run trend of increasing brightness." [27] Even Dwight Eisenhower and Eugene McCarthy, who spoke out against expansive and possessive presidential leadership, venerated the possibilities for moral leadership in the office and assumed that presidents should unify and uplift the American people and liberate them from their weaknesses. Here, for example, are Eugene McCarthy's conceptions of the presidency from the 1968 campaign: "The role of the President must be to unite the nation. But he must unite it by inspiring it, not unite it by just adding it up or piecing it together like some kind of jigsaw puzzle. Rather than trying to organize the nation, he must try to encourage the common purpose of creating an order of justice in America. . . . He should understand that this country cannot be governed by coercion, and that it needs a special kind of leadership, which itself recognizes that the potential for leadership exists in every man and woman." [28]

From 1953 to 1972 the incumbent president was first in the Most-Admired Man Poll annually conducted by Gallup except in 1967 and 1968, when a war-weakened Lyndon Johnson lost out to former president Eisenhower. Apparently, the view that "if they were not the most-admired men in the country they wouldn't have been elected president" is widely respected. Perhaps because of our need for reassurance that things will work out satisfactorily, we admire more readily the dramatic actions of people in high places who are willing to cope with the exigencies of crisis and perplexity. As political scientist Murray Edelman puts it: "Because it is apparently intolerable for men to admit the key role of accident, of ignorance, and of unplanned processes in their affairs, the leader serves a vital function by personifying and reifying the processes." [29]

POLITICAL AND ELECTORAL-SYSTEM VALUES.   A president may be elected by a small margin, but after election he is supposed to speak for all the people. Textbooks suggest that one may question a presidential candidate vigorously, but not a new president; after the election, it is one's duty to unite behind the legitimized winner because united we stand, divided we might not. The mood is one of beginning anew, of reasoning together, and of joining together with renewed support for both presidency and nation. It is as though the president were the pilot of an aircraft and the rest of us passengers, whether we like it or not. Hence, we all have a stake in his success. We feel that we must give the man a chance; to behave otherwise is unpatriotic or smacks of unsporting partisanship. The losing party receives little sympathy during post-election periods; the time for complaints is the next election, or at least not the first year or so while the new man is trying hard to get on with the job.

Some political scientists point out that childhood romanticisms and deferential respect for the presidency may be blessings in disguise in terms of national stability. A study of children's images of the presidency has argued:

> *From the point of view of the stability of the American political structure, some such attachment early in life has positive consequences. As the child grows to adulthood, he is exposed to considerable debate and conflicts over the merits of various alternative incumbents of the Presidency and of other roles in the political structure. There is constant danger that criticism of the occupant will spill over to the role itself. Were this to occur under certain circumstances respect for the Presidency could be seriously impaired or destroyed. But the data here suggest that one of the factors that prevents this from occurring is a strong parental-like tie with respect to the President's role itself, developed before the child can become familiar with the contention surrounding the incumbent of the office.*[30]

Our system of adversary elections in which ambitious and competing hopefuls strive to outdo each other in their promises and denunciations is counterbalanced, then, by an institution of ritualistic unification. The presidential role symbolically absorbs much of the discontinuity and tension promoted during the often hectic election period.

THE COMMERCIAL AND POLITICAL GOALS OF TEXTBOOK AUTHORS.

The commercial aim of a textbook is hard to ignore. Several authors of texts unabashedly, though privately, cite financial remuneration as a major incentive not only for writing a text but for its substantive orientation as well. This is especially true of high school texts, which generally must be approved by state or local authorities. It is also difficult for a text author to achieve genuine detachment from contemporary developments; his or her ideological orientation usually can be detected in the resulting analysis of and in the normative images used to describe presidential leadership. This widespread phenomenon may not be amenable to easy improvement, nor may it be entirely undesirable.

Most text writers probably would agree that introductory American government texts have two preeminent functions: to enlighten students and to train citizens. Text authors are certainly motivated by the goal of instructing students about the realities of the highly competitive, complex, and inchoate process of determining national policy. In addition, they and sometimes their editors are motivated by the goals of socializing students by teaching them the norms of their culture and of cultivating respect for their society's political institutions. Often, the latter goal seems to require a glossy, controlled picture of the institutions of national leadership, one that inspires loyalty but conflicts with reality. When this occurs, as one text writer remarked in conversation, the author almost invariably emphasizes citizen training, usually at the expense of instruction. On balance, most authors willingly accept the assignment of combating student cynicism by stressing the practicality of the democratic system and pointing out the benefits and opportunities of the American Dream. Disconcerting realities are deemphasized, the positive is affirmed.

Not surprisingly, most text writers identify with the considerable liberal faith in the possibilities of structural reforms. This liberal viewpoint has it that better and faster reforms are more likely to be achieved through a vigorous chief executive than through alternative institutions. In the 1950s and 1960s academics frequently turned to the presidency in despair because Congress, dominated by southerners or a conservative coalition, held out such little hope for those progressive, redistributive reforms that intellectuals believed were urgently needed. Moreover, many of them believed, in part correctly, that the biases of the electoral college would usually encourage more liberalism in the White House than on Capitol Hill. They expected White House leaders to respond better than local politicians to the public interest because the federal government enjoyed an expanding and more progressive tax base. One result of these shared values among text authors is that text discussions of the presidency move back and forth between what the presidency is to what it ought to be, and it becomes difficult to separate the factual from the normative. Many authors also may be persuaded that the high expectations of the presidency are useful, even as something to strive toward. At least the public *may* aspire and perhaps the parties *may* try to come as close to the ideal as possible. If presidents were expected to be mediocrities, goes the argument, would they not be selected on that basis, and would not the public be substantially worse off?

Part of this favorable and indulgent disposition toward the presidency may lie in the ideological heritage of recent generations. In the 1930s and 1940s it doubtless was hard *not* to identify with American political institutions, perhaps symbolized in the presidency, because at the time they were coming under international attack.

Across the sea, Hitler defiantly taunted the democracies as impotent. Praise for the efficacy of the Fascist dictatorship in Italy was heard in surprisingly high places in the democracies. Some doubts were being expressed as to the ability of the presidential system to supply the bold dynamic leadership required for solution of the problems of modern government. A question was raised as to whether efficiency and democracy were compatible. Was constitutional government under a President and a Congress a luxury of an earlier age that could not be afforded in modern crisis government? [31]

One reaction to this was to feel that the presidency should be more of a place for strong, activist, vigorous leadership. The personal magnetism of Franklin Roosevelt seemed to fill this need. FDR upstaged his colleagues and most world leaders as he magnified the personal role and heroic style of a confident, competent persident in the context of tumultuous times. The mantle of world leadership was passing to the United States, isolationism had been defeated, and the American era had begun. Understandably, these developments, especially the dramaturgy of the New Deal presidency, affected young liberal academics and their future interpretations of the presidency. For example, "Under Roosevelt, the White House became the focus of all government — the fountainhead of ideas, the initiator of action, the representative of the national interest." [32]

The idealized view of the Roosevelt years — a halo effect that characterizes most of the recent treatments of the presidency — seems to have emerged more distinctly in the 1950s and 1960s than during the years FDR was in office. Such students of the presidency as Edward Corwin, Pendleton Herring, Richard Hofstadter, and Harold Laski, who wrote during or immediately after the Roosevelt presidency, offered more restrained evaluations of the presidency in general and of Roosevelt accomplishments in particular.[33] Perhaps a delayed reaction was at work; members of the older generation may have been less inclined to idealizing a hero than a younger, more impressionable generation of writers who may have been more easily mesmerized by the Roosevelt performance. Many of the textbook writers of the 1950s and 1960s were teenagers or young adults during the depression years, and many became involved in one way or another in the executive branch helping to fight or manage World War II. It is also plausible that myths of Roosevelt's ability reached a peak only well after he was removed from the continual congressional and journalistic barbs to which he certainly was subjected in his day.

In fairness, factors other than the impressionability of youth were at work, including great and genuine respect for Roosevelt's wartime policies and leadership. Arthur Schlesinger, Jr., for example, even though he now admits that he, along with other historians, devised exaggerated views of presidential omniscience, points out that the whole thrust of the cold war seemed at the time to compel the growth and superordinate status of the presidency: "Above all, the uncertainty and danger of the early cold war, with the chronic threat of unanticipated emergency always held to require immediate response, with, above all, the overhanging possibility of nuclear catastrophe, seemed to argue all the more strongly for the centralization of the control over foreign policy, including the use of the armed forces, in the presidency." [34]

RESEARCH METHODS AND AVAILABLE DATA. The textbook presidency emerges also from the modes of analysis employed by the typical textbook writer. Normally, an author relies on some combination of the public record, prior texts, cabinet and White House staff memoirs, and perhaps some interviewing of Washington officials. Newspaper and magazine commentary serves as a supplement. Reliance on such sources usually will encourage a positive orientation toward presidents and the office. Those who have worked closely with presidents are unlikely to downgrade their experiences. As Theodore Sorensen said: "The inaccuracy of most Washington diaries and autobiographies is surpassed only by the immodesty of their authors." [35] Frequently, former members of the White House inner circles are modest about neither their own role nor their claims for the strengths and virtues of their presidents. Literate members of the White House press corps, referred to by some presidents as their "newspaper cabinet," are similarly afflicted. To preserve their access to the president, a requisite for their economic survival, they must treat presidents graciously, or else risk becoming victims of intensified White House animosity and manipulation. Then, too, upon the inquiry of the outside academic, insiders may "forget" those plans or strategies that did not work and unwittingly embellish the record of presidential and personal performances. Any mention of mistakes or uncertainties, shortcuts, or foul play is usually off the record — or "stonewalled" as the Nixon people came to say.

Another methodological technique that leads to overdramatizing the presidency is the reliance on exciting case histories of international crises and domestic emergencies. Case studies of Roosevelt's first hundred days; of Truman's decisions to drop the atomic bomb, enter Korea, and create the Marshall Plan; of Eisenhower's summit conferences; of Kennedy's Cuban missile blockade and "victory" over the steel price-rise; and of Nixon's journey for peace to China come to mind. To be sure, documents, press accounts, and memoirs about these incidents are readily available. But to study presidential performance only in the context of crisis or presidential summitry is to magnify the importance of the job and the man at the expense of other major determinants of policy.

THE INSTITUTIONAL FOCUS. Large introductory American government texts expose students to the whole spectrum of political institutions and processes. Almost always, the authors treat each institution separately: there may be one chapter on the Constitution, another on elections, perhaps a chapter on political parties and interest groups, two on Congress, one on the courts, and so forth. Unfortunately, the resulting compartmentalism often gives the impression that the men and women who populate these institutions and the processes in which they engage are not only distinctly different but also largely unrelated. A chapter may stress the informational and representational roles performed by interest groups and lobbyists, but only scant mention will be made of their activities in relation to the presidency. Likewise, little attention will be paid to the way in which federal bureaucrats or mayors and governors become involved in the implementation of presidential policy. In the chapter on Congress and the president, the student learns that a major function of Congress is to question and review presidential program requests and occasionally to oppose — in short, not to be taken in by the president's overtures. A chapter on the presidency suggests the centrality of the office and its paramount role in initiating and controlling public policy and leaves the impression that national policy is almost entirely the product of a president and the "best and the brightest" at his command. This picture of government is overly hierarchical and neat: a nearly omnipotent presidency really runs the country, but because this is a democracy rather than a monarchy, such institutions as Congress and the court system serve occasionally as the nation's insurance policy between elections.

Of late, analysis of White House staffs and presidential advisory processes has greatly improved. It has moved beyond the image of a lonely president making inspired decisions in the quiet of his Oval Office. Yet, a misplaced emphasis and oversimplification remain in the portrayal of presidential counselors and staff associates as the real policy makers. Hence, the Bay of Pigs defeat is credited solely to overzealous and misinformed CIA leaders. The unsuccessful North Vietnam bombing policy is blamed on Dean Rusk and Walt W. Rostow because they championed it. And innovative peace negotiations are credited to Henry Kissinger, who is possessed, so the argument goes, of a vision so clear and a grip on reality so tenacious that the achievements of the Nixon administration in foreign policy must be labeled brilliant. The ineffectiveness of the war on poverty is explained in terms of the defective or myopic vision of a small band of social science advisers and a few presidential aides. The Watergate mess was blamed, at least initially, on overzealous underlings. The net impression is that public policy is controlled, if not by the president, then by a handful of presidential intimates. The student remains grievously ignorant of the large number of elite and institutional forces behind policy formulation and implementation and of the complex transactions and ambiguities that more accurately characterize most national policy developments.

THE EXPANDED ROLE OF GOVERNMENT. Government today does vastly more in domestic and economic affairs than it did in the nineteenth century, and a president is the most visible leader of that level of government, the national establishment, which nearly monopolizes the rich and expanding monetary resources made up of the personal and corporate income tax and social insurance taxes. Proponents of the textbook presidency feel that in the absence of a strong president, our system of checks and balances simply does not produce decisions quickly enough. Most high-level fights within the executive branch come to the president. Legislation often languishes without his support. The presidential voice is amplified so that it looms larger and louder than that of any rival. Presidential leadership is an absolute necessity, or so it seems to them, if the system is to work at all. To them, the concept of the all-powerful presidency is rooted in experience as well as in fancy. This is where national goals must be set — where else? Who else could determine national priorities in such a fast-paced, complex era?

PUBLIC CELEBRITY NUMBER ONE

Textbooks are not alone in elevating and distorting public expectations. Television, journalists, and political campaigns increasingly help to structure the expectations not only of the public but also of the candidates themselves. The personalization and dramatization of the presidency is a central feature of the present. The American public has become conditioned by the media not to believe in the reality of a public act until it has been transformed into a dramatic or theatrical gesture. National personalities, including presidents, know they must try to acquire the attributes of show business.

Part of the problem is the oversell quality of political language. Candidates and their publicists necessarily adopt the language of promise; they pledge that they can accomplish objectives that are either nearly impossible or unlikely. Recall the early declarations about the war on poverty, the Great Society, Model Cities, the Alliance for Progress, the war on behalf of safe streets, President Nixon's New American Revolution, or President Ford's WIN program. Initiatives and programs are repeatedly packaged in military language — a war on this, a battle or crusade against that, a new corps here, a new campaign there. It is as if politicians and speechwriters think that rational but less dramatic plans clothed in ordinary civilian language do not suit a presidential command performance or would be ignored by a citizenry now immune to any but the most startling of proclamations.

So much media news time is devoted to the presidential elections that people might well expect an election to produce a savior rather than a president. The net result, Anthony Howard points out, is cause for alarm: "For what the nation has been beguiled into believing ever since 1960 is surely the politics of evangelism: the faith that individual men are cast to be messiahs, the conviction that Presidential incantations can be substituted for concrete programs, the belief that what matters is not so much the state of the nation as the inspiration-quotient of its people." [36] Television has downgraded local news and elevated national phenomena. Presidential travels and addresses are accentuated, and events are divorced from interpretation. Particularly advantageous for a president is the fact that in this era of televised communication the symbolic actions and the appearances of action often are as effective while they last as concrete action itself.

Another factor is the customary first-year grace period during which serious criticism of the president generally is considered off-limits. The presidential honeymoon is traditionally characterized by an elaborate press buildup of the candidate into a textbook president, the "great man incarnate." Glowing human-interest stories about the president and his family and Horatio Alger or boy-wonder tales extolling his unique skills fill the air. Thus, the *New York Times* published President Ford's picture twelve times on the front cover in the first fourteen days of his White House tenure. Early appointments to the cabinet and major agencies customarily elicit high praise and congratulatory press coverage. The new president's capabilities, his first State of the Union address, and new proposals are greeted by the predictable ritual acclaim describing them as bold, courageous, historic, and not to have been achieved by his predecessor. (Occasionally, of course, this last may be quite true: time in office does foreclose options.) Indeed, all of the initiatives of the honeymoon period may sound impressive, but the president has yet to implement anything. Presidents, of course, are also at fault. What president has refused the personal accolades issued during his honeymoon? What president has avoided the temptation of trying to perpetuate his honeymoon by manufacturing elevated expectations and success stories of one kind or another? (Ford's pardon of Nixon and his unusual modesty in his first year are indeed a striking exception, but the pardon may well have been forced on him in some way and perhaps Ford did have much to be modest about.)

Somewhere along the line the myth developed that the presidency inherently, even if mysteriously, strengthens and elevates. It has long since been popularly accepted that any person who becomes president is ennobled merely by becoming president, quite apart from his past performance or questionable preparation for the job. It is assumed that people of otherwise meager talents and undistinguished administrative careers will grow rapidly and that their talents will blossom. Newscasters and editorial writers have seldom questioned this simplistic assumption, and it might be argued that they have done more than their share of perpetuating and nurturing the legend. (But doesn't the press give the public what is wants? If so, then we are all in some way responsible.)

This myth may have had some valid basis in the nineteenth or early twentieth centuries; but particularly since the cold war era, it is possible that the opposite could also be true. Is it not plausible that the office may now tempt (harsher critics would say corrupt) presidents to take actions they might not have considered in other offices? Could it be that the office and the institution, and perhaps the great legacy against which they are now being judged, now weaken incumbents and nourish tendencies toward personal smallness on the one hand and a swelling sense of personal absolutism on the other? Of course, this interpretation would be hard to document and doubtless sounds like hypocritical carping when one sees the very critics who condemn high-handed actions by a Johnson, Nixon, or Ford regarding some similar actions as far more acceptable in a Washington, Jefferson, or Lincoln.

In any event, the assumption that the office ennobles and that the presidency always brings out the best in the occupant needs to be dealt with empirically and not just handed down to our young as certitude or platitude. In the opinion of popular historian Barbara Tuchman — and her concerns at least deserve consideration, if not acceptance — the presidency has become a greater risk than it is worth and the office has "bewitched the occupant, the press and the public. . . . While this process has been apparent from John F. Kennedy on, it took the strange transformation of good old open Presidency Gerald R. Ford to make it clear that the villain is not the man but the office. . . . Hardly has he settled in the ambiance of the White House than he began to talk like Louis XIV and behave like Richard M. Nixon. If there was one lesson to be learned from Watergate it was the danger in overuse of the executive power and in interference with the judicial system. Within a month of taking office Mr. Ford has violated both at once." [37] Are Ms. Tuchman's views too harsh? Were they an overreaction to the Ford pardon of former president Nixon? Perhaps; however, few can deny that the problem she singles out deserves critical examination.

Presidents, themselves the captives of many of these illusions and exaggerated expectations, become conditioned, during their campaigns if not earlier, to be stage actors. Seldom do they begin executive training or sharpen their executive skills until well after they have taken office. Their habit as politicians has been to sell themselves, to promote new ideas, to move on to seize new opportunities — what has been called "the politics of motion" or "the curse of activism." The emergence of what might be called the "acting-president" syndrome results in part from the difficulty and sometimes even the impossibility of governing:

acting is substituted for action; governing symbolically substituted for the more painful task of governing substantively. (An elaborate script for, and the consequences of, this posturing are examined in Chapter 5.)

But when the Camelot atmosphere of the first few hundred days fades away, a president is held personally accountable for what is not going smoothly. Inevitably, he is seen to be putting certain partisan interests above national ones. Soon he is discredited for not holding enough press conferences or for managing the news. The second round of appointments is questioned as overt patronage or as unworthy of the presidential imprimatur. Congressional committees prove recalcitrant. Unsuccessful international entanglements are associated with the president personally. Predictably, by the second year, reports spread that the president has become isolated from criticism.

MORAL AND RELIGIOUS TRAPPINGS

Most Americans now agree with Theodore and Franklin Roosevelt's celebrated assertions that the presidency is a bully pulpit and preeminently a position of moral leadership. Few citizens wince at James Reston's observation that "the White House is the pulpit of the nation and the president is its chaplain." British Prime Minister Harold Macmillan quipped, however, that if the people want a sense of purpose, they should get it from their archbishops. Americans do look to their presidents to articulate national goals, to unite the nation, to explain the state of the nation and the state of the world, to forecast the future and protect them from alien ideologies, and to involve the public in visions of a more just society. We are accustomed to regard our sense of purpose and pious presidential pronouncements as nearly one and the same. Richard Nixon's first Inaugural Address, in 1969, invoked God numerous times and talked often of spirit and the nation's destiny: "To a crisis of the spirit, we need an answer of the spirit. . . . We can build a great cathedral of the spirit. . . . We have endured a long night of the American spirit. But as our eyes catch the dimness of the first rays of dawn, let us not curse the remaining dark, let us gather the light. . . . Our destiny offers not the cup of despair, but the chalice of opportunity." [38] These exhortations appear to be calculated to reclaim the role of a pre-Reformation ecclesiastical mentor by proclaiming a nationwide crusade of spiritual renewal.

This inflated stress on the moral leadership of the presidency invites the type of response made by Nixon's own presidential Commission on Campus Unrest in 1970. Commission members evidently presumed that the vast moral powers of the presidency could somehow still student unrest around the nation. Accordingly, their most important recommendation was that "only the President can offer the compassionate, reconciling moral leadership that can bring the country together again. Only the President has the platform and prestige to urge all Americans. . . . Only the President, by example and by instruction can effectively calm." [39] Did the commission actually feel that the president was the only person who could serve as chief arbiter and conciliator in campus disturbances? Quite apart from the practicality of bringing presidential guidance to the nation's campuses is the question of how often a president can effectively offer his moral leadership to the nation.

Those persons who argue the need for more moral leadership from the presidency may not like the moral values individual presidents may promote. What is and is not moral — as when a president proclaims his support for or against prayer in the schools, abortion on request, religious services in the White House, amnesty for war resisters, birth control for the unmarried, legalization of pornography, or aid to Catholic schools — remains debatable. Those urging more moral leadership may find that they are getting more of it but liking it less. Moreover, civil religion is not always practiced in pursuit of the most laudable ends. Some presidents apparently have justified particular strategies on the grounds that they are the righteous courses of action, and it is evidently easy to find some scriptural legitimacy (and clerical blessing) for whatever one wants to do. Principled justifications, especially when they fuse country, flag, and God, can become hardened into rigid behavior. For example, Wilson's attempts to help set up the League of Nations became imbued with a moralistic fervor; the moral environment that generated the commitment was allowed to expand; and Wilson's role as the nation's spiritual leader expanded, until there was virtually no room for the role of political negotiator, for a nonmoralist Wilson to transform the idea into a reality. Perhaps Herbert Hoover's moral and ideological commitment to rugged individualism similarly inhibited alternative responses to the depression. President Johnson drummed up a great moral and patriotic support for U. S. involvement in Vietnam that ultimately was to weaken his subsequent efforts to reverse his course. And who will ever forget the priestly and rabbinic defenses of himself that President Nixon proudly mustered in 1974, or Gerald Ford's celebrated Sunday pardon and disquieting remark that "the ethical tone will be what I make it. . . ."

CONSEQUENCES OF THE CULT AND THE HALO

The textbook presidency may appear simple and useful to many, and its oversimplifications and distortions may strike some as amusing. Its exaggerations are not, however, without cost to society. It is difficult to separate out the impact of traditional patriotism, nationalism, and hero-worship from the reinforcing influences of the textbook images of presidential capacity and performance. But some consequences of the teachings of the textbook presidency are reflected in the quality of civic participation, in the potential for cynicism toward government, and in the distorted perceptions within the presidential establishment itself.

THE EFFECT ON CITIZEN POLITICS. The relationship between moral leader and layman is often viewed as a one-way street. If the president is indeed the national chaplain, how is it possible to cultivate a democratic citizenry that is active and not passive, that may, on selective occasions, responsibly dispute with this national moral eminence? The average citizen, nurtured in the belief that presidents are personally powerful enough to end war, depression, corruption, and all like manner of civic malaise, finds it difficult to disagree strongly with the president under any circumstances. Students are instructed that it is proper to state one's differences in a letter to congressmen or even to the White House. But because of the almost certain deference to his textbook image, the president usually can expect four- or five-to-one ratios in telegram and mail responses and about a two- or three-to-one ratio in national opinion-poll responses in favor of his handling of the presidency (except during the last year or two in office).

There are, of course, those who engage in protest, perhaps to discredit presidential claims or to weaken the incumbent president, hoping to obtain a more suitable leader — probably one more like the textbook version — or more suitable policies at the next election. But protestors and demonstrators are dismissed by large numbers of Americans as self-righteous and unpatriotic critics, elitist easterners, or congenital defeatists. The "love it or leave it" slogan includes a basic respect for the presidency as well as the country.

The most popular course of action is to quietly rally around the president and offer him permissive support, hoping by such action — or inaction — to strengthen his and the nation's resolve to meet the present challenge. A related pattern of behavior, that of apathy and indifference, is selected by citizens who feel secure in the belief that presidents know best. Thus, a president usually may assume that when major difficulties are faced, most Americans, at least for a while, will trust and follow him, often tendering him even increased support. In the process a citizen's loyalty to the nation often mindlessly blends into loyalty to his president, a confusion much to be desired by incumbent presidents and indeed often promoted by them. As a result public support comes not only from those who feel the president is right but is also measurably inflated by those who, regardless of policy or situation, agree with their president merely because he is the only president they have.

Presidents and press alike might be well advised to de-escalate claims that the American people or the great silent majority of middle Americans are strongly behind the president on a certain policy matter. This may or may not be the case, regardless of the polls; in all likelihood, a substantial portion of the people really do not know much about the subtleties — or crudities — of the policy or do not much care. For those few who are inclined to protest the actions of their president, textbook wisdom seems to encourage a direct, personal confrontation. If the president personally is so powerful and independent, it appears logical to picket him, march on his White House, or try to break or get rid of him in order to change policy; but breaking or changing presidents does not necessarily insure any major shift in specialized policy subsystems. Cast as superhuman, presidents and even presidential candidates are supported passionately, but they also run the risk of assault and assassination.

Thus, although the vast majority of Americans support and honor their presidency, presidents are prime targets for psychotics and extremists. Regrettably, presidents become deeply loved and roundly hated, unduly worshiped and unduly feared. On both sides of the presidential popularity equation, the president's importance is inflated beyond reasonable bounds. On one side, there is a near-mindless faith that a president enjoys a monopoly of national civic virtue and wisdom and that any detractor must be an irreverent effete snob or a nervous Nellie. On the other side, a president becomes the most crooked of all politicians, the perpetuator of poverty and racism, the tool of the establishment, and the primary source of a choleric national disposition.

AN INVITATION TO CYNICISM AND DESPAIR.   The idealized textbook view has it that the president as the architect of policy is the lobbyist for all the people, the representative of the otherwise unrepresented. Pointing out that often he is quite dependent on one or another political and policy elite both inside and outside the federal government is regarded as indecorous. Perhaps textbook writers, along with many political scientists of the 1950s and 1960s, overreacted defensively to the allegations of sociologist C. Wright Mills and others about the existence of a cabalistic power elite.

But what happens when the citizen who was raised on the sanitized textbook version of the presidency learns that the presidential establishment sees to it that the government extensively subsidizes corporate farmers, opposition political forces in Chile, Lockheed Aircraft, home-building companies, and the like; or that the presidency is sensitively deferential to monopolistic organizations such as ITT and the Teamsters' Union because of their political and financial clout? What happens when the student learns too about deliberate government suppression of information about massacres of Vietnamese citizens, irregularities in defense contracting, illegal campaign practices, political fixes, Watergate conspiracies, and advertisements and telegram campaigns rigged to give the appearance of public support for devious presidential policies? Cynicism, a crisis of confidence, and a diminution of the feeling of legitimacy in the institution of the presidency seem inevitable, and indeed these have occurred. The paradox is that when misunderstood and misused, those very characteristics that nourish the potential for responsible leadership in the presidency — its pronounced visibility, its mystique, and its exalted legacy — can also undermine it.

DISTORTIONS OF PRESIDENTIAL PERCEPTIONS. If the mythical textbook image of the presidency has costly implications for the quality of the relationship between citizens and the presidency, it affects fully as much the ways in which presidents and their associates conceive of themselves and of their jobs. The reverence and loyalty rendered a new president are a rich resource, but an overindulgent citizenry can distort the president's psychological perspective and sense of balance. Though some of his observations are overstated, former presidential press secretary George Reedy's acrimonious criticisms of the monarchial trappings of the contemporary White House deserve attention:

> *The atmosphere of the White House is calculated to instill in any man a sense of destiny. He literally walks in the footsteps of hallowed figures — of Jefferson, of Jackson, of Lincoln. The almost sanctified relics of a distant, semi-mythical past surround him as ordinary household objects to be used by his family. From the moment he enters the halls he is made aware that he has become enshrined in a pantheon of semi-divine mortals who have shaken the world, and that he has taken from their hands the heritage of American dreams and aspirations. Unfortunately for him divinity is a better basis for inspiration than it is for government.* [40]

The Gaullist image of the American presidency that was allowed to grow up in the Nixon White House — so obvious from the deference shown him by oversolicitous and overzealous sycophants — is an illustration of this type of distortion. The quality of advice necessary to balanced presidential decision making can be adversely affected by too respectful an attitude toward the chief executive. So acute did this problem become in the Nixon presidency that John Ehrlichman's Watergate testimony conjured up the image of a paper presidency. From notions that the president is too busy to be bothered, that bad news should be kept away, and that the dignity of the office somehow was demeaned or compromised if heated debate and advocacy were allowed to occur in the presidential presence, it was only a short step to the autocratic views that "the President is the government," to quote Ehrlichman, and that "every President has a right to conduct foreign policy in a way *that helps him most*" (italics added), to quote Henry Kissinger. [41]

Protecting a president and his power too assiduously sometimes can lock the president into a disastrous policy. [42] Thus, former Nixon White House aide Egil Krogh led the plumbers operation because he believed sincerely that "freedom of the President to pursue his planned course was the ultimate national security objective." Only after his conviction did he recognize that sincerity and loyalty "can often be as blinding as worthy." His advice to future young people in high governmental posts sums up the classic problem: "I hope they will recognize that the banner of national security can turn perceived patriotism into actual disservice. When contemplating a course of action, I hope they will never fail to ask, 'Is this right?' " [43]

Chapter I posed the question: "Is the presidency strong enough to direct and manage the domestic side of government?" To look at the illusions generated by the textbooks and often by the mass media, the answer would appear to be an unqualified "yes!" But the answer, as we will see in following chapters, really is not so sanguine. The illusory notion must be put to rest that the right person in one job almost single-handedly can *solve* the nation's problems. Alternatively, the competency of the presidency in planning and implementation must be improved radically. In fact, both steps are necessary if we are to make the presidency safe for democracy, and, conversely, if we would make democracy safe from weak or unaccountable presidential performance.

NOTES

1. Fifteen introductory college texts on American government and another twenty more specialized studies of the presidency or national policy making were examined, with special attention to the types of images, perception, and facts given about presidential performance. The case made in this sction is merely illustrative; no claim of exhaustive quantitative analysis is implied. Any definitive exercise of that kind would require a quantitative analysis of the content of textbook images over time and of the degree of variation among them. These would then be counterbalanced by an extensive number of cases demonstrating that these images are incorrect or misleading for an understanding of actual presidential performance. Although such a study is feasible and would be of value, the scope and intent of this chapter are, respectively, more limited and modest.

   An earlier version of this chapter was presented as a paper, "The Textbook Presidency and Political Science," to the Annual Meeting of the American Political Science Association in September 1970; the paper was reproduced in U.S., Congress *Congressional Record,* 1970 vol. 116, pp. 517102–15. Senate, 91st Congress, 2nd session.
2. David Easton and Jack Dennis, *Children in the Political System* (McGraw-Hill, 1969); and Fred I. Greenstein, *Children and Politics* (Yale University Press, 1965).
3. See the discussion in Byron G. Massialas, *Education and the Political System* (Addison-Wesley, 1969), chap. 3.
4. Educational films about the presidency and recent presidents usually outdo even the texts in overstating and romanticizing presidential influence and greatness.
5. Robert Carr, Marver Bernstein, and Walter Murphy, *American Democracy in Theory and Practice,* 4th ed. (Holt, Rinehart and Winston, 1965), p. 447.
6. William A. McClenaghan, *Magruder's American Government* (Allyn and Bacon, 1962), p. 262.
7. Robert A. Dahl, *Pluralist Democracy in the United States* (Rand McNally, 1967), p. 90.
8. William H. Young, *Essentials of American Government,* 9th ed. (Appleton-Century-Crofts, 1964), p. 251.

9. Rowland Egger, *The President of the United States* (McGraw-Hill, 1967), p. 4.
10. James M. Burns and Jack W. Peltason, *Government by the People,* 5th ed. (Prentice-Hall, 1964), pp. 434–35. For a similar point of view, see Kenneth M. Dolbeare and Murray J. Edelman, *American Politics* (D. C. Heath, 1971), p. 296.
11. James M. Burns, *Presidential Government* (Avon Books, 1965), pp. 326–27.
12. Theodore H. White, *The Making of the President 1960* (Pocket Books, 1961), p. 441.
13. Theodore H. White, "The Action Intellectuals," *Life,* 9 June 1967, pp. 43–76; 16 June 1967, pp. 44–74; 23 June 1967, pp. 76–85. For a later study that shatters such illusions see David Halberstam's *The Best and the Brightest* (Random House, 1972).
14. Clinton Rossiter, *The American Presidency,* rev. ed. (New American Library, 1960), pp. 250, 84, 68–69, 17.
15. *Ibid.,* p. 102.
16. Richard E. Neustadt, *Presidential Power* (Wiley, 1960). This pioneering analysis of New Deal and post-New Deal presidential performance had an important influence on political science. Neustadt's thesis that a leader's power hinged upon his capacity to persuade, and that his capacity to persuade rested upon his image and reputation, was provocative. Neustadt's optimism about the potential for effective presidential leadership, however, is more tempered in later writings, especially *Alliance Politics* (Columbia University Press, 1970). See also the assessment of his argument by Peter W. Sperlich, "Bargaining and Overload: An Essay on Presidential Power," in Aaron Wildavsky, ed., *The Presidency* (Little, Brown, 1969), pp. 168–92.
17. Neustadt, *Presidential Power* (John Wiley & Sons, 1960), p. 43.
18. See, for example, Nelson Polsby, *Congress and the Presidency,* 2nd ed. (Prentice-Hall, 1971), p. 25; and Garry Wills, *Nixon Agonistes* (Houghton Mifflin, 1970), pp. 221–22.
19. Burton P. Sapin, *The Making of United States Foreign Policy* (Brookings Institution, 1966), p. 90. (Emphasis added.)
20. James David Barber, *The Presidential Character* (Prentice-Hall, 1972), p. 446.
21. Erwin C. Hargrove, "Presidential Personality and Revisionist Views of the Presidency," *American Journal of Political Science,* November 1973, p. 826. See also Alexander L. George, "On Analyzing Presidents," *World Politics,* January 1974; and Erwin Hargrove, *The Power of the Modern Presidency* (Random House, 1974). Also useful are articles by James David Barber, "Strategies for Understanding Politicians," *American Journal of Political Science,* Spring 1974, pp. 443–67; and Arthur Schlesinger, Jr., "Can Psychiatry Save the Republic?" *Saturday Review/World,* 7 September 1974, pp. 10–16.
22. Nelson A. Rockefeller, *Unity, Freedom and Peace* (Vintage Books, 1968), pp. 152–53.
23. Lyndon B. Johnson, *My Hope for America* (Random House, 1964), p. 14.
24. Theodore H. White, *The Making of the President 1960,* pp. 450–51.
25. Theodore H. White, *The Making of the President 1968* (Atheneum, 1969), p. 428.
26. Michael Novak, *Choosing Our King* (Macmillan, 1974), p. 5.
27. William H. Riker, *Democracy in the United States,* 2nd ed. (Macmillan, 1967), p. 188.
28. Eugene McCarthy, "Thoughts on the Presidency," *New York Times,* 30 March 1968.
29. Murray Edelman, *The Symbolic Uses of Politics* (University of Illinois Press, 1967), p. 78.
30. Robert D. Hess and David Easton, "The Child's Changing Image of the President," *Public Opinion Quarterly,* 24 (Winter 1960):644.
31. Herbert Emmerich, *Essays on Federal Reorganization* (University of Alabama Press, 1959), p. 62.

32. William E. Leuchtenberg, *Franklin D. Roosevelt and The New Deal* (Harper and Row, 1963), p. 327.
33. See Edward S. Corwin, *The President: Office and Powers* (New York University Press, 1940); Pendleton Herring, *Presidential Leadership* (Farrar and Rinehart, 1940); Richard Hofstadter, *American Political Tradition* (Knopf, 1948); Harold Laski, *The American Presidency* (Grosset and Dunlap, 1940).
34. Arthur M. Schlesinger, Jr., "Congress and The Making of American Foreign Policy," *Foreign Affairs,* Fall 1972, pp. 94–95. See also his *The Imperial Presidency* (Houghton Mifflin, 1973).
35. Theodore C. Sorensen, *Decision-Making in the White House* (Columbia University Press, 1963), p. 75.
36. Anthony Howard, "No Time for Heroes," *Harper's,* February 1969, pp. 91–92.
37. Barbara Tuchman, "The Villain Is The Office Not The Man," *Boston Globe,* 21 September 1974.
38. Richard Nixon, Inaugural Address, 20 January 1969. *Public Papers of the Presidents 1969* (U.S. Government Printing Office, 1970), pp. 2–4.
39. *Report of The President's Commission on Campus Unrest* (September 1970), chap. 7, p. 30. (U.S. Government Printing Office.)
40. George E. Reedy, *The Twilight of the Presidency* (World, 1970), pp. 14–15.
41. John Ehrlichman, quoted in *Time,* 30 July 1973; Henry Kissinger, statement before the Senate Foreign Relations Committee, quoted in *Los Angeles Times,* 9 September 1973.
42. See the useful elaboration of this point in Alexander L. George, "The Case for Multiple Advocacy in Making Foreign Policy," *American Political Science Review,* September 1972, pp. 762–63.
43. Statement by Egil Krogh, Jr., released by his attorney after he was sentenced in U.S. District Court for his role in the plumber's break-in of the office of Daniel Ellsberg's psychiatrist. *New York Times,* 25 January 1974, p. 16.

CHAPTER 3

PREROGATIVES
DISCRETION WITH CONSTRAINTS

*The powers of the Presidency are often described. Its limitations
should occasionally be remembered.*

— *President John Kennedy, 26 October 1963.*
   Public Papers of the President
   (*Government Printing Office, 1964*), *p. 815.*

*It is a tragic fact that a President can hardly ever have a friend.
There are enough, always, of those who aspire to his intimacy; but
even those he has known the longest will often betray him;
sometimes without realizing how serious the breach of confidence
has been. . . . They will not understand, as a friend must, the casual
allusion in conversation, the reference to this or that which it
would be tiresome to explain. . . . Sometimes they will get on a
moral high horse and ride away from a man who must always be
guided by political possibilities.*

— *Rexford G. Tugwell,* The Democratic Roosevelt
   (*Penguin, 1957*), *pp. 361–62.*

*It is in the President's interest to put the best gloss he can on things,
and the reporters' vocation to find out what is "really happening."
. . . Social prizes may go to the reporter who goes along, but
Pulitzer prizes go to the reporters who get things they are not
supposed to have.*

—*Aaron Wildavsky,* Perspectives on the Presidency
   (*Little, Brown, 1975*), *introduction.*

An appealing but deceptive notion is that any strong, determined president — "the type who knows what leadership is all about" — can overcome the constraints on the office. Thus, only a reluctant, passive president, one uninterested in power and indifferent to results, will resign himself to the frail authority and narrow boundaries so often prescribed by Congress, the courts, conservatives, and critics of presidential activism. Conventional wisdom holds that any president who genuinely wants to overcome the resistance of Congress, the bureaucracy, or special interests has virtually all the required resources or formal tools. In the words of veteran *New York Times* columnist Arthur Krock: "A President has a vast store at his command of rewards and punishments for members of Congress, Governors and local bosses. They reach from patronage, instant television time if and when he wants it, and the front page of the press for almost every act and word, to access to income tax returns, command of the armed forces, and moral leadership." [1] This and similar listings of presidential resources often leave the impression of extraordinary influence. They can also heighten expectations of a wonder-working presidential performance. Such expectations often diminish rather than enhance the power of the office.

The understandable tendency to examine the presidency in the context of crisis usually adds to this impression of presidential strength. Emergencies enlarge the catalogue of leadership resources available to presidents. Congress is, if the crisis is not too drawn out, more generous than usual. Crises relax the settled bounds of public opinion, special-interest lobbying, and standard administrative procedures. Hence, a president, even when he loses, appears more powerful than he really is when confronting the steel industry or the Russians, or mobilizing the National Guard, or putting the country on nuclear alert. To look at American intervention in Vietnam is to observe the substantial and often unbridled exercise of presidential prerogatives. And yet, even in this last instance, presidents have never succeeded in achieving what they had intended. Examining the great bulk of what presidents attempt to accomplish in the day-to-day conduct of business reveals a constellation of *brakes* that limit a president's influence. The value of even the most valuable prerogative is lessened with too frequent use, and many strategies theoretically available for leadership may not actually be usable when a president would like to deploy them. Still other resources are underused or misused.

This chapter and the one following examine how presidential discretion is more easily imputed than realized. Five major prerogatives in the presidential arsenal are assessed: (1) appointments, (2) advisers, (3) reorganization, (4) publicity, and (5) the veto. To be sure, a president has many other prerogatives but an examination of these will suffice to show that the panoply of strategies, props, and prerogatives thought to be his for leadership may or may not actually be usable when a president would like to use them, and that often these resources are abused. Chapter 4 will argue that even when presidential prerogatives are deployed creatively, they usually are braked by the countervailing constraints of such institutions as Congress, professional and bureaucratic elites, or public opinion. In short, checks and balances are alive and mostly well, and retainer walls of one kind or another are particularly constraining for the president who undertakes to achieve progressive, redistributive goals.

APPOINTMENTS

A president's most strategic formal resource is the ability to recruit able people, who share his convictions, to fill high-level positions. According to what might be called the good-person theory, a presidency is only as good as its staffs, cabinet, and counselors. Quality and loyalty are what is wanted. In practice, however, former White House aides attest that many mistakes are made in recruitment and that seldom is enough time given to it. One Kennedy aide said, in retrospect, "Our recruitment effort was pretty accidental and backward. . . ." Several Nixon aides reported that their patronage and recruitment efforts verged on the disastrous during the first two years.

After running for the presidency for several years the successful candidate often finds that the people he courted during the campaign — delegates, press, financial contributors, machine leaders, advance men, or political strategists — do not have the skills needed to manage the executive branch. Kennedy repeatedly complained, "People, people, people! I don't know any people [for the cabinet and other top posts]. I only know voters! How am I going to fill these 1,200 jobs?" [2] In fact, Kennedy eventually appointed a cabinet almost half of whom he did not even know.

In the post-election rush many appointments are made on the basis of subjective judgments or ethnic or geographical representation and from too limited a field of candidates. Ironically, at the time when a president has the largest number of jobs to fill and enjoys his greatest drawing power, he has less time and information available than at any other point in his administration to take advantage of this major prerogative. Later in his term he has fewer vacancies and usually less prestige; candidates from outside the government are wary about being saddled with troubled programs and recognize that little can be accomplished in an administration's last year or two. During the post-election rush there is also the need to deflect an avalanche of unsolicited job requests — many from local campaign persons — without giving offense.

Too frequently appointees are not carefully related to policy. Many sub-cabinet appointments, for example, are made by subordinates, with the president hardly aware of whether the appointee is matched with the position. Just after election the views of the president and of his appointees are in a state of evolution. Once in office many appointees adopt new attitudes as a result of new institutionalized responsibilities; or some, perhaps ill-suited for institutional management, may become rigidly wedded to the views of the interest groups with which they most frequently interact.

Presidential appointments may and often do err in the opposite direction as well: a president can be surrounded by such like-minded appointees that an amiability and conformity in thinking can develop all too easily. Social psychologist Irving Janis points out that when this occurs there is a dangerous inclination to resort to seeking concurrence and *groupthink* at the expense of critical judgment.[3] The cult of loyalty to President Nixon doubtless encouraged the suspension of critical and objective thinking on the part of many of the people involved in the Watergate affair.

Many other circumstances limit the presidential appointment prerogative. Some potential appointees just do not want to live or even be near Washington, D.C. Others balk at the idea of having to disclose their financial background and income. Involvement with past administrations or too close an association with past scandals or major industries connected with a new assignment may be enough to occasion congressional hostility to a presidential nomination. Nelson Rockefeller's wealth and personal gifts became a major obstacle in his nomination for vice president. Several former Nixon aides, such as Peter Flanigan who was nominated by Ford as ambassador to Spain, were unable to overcome senatorial opposition and subsequently Ford withdrew these nominations. And Congress is becoming more and more sensitive these days to any kind of potential conflict of interest, especially when it will directly affect American consumers. In short, then, the pool of available appointees is often smaller than people assume.

APPOINTMENTS TO THE COURT. The selection of judges who have a constitutionally prescribed independence from the executive, as distinct from appointments nominally under a president's line of authority, can also lead to major disappointments. Historically, for example, the Senate has rejected nearly 20 percent of presidential nominees to the Supreme Court, most recently including one each in 1968, 1969 and 1970. Political scientist Robert Scigliano suggests that one Supreme Court justice in four consistently rules quite differently from what the president who appointed him expected and that numerous other justices fail to conform to expectations in cases of particular importance.[4] Some presidents apparently have thought the people they appointed held views different from those they actually held. In other instances the liberating conditions of court office — life tenure, high salary, and responsibility to the Constitution and legal tradition — may have altered the views of justices.

Harry Truman is alleged to have said that his appointing of Tom Clark to the Supreme Court was one of his biggest mistakes. It is known that Eisenhower was retrospectively displeased that his appointees, Earl Warren and William J. Brennan, created a Supreme Court libertarian majority. An Eisenhower contemporary wrote:

> ... Eisenhower felt increasing disappointment at Warren's increasing show of finding law for libertarian political doctrine where there was none in the books, and at the support of this practice by his first Democratic appointee to the Court, Justice Brennan. The President told his friends that Chief Judge Arthur Vanderbilt of New Jersey, who had an enviable reputation for decisions based on the law of the cases, had assured him that Brennan had the same "ideal judicial concept," and said the President, "he had got the same mistaken impression of Brennan in a conversation prior to the appointment." [5]

Justice Byron White has voted far more conservatively than Kennedy forces expected. But the Kennedy difficulties were greater in the selection of federal circuit and district judges in the South. In large part these choices "were the products of the preexisting judicial selection system which the Kennedys inherited and more or less perpetuated without much question. . . ." [6] As is traditional, of course, regional senators had offered nominations for these regional posts. With a slim working majority in Congress, Kennedy was constantly aware that his legislative program could suffer at the hands of disgruntled southerners. Accordingly, the Kennedy brothers learned that "you have to play ball with the senators and do the best you can." But it seems clear in retrospect that no one aspect of the Kennedy performance in the civil rights area is more vulnerable to criticism than the exercise of the appointment prerogative. Simply stated, they gave in too readily; for the Kennedys bypassed civil rights legislation in favor of litigation, yet they turned right around and appointed individuals dedicated to frustrating that very litigation. "[One result was that] the Kennedy Justice Department was forced to devote thousands of dollars, untold energy, imagination and brilliance, all to counteract the obstructionist tactics of its appointees, five of whom decided over one hundred cases against the Negro, the Civil Rights Division, and the Constitution. . . ." [7]

Nixon, of course, had considerable trouble trying to appoint a southern conservative to the bench. Twice he was thwarted and only after appointing two northerners was he able to succeed with his nomination of Justice Powell, a Virginian moderate and an esteemed past president of the American Bar Association.

THE CASE OF DR. JAMES ALLEN. Several problems that may arise in presidential recruitment can be seen in the case of Nixon's first commissioner of education, Dr. James E. Allen. Allen had been commissioner of education in New York State for more than a decade, serving both the Harriman and

Rockefeller administrations. A registered Republican, he was widely regarded as one of the nation's leading educators. "He was at the top of everybody's list of suggestions."

It was well known that Allen had turned down President Kennedy's invitation for the same post, and administration officials believed, correctly, that they could earn the confidence of the national educational community, as well as favorable attention in the eastern press, if they could overcome his initial reluctance to accept the job. The president himself called and invited Allen to the White House, where the president stressed that he admired Allen and wanted him. Allen was surprised that neither HEW secretary Robert Finch nor the president seemed to know or care much about specific major educational issues. Except for Nixon's animated talk about the imperative of bringing more discipline back into the public schools, Allen could not detect that Nixon had any special educational programs or policies that he wanted to promote. He was led to believe he would have a major say in the administration's educational policies. Allen, with some ambivalence, accepted. He reasoned that if he did not accept the job, someone less progressive and less responsive to the educational community would do so.

Once on board, Commissioner Allen's tenure became unusually turbulent. Allen was both a political and educational liberal, a progressive and outspoken advocate of desegregation and integration. He regarded busing as a reasonable technique to achieve such ends and advocated a more tolerant stance on student dissent and unrest. Above all, Allen championed the goal of an activist federal commitment to all levels of public education. Actually, Nixon and Allen were in accord on few politically salient issues in educational policy.

Allen made no effort to conceal his contempt of White House and Republican party suggestions for key staff and deputy positions. Regarding himself as an advocate, Allen time and again spoke out in behalf of a higher priority for education, noting that the educational needs of the nation were being downgraded, bypassed, and virtually ignored by the White House. Occasionally he rejected the advice of senior White House aides; he accepted other decisions with ill-disguised resentment. As time went by, Allen's advice was sought less and less frequently by the White House. Then, about a year after he had joined the administration, he publicly criticized presidential foreign policy: "I find it difficult to understand the rationale for the necessity of the move into Cambodia as a means of supporting and hastening the withdrawal from Viet Nam — a withdrawal that I feel must be accomplished as quickly as possible. What concerns me most now is what our responsibility is in dealing with the disastrous effects that his action has had on education throughout the country and on the confidence of millions of concerned citizens in their Government." [8] Political counselors to the president immediately urged that Allen be replaced; he was fired twenty-one days later.

Patronage factors enter more into appointments in the federal regional and field offices of domestic departments than into those in Washington. Patronage concerns often are accentuated in new and controversial program areas, presumably because of the need for political support. In many such instances congressmen and interest groups seek appointments for their nominees to advance their own interests in regional and regulatory areas. An entire spectrum of traditional patronage posts — judgeships, U. S. marshals and attorneys, collectors of the customs, members of selective service boards, and regional white-collar jobs — are claimed by congressmen, governors, or state party leaders as a matter of right. Presidential resistance invites disloyalty and disaffection. It is generally accepted, also, that high cabinet and political appointees need a few aides to serve at their own pleasure. Some important administrative positions are the private preserve of congressional committees, well-organized interest groups, or professions.

AFL-CIO officials often have dictated top Labor Department appointments. Nixon's second secretary of labor, James D. Hodgson, complained after being forced to resign in 1972 that AFL-CIO President George Meany insisted on a cabinet member who would be "100% for labor's point of view regardless of how the Secretary himself feels as a member of the President's Cabinet." Hodgson added that "what Meany really wanted was for me to be the Earl Butz for organized labor." [9] During the Johnson administration, the AFL-CIO was able to keep favored subcabinet members in their posts despite the wishes of the president and cabinet secretary. Similarly, the American Medical Association has enjoyed a special voice in the selection of high-level federal health officials, especially under Republican administrations. The absence of lateral-entry opportunities in certain government services also works to limit the scope of presidential appointment; for example, all appointees for the chairmanship of the Joint Chiefs of Staff must be designated from among a select few of the senior career military officers.

The liabilities of the appointment prerogative are recalled by the political maxim, "Filling a political job creates nine enemies and one ingrate." President Kennedy's lieutenant, Theodore Sorensen, wrote that patronage caused more headaches than anything else. "Patronage squabbles in several states earned the Kennedy administration more enemies than friends. Only occasionally did a specific personnel opening at the time of a crucial vote enable both the president and a key legislator to please each other." [10] Kennedy himself played down the importance of patronage for the presidency, noting that most of the jobs belonged to members of Congress anyway.[11] Kennedy also quipped, "When I was a Congressman I never realized how important Congress was. But now I do."

Efforts to plant "friends" of the president or the party in the departments usually meet with considerable resistance. The departmental view is either to promote from within or recruit from among their own "friends." Some of the problems probably stem from hasty or heavy-handed White House tactics. One Nixon staffer alluded thus to the difficulties:

We had a very good working relationship with the cabinet before the inauguration and in the first days of the Administration they seemed quite happy to have our help in suggesting and referring people to them. But soon after they had taken office in their departments, the cabinet members became very upset at us and very ill at ease working with us at the White House. They wanted their own people, they wanted to lean on people that they knew, and they didn't want patronage people being pushed on them. After a while and for most of the first year of the Administration we were at each others throats ... and with certain departments such as HEW and Agriculture the battles were bloody.

Many other White House aides in recent administrations complained of department leaders who protested that White House staff nominees were not qualified. One former White House aide caustically complained about the "pious fraud of guys who claim to be public administration specialists — every time you turned around they were promoting each other." This same aide recalled the time he was assigned to secure a routine middle-grade job for the husband of one of the president's secretaries: "Planting him in the Defense department sounds as though it would be easy, but what a stink it turned out to be. That's about the hardest thing to do in Washington." Once hired it is usually costly to fire administrators from responsible positions, although in theory presidents can fire whomever they wish among executive branch political appointees. One of Lyndon Johnson's former cabinet members said that he believes the president wanted to fire at least three of his cabinet members in 1968; but because several key cabinet members already had resigned by late 1967, the firing of others would have confirmed suspicions of weakness and conflict.

Administration dismissals can backfire in the news media; a presidential firing, rather than removing an official's public platform, actually can attract substantially greater public attention to the man and issues in question. Harry Truman's firing of General Douglas MacArthur is an example of the severe political fallout that can accompany the dismissal of high officials. President Nixon's first-term firing of Interior secretary Walter Hickel and second-term firing of Special Prosecutor Archibald Cox and Deputy Attorney General William Ruckelshaus prompted fusillades of charges in the press that the administration was isolated from the views of the people and that Nixon was violating the open presidency pledge made in his campaign. The Nixon administration's determined efforts to fire A. Ernest Fitzgerald, an Air Force deputy assistant secretary who had told Congress of vast cost overruns in defense contracts, were reversed by the combined efforts of numerous journalists, a vigorous campaign for his reinstatement by Senator William Proxmire and the American Civil Liberties Union, and, finally, by orders from the chief appeals officer of the Civil Service Commission. Fitzgerald, a civilian employee, lost his $32,000 a year job after testifying before Congress about outlandish cost over-runs, which his superiors were dismissing as of minor concern. At one point, President Nixon personally advised that Fitzgerald should be fired and he publicly stated his intention to stick by that directive. The president's efforts were in vain, however, for in 1973, after a long and highly publicized campaign, Fitzgerald resumed his previously abolished job in the Pentagon. Highly publicized resignations such as those of Elliot Richardson during the Watergate scandals, of Ford's press secretary Gerald terHorst during the Nixon pardon episode, or of his energy administrator John Sawhill, can shake public confidence in a president. Ironically, Ford also lost ground because he refused to quickly fire or othewise rid himself of many former Nixon aides. It seemed initially that Ford just did not know people to recruit and that he was unable to develop a strategy for recruitment.

ADVISERS

Presidents, it is generally thought, can command the help and advice of just about anyone in the country. The "best and the brightest" and other "available" intellectuals are at their disposal. But this new priesthood has liabilities for a president; the use of experts and intellectuals is almost always a complex political exchange. John Kennedy's fury at the so-called "specialists" in the aftermath of the Bay of Pigs episode well expresses the dangers of relying on the experts: "All my life I've known better than to depend on experts. How could I have been so stupid, to let them go ahead?" [12] One result of this experience was an attempt to broaden the president's base of information by going beyond organization charts and outside formal hierarchic channels and by encouraging the presentation of competing points of view. Kennedy found time and again, however, that his advisers were divided; and it was far easier for advisers to make speeches and speculate about possible outcomes than it was for him to make final judgments. Kennedy liked to observe wryly that he, the president, must bear the burden of responsibility; his advisers could move on to new advice.

Former President Nixon's reliance on a band of former CIA agents and assorted public relations experts to mastermind his 1972 reelection bid also illustrates the liabilities of depending on the so-called experts. Nixon became dependent on his dependents, and his dependency continued even as many of them became defendants. In the end, as is now well known, Nixon's role as chief defendant gradually superseded that of chief executive, and he was forced to resign just short of being impeached.

Sometimes the best adviser is not simply the person who has the most expertise and is the most articulate. As one senior White House aide said: "The more specialized in a single area you are, the less likely you are to be effective. It very easily happens that you become a lobbyist. On the other hand, those who stay as generalists are likely to be turned to by a president, to pick up and deal with day-to-day problems that face him. It's a *problem* orientation rather than a *specialized program* orientation that earns presidential respect and sustained access." A Kennedy aide described the president's antipathy to staff advocates in similar terms:

The President did not like advocates and hence two of his early appointments as civil rights staff assistants didn't work out at all, not so much because of their style or personality but because the President didn't like being pushed. He was sensitive to lobbyists: in fact, he often shuddered when lobbyists were even visiting elsewhere in his White House. If it were known that you favored or occasionally acted as an agent for special interests, it reduced your effectiveness under Kennedy. The President, for example, viewed [a national security "expert"] as too much of an advocate. He was bothered and irritated by . . . [a staff assistant for minority problems] because of his overlong and trivia-heavy memos urging too much too fast. And, the intervention of . . . [an activist policy aide] and his over active role in certain Brazilian and Venezuelan policy questions made JFK really mad. . . .

Self-assured advisers can distort by drastic oversimplification, which demonstrates little more than a disregard for complexity and an incapacity for modesty. Presidential counsel Theodore Sorensen put it this way: "The most rational, pragmatic-appearing man may turn out to be the slave of his own private myths, habits, and emotional beliefs. The hardest working man may be too busy and out-of-touch with the issue at hand, or too weary to focus firmly on it. The most articulate, authoritative man may only be making bad advice sound good, while driving into silence less aggressive or more cautious advisers." [13]

Most outside advisers are advocates of special theories or models; most also are particularly mindful of the resource needs of their disciplines or institutions; and most favor an increase in federal funds for these pet interests. Outsiders may also not understand or accept the intra-administration rules of the game. Many professionals share the Galbraith and Moynihan opinion that personal modesty is a vastly overrated virtue. Bright people not uncommonly want credit for their ideas and are more uncomfortable than most people about putting their advice to use in lobbying or public relations charades. Despite the initial glamor of being called upon to advise a president, they maintain an independence, sometimes irreverent, that makes it difficult for presidents to discipline or at times even to work with them.

Vannevar Bush, who worked with several presidents, wrote that, "Neither Truman nor for that matter Eisenhower at first understood the art of effective relations between the President and the scientific and engineering fraternity." [14]

Despite temporary improvement in these relations late in the Eisenhower and in the Kennedy periods, detachment and distrust developed in the late 1960s, culminating in Nixon's disbanding of the Office of Science and Technology and abolition of the once prestigious President's Science Advisory Committee. Another illustration of the potential difficulties of employing outside advisers is Nixon's appointment of Chancellor Alexander Heard of Vanderbilt University during the summer of 1970 as a short-term adviser on student unrest and related campus problems. Heard's report implicitly criticized various White House policies and urged more presidential concern and more effective leadership. Not surprisingly, the White House was disappointed by Heard; it felt that, rather than offering plausible solutions, he was in essence giving widely publicized sermons to the president — at the president's expense and on a presidential platform.

Presidents are pressed constantly to add advisers for specifically delimited areas of policy: a special assistant for disarmament, for minorities, for consumers, for women, for wage and price negotiations, for students and youth, for cultural affairs, for higher education, for senior citizens, or for energy matters. Such specialized advisory units develop a clientele in and out of government; more often than not, they begin and continue as advocates and promoters, ambassadors to the White House from particularistic constituencies. Soon they even start acting like agencies, "doing" rather than advising the president. And the very establishment of every one of these special staff positions invariably generates requests by other special interests — why, they wonder, can't they have someone with their views involved too? — thus opening the door to a potential endless diffusion and fragmentation within the presidential entourage.

ADVISORY COMMISSIONS: HELP FROM THE OUTSIDE. A prominent Senator once complained:

> *It seems as though most Presidential Commissions are merely so many Jimminy Crickets chirping in the ears of deaf Presidents, deaf officials, deaf Congressmen, and perhaps a deaf public. They could be the nation's conscience, spurring us on to do what we know ought to be done, showing us the way, strengthening our determination to build a just and peaceful productive society. But all too often we reject them, or ignore them, or forget them....*[15]

Yet presidents have often become similarly exasperated with advisory commissions. Henry Fairlie, in *The New York Times Book Review,* quotes President Johnson as saying to an aide in 1966: "No more White House conferences. I'm having no more White House conferences." He might have said the same about advisory commissions too, although he continued to appoint them right up to the end of his term; for he had appointed a number of them whose final reports, because they implicitly indicted him for not doing more, irked and distressed him.

"In politics there are no friends, only allies," John Kennedy once said. The politics of advice is subject to all of the same vagaries and uncertainties of partisan politics at its most competitive. If a president tries to appoint safe or friendly commissioners, he invites criticism that the commission is not representative, bipartisan, or democratic in make-up. If a president avoids using commissions and advisory task forces, he invites criticism that he is not utilizing all the resources of his office. If a president enjoys the support or deference of members of a study commission, he still cannot be sure that the commission's staff may not promote counterproductive measures.

Presidential commissions as yet another means to gather and distill useful policy ideas are now viewed as an extension of the presidential office, even if a president often has little control over them. A president is under relentless pressure to find solutions and come up with new ways to solve old problems. "Expected to respond to every public misfortune, the President has found that he can always respond on the plane of symbolic politics if not on the plane of action. He can appoint a commission. This has become one of the principal technologies by which he tries to fill the gap between that which he is held responsible for and that which he can actually do." [16] Such commissions are often appointed, of course, as a means to delay or deflect heated political issues. The reasoning seems to be: when in doubt, form a study committee. But the reports of these commissions often take on authoritative casts, which invites presidential critics to find inconsistencies between a president's performance and the suggestions of his commissions.

A president naturally tends to publicize widely those reports that reinforce his own convictions and to downplay those that differ or might prove embarrassing. President Eisenhower, although tolerant toward the Gaither Committee's conclusions about the nation's defense, discovered that what he believed to be an off-the-record private document for purposes of internal discussion had become a public document embarrassing to his administration. John Kennedy's public advisory panel on foreign aid had the effect of inspiring opponents of foreign aid to greater energy. Lyndon Johnson's commissions on technology and on civil disorders urged policies that he viewed as indictments of his own. Richard Nixon had his share of troubles with the Commission on Student Unrest headed by William Scranton and White House conferences on food, health, and nutrition and on children and youth. The report of the presidential commission on obscenity, appointed by President Johnson, was denounced by the Nixon White House even before it was published.

The National Commission on the Causes and Prevention of Violence, chaired by Milton Eisenhower, worked at a back-breaking pace for a year-and-a-half (June 1968–December 1969). Its thirteen members were a blue-ribbon, bipartisan group comprised of two judges, a cardinal, four members of Congress, and several nationally esteemed lawyers. They commissioned several books, took testimony from over 150 expert witnesses and produced very valuable recommendations for public policy change. President Nixon listened attentively to a capsule summary of their major findings and recommendations. But their report soon was buried in some obscure White House file. Nixon never made a single public comment about the commission's findings. The commission's chairman was astonished at Nixon's complete refusal to offer leadership in this area. He concluded that it was easier for Nixon to talk about attacking crime and violence than it was for him to do something about it. "Politicians always quote scare statistics when they are running for office but, once elected, they limit their attack on crime to finding ways of interpreting statistics to show that the situation is improving." [17]

Presidents are contemptuous of advisers who cannot produce newsworthy new policy solutions, and yet they are irritated when commissioners exhort them to activism or moral leadership beyond what they feel is reasonable. One obviously overtaxed former cabinet member summed up the frustrations this way:

Outside advisers can sometimes be used, but it's tricky because free advice is just that: the advisers go home and don't have to live with the implications and operation problems. There is a big world of difference between the world of decision and the world of opinion. One of my predecessors was adamantly against the use of outside advisers and never, if possible, used them, viewing them as "just another bunch of out-of-town-bastards." My own view is less severe, but as an outsider and observer you don't have to live by your opinions and views. Added to all this is the problem of their embarrassing presidents, which has happened increasingly in recent years. . . .

PROGRAM EVALUATION.   One area in which presidents seldom get adequate advice is program planning and evaluation. A president often does not have the staff resources to perform these functions effectively. Existing arrangements for program development rely heavily on ad hoc efforts by collections of executive office aides and part-time outside advisers. Moreover, quantitative indicators of performance in domestic programs are difficult to obtain, and what measurements are available often are not transmitted swiftly or accurately to the White House. Until recently, most domestic bureaus and agencies have assessed their programs in such a way as to praise them rather than analyze them.

Another difficulty is that departments and agencies have routinely "measured" their own performance by adding up program inputs, that is, the number of dollars spent, the number of people employed, or the number of local projects in operation. Departmental officials until recently seldom were trained or required to view their programs in terms of outcomes, that is, as performance results, or as comparisons of one program with that of others. Program evaluation reports coming from departmental bureaus are still suspect, however, because to a considerable extent the success of the programs they administer puts their own performance on the line. As Navasky points out: "It is an unwritten law of annual report writing in the federal bureaucracy that every agency's statistics are better than those of the previous year and far better than those of the previous administration, so the statistics trotted out at such moments prove nothing." [18] Agencies and bureaus such as the FBI annually must show an increased problem in their areas if their funding is to be raised accordingly.

Not only are available statistical indicators crude but the political implications of the available data must also be gauged. Evaluation is never entirely apolitical; it will be used by one party or branch of government against another, and evaluators may become passionate advocates of programs that their analyses support, thereby risking their neutrality. But statistical information on young pilot programs must be interpreted cautiously; ambiguity must be confronted with a sense of balanced perspective; short and long-term effects may appear contradictory. These are complex assignments for both social scientists and public officials. A former commissioner of the Bureau of Labor Statistics, Arthur Ross, explained that officials can easily deceive themselves with statistics of impeccable quality:

> The trouble is that the unmeasured, or unmeasurable aspects of a problem may be vastly more important than those that have been, or can be, measured. And even with measurements that are known to reflect on the core of a problem, the rate of change in the United States has become so swift that "good" statistics, intelligently used in decision-making, may be rendered irrelevant or obsolete by the time action results from an official decision.
>
> These margins for misjudgment are not always stressed to the policy-maker. Attracted by the appearance of objectivity and precision, he keeps his eyes fixed on charts and tables that may be incomplete, obsolete, or both. Eventually he may come to believe that poverty really is a condition of having less than the current cut-off point of $3,335 in annual income, that full employment really is a situation where the national unemployment rate of 4 percent or less, and that Vietnam really is a matter of body counts and kill ratios.[19]

THE REORGANIZATION PREROGATIVE

In his 1971 State of the Union address, President Nixon proposed abolishing seven domestic cabinet departments and establishing instead four new broad-ranging superdepartments. The reorganization was billed hyperbolically as the beginning of a New American Revolution. The attorney general hailed the address as the most important document since the Constitution. The Agriculture;

Commerce; Health, Education and Welfare; Housing and Urban Development; Interior; Labor; and Transportation departments would have been abolished, and new departments would have been created for human resources, national resources, community development, and economic affairs.

Almost a year elapsed, however, before congressional leaders were willing to hold hearings on even one small portion of the package. Even then, the chairman of the House Government Operations Committee explained that it would be a long time before Congress could act: "I'm overwhelmed by the magnitude of the task. There are so many lines to other departments and agencies; we'll have to take a piece at a time. A lot of special-interest groups want to testify; there will be a great deal of opposition from them." [20] Two years later the reorganization proposals had been forgotten. There was no expectation that Congress was seriously interested in streamlining the executive branch according to the Nixon design. Critics complained that Nixon had chosen to make a low-profile technical reorganization the centerpiece of his State of the Union message while ignoring unemployment, housing, crime, or civil rights. The charge was even advanced that Nixon, knowing full well that Congress would not act, seized the issue so that he could blame Congress by claiming that it had denied him the tools to do his job properly!

Of course, the form of organization seldom stands in the way of the ablest people, and reorganization can never convert mediocrity into excellence. A Nixon aide whose primary responsibility was reorganization conceded that recruiting able people was always more important than structural rearrangements. Still, even more important, however, is combining organizational and personnel changes, putting the "most talented people you can trust" in critical positions. A Kennedy White House aide said, "I have never believed in reforms other than getting competent people and a network of allies whom you can trust and work with around town. . . . I would get one trusted person in each of the agencies whom you can rely on, who can tell you what's going on and evaluate things in advance [sic] for you."

A president can never completely avoid vesting discretion in the officials who are to implement programs. An exceptional instance of bureaucratic independence occurred in 1971–72 when General John D. Lavelle initiated bombings of North Vietnam under conditions contrary to presidential orders and then falsified official reports. As Francis Rourke commented:

> [*This case*] *revealed as had so many other earlier occurrences in Vietnam . . . the risks that a president takes when lower-level officials enjoy wide discretion in carrying out policies that are general and often ambiguous in character. Very often, the outcomes that result when complex and highly specialized organizations take over the task of executing these orders differ considerably from the president's original intent.*[21]

Presidents Nixon and Ford suffered from similar problems as they tried to reorganize and staff a series of federal energy organizations. Ford, irked at the independence of his first energy czar, John Sawhill, fired him outright and transferred his responsibilities to a dependable old congressional buddy, Rogers Morton, who headed up the Department of the Interior.

The pressures on a president to streamline the government are many. New priorities, new laws, and rapidly changing social and economic conditions make it necessary to realign agencies and shift certain functions from one department to another. New circumstances often make it desirable to create a new department or eliminate an old one. He is pressured to revitalize the departments and give them the flexibility to get things done, or set up new agencies because he will not be able to force recalcitrant federal bureaus to be responsive to his priorities. A person who served in high posts in four successive administrations, from Kennedy's through Ford's, put it this way: "Few modern Presidents have made any impact on the federal bureaucracies save by creating new ones. The bureaucracies are unfamiliar and inaccessible." [22]

Presidents push for the establishment of new departments and agencies as a means to push particular policies, for example, Kennedy's Peace Corps, Johnson's Department of Transportation, Nixon's Federal Energy Administration, or Ford's Economic Policy Board. Franklin Roosevelt was the grand master of initiating reorganizations and creating new units, and at times he "acted as if a new agency were almost a new solution. His addiction to new organizations became a kind of nervous tic which disturbed even avid New Dealers." [23]

Congress holds enormous power over almost any kind of executive reorganization. The Congress, not the White House, determines the mission and structure of all executive departments. The Constitution makes the president responsible for the faithful execution of the laws, yet Congress jealously limits a president's leeway to deal with organizational problems. Milton Eisenhower, who served for eight years as an adviser to his brother on administrative matters, complains:

One might reason that, since the executive, and judicial branches of the government were very deliberately created to be separate and equal, the President should have complete authority to shape the executive structure in ways that make it possible for him to execute the laws most effectively and most efficiently. Not so! Although the President cannot tell the Congress what its committee structure and procedures should be, the Congress can and does dictate, to a considerable extent at least, how the executive branch is to be organized. Then, having done so, it holds the President responsible for the effective management of the executive branch as the Constitution requires.[24]

Since the New Deal, for example, Congress has rejected about 30 percent of formal reorganizations submitted by presidents.[25] And, of course, that figure would be much higher if presidents submitted plans they would very much like to see approved but realized that Congress would not consent.

Reorganization may suggest, falsely, that fundamental conflicts over values, difficulties with a program's delivery system, or vagueness about the scope and substance of the law are being seriously addressed. But critics have charged that reorganization may be intended not so much to improve policy performance, but as a means of survival — as a rationale necessary for a president to continue supporting an embattled program or for a congressman to vote for a program.

The frequent reorganization and renaming of the foreign aid agency reflected efforts to bolster congressional support and to demonstrate Presidential interest, rather than to introduce new policies and improve management. There have been no less than eight successive foreign aid agencies — from the Economic Corporation Administration in 1948 to the Agency for International Development in 1961 — until 1961 an average of a new agency oftener than every two years.[26]

And if a department or agency becomes a favorite target for reorganization, as have the Defense Department, AID, OEO, the Bureau of Indian Affairs, and the U. S. Office of Education, morale within the department may suffer.

THE TRIPLE ALLIANCE. Special-interest groups often effectively capture administrative as well as legislative officials and succeed in fragmenting the organization to their own ends. John W. Gardner, former secretary of Health, Education and Welfare, told the Senate Government Operations Committee:

As everyone in this room knows but few people outside of Washington understand, questions of public policy nominally lodged with the Secretary are often decided far beyond the Secretary's reach by a trinity consisting of [1] representatives of an outside body, [2] middle level bureaucrats and [3] selected members of Congress, particularly those concerned with appropriations. In a given field these people may have collaborated for years. They have a durable alliance that cranks out legislation and appropriations in behalf of their special interest. Participants in such durable alliances do not want the Department Secretaries strengthened. The outside special interests are particularly resistant to such change. It took them years to dig their particular tunnel into the public vault, and they don't want the vault moved.[27]

Congress, even when it is dominated by the president's party, often does not want to increase presidential discretion within executive agencies. The congressional committee structure in large measure parallels executive branch organization, and what often appear to be structural absurdities in the executive branch may persist because of long-standing jurisdictional disputes within the Congress. Citing their responsibility of administrative review, these committees jealously protect what they consider to be their prerogative to determine how the departments and agencies they oversee are to be restructured. In addition, congressmen guard those areas in which they have developed expertise and close relations with government officials and extragovernmental clientele. A committee reorganization could diminish a member's sources of campaign finance or even jeopardize his chances for reelection.

Congressional opposition, no doubt mirroring labor and agricultural interest groups who feared losing functional representation and symbolic status, helped doom Johnson's attempt to abolish the Labor Department in 1967 and Nixon's 1971 attempt to restructure the executive departments. Influential congressmen have undermined repeated attempts to shift the civil functions of the Army Corps of Engineers to the Interior Department. Influential members of Congress also blocked the establishment of Nixon's proposed Department of Community Development in 1972, even though it had been reported out favorably by the House Government Operations Committee. Time and again, duplication, inefficiency, and anomalies in the executive-branch organization chart have been allowed to persist because particular committees have demanded that programs remain in departments under their control. Regrettably, Congress is far less aggressive and imaginative in reforming itself so as to defend its own institutional integrity than it is in fighting executive reorganization that threatens committee jurisdictions. Congress as an institution could be strengthened by strengthening those executive agencies that might more effectively provide it with a national perspective on national issues.

The move to create a Department of Health, Education and Welfare was thwarted under President Truman because of pressures brought to bear by the American Medical Association and congressional antagonism toward incumbent federal security administrator Oscar Ewing, who was considered most likely to head the new department. A few years later, President Eisenhower succeeded in establishing the department during his honeymoon period. Ewing had departed, and the AMA knew Eisenhower would not advocate socialized medicine. But even so, the president had to make concessions that restricted the authority of the HEW secretary to interfere in certain internal departmental matters, for example, in the authority of the surgeon general. Only when the president was prepared to keep authority vested in the separate components of HEW, rather than in his cabinet member, was Congress prepared to approve the plan.

THE DEPARTMENT OF HOUSING AND URBAN DEVELOPMENT. The long gestation of the Department of Housing and Urban Development illustrates some of the problems inherent in the president's reorganization prerogative. Spokesmen for housing and big-city interests had advocated some kind of department of urban affairs or urban development throughout the 1950s; bills to this effect were submitted in Congress as early as 1955. The Democratic platform of 1960 endorsed the idea, and John Kennedy campaigned in behalf of a broad-scale program of community development under a cabinet department. After his election, he twice sent such a measure to Congress but twice failed to get the department approved.

Interest groups were divided; government officials held mixed views; congressmen from rural areas were suspicious; and southern congressmen feared the big-city constituency that such a department would have and were cool toward Robert C. Weaver, a black economist-administrator who probably would become the cabinet secretary. Kennedy found himself running an obstacle course:

> ...different groups were supporting the measure for different reasons. What would serve the mayors and their allies might not please housing spokesmen, nor were housing groups themselves in complete accord.... Departmental status was of some urgency to some interest groups, but in fact had rather low priority at the White House.... Within the Washington community jealousy was quietly coming to life in existing departments, where many tended to view an additional cabinet unit as another competitor for the President's ear.[28]

Kennedy, already under intense pressure from civil rights groups, felt he could not afford to abandon Weaver. "The position of the Southern Democrats was clear. However loyal they were to President Kennedy, or to government housing, or even to help for big cities, most Dixie members just could not afford to cast a vote that might be construed as favoring a place for a Negro in the cabinet. None made any comment on the floor about Weaver's race, and indeed few of them participated at all during the floor debate. But the votes of the southern delegations spoke louder than their words." [29] Only three senators and four House Democrats from the Old Confederacy states voted for the Kennedy bill to create a department of housing and urban development. Another four years, a president from the South, an election landslide in 1964, and much wider support within Congress and without were required before the Department of Housing and Urban Development could be created in 1965.

The campaign to bring about a cabinet-level urban development department took nearly a decade. But in its first decade of existence the department fulfilled few of the expectations once held for it. It remained a Department of Housing that catered to the National Association of Home Builders and similar groups. Neither had it been an effective coordinator of national urban policies, nor had it met with success in integrating federal social programs with traditional brick-and-mortar housing programs. The Nixon administration's low regard for it was demonstrated by the establishment of a White House Urban Affairs Council in 1969 and the proposed abolition of HUD altogether in 1971. The history of HUD shows a cyclical quest for, at first, distinctive cabinet autonomy and then a later shift toward integration and centralization. Even the layman must ask: what differences have the predepartment and department phases made, or will, potentially, the postdepartment phase make, to the urban communities?

Thus, although a president is held accountable for the performance of the executive branch, he seldom has the legal or political authority to redesign and reorganize the executive branch structure. Even when reorganization is permitted, the subsequent rearrangements of the boxes on the organizational charts may give the appearance of progress when real progress is minimal. The reorganization prerogative, while important on occasion and sometimes quite helpful to a president, is seldom the solution to major socioeconomic problems, which require sustained attention to such nonorganizational matters as tax reform, a national income strategy for the poor, revenue sharing, automatic formulas for taxing polluters, and other financial incentive plans. Improvements in structure usually are poor substitutes for clarification of program goals and genuine economic reform.

PUBLICITY PREROGATIVE

Clinton Rossiter claimed that the president is "at the same time if not in the same breath, the Voice of the People, the leading formulator and expounder of public opinion in the United States. While he acts as a political leader for some, he serves as moral leader for all. . . . The coming age of radio and now television has added immeasurably to the range and power of the President's voice, offering the man who occupies this 'bully pulpit' an opportunity to preach the gospel of American in every home, and indeed, in almost every land." [30] A former Kennedy White House aide elaborated further that "our presidents today have to be a personal model, a cultural articulator, and a semi-priest or semi-tribal leader. It will be less important in years to come for presidents to work out programs and serve as administrators than it will be for presidents through the means of television to serve as educational and psychic leaders."

Although these opinions may be somewhat overstated, there is little doubt that adroit presidential use of television embellishes the textbook image of the presidency. Radio and television have strengthened the presidency in relation to Congress, political machine leaders, editors, and nearly all other strategic opinion-shaping elites. To the layman, the president can seemingly go on television anytime and say whatever he wants, whereas other leaders have to scramble for attention. The contemporary president *seems* to possess a near-limitless capacity to make and dominate the news. The president can use an FDR-style fireside chat, a JFK-style news conference, informal briefings, or lengthy personal interviews with favored members of the White House press corps to pre-empt his opponents.

However, the publicity prerogative of a president is a tricky device to use — people tire of evasive rhetoric and do not suffer superficialities gladly. Winning sustained political support from the public for important policy changes is difficult. John Kennedy's able use of television and news conferences won him much popularity but could not translate his legislative proposals into legislative victories. More than publicity campaigns is needed to overcome hardened opposition. Nixon tried just about every public relations ploy in his attempts to disassociate himself from the Watergate scandals, but each of his major television talks on the subject actually increased rather than diminished the number of people who felt that he was lying.

Television appearances have been more useful in enhancing a president's position on issues which he already has authority to act upon than in generating pressure on Congress to embark upon some new course of social change. Truman was unable to generate much support for his Fair Deal. And no president has been able to sell foreign aid programs that way. Ford's public attempts to garner support for his WIN (Whip Inflation Now) program were unheeded. Kennedy's call for fallout shelters at the height of the Berlin crisis fell on deaf ears; in fact, describing the public response as unenthusiastic would be generous, and the effort was soon abandoned. British observer Henry Fairlie assesses the limits of the publicity prerogative this way:

Whenever there was something which [President Kennedy] wished to do, he went before the television cameras and could rely on obtaining the desired popular reaction; the expression was aroused, and the expectation was supported; but on the following morning the thing had still to be done. There is in fact very little that the people can do to assist a President while he is in office; brought together at a general election, they are dispersed between elections; brought together in the evening by a television address, they are dispersed the next day. Popular leadership can bring only small returns; and it should be used sparingly.[31]

On the other hand, a president, by accident of style and temperament, simply may not be effective on television. Lyndon Johnson, for example, came across as syrupy: "He stuck to the lens," as Joe McGinniss put it.[32] Nothing could lessen Johnson's discomposure on television, even though he and his staff tried desperately to improve his delivery. Said one former Johnson counselor: "He just didn't speak well enough, and even though we tried to get him to work with television and overcome his problems with it . . . he personally disliked television. It was not enough to speak to business leaders at the White House; hell, we had the business leaders in our pocket — that's not adequate — you can and still have to go over the wall to the people."

Overexposure is another pitfall. A daily diet of Arthur Godfrey or Johnny Carson may be a comfort for some people, but the president who regularly asks for support or personal sacrifice is stronger medicine. It is easy to forget that on the average Franklin Roosevelt held only two of those celebrated fireside chats each year, and he seldom used them to ask for support of his legislative programs. John Kennedy, mindful of not wearing out his welcome in the living rooms of America, gave only nine major television addresses in almost three years, yet he was criticized for relying too much on the direct media connection to the people. George Reedy, a former Johnson press secretary, pointed out that the one-way communication via television can be deceptive: "It is a means by which a man can conduct a monologue in public and convince himself that he is conducting a dialogue *with* the public." [33] In Reedy's view, nothing can be more damaging to the pysche of a president.

Just as television can magnify a president's image and views, so it can also amplify his problems. The televised Watergate hearings, documentaries on inflation and recession, and those seemingly endless nightly news reports on Vietnam in the 1960s induced public yearnings for better and faster solutions. Thus, the gap between popular expectations and popular perception of reality is encouraged, largely by the very medium of communications that has made the voice of the president loom so large in America.

PRESS RELATIONS. The presidential press conference invites mistakes — or dangerous imprecisions — especially in the delicate area of foreign relations; for presidents have long since done away with the old custom of reviewing press conference transcripts before release. And retractions such as the Nixon White House used to put out — that some statement was "inoperative" or that someone "misspoke" — only weakened credibility. A former assistant secretary of defense pointed out some of the liabilities of press conferences:

> *Twenty-nine minutes of thoughtful, informative, well-planned exchange could go down the drain with one too-rapid exchange with a single reporter. We looked upon news conferences as potential booby-traps and excellent opportunities for disaster. Any sentence could be picked up and disseminated around the world. One remark spoken too hastily or taken out of context could plague a top official his entire time in office — or for the rest of his life ... [hence] it was not uncommon for us to work together for eight or ten hours prior to a session with the Pentagon press, and twenty or more hours getting ready for a Sunday panel show on national television.[34]*

President Nixon regularly called news conferences during his first two years in office, but later he studiously avoided them. Staff aides to Nixon frankly admitted that their decision was based in large part on Nixon's wish to appeal over the heads of professional Washington reporters, many of whom were viewed as unfair and hostile. Regular White House press conferences not only invited embarrassing questions but also increased the prestige of the regular White House press corps as a register of important issues. Nixon wanted to dictate what issues were important, not to be dictated to. Rather than having what he said filtered through the allegedly subjective Washington press, Nixon increasingly opted to speak directly, and unilaterally, to the American people on carefully selected occasions. This, of course, infuriated members of the press and doubtless made them even more hostile than they might otherwise have been.

Presidents and the press are almost constantly at odds with one another, and this is now accepted as routine. Presidents want to be loved, they want praise, and they want sympathetic stories written about their achievements. Members of the press seldom want to be relegated to the cheerleader role, and they are respected by their peers more for exposé than for merely retyping White House press releases. Some presidents, such as Franklin Roosevelt and John Kennedy, gave the impression of enjoying the give-and-take with the White House press, although aides report that even these presidents were very thin-skinned when it came to personal criticism. Harry Truman, perhaps our most candid president in recent times, was outspoken about certain members of the press: "I'm saving up four or five good, hard punches on the nose, and when I'm out of this job, I'm going to run around and deliver them personally." [35] Nixon and Agnew, of course, spent three or four years actively attacking the press, which left little doubt about how they felt toward the press.

Presidents have become almost paranoid about the power and the cynicism of the press. But it is only the Washington reporter's intimate awareness of a president's political problems that has made the press a paramount political problem for presidents. Of course, many of the press are highly idealistic; while others have developed a becoming skepticism toward presidential and other governmental statements. Former White House correspondent Max Frankel argued:

It is the damnable tendency toward manipulation that forces us so often into the posture of apparent adversaries. We have progressively lost our naivete about the truthfulness of Presidents and Government, starting with the U-2 affair a decade ago, A. J. Liebling found the awakening after U-2 to be the "beginning of wisdom" in the country and in the press. We lost the habit of reporting as fact what was only a contention or claim of our highest officials. And there is nothing in the record of the current Administration, ten years later, to break us of the habit of treating virtually every official utterance as a carefully contrived rendering that needs to be examined for the missing word or phrase, the sly use of statistics, the slippery syntax or semantics. [36]

Just as a president is unlikely, as a professional politician, to leave the news unshaped to his own purposes, so too are the more professional among the contemporary press corps highly unlikely to serve as the administration's flacks.

Every effort by Lyndon Johnson to rid himself of the credibility gap seemed to further that very affliction. Apparently, he overreacted to mistakes or criticism by making himself too accessible; gradually, members of the press, even in their own opinion, knew too much of what went on. As *Time* correspondent Hugh Sidey reported: "Johnson compounded his troubles because of his naivete as to how the Washington press corps operated — this after thirty-six years in the city. He was, strangely, an alien in the journalistic thicket. He did not comprehend the camaraderie of reporters, or their conviction that virtually everything said in and around Washington — whether in one's home or on the street — somehow bore on the public's business and was, at one time or another, for use." [37]

Controlling the press relations of the executive branch bureaucracies is another problem. Numerous developments are brought to the attention of cabinet secretaries or the White House only when it is too late to head off embarrassing exposés in the press. When brought to light by the press, the intricate coverup of the Mylai massacre, for example, apparently was as much a surprise to the White House as to the general public. One former cabinet-level public information officer commented: "I'm not at all sure that the tendency to hide instances of corruption, disaster or grievous human error from one's superiors is more pronounced in the military than in the Department of Agriculture or a giant nongovernment organization, but I do know that it is too great." [38]

At the same time, the White House staff sometimes has difficulty extracting hard news from departments and agencies. Despite White House efforts to influence the appointment of friendly public information officers, most of the government's thousands of public information officers are career civil servants. Their primary loyalties, understandably, are with their agencies; they view the working press as their clients and often resent White House aides who want information only to make a president look good. White House aides, for their part, often become disappointed with the seemingly unimaginative and unresponsive work produced by departmental public information officers, and, over time, the relation gradually deteriorates.

Presidents and their staffs spend vast amounts of time on image-tending and the exercise of the publicity prerogative. If popularity ratings slip, the resuscitation of the president's image becomes a consuming pursuit. Precisely because of the claims of the media that the administration is becoming isolated, is attempting to manage the news, or is widening a credibility gap, it becomes more difficult to refuse television interviews, public appearances, or news briefings. When the Watergate crisis became so intense, Nixon found that, although he was eager to avoid news conferences, nothing else would satisfy the press, public, and even leading spokesmen in his own party. In such cases, talented staff within the White House are diverted from program development, legislative planning, or strategy work to the more immediate publicity need. No quest becomes more pressing than the effort to sell and resell the White House story.

THE VETO POWER

The veto power, which is almost always cited as a major source of presidential strength, is often a clumsy instrument. Today, it hardly amounts to a viable ultimate weapon, a most formidable prerogative, or one of the most powerful weapons in the arsenal of Presidents; it is hardly so efficacious that Congress can seldom succeed in enacting legislation to which the President really objects.[39] Too much has been made of Franklin Roosevelt's inimitably robust assertion that the veto power was among the presidency's greatest attributes and was an important means of enforcing congressional and agency respect for presidential preferences and programs.

Two misleading generalizations help account for this misrepresentation. Textbooks often stress that strong presidents, such as Grover Cleveland and Franklin Roosevelt, vetoed hundreds of bills — more than 1,200 between them. Then, they often emphasize that vetoes usually stick: of the nearly 3,000 vetoes since Washington took office, Congress has overridden only about 85, or about 3 percent. But the unimportance of perhaps 90 percent of all vetoed bills discounts these statistical claims. The overwhelming bulk of vetoes have been directed against private relief, special immigration permissions, and individual pension claims, such as "to grant increase in pensions to certain widows of veterans of the Civil War"; "for the relief of the Bankers Reserve Life Co. of Omaha, Nebraska, and the Wisconsin National Life Insurance Co. of Oshkosh, Wisconsin"; or "to permit Raymond Baurkot to receive a refund claim for taxes paid on beer destroyed in a 1955 flood." [40] In most cases questions of public policy really were not involved. The White House may sometimes even be informed by the congressman sponsoring the original private bill that he introduced his bill only in deference to good public relations with his constituency.

Seldom, however, do presidents veto major tax and appropriations legislation. When they do, they sometimes win, but the ratio of successes to defeats is in marked contrast to the one for vetoes on private bills. Vetoes of major appropriations bills were sustained thirty-two times between 1789 and 1972. On tax legislation the White House has judiciously learned to accommodate rather than threaten. As tax expert Joseph Pechman noted:

By the time the bill reaches the President's desk administration forces in Congress have tried every legislative device to modify it to meet his requirements. For this reason, the President rarely vetoes a tax bill, even though very few of them satisfy him in every detail. In the past thirty years, only two important bills have been vetoed. Congress passed both bills over the President's veto by the necessary two-thirds majority. Since 1948, the President has signed every major tax bill that has passed both houses.[41]

Until the Nixon presidency, the veto had been used relatively infrequently in recent years. Its usefulness has been diluted by omnibus bills in such areas as public works, which a president must either accept or reject in their entirety; by the increasingly late passage of strategic appropriations bills which must be accepted to prevent financial chaos, and by the tendency of Congress to stay in session, except for irregularly scheduled vacation breaks, for nearly the entire calendar year, thereby undermining the utility of the pocket veto. Congress, in fact, has its own equivalent of the presidential veto: bottling up presidential measures in committee, adding riders, filibusters, congressional resolutions, and rejection or embarrassingly minute examinations of presidential nominees.

Presidential ambivalence toward using the veto prerogative is illustrated by President James K. Polk's apprehensions on signing the bill that created the Department of the Interior: "Had I been a member of Congress, I would have voted against it. Many bills pass Congress every year against which the President would vote were he a member of that body, and which he yet approves and signs." [42] For recent presidents who have wanted to pass progressive domestic legislation, the veto has been an inappropriate tool of influence. During his almost three years in office, President Kennedy vetoed only twenty-one bills. Lyndon Johnson vetoed even less often — a total of thirty during his more than five years in office. And most Kennedy and Johnson vetoes were applied to relatively unimportant legislation (see Table 3-1).

Even when a presidential veto has been sustained on a major piece of legislation, Congress may simply resurrect and pass substantially the same bill at a later session or even later in the same year. Although President Eisenhower twice vetoed earlier versions of the Housing Act of 1958, Congress persisted, passed the bill a third time, and prevailed. Carolyn Griffis concluded that "the veto both as a threat and as a power to negate the will of Congress was not successful in accomplishing the major policy changes advocated by the President, though it did elicit minor modifications in the housing legislation." [43] President Eisenhower vetoed the public works appropriation bill of 1958 on the ground that it included too many projects not approved by his Bureau of the Budget. Congress at first upheld the veto by one vote in the House; but after appropriations were reduced slightly, the bill was repassed by both houses.

TABLE 3–1 RECENT PRESIDENTS AND THEIR VETOES

	Vetoes	Private/Public[a] Bills	Pocket Vetoes	by Congress Overridden
H. S Truman	250	153/97	70	12
D. D. Eisenhower	181	107/74	108	2
J. F. Kennedy	21	12/9	9	0
L. B. Johnson	30	15/15	14	0
R. M. Nixon	43	3/40	19	5
G. R. Ford[b]	28	3/25	11	4

[a] Compilers say that some margin of error must be allowed in the private/public split, because it is not always possible to determine the exact nature of the bills.
[b] As of April 1975.

Congressional Research Service.

A second presidential veto was overridden largely on partisan lines, with enough Republicans defecting from the president to support their pet projects.[44]

Democrats in early 1973 were frustrated at being unable to reject Roy Ash, Nixon's nominee to be director of the Office of Management and Budget, whose Litton Industries conglomerate was in trouble with several huge cost overruns on government contracts. They were also upset at not having a chance to approve of Frederic Malek who came to OMB's deputy director post directly from the controversial Committee to Reelect the President. A bill was passed that would have required Ash and Malek to have Senate confirmation before taking office. President Nixon's veto of that bill was sustained by the Congress. But in short order Congress passed a similar bill that made all future directors and deputy directors of OMB subject to confirmation. This time the bill passed in Congress with an overwhelming vote, so decisively in fact that Nixon decided against the veto, plainly knowing that a veto had no chance of working that time.

On occasion, a president may veto an appropriations bill to strike an anti-inflationary posture even though he knows that Congress will probably override him. This gives the opposition party a chance to campaign against a do-nothing incumbent, as in the Kennedy campaign against the Eisenhower-Nixon record on domestic legislation during the late 1950s.[45] Of course, Congress can play the same game on pieces of legislation it dislikes, as it did when congressional activists successfully assailed Nixon's 1970 recommendations on the supersonic transport and the 1974 defense budget as being inflationary steps.

What is the effectiveness of the threat of the veto? It is said that Congress, especially members of the president's party, often act with White House reaction in mind. Warnings expressed by a president or conveyed through aides can prompt a measure to be modified or rewritten so as to avoid executive disapproval. But the gun-behind-the-door threat of a veto often devalues a president's hand. As Kallenbach cautioned: "On the whole a President will find that the threat of a veto . . . must be used with caution and circumspection. A too truculent, uncompromising voicing of his objections in advance . . . may be treated by legislators as a challenge and lead them to take a more recalcitrant stand than they would if the issue had not been thrust upon them in so stark a fashion." [46] The immediate override of President Nixon's veto of a $24.6 billion water-pollution control bill in 1972 was occasioned in part by Nixon's strident efforts to clothe only himself in the robes of fiscal responsibility.

Congressmen may rebel heatedly if the public begins to view them as rubber stamps of administration policy or as pushovers for presidential vetoes. Thus, even the pocket veto of a minor authorization bill during a brief Christmas recess in 1969 occasioned acrimonious hearings about executive encroachments on congressional prerogatives. A dramatic act of rebellion occurred in 1944 after Franklin Roosevelt vetoed a major revenue bill. A furious Senate Majority Leader Alben Barkley, usually characterized as a White House errand boy, dramatized his opposition by resigning from his Senate leadership position and denouncing the president's act publicly as a "calculated and deliberate assault upon the legislative integrity of every Member of Congress." [47] Congress revolted by overriding FDR's veto by wide margins.

Nixon exercised the veto prerogative somewhat more often than his two predecessors, having, unlike them, an opposition Congress. His vetoes, however, were not without costs. Not only were several overridden by Congress, but one thorny pocket veto actually was ruled unconstitutional by a U. S. district judge. By 1973, after the Watergate crisis began to take its toll, Congress often challenged presidential vetoes, and the White House adopted an increasingly conciliatory stance. One member of Congress noted in the *Wall Street Journal* in the spring of 1973 that the "disdain and defiance" of the White House hierarchy were softening because of Watergate. This attitude was confirmed, in the *Wall Street Journal,* by a senior Agriculture Department official: "The standards for signing have dropped considerably in the last few weeks." Although Nixon enjoyed acceptance of his foreign policy measures, his domestic record was distinguished by his asking little and his having to accept, after compromises of one kind or another, numerous measures generated and pressed on him by Congress. Even in national security areas Congress began reasserting itself — to the surprise of many and perhaps of Congress as well — by forcing the president to end the bombing in Cambodia. Congress also successfully overrode Nixon's veto of the congressional resolution limiting the president's power to wage war without congressional approval. An even more assertive Congress vetoed four out of fifteen of Gerald Ford's vetoes within his first few honeymoon months in office. Three times they did so within a period of three weeks!

On occasion a useful weapon, especially in the hands of a president who is dedicated to halting ill-drawn legislation or unusually expensive legislation in inflationary periods, the veto in reality, like most other constitutional powers assigned to the presidency, is circumscribed by powerful limitations. In short, a president can seldom lead or shape national policy by relying on his veto power. Thus this resource, like the other presidential prerogatives that in theory are available, may not be usable when a president wishes to employ it.

The costs and constraints associated with the use of all of the president's prerogatives nearly always are underestimated. The prerogatives of the presidency are more fragile than is imagined. Perhaps nowhere is this better illustrated than the clumsy and often inefficient way presidents employ their executive office staff units to review policies and oversee program implementation. Recent studies repeatedly find that a surprisingly large number of presidential policy decisions are made without effective consideration of the future costs of present decisions. In a trenchant evaluation of the budgetary and policy review processes of the national government, one former assistant director of OMB claims that "after more than fifty years of experience with the executive budget process . . . the Executive Office of the President has yet to organize an effective policy formulation and review process." [48] The view is now widespread that White House decisions are generally made by default, in ad hoc and hurried response to decisions or events originating elsewhere. Thus budget specialist Allen Schick says that the presidential prerogatives in the budget process have diminished markedly in recent years, noting that "while no President can afford to ignore or withdraw from the budget process, budgeting has become less useful to the President than it once was. In fact, the budget process tends to operate as a constraint on presidential power rather than as an opportunity for the development and assertion of presidential policies and priorities." [49]

Outsiders and insiders differ about the causes of the presidential ordeal as a manager of the sprawling executive branch. Some claim that inertia and past habits, usually bad ones, create an environment that promotes ad hoc management rather than systematic management by clearly understood presidential objectives. Others, like Marver Bernstein, suggest that presidents have consciously ignored the managerial side of their responsibilities because there seemed to be no incentives in trying to make headway there. "No President has been able to identify any significant political capital that might be made out of efforts to improve management except for the conservative purpose of economizing or reducing costs." [50] A Lyndon Johnson lieutenant, Joseph Califano, sums up the view of those who have worked in the White House:

The President's power to achieve his goals is remarkably limited. In the budgetary area, he can propose Federal expenditures and tax policies, but it is the Congress that must enact them if they are to become national policy and the law of the land....

Smaller agencies respond to Presidential leadership only in the minds of the most naive students of government administration. Under the myth of reporting to the President, more often than not these agencies operate as independent fiefdoms....

No President, no matter how hard and long he works, can hope to have more than a superficial knowledge and control of the enormous bureaucracy over which he presides.[51]

In sum, the array of formal powers and accumulated prerogatives that we commonly associate with the modern presidency in fact do not guarantee the achievement of very much. We have traditionally overestimated the significance of presidential prerogatives and underestimated the number and importance of the brakes on presidential leadership.

NOTES

1. Arthur Krock, *The Consent of the Governed and Other Deceits* (Little, Brown, 1975), p. 179.
2. Quoted in Arthur M. Schlesinger, Jr., *A Thousand Days* (Houghton Mifflin, 1965), p. 127.
3. See Irving L. Janis, *Victims of Groupthink* (Houghton Mifflin, 1972).

4. See Robert Scigliano, *The Supreme Court and the Presidency* (Free Press, 1971), pp. 96–99, 146–58. The author shows persuasively that both partisanship and the timing of appointments are critical factors, especially in combination.

5. Arthur Krock, *Memoirs* (Popular Library, 1968), p. 282.

6. Victor Navasky, *Kennedy Justice* (Atheneum, 1971), p. 256.

7. *Ibid.,* p. 245.

8. U.S., Department of Health, Education and Welfare, Office of the Assistant Secretary of HEW/Commissioner of Education, press release, 11 June 1970, containing statement made in May.

9. James D. Hodgson, interview in the *Los Angeles Times,* 30 November 1972.

10. Theodore Sorensen, *Kennedy* (Bantam Books, 1965), p. 291.

11. John F. Kennedy, radio-television discussion on the ABC, CBS, and NBC networks, 17 December 1962, *Public Papers of the Presidents,* U.S. Government Printing Office (1963), p. 892. For a different view see Martin and Susan Tolchin, *To the Victor . . .* (Random House, 1971), pp. 187–297.

12. Quoted in Sorensen, *Kennedy,* p. 346.

13. Theodore Sorensen, *Decision-Making in the White House* (Columbia University Press, 1963), p. 76. For an excellent discussion of a variety of other potential advisory-system inadequacies, see Alexander L. George, "The Case for Multiple Advocacy in Making Foreign Policy," *American Political Science Review,* Sept. 1972, pp. 751–785.

14. Vannevar Bush, *Pieces of the Action* (Morrow, 1970), p. 305. See also Joel Primack and Frank von Hippel, *Advice and Dissent: Scientists in the Political Arena* (Basic Books, 1974).

15. Edward M. Kennedy, statement before the Senate Judiciary Committee, Subcommittee on Administrative Procedure, *Hearings on Presidential Commissions* 1st session, 25 May 1971. 92nd Cong., sess., 1971, p. 3.

16. Martha Derthick, "On Commissions — Presidential Variety," *Public Policy,* Fall 1971, p. 630.

17. Milton Eisenhower, *The President Is Calling* (Doubleday, 1974), p. 460.

18. Victor S. Navasky, *Kennedy Justice,* p. 443.

19. Arthur M. Ross, "The Data Game," in C. Peter and T. Adams, eds., *Inside the System* (Praeger, 1970), pp. 259–60. See also Ewan Clague, *The Bureau of Labor Statistics* (Praeger, 1968).

20. Chet Holifield, quoted in Dom Bonafede, "Bureaucracy, Congress, Interests See Threat in Nixon Reorganization Plan," *National Journal,* 8 May 1971, p. 985.

21. Francis E. Rourke, "The Domestic Scene: The President Ascendent," in Robert E. Osgood et al., *Retreat from Empire?* (Johns Hopkins Press, 1973), pp. 102–3. See also Herbert Kaufman, *The Limits of Organizational Change* (University of Alabama Press, 1971).

22. Daniel P. Moynihan, "The Presidency and the Press," *Commentary,* March 1971, p. 44.

23. Arthur Schlesinger, Jr., *The Coming of the New Deal* (Houghton Mifflin, 1959), p. 535.

24. Milton Eisenhower, *The President Is Calling,* pp. 275–76.

25. Harvey C. Mansfield, "Federal Executive Reorganization: Thirty Years of Experience," *Public Administration Review,* July–August 1969, pp. 332–45. See also Harvey C. Mansfield, "Reorganizing the Federal Executive Branch: The Limits of Institutionalization," *Law and Contemporary Problems,* Summer 1970, pp. 461–95.

26. Harold Seidman, *Politics, Position and Power* (Oxford University Press, 1970), p. 26.

27. John W. Gardner, testimony before the Senate Government Operations Committee,

reprinted in *Congressional Record* 1st Session, 92nd Congress (3 June 1971), Senate p. 8140.

28. Judith H. Parris, "Congress Rejects the President's Urban Department 1961–62," in Frederic Cleaveland, ed., *Congress and Urban Problems* (The Brookings Institution, 1969), p. 188.

29. Parris, *ibid.,* pp. 213–14.

30. Clinton Rossiter, *The American Presidency,* rev. ed. (Mentor, 1960), pp. 29–30. See the balanced discussion of this point in Elmer E. Cornwell, *Presidential Leadership of Public Opinion* (University of Indiana Press, 1965); see also Bernard Rubin, *Political Television* (Wadsworth, 1967).

31. Henry Fairlie, *The Kennedy Promise* (Doubleday, 1973), p. 150.

32. Joe McGinniss, *The Selling of the President* (Trident, 1969), p. 30.

33. George Reedy, *The Twilight of the Presidency* (World, 1920), pp. 165–66.

34. Phil Goulding, *Confirm or Deny* (Harper and Row, 1970), pp. 344–45.

35. Quoted in William J. Small, *Political Power and the Press* (Norton, 1972), p. 62.

36. Max Frankel, letter to the editor, *Commentary,* July 1971.

37. Hugh Sidey, *A Very Personal Presidency* (Atheneum, 1968), p. 190.

38. Goulding, *Confirm or Deny,* p. xi.

39. See the discussions in Charles J. Zinn, *The Veto Power of the President* (Government Printing Office, 1951), pp. 4–8; Daniel M. Berman, *In Congress Assembled* (Macmillan, 1964), pp. 311–18; William Keefe and Morris S. Ogul, *The American Legislative Process* (Prentice-Hall, 1968), pp. 403–4. See also Woodrow Wilson, *Congressional Government* (1885; reprinted. Meridian, 1956), p. 53.

40. See Senate Library, comp., *Presidential Vetoes* (Government Printing Office, 1961).

41. Joseph Pechman, *Federal Tax Policy,* rev. ed. (The Brookings Institution, 1971), p. 44. See also John Manley, *The Politics of Finance* (Little, Brown, 1970), especially chap. 7.

42. Allan Nevins, ed., *Polk: The Diary of a President 1845–1849* (Capricorn Books, 1968), p. 387.

43. Carolyn S. Griffis, "Selected Variables Affecting the Efficiency of the Presidential Veto" (Ph. D. diss., University of Florida, 1969), p. 197. For the magnitude and type of congressional opposition raised by the first Eisenhower veto of the housing act of 1959, see U.S., Congress, Senate, Subcommittee on Banking and Currency, Senate, *Hearings before a Sub-Committee on Banking and Currency on the President's Message Disapproving S. 57,* 86th Cong., 1st sess., 1959.

44. See Richard Fenno, *The Power of the Purse* (Little, Brown, 1966), p. 676.

45. It must be admitted, of course, that a president who realizes that he cannot normally persuade Congress to enact his preferred legislation can, for a while, as in Eisenhower's case, "effectively block or force into compromise the legislation a clear majority of the House and Senate would otherwise enact into law" (Neil McNeil, *Forge of Democracy* [McKay, 1963], p. 245). See also Glen Gordon, *The Legislative Process and Divided Government* (Bureau of Government Research, University of Massachusetts, 1966).

46. Joseph Kallenbach, *The American Chief Executive* (Harper and Row, 1966), p. 361. See also the useful study of the veto power at the state level in Roy D. Morey, "The Executive Veto in Arizona: Its Use and Limitations," *Western Political Quarterly,* 19 (September 1966) :504–15.

47. See the discussion of this episode in James M. Burns, *Roosevelt: The Soldier of Freedom* (Harcourt Brace Jovanovich, 1971), pp. 433–37; and in Carlton Jackson, *Presidential Vetoes, 1792–1945* (University of Georgia Press, 1967), pp. 220–23.

48. William A. Niskanen, *Structural Reform of the Federal Budget Process* (American Enterprise Institute for Public Policy, 1973), p. 55.

49. Allen Schick, "The Budget Bureau That Was: Thoughts on the Rise, Decline, and Future of a Presidential Agency," *Law and Contemporary Problems* (Summer, 1970), p. 521.

50. Marver Bernstein, "The Presidency and Management Improvement," *Law and Contemporary Problems* (Summer, 1970), p. 516. See also: Otis L. Graham, Jr., *Toward a Planned Society: From Roosevelt to Nixon* (Oxford University Press, 1976), and Richard Rose, *Presidential Objectives: The Politics of Presidential Management* (forthcoming, 1976).

51. Joseph A. Califano, *Reorganization of Executive Departments,* Hearings before a subcommittee of the Committee on Government Operations, House of Representatives, 92 Congress, 1st session (June 14, 1971), pp. 392–393.

CHAPTER 4

THE BRAKING
OF THE PRESIDENCY

Well, I agree with you, but I'm not sure the government will.

— *President John F. Kennedy, quoted in Roger Hilsman,*
    The Politics of Policy Making in Defense and Foreign Policy
    (Harper & Row, 1971), p. 1.

*The federal government today is almost unmanageable. It is filled
with inefficiency. Obsolete activities, or ones of diminished
importance, are carried on in sheer inertia. An entrenched civil
service has become a burden....*
    *The presidency has become an impossible post. That changes
are needed at once to make it an effective position of leadership
in the face of modern complexity and enormity of government no
one can deny.*

— *Milton Eisenhower,* The President Is Calling
    (Doubleday, 1974), pp. 272, 562.

*Most of the problems he will encounter are, in their ultimate
foundations, shaped for him by the great, impersonal forces of past
history; he will be able, proportionately whatever his ability and
energy and good will, to affect them in but a small way. He will
be dealing with people who, on any showing, are mainly wrapped
up in their private lives.*

— *Harold Laski,* The American Presidency
    (Grosset & Dunlap, 1940), p. 264.

So highly decentralized and slow in operation is the American governmental system that it seems designed for the protection of the status quo and the compromise of any crusade for redistributive change. Fundamental reforms depend on the status quo's becoming significantly more painful than change or on the occurrence of crises. Short of such dramatic crises as the depression, Pearl Harbor, and the Cuban missiles in 1962, presidents usually have felt the muscular disapproval of interest groups whenever they have embarked on new policy ventures that in any way threatened the existing distribution of power. Veteran White House counselors consider it almost axiomatic that crises must be exploited because of the special but quite temporary support that coalesces for the president at such times. Under more usual circumstances, presidential policies will become greatly adjusted and compromised as they proceed through legislative and, later, a variety of administrative processes.

In attempting to make innovations in domestic policy, the American presidency operates within a system of shared power, one in which the claims of many groups constantly compete. Presidential struggles with other governmental and extragovernmental centers of power stem from the larger societal conflicts over values and the allocation of wealth and opportunity. As a result, the presidency becomes a place in which few radical decisions are made; most of its domestic policies are exploratory, remedial, or experimental modifications of past practices. This chapter examines the brakes on presidential efforts to bring policy performance into line with enunciated goals. These braking actions are applied by Congress, the bureaucracy, special interests, the courts, and the public.

Limitations on a president's freedom of action are, to be sure, often desirable. Many of the checks and balances that are still at work today were deliberately designed by the framers of the Constitution. And in some measure, presidents should be the captives of their campaign commitments, their parties, and their announced programs. They should be responsive most of the time to the views of the majority of the American people. Presidential behavior should be informed by the Constitution, existing laws, and the generally understood, albeit hazier, values that define democratic procedure. The notion that party programs, spelled out in campaigns, allow the public some control over policy through the election process, is a valuable brake, one that needs, if anything, to be revitalized. Other brakes that limit presidential discretion may be viewed as positive or negative, depending on an individual's political and economic views.

CONSTRAINTS IMPOSED BY CONGRESS

With rare exceptions, presidents have substantial difficulty getting Congress to pass their programs. In President Nixon's first three years, only 33 percent of his publicly requested programs were approved; and in about the same time in office, President Kennedy, with 40 percent approval, fared little better. Part of the problem is that the first year, when a president wants to spend his time organizing his own household and studying policy recommendations, is the best year for him to entreat Congress to act upon his programs. As President Johnson noted: "You've got to give it all you can, that first year. . . . Doesn't matter what kind of a majority you come in with. You've got just one year when they treat you right, and before they start worrying about themselves. The third year, you lose votes. . . . The fourth year's all politics. You can't put anything through when half the Congress is thinking how to beat you." [1]

But a president's proposals may be arrested by a Congress even fresh on the heels of a triumphant election. Franklin Roosevelt, after his election in 1936 by the largest plurality in electoral history, suffered his most embarrassing congressional rebuff in the defeat of his bill to enlarge the Supreme Court. For a different set of reasons, immediately following his electoral landslide in 1972, President Nixon experienced a strikingly similar congressional stubbornness. *Congressional Quarterly* reported that Congress opposed Nixon more often in 1973 than it had opposed any president in the previous twenty years.

The skills and resources requisite for winning office are not necessarily those useful in dealing with legislators. John Kennedy, in spite of fourteen years in Congress, had little taste for effectively courting Congress. From the perspective of the presidency, he saw the collective power of Congress as a bloc as far stronger than he had thought when a senator:

> It is very easy to defeat a bill in the Congress. It is much more difficult to pass one. To go through a subcommittee . . . and get a majority vote, the full committee and get a majority vote, go to the Rules Committee and get a rule, go to the Floor of the House and get a majority, start over again in the Senate, subcommittee and full committee, and in the Senate there is unlimited debate, so you can never bring a matter to a vote if there is enough determination on the part of the opponents, even if they are a minority, to go through the Senate with the bill. And then unanimously get a conference between the House and Senate to adjust the bill, or if one member objects, to have it go back through the Rules Committee, back through the Congress, and have this done on a controversial piece of legislation where powerful groups are opposing it, that is an extremely difficult task.[2]

One of the misleading indications of presidential power or success is the so-called presidential box score used by the *Congressional Quarterly* to indicate successes and failures in legislative programs. If Congress has approved a majority of a president's legislative program, the *Congressional Quarterly* may headline their story "Congress Acts Favorably on President X's Requests." The impression often given is that a president is not only devoted to high principle but has also given independent, creative, galvanizing impetus to legislative progress. The president is the chief legislator; the Congress is mainly passive and has yielded its legislative authority.

However, these box scores must be regarded cautiously. In the first instance, they are always deceptive because legislative measures are by no means equal in importance. Such box scores, moreover, fail to distinguish between measures that were central and those that were peripheral to presidential priorities. In addition, they are skewed by the high percentage of presidential requests in the areas of defense and foreign policy, which Congress traditionally approves. Finally, they show nothing of those programs that a president wanted but, recognizing the overwhelming likelihood of defeat, never requested at all. Much of what a president does not achieve consists of what he never requested, rather than of what he proposes but does not get passed.

The relationship between the president and Congress is designed as much for conflict as for cooperation. As already mentioned, Congress enjoys substantial authority over confirmation, government organization, and, of course, authorizations. Moreover, the quality of the congressional staff has increased impressively in the past thirty years. More than sixteen thousand employees now serve the Congress. Moreover, more professionals and professional organizations now render assistance to Congress as well as to the executive branch: "The nation's corps of expert professionals . . . has long given primary allegiance to the executive branch, and has often been scornful of Congress. But today even that pendulum has begun to swing. Former State Department and Presidential advisors are seeking congressional outlets for their services in unprecedented number. Ex-ambassadors, analysts and White House staffers abound on Capitol Hill. The powerful staff of the Senate Foreign Relations Committee consists almost entirely of refugees from the Foreign Service." [3] Reports of Congress' death are greatly exaggerated. It may not be the fountainhead of reformist and redistributive leadership; but, when it wants to be, it can play a relatively active role in the determination of particular policies. It has clearly played such a role in tax matters, in policies determining freedom of information, and in the procurement, development, and evaluation of weapons systems. [4]

Textbooks tend to emphasize the legislative triumphs of Wilson, Roosevelt, and Lyndon Johnson. But a closer examination of these presidential efforts suggests that they occurred usually during very brief periods (1913–1915, 1933–1935, 1964–1965). A development just as important, but seldom given as much attention, has been the rise of the conservative coalition in Congress, which refers to the tendency of southerners to join with Republican colleagues in the Congress in resisting social and economic reform measures proposed by the White House. Since 1936 this coalition has been an important political force in tempering White House leadership efforts. All of our recent presidents, including the conservative ones, have had programs undermined, if not buried, by the conservative coalition.

Congressional barriers to presidential initiatives are particularly apparent in the important areas of budget and tax policies, both of which must be approved by Congress. Timely presidential fiscal initiatives, particularly counter-cyclical fiscal actions, become difficult to carry through because Congress generally resists any raising of taxes and, at the same time, any cutting of spending for federal programs. Even the threat of the latter brings an avalanche of protests from interest groups inside and outside the government. Thus, for example, tax cuts passed in 1964, 1969, and 1971 were coupled with actual expansions of existing programs, which sharply reduced federal revenue receipts and strongly braked the ability of either the president or Congress to launch significant new social action programs.[5]

Another area in which Congress influences presidential initiatives is in the shaping of legislation. Much of the recent literature about the presidency suggests that Congress merely delays and amends and is basically incapable of creating legislation or formulating policy. In actuality, however, Congress sometimes plays the dominant role in initiating legislation, and the formulation as well as the enactment of virtually all major legislation relating to domestic and economic policy is the result of extensive conversations between the presidency and Congress, and between both of these institutions and pivotal interest groups.

Much of the policy that presidents supposedly formulate and propose as their own is derived directly from traditional party priorities, from previous presidents, or from Congress. Just as the celebrated New Deal legislation had a fairly well-defined prenatal history extending back several years before its espousal by FDR, so also recent investigations into the origins and enactment of most of the New Frontier and Great Society legislative programs — for example, broader medical care programs, federal aid to education, and the more activist stance on civil rights — indicate that they were the fruition of past recommendations by the Democratic party. James Sundquist noted that most of John Kennedy's legislative program was in fact handed to him: "In any case, the Democratic program that was presented to the country in 1960 was truly a *party* program. The platform writers and the presidential nominee contributed emphasis, style, and form, but the substance of the program had been written with unusual precision and clarity during the eight years out of power — eight years that at the time seemed endlessly frustrating but were, it is clear in retrospect, extraordinarily fruitful." [6]

Most of the Johnson legislation — notably that of the Eighty-ninth Congress, which passed more social action legislation than any recent congressional session — was neither entirely new nor solely presidential in initiative.

And, as David Price pointed out, Congress was a most instrumental and durable partner with the president:

Formulation, instigation and publication were widely shared functions; executive resources were in many ways superior, but Congress often displayed greater flexibility and permeability. If it was wise for executive formulators to touch bases on Capitol Hill, it was virtually impossible for congressional formulators to proceed without the assistance of the bureaus already operative in the field. Nor was any publicizing move more important than securing a place for one's bill on the presidential agenda. But the case studies suggested that congressional activists had some advantages of their own. A proposal could become visible much more quickly in the legislative branch. This not only gave legislators and their staffs an incentive to assume the instigator role; it also made it likely that instigators from outside like ... Ralph Nader ... would seek congressional alliances. A legislator with a permissive chairman and access to committee resources could develop a proposal and get it into the newspaper with relative ease. Ideas rose to the top with more difficulty in the executive branch.[7]

Nelson Polsby defines the concept of policy incubation in Congress as "keeping a proposal alive while it picks up support, or waits for a better climate, or while the problem to which it is addressed grows."[8] The best way to get a bill on a president's legislative agenda may be to hold a series of well-run congressional hearings and to have the bill sponsored by respected senators who already have begun generating publicity and support for the "new" proposal.

In practice, then, Congress serves not only as a broker between the presidency and the people but also as a brake on presidential initiatives that are either not yet well enough developed or not yet acceptable to a majority of the public. To picture the presidency as representing the national interest or general welfare is as naive as to picture Congress as being merely the tool of special or particularistic interests. Any new presidential initiative, whatever its motivation, invariably promotes certain interests at the expense of others, or gives advantage to some new elite as it no doubt disadvantages a previously favored elite. The welfare and regulatory legislation enacted in the 1930s was vitriolically opposed by a wealthy elite, who cried that socialism was taking root and predicted grave economic disaster. Most such legislation represented joint presidential-congressional efforts. In the case of Nixon, on the other hand, tax credits, authorized price rises, subsidies, and controversial loans to such large corporate interests as Lockheed and the dairy industry, nearly always have represented presidential initiations.

Congress, of course, is often unable to make up its collective mind; certainly, it does not readily speak with one voice. By and large, however, this is because Congress is, in part, designed as a forum in which the diverse views of heterogeneous publics are to be registered. The division and apparent slowness of Congress should not lead to the belief that Congress is no longer a significant partner in setting and settling national priorities or in nurturing policy innovations. If national policy making is seen as a continuing process, which it surely is, as being as active and full of potential during both the implementation and the later stages of evaluation and alteration as it was in the original battle for passage, then the role of Congress in incubating, clarifying, and overseeing policy looms markedly larger than is usually acknowledged. Congressional supervision of the implementation of federal policy is intermittent at best and unsystematic. Supervising the execution phase of national policy is most of the time not a high priority for most members of Congress. But much of the supervision that does occur is not recognized as such. "Because a session is called a legislative hearing, or because processing of constituent complaints is called casework does not mean that these activities are unrelated to oversight." [9]

Oversight and congressional impact on implementation must be viewed from a broader perspective than that of formal investigations or explicit amendments. Time and again, members of Congress and their staffs are able to dilute or strengthen innovative initiatives by cajoling the public servants who administer the program, by appropriating fewer (or more) funds, by threatening to abolish the program if certain aspects of it are not changed, or by insuring that people with different values are promoted into strategic administrative positions. The war on poverty and the model cities programs provide classic illustrations of how significant changes were imposed on programs after initial passage. In these instances the presidential version, as is often the case, won passage, but congressional intent crept in and became dominant after passage.[10]

CONSTRAINTS IMPOSED BY THE BUREAUCRACY

The federal bureaucracy, greatly swollen by the New Deal and the cold war agencies, as well as by the Great Society, is one of the most visible checks on a president. Indeed presidents are quick to fault the bureaucracy for the many problems that beset the implementation and evaluation of presidential programs. One is reminded of Harry Truman's observation about what it would be like for his successor to be a president rather than a general: "He will sit here and he'll say, 'Do this! Do that!' *And nothing will happen.* Poor Ike — it won't be a bit like the Army! He'll find it very frustrating." [11]

The problem of how to control the bureaucracy has become a major preoccupation for presidents. Even persons who championed the New Deal now recognize that the executive bureaucracy can be a presidential curse. Arthur Schlesinger, Jr., writes that "as any sensible person should have known, the permanent government has turned out to be, at least against innovating Presidents, a conservatizing rather than liberalizing force." [12] Concern about taming the bureaucracy comes from the right, from the revisionist left, and from moderates. Participants in the Nixon administration constantly embraced the same themes, even to the extent of claiming that their programs were being sabotaged from all directions. One of the key factors in former president Nixon's continuing attempts to centralize more authority either in the White House or in the hands of a few trusted and strong cabinet officials was this very suspicion about the loyalties and parochialism of federal civil servants.

Gaining control over existing bureaucracies and making them work with and for the White House is an enormous burden on the president. He must constantly delegate, he must be most precise about what he is delegating, and he must know whether and for what reasons the agencies to which he is delegating share his general outlook. He must be sensitive to bureaucratic politics, to the incentives that motivate bureaucrats, and to the intricacies of their standard operating procedures. He must have some assurance (and hence an adequate intelligence system) that what he is delegating will be carried out properly.

Recent presidents, doubtless because they were trained as legislators and not as executives, have tended to misunderstand the workings of bureaucracy. They have little appreciation for bureaucrats' considerable concern about organizational essence, organizational morale, and organizational integrity. Presidents mistakenly but invariably look upon the executive branch as a monolith, and they are especially offended when senior bureaucrats differ with them or otherwise refuse to cooperate. Presidents quickly become defensive and critical of the bureaucracy. They fear, sometimes with reason, that their pet programs will get buried in the inert custodial hands of old-line bureaucracies. As a result, as mentioned in the previous chapter, presidents have often sought short cuts by setting up new agencies for each of their pet projects and relying increasingly on separate advisory and staff units within the executive office. However, the creation of a new agency does not guarantee presidential control. Indeed, some of the most independent, even maverick, federal agencies were originally set up to by-pass the so-called old-line departments. Among such agencies are the Atomic Energy Commission, the Office of Economic Opportunity, and the Federal Energy Administration.

Bureau chiefs and career civil servants often do avoid initiative, taking risks, and responsibility, opting instead for routine and security. The bureaucracy most assuredly has its own way of doing things, often more conservative or more liberal than what the president wants. But the fact that bureaucratic interests and presidential interests often differ does not mean that the permanent employees of the federal executive branch constitute an active enemy force. Bureaucratic organizations act, rather, in reasonable, rational ways to enhance their influence, budget, and autonomy. And they generally believe that in doing so they act in the nation's interest.

Thus, the bureaucracy often defines the national interest quite differently from the way it is defined in the White House. But a close examination of these two definitions often reveals that both are valid and representative views of what is desirable about which reasonable people can legitimately differ. The task for a president, then, is to understand the strategies and tactics of federal bureaus and appreciate the underlying motivations. Properly diagnosed, the bureaucratic instinct for competition, survival, and autonomy can be creatively harnessed by the White House both to educate itself and to develop cooperative alliances.

Examination of bureaucratic habits and folkways suggests that certain patterns show up repeatedly. For example, the quest for autonomy has a significant impact on the views and behavior of organizations. Morton Halperin, a former White House aide and Defense Department official, points to four predictable patterns:

1. *In negotiating among organizations about desirable actions, each prefers an agreement which leaves it free to pursue its own interest even if this appears to an outside observer to lead to an uncoordinated and hence inefficient policy....*
2. *In devising options for senior officials, organizations tend to agree on proposals which exclude any joint operations and which leave each free to go its own way and continue to do what it prefers to do....*
3. *In presenting policy proposals to senior officials, organizations typically indicate that the proposed course of action is infeasible unless they are given full freedom to carry it out....*
4. *Organizations seek to guard their autonomy by presenting to the President or Cabinet officials only a single option so that he cannot choose among options interfering with their preferred course of action.*[13]

BUREAUCRATIC VETOES. One major cause of the distance and frequent distrust between the presidency and the executive branch lies in the nature of the bureaucracy and of bureaucrats.

Consider the official who directs the day-to-day operations of even a broadly defined program; let us call him the bureau chief. He directs the work of large numbers of people, he disposes of large sums of money, he deals every day with weighty, intricate, and delicate problems. He has probably spent most of his adult years in the highly specialized activity over which he now presides. He lives at the center of a special world inhabited by persons and groups in the private sector who stand to gain or lose by what he does, certain members of Congress who have a special interest in his actions, and a specialized press to which he is a figure of central importance. The approbation which is most meaningful to him is likely to be the approbation of the other inhabitants of this special world. The rest of the federal government may seem vague and remote, and the President will loom as a distant and shadowy figure who will, in any event, be succeeded by someone else in a few years. It would be unreasonable to expect this official to see his program in the Presidential perspective.[14]

Seldom is there a passion as keen as that of functionaries for their functions. The bureaucrats whose basic loyalty is to the established way of doing things and whose job survival and promotion are tied directly to program survival and expansion, instinctively, but rationally, resist threats to program control or coordination from the White House.

Consequently, although the bureaucracy was intended to be neutral and nonpolitical, the bureau chief will extend his allegiance to persons or groups who will aid and abet the enlargement of his program or, at the least, its stability. Knowing that presidential and congressional support are only won when the bureau can demonstrate widespread and intense public support, that a president wants to be associated with popular programs, many bureaus and even departments willingly invite capture by special interests in order to gain what they perceive as indispensable clientele and grassroots support. Where little special-interest support exists, shrewd bureau chiefs do everything possible to create it. Moreover, they spend considerable time forging alliances with well-situated members of Congress and their staffs.

Figure 4-1 illustrates the central alliance-building role played by bureau chiefs and the triangular relations of which they are a part. How entrenched these relations can become can be inferred from the fact that, whereas tenure on the White House staff averages less than three years and even less than that among cabinet appointees, the bureau chiefs, senior members of Congress and senior staff in Congress, and veteran Washington lobbyists often endure in their posts for ten or fifteen years or more. As a former Johnson White House aide points out, these alliance-building tactics create major antagonism to presidential leadership:

> *Coagulations of power cut across the formal branches of government and incorporate participants, highly effective participants, outside of government. There was, in fact, a tendency toward sub-governments in Washington. Key operatives in the executive branch, key committee heads or sub-committee heads in Congress, and key participants outside the formal structure of government were working in arrangements of their own to exercise power over vast areas of government. These are not simply old fashioned pressure groups. These are arrangements of men and of offices which are able; unless effectively challenged, to make decisions and to exercise power. The chief problem of policymaking in modern government is to try to bring the various sub-governments into a working unity. The problem is to establish priorities which can override the priorities that are set by the sub-governments.[15]*

Practically any new presidential initiative, therefore, faces a strategically placed veto group within the executive branch itself: a social services bureaucracy to resist a negative income tax; an Office of Education to resist measures that would undermine traditional school-of-education training programs; a defense establishment to resist disarmament agreements; and so forth.

The professionalization of many sections of the federal government has created another potentially powerful constraint on presidential action. Professionals in government — for example, senior engineers and physicists in the National Aeronautics and Space Administration or the Defense Department, physicians and biologists at the National Institute of Health, and economists throughout the government — ordinarily are more committed to the values of their profession than to the political fortunes of presidents. Professionals are more likely to move in and out of government than are other career civil servants. Once outside, the professionals can use their inside knowledge to become effective critics of official decisions as well as lobbyists for interest groups. Those remaining inside can resist the administration by leaking documents or key findings or by threatening collective resignations.

The Nixon administration, for example, was challenged on the usefulness and desirability of the supersonic transport by some of its leading science

FIGURE 4–1 BUREAU CHIEFS AND THEIR WORLD

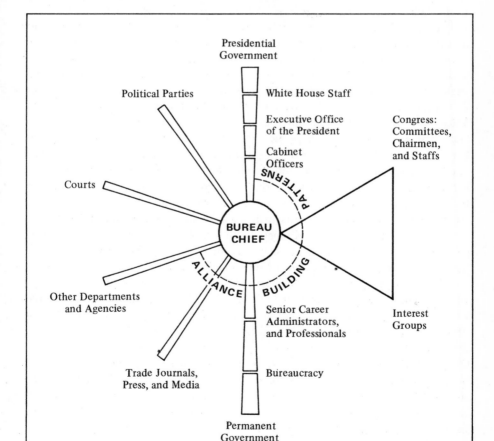

James MacGregor Burns, J. W. Peltason, Thomas E. Cronin, *Government by the People,* ninth edition (Englewood Cliffs, N. J.: Prentice-Hall, 1975), p. 483.

counselors, who made their professional views public. During the debates over antiballistic missiles, one member of the president's Science Advisory Committee questioned the feasibility of the proposed limited ABM. Similar instances of professionals voicing independent views occurred with respect to the war on crime and various environmental protection issues. In the Watergate episodes those persons who attempted to curb the various excesses or who stood firm against egregious coverup activities were senior professionals in the FBI, CIA, and Justice Department, who were supported by the professional code of standards of their bureaus and colleagues.

OPPORTUNITIES FOR PRESIDENTIAL DIRECTION. The great reservoir of respect for the presidency that does exist within the bureaucracies is predicated on the belief that bureaucrats can be heard and taken into account. Federal civil servants believe, understandably, that they have significant expertise in their substantive areas. Although not elected, they often feel that they are more representative of the American people than Congress, White House staffs, or even leaders of political parties. Hence when a vacuum occurs in holding presidents accountable, career public servants often feel compelled to protect their professional interests, particularly from interference by junior White House aides or faceless, unknown, and unconfirmed executive office officials. They may be uncertain of a particular presidential objective until the president's own voice can be heard. Intervention by a White House staff motivated by partisan politics or public relations may be considered personally degrading. And when bureaucrats disagree strongly with the policy goals of the White House, they may not comply or may overtly defy them.

During the 1960s civil servants in most domestic departments did not consciously obstruct most of the Kennedy-Johnson objectives. At times there was considerable euphoria within the Department of Health, Education and Welfare because of the large number of new missions assigned to it as part of the Great Society program. Labor Department officials also were often most supportive of new manpower-training initiatives, and notable increases in morale occurred in such expanding agencies as the National Institute of Health, the Office of Economic Opportunity, and the National Aeronautic and Space Administration. The most frequent difficulty was that for such significant new departures as antipoverty agencies, reforms in criminal justice, or environmental protection efforts, no competent federal civil service organizations existed at the time. Time was required to create effective organizations, which were made up mostly or wholly of outsiders, as in the case of the Teacher Corps, the Law Enforcement Assistance Administration, and the Environmental Protection Agency.

This circumstance underscores the fact that the United States has never developed a corps of versatile and flexible public administrators who, on stepping into newly organized public service organizations, can carry through on a policy objective enunciated at the political level. One of the problems, of course, is that so many of these new initiatives have been set up as crash programs and were expected to achieve or overachieve in an unrealistically short time. To no one's surprise, many of these programs did indeed experience crash landings of one kind or another. Nonetheless, a significant factor is that during the past dozen years or more, career staffs have been downgraded steadily and supplanted at the top level by political appointees. Political appointees always are set apart from the career public servants, and eventually many of the ablest of the latter choose to leave. Because a president is dependent on finding literally crowds of competent people dedicated to the public interest (as well as to him) to come in and run first-priority programs, this situation severely limits his ability to achieve critical program objectives — as was clearly the case in the Department of Housing and Urban Development and in the Office of Education during the Great Society years.

The main complaint in the Kennedy-Johnson years, one raised as well by many persons in the Nixon-Ford administrations, was the inertia of the bureaucracy; it was sluggish and too reluctant to try new ways of doing things. White House aides, however, repeatedly failed to understand the virtues of the bureaucracy, the experience and wisdom that lay behind its warnings and reluctance. Speed is not always the pace of prudence, and the all-too-frequent decision to by-pass the bureaucracy rather than to take hold of it and work with it often served the White House and the nation poorly. A British observer aptly perceived the defects of this strategy: "The tension between the politician who wishes to act and the bureaucracy whose instinct is to warn against action is one of the more important of the conservations, if one may so put it, which should be continuous within the life of politics. One must believe that the bureaucracy — the departments — know something which is not known elsewhere in the political process; because they do. They have been there a long time, they will be there longer still; and, unless one believes that experience confers no wisdom, it is sensible to heed their lore." [16]

A bureaucracy properly staffed and motivated can act, evaluate, and implement creatively. Often, it is not the encrusted old-line bureaucracy so often denigrated in conventional public administration courses (but which rarely is involved in new programs anyway) that most brakes the momentum of a new presidential initiative, but rather the absence of any competent professional bureaucracy whatsoever in the innovative areas. In short, far more attention should be paid to the question of how to create and sustain large pools of talented public executives.

Much of the contemporary debate about the federal bureaucracy paints a rather dismal picture. One president compared dealing with the bureaucracy to wrestling with a featherbed. Nixon complained that there was no discipline in the bureaucracy. Others argue that the executive departments are filled with people who are inherently irresponsible because their jobs are so specialized that neither the president nor the American voter can understand what they are doing. Two political scientists, after extensive interviewing of senior bureaucrats, concluded President Nixon's belief that the bureaucracy was resisting him was valid. They found that Nixon's perception was indeed very accurate; the federal bureaucracy was not fertile soil in which to plant conservative Nixon social policies. They found "a career bureaucracy with very little Republican representation and a social service bureaucracy dominated by administrators ideologically hostile to many of the directions pursued by the Nixon administration in the realm of social policy. Democratic administrators in the social service agencies were the most hostile, but even Republican administrators in these same agencies ... held attitudes that were not wholly sympathetic to the social service retrenchments sought by the Nixon administration." [17]

Nixon sought to make the bureaucracy accountable to the White House, but his efforts failed. Are presidents inescapably trapped by bureaucrats now so powerful in their own right that they are unlikely to listen seriously to White House aides? In practice this depends on what policy objectives are involved and what kind of political support is given to the bureaucracy by interest groups, Congress, and the courts. Experience indicates that a president who uses his office and his authority for noble ends can lessen many of the bureaucratic obstacles discussed here. Presidential success with the bureaucracy depends in part on ideological and political realities, but executive skill and adroitness are also involved. Thus, the following qualities are all necessary: (1) knowing what he wants to do and what he can do, displaying a serious commitment to the intended goals; (2) communicating his views effectively and thereby strengthening the hand of those in and out of government who share them; (3) devoting considerable time to both the formulation and implementation stages of his priorities; and (4) transforming both the departments and his own executive office into far more sophisticated educational institutions, which would learn from mistakes and experiment carefully, and which could establish machinery capable of producing the feedback needed to alter, amend, and redirect ongoing programs.

Even if the president possesses the skills, in practice the bureaucracy is an important check on presidents. The permanent government in the executive branch is as much attuned to congressional committees and their powerful chairmen as to the White House. Many people believe that this is a virtue. They view the bureaucracy as an arm of Congress as much as it is an extension of presidential power.

Whether more or less dependent upon the agencies, no president has the authority or power to control them in a manner similar to the president of a corporation dealing with lower echelons in his organization. . . .

The bureaucracy is a fourth branch of the government, and, like the original three, not entirely independent of or dependent upon coordinate branches. Created by Congress, the administrative agencies necessarily must be responsible to congressional inputs. Agencies are the agents of the legislature and are supposed to carry out the mandates set forth in legislation.[18]

In fact, the bureaucracy is at least as accountable and controlled as the three original branches. It sometimes exercises discretion, but so do the other branches. It is checked by and acts as a check upon the other branches. It is not elected, but is responsive to political constituencies, some of the components of which are elected. It is often rigid and wrong, but these traits are not exclusively those of bureaucrats. Presidents and congressmen, too, have been known to possess them.[19]

CONSTRAINTS IMPOSED BY SPECIAL INTERESTS

The American political system is deliberately designed to enhance the chances of special interests to veto policies that affect them. Although the various economic and professional elites may not be as cohesive and omnipotent as the power-elite school suggests, the better-armed and wealthier interest groups have perpetuated decidedly favorable governmental privileges to advance their business and professional goals. Although at times of crisis there are substantial incentives for subordinating special claims to the nation's well being, such times are a presidential luxury. Under normal conditions, an elaborate network of influences and obligations may frustrate presidential objectives, especially in the area of domestic policy.

Multiple strategies are available to well-financed interest groups for representing policy ideas that may contravene the president's. They may appeal to Congress or to the White House staff, to friends in the cabinet or in departments and agencies, to advisory commissions, or to the press. Wealthy special-interest groups can hire lawyers to represent them in courts, lobbyists to advance their interests in legislatures, and a variety of other specialists and public relations consultants to plead their causes to the administrators responsible for implementing federal policy. As the growing White House and executive office bureaucracies subsume a growing number of interest-group representatives — that is, staffs or offices established to deal with various industrial, regional, professional, minority, or class interests — a mosaic of symbiotic professional and consulting ties emerges between public officials and special-interest and policy elites. Other opportunities to influence the formulation and implementation of policy include: helping to recruit and approve executive branch advisers; suggesting the framework within which policy changes are made; proposing and framing special legislation; building coalitions of support for, or opposition to, policy changes; and influencing the research and evaluation that take place in particular policy areas. These affiliations and activities substantially affect the manner in which policies are adopted, perpetuated, and administered. Invariably, new ideas seldom compete solely on their merits; and who will have the advantage or disadvantage, who pays and who holds the political clout, is always taken into account as well. To see that this is the case, more than five thousand full-time lobbyists are currently operating in Washington, D.C.

To believe that as a representative of an outside elite comes closer to the center of national policy making the more he will temper the blatantly selfish goals of his interest group, is as much an illusion as the schoolbook myth that an ordinary citizen on becoming president is somehow transformed into one of the wisest and most informed of human beings. Former senator Paul Douglas wrote about the role of Senator Robert Kerr during the Truman and Kennedy presidencies:

> *The uncrowned king of the Senate for some years was Robert S. Kerr. This son of a Baptist preacher early fused piety with great wealth, which came from the oil business. . . . In the main, this wealth was acquired by shrewdness and good management, but Bob was not one to worry about ethical implications in uranium and other materials needed for the atomic energy and space programs. As chairman of the Joint Congressional Committee on Space, he controlled the latter programs. He even placed his former chief of operations at Kerr-McGee as the administrative head of the new agency. He also became the chief legislative representative of the oil, gas, lead and zinc industries. The most powerful figure on the Public Works Committee, he dotted Oklahoma with dams and lakes and spoke of the time when he would transform the shriveled Arkansas River into a great artery of commerce, with steel mills and basic industries lining its banks.*
>
> *Stating that he was opposed only "to any deal I am not in on," and acting on this philosophy in the Finance Committee, he was a keen and remorseless bargainer, who usually won the lion's share of any spoils that were divided.*[20]

Many like Kerr enjoy close relations with presidents. President Nixon's second secretary of the treasury and close ally, John Connally, evidently was effective in reinforcing Nixon's supportive view toward oil-depletion allowances. At the Connally ranch in Texas Nixon declared to a throng of Texas businessmen: "I strongly favor not only the present ratio, but going even further [sic] than that." [21]

Presidents must live with a vast array of venerable subsidy programs that are well protected by Congress and influential interests. These programs inhibit serious reconsideration of the distribution of economic and political power. Corporate dairy farmers, the oil industry, home-builders associations, and the maritime industry, for example, carefully protect their cherished governmental shields. The highway, farm, and public works lobbies also look more powerful from within than from outside the White House. White House aides in every administration learn quickly, if they did not already know, how deep and wide-ranging is the political opposition to foreign textile imports, not only from outside the government but also from the Commerce, Labor, and Treasury departments.

Throughout the 1960s, administration efforts for tax reform were frustrated or stillborn. Kennedy administration proposals for the deregulation of transportation made no progress. Johnson and Nixon administration attempts to curtail federal largess in impacted-area educational grants were repeatedly defeated. Congress regularly fails to move on administration initiatives for higher charges for use of federal facilities. One of Johnson's economic advisers summed up the unpromising outcomes of nearly all such attempts as follows:

> Particularly in the early 1960's, far greater gains were to be made by fighting to enlarge the size of the economic pie than by pressing proposals to increase equity and efficiency in sharing the pie. Improved overall performance of the national economy could be legitimately sold as a good for everybody, and thus fitted into the Johnsonian consensus approach. Thus for understandable — though regrettable — reasons [the strength and the bitterness of the opposition], the shields and subsidies continue on the statute books into the seventies.[22]

Often, local special interests who run federal grant programs are the most intense supporters of the status quo; they have high investments in specific policy options and explicitly desired outcomes. Often, too, they benefit as much, if not more, than the intended beneficiaries. As economist Alice Rivlin sees it:

> Most of these programs support the services of particular professional groups — librarians, vocational education teachers, veterinarians, psychiatric social workers, sanitary engineers. Each of these groups believes it is doing something important and useful — and it doubtless is — and fights to preserve and expand the programs it knows will support its activities. The professionals tend — far more than the beneficiaries — to be articulate, conscious of their joint interest and able to impress a Congressman with the importance of what they do.[23]

A president's latitude for achievement can be determined by the degree to which consensus or conflict exists among elite interest groups within a particular arena of public policy. If the policy elite of a given profession or industry agrees on a particular issue, it is nearly impossible for a president to effect an opposing point of view. Exceptions such as Medicare, automobile safety devices, and antipollution legislation are not persuasive, because the profession or industry in question seldom lost much and the costs for such programs were in each case passed on in some way to the consumer or taxpayer. If, however, cleavage or confusion occurs over substantive or procedural matters, a president has some independent influence; although even then, the scope and type of his influence will be shaped by the character of the conflict among these elite. Thus, Johnson's efforts to create model cities as demonstrations of how social and physical planning could produce decent and livable cities soon was heavily influenced by determined pressures from home builders, developers, real estate associations, big-city mayors, and other strategically positioned interests. Likewise, despite widespread public support for rapid progress on the environmental front, Nixon's environmental protection recommendations soon became influenced by the views of the automobile manufacturers as well as by the unions potentially affected by stringent standards and too rapid implementation. Sometimes, a consensus among policy elites may be the product of presidential commitment, but the reverse is more likely to be the case.

Prior commitments to special interests inhibit planning, brake a president's capacity to focus on new problems, and help to exhaust his political credit. Despite high expectations, a president may find himself merely a strategically situated broker for his own party, able only in a limited way to affect existing patterns of grants or subsidies. The president, as Nixon did, may find his hands tied when it comes to changing the federal delivery system or shifting funds from one project to a new priority, or consolidating categorical grants into bloc grants, or using federal funds to provide a floor for personal income.

Every grant program generates concrete benefits to a particular group, and possessiveness characterizes nearly every group that has participated in the growth of federal aid programs since the New Deal. According to the doctrine of interest groups, the unorganized are left out of most policy-making equations. In fact, seldom does an interest group emerge that has as its aim the promotion of the public benefit, a program that would benefit everybody. Theodore Lowi lamented the eventual consequences: "Liberalism has become a doctrine whose means are its ends, whose combatants are its clientele, whose standards are not even those of the mob, but worse, are those the bargainers can fashion to fit the bargain." [24] At the same time, the standards of justice and respect for law deteriorate amid informal, frankly feudal negotiations among those stronger interests who can adjust the laws to their own advantage and profit.

This nation was founded on the belief that the essence of democracy was the judicious division of power among three branches. Nearly all proposals to make the national government more responsive to the have-not sectors of society have centered around the idea of strengthening one of those three branches; and short-term advantages have come from such strategies. Elections, for the most part, have become more open than in the days of smoke-filled backrooms at conventions, and a better means of financing them is at last being attempted. Better procedures for judicial selection and legal assistance for the poor have had ameliorative and constructive effects. And strengthening the presidency and abolishing the spoils system at certain points have also had positive effects.

But such tinkering with the existing system may never be enough to offset the decided advantages that wealthy segments of society can buy, retain, and nurture. For in the end all three branches of government and the bureaucracy listen more attentively and usually yield to the arguments and ideas from those segments of society able to represent themselves, able to shape the character of those branches, and able to supply precisely that information and argumentation needed to make the system move. So it is that the many well-heeled interests continue to enjoy a special advantage in any contest with a president who genuinely is a redistributionist. As historian Bert Cochran observed in speaking of the net impact of the New Deal: "When the smoke of controversy cleared, the social and economic contours of the landscape were essentially undisturbed." [25] So, too, after the Great Society various minorities had gained opportunities and access to desired goods and experiences, but the inequitable distribution of wealth in the nation remained fairly constant. Nixon aide Jeb Magruder put it this way: "We didn't spend time on the disadvantaged for the simple reason that there were no votes there. . . . We don't have a democracy of the people. We have a special-interest democracy." [26]

CONSTRAINTS IMPOSED
BY THE FEDERAL JUDICIAL SYSTEM

Although the federal judicial system is usually less of a check on presidents than Congress, public opinion, and other institutional forces, courts can act to constrain, as well as to provoke, presidential leadership. The courts must work within the boundaries of various restrictions: the Constitution, precedents, and the dominant alliances of the times. But if the judicial system is vulnerable, it also can be powerful. The courts, and the Supreme Court in particular, enjoy a special legitimacy not shared by Congress or the presidency. They are viewed uniquely: as that branch which interprets and protects the Constitution. In this sense, as guardians of the law, as conferers of legitimacy, and as the arbiters of last resort, courts become as inescapably involved in legislative and administrative functions as in their more formal legalistic or judicial functions.[27]

Scholars have demonstrated persuasively that in many respects the courts have enabled and even encouraged the presidency to enlarge its prerogatives, especially in the sphere of national security. And there is evidence, too, that through appointments a shrewd president can bring about gradual changes in the voting blocs within the Supreme Court as well as in lower courts. Still, the courts have a power base that is semi-independent, and although more often than not they may go along with the dominant alliances of the day — which, not surprisingly, are likely to wield great influence in Congress and the executive branch as well — they often have curbed excesses, ruled laws unconstitutional, and enjoined lesser executive branch officials to halt, alter, or strengthen certain kinds of administrative activity. Much like the Congress, then, they can dilute or strengthen an innovative or redistributive initiative. The courts

undeniably are highly political institutions. Judges recognize that their legitimacy depends in large part, if not entirely, on winning favorable support
both from the general public and from the administrative officials to whom
many of their directives are issued. Thus, although the Supreme Court seldom
issues explicit orders to a president, it has innumerable opportunities not
only to interpret and modify laws but also to influence the substance and scope
of national program implementation.

Many classic instances of this kind in domestic policy took place in the
heyday of the New Deal. It took about two years for much of the emergency
legislation of the New Deal to work its way up to the Supreme Court. When
many of the more controversial proposals finally arrived, they were invalidated
by a none-too-friendly bench. One after another, measures were struck down
— some on nearly unanimous votes, others by five-to-four decisions — the
National Industrial Recovery Act, the Railroad Retirement Act, the Frazier-
Lemke Act, the Agricultural Adjustment Act, the Bituminous Coal Conservation Act, and so on. Herman Pritchett wrote that "the resulting constitutional
crisis was by no means the first executive-judicial clash in American history,
although it was easily the most important, since it was the first time that the
Supreme Court imposed such a blanket veto on executive and legislative powers." [28] Soon thereafter Roosevelt tried to purge the court by enlarging its
membership; not only was he soundly defeated but in the process he lost substantial public support. Few of Roosevelt's strategies proved so damaging.

President Truman suffered a notable defeat at the hands of the Supreme
Court in the case of *Youngstown Sheet & Tube Co.* vs. *Sawyer,* more commonly known as the steel-seizure case of 1952. Rarely does the Supreme Court
direct a president not to do something; indeed, not only not to do something
but to reverse ongoing implementation activities immediately. Truman's position was an unusually vulnerable one: he was near the end of his tenure, his
popularity ratings were low, the Korean War had divided and diminished his
personal reputation, and he had acted quite contrary to congressional provisions for the situation that the country then faced. Truman immediately
backed down and his policy was reversed.

President Eisenhower had a quite different set of difficulties with the Supreme Court. His appointees were at odds with what he had intended and
were more activist and progressive ideologically than his administration. No
sooner had Governor Earl Warren been confirmed as chief justice, than the
nation was rocked by the landmark unanimous *Brown* vs. *The Board of Education* decision of 1954, which overturned long-standing traditions of school
desegregation. Like it or not, this and subsequent Supreme Court decisions
provoked continuous presidential and congressional program implementation
and still affect the state of the presidency.

The Supreme Court in this instance had stepped into a leadership vacuum.

In a sense, it was operating under that unwritten political rule in Washington which holds that any branch has an inherent right to move into such a vacuum. The Warren court proved that it could follow this practice in several areas, and its legislative and administrative impact was great in the areas of civil liberties, defendant's rights, church-state relations, reapportionment, and voting rights. Repeatedly, the Eisenhower administration and, to a lesser degree, those following found that their hands were being restrained or forced and that, their own intentions notwithstanding, certain initiatives were legitimized and given a momentum of their own. This is not to say that the court acting alone can force its values on a president on a large number of issues most of the time. Clearly, the Supreme Court alone is unable to implement policies requiring sustained program development and administration. But the Warren court, regardless of whether or not one believes it overextended itself, constrained presidential behavior and shaped national program implementation.

The history of the Nixon administration demonstrates how great a check the Supreme Court can be on presidential initiatives. This court and all courts, of course, try hard to avoid political questions; and they especially try to avoid issuing orders to a president. Time and again, however, the Nixon administration found itself reversed or overruled or certain of its administrative actions amended because of court decisions. Many issues were settled in lower courts or even before direct courtroom confrontation took place, in part because the president did not want to risk a severe and well-publicized setback. Yet, ill-disguised efforts to curtail and redirect major programs of the Office of Economic Opportunity, especially legal assistance activities, suffered setbacks in the lower courts, as did the administration's attempts to impound congressionally appropriated funds for environmental protection and highway construction programs.

President Nixon found his performance and many of his emotionally argued stands undermined by the federal judicial system. He lost the highly publicized battle to restrain the *New York Times* from further publication of the Pentagon Papers. In several unanimous decisions in 1970, the Burger court, as it had come to be called, actually extended certain Warren court decisions by condoning the use of busing and similar devices to end dual school systems in the South. Many of these decisions were unanimous despite the attempts by Nixon aides to go a different route. The Nixon administration lost other major cases before the Burger court: a 1972 ruling that in effect struck down the death penalty; a 1973 ruling that denied tax relief to parents who send their children to parochial schools; another 1973 ruling that held abortions to be legal during the first three months of pregnancy; and the celebrated tapes case, *The United States* vs. *Richard M. Nixon*. In each instance, Nixon had endorsed or campaigned for different outcomes. And throughout the Watergate affair federal district court judge John Sirica demonstrated time and again that a federal judge can countervail self-assumed presidential prerogatives that go beyond the doctrine of self-restraint implicit in the Constitution.

CONSTRAINTS IMPOSED BY THE PUBLIC AT LARGE

The presidency has enjoyed a unique status as a symbol of the nation, and it is a reasonably simple handle by which many Americans can grasp the complexities of government and national politics. The public esteem granted to the presidency and most presidents is not, however, withheld from other governmental institutions, but it is subject to rapid shifts. Issues can change quickly, and the American people find it convenient to blame their presidents for a whole range of problems, many of which are well beyond presidential control. Jim Bishop, the popular writer of the "A Day in the Life of . . ." books, has a valid, although overstated, point: "He [a president] has become the dispenser of all good and evil. The quality of these adjectives is determined by the people. They may withhold applause when his work is good, but they never fail to hiss his blunders. Public scrutiny of the office, and every act of the President, is what makes the position impossible today. An intelligent patriot is not enough for this job; he must be without stain, past and present, and be desensitized to criticism." [29]

No matter what presidents do, their popularity declines. It hardly seems to matter what they attempt or even who is president. When news is good, a president's popularity goes down; when news is terrible, it merely goes down faster and further. The decline in approval of the president is no doubt in part a function of the inability (and unlikelihood) of a president to live up to the buildup he receives during the presidential honeymoon. In the now-classic cycle, discussed in Chapter 2, heightened textbook expectations of a heroic wonder-worker are predictably followed by disappointment. Sometimes the disappointment occasions despair and retribution; people turn on a president almost as if he were the sole cause of everything that is wrong in their lives.

A national survey conducted in 1969 indicated that close to nine out of every ten adult Americans considered that it "makes a lot of difference" to them who becomes president. [30] Contrary to the radical view that politicians cannot be trusted, most adult Americans believe that the president can be trusted "to do what is good for people like me." But respect and deference toward the presidency is matched by public respect for other governmental institutions. The general public places a similar, though not quite so great, trust in their governors, U. S. senators, and the Supreme Court. That the court is slightly less trusted may be due to the fact that the people do not elect its members and feel less able to hold it accountable. The public may also have resented the Warren court's extended policy-making activities in °civil rights and the civil liberties of defendants. In any event, Americans, while trusting their presidency, apparently do not thereby lessen their trust in alternative sources of government leadership.

In this same survey the sample of adult Americans was asked whether the president or other government institutions had the power to get people to do what they wanted. Forty percent of the sample agreed that the president could get almost everyone to do what he wanted. Interestingly, the Supreme Court was viewed as equally powerful; governors and U. S. senators were ranked as more restricted wielders of power. Apparently, many adults now reject a naive view of presidential omnipotence; for a majority of Americans feels that governmental institutions, including the presidency, do not now have the power to get people to do what they want.

Surveys and polls conducted in the mid-1970s revealed a widespread distrust and lack of confidence in political institutions, and loss of confidence in the presidency was approximately matched by increased public disapproval of Congress, political parties, and related governmental institutions.

Other surveys have suggested that Americans value a shared, multiple-leadership form of government, in which no institution is permitted unrestrained dominance. In response to a national Harris poll conducted in late 1968, approximately 60 percent of those interviewed felt that the primary responsibility for the formation of public policy should be equally distributed between Congress and the executive (see Table 4-1). Of those preferring to ascribe a major responsibility to one branch over another, a greater proportion favored a policy-making relationship dominated by Congress. This data is doubtless somewhat influenced by when the poll was taken — it could reflect a reaction against Lyndon Johnson's seeming dominance over the legislative branch — nonetheless, it points up the extent to which the public prizes a sense of balance. The glorified textbook visions of presidential greatness do not seem to have completely maligned the perceived leadership capabilities of the other institutions in our multi-branched system of government.

Certain segments of the public are more likely to rally around the presidency, both in crisis periods and in general. Three University of California political scientists have suggested that future presidents may have less such support as many of these groups diminish in size and importance:

Our analysis suggests that generalized support for presidents among citizens can be expected to decline over time. The kinds of people who are disposed to give the most support make up an increasingly smaller proportion of the total public while those least supportive are growing. Presidential support is disproportionately located among citizens who are older, of fundamentalist religious persuasion, have fewer years of formal schooling, and may be described as psychologically inflexible. Yet the population is becoming younger, less likely to belong to fundamentalist sects, possessing additional years of formal education, and is more likely to be psychologically flexible. Other things being equal, therefore, these long term secular changes in the population would lead to a drop in support for presidents.[31]

The authors concede, however, that things are not necessarily equal. Changes do occur, and presidents who can discern the difference between popular and political leadership and who can use the presidency for the noble ends that will best serve the nation, can affect how the public will regard them, as well as the office of the president.

CYCLES OR TIDES OF PUBLIC SUPPORT. Lyndon Johnson concluded that "a man who uses power effectively must be a realist. He must understand that by spending power he dissipates it.... I was under no illusion that I had as much power in 1968 as I had in 1964." [32] Several presidential resources wane as the years in office roll by. The presidential honeymoon comes to an end, if it has not already done so, by the time the congressional elections take place late in the second year of a presidential term. With the exception of Eisenhower, who experienced only a slight drop, presidential incumbents since 1945 have invariably lost popularity as their presidency neared its completion. As prominent politicians begin to attack a president's positions, partisan followings crystallize and the ranks of those who disapprove of the way a president is doing his job begin to swell, as can be seen in Figure 4-2. Presidential legislative box-score successes, albeit a misleading indicator, are related to length of time in office. His diminishing potency also has an effect on personnel recruitment.

TABLE 4–1   PUBLIC VIEWS OF PRESIDENTIAL AND CONGRESSIONAL POLICY-MAKING RESPONSIBILITIES, IN PERCENTAGES (DECEMBER 1968)[a]

	Foreign Policy (N = 1518)	Economic Policy (N = 1514)	Racial Policy (N = 1513)
President	14	7	11
Equal	60	58	63
Congress	23	31	23
Not sure	3	4	3
Total	100	100	100

[a] Question asked: "Some people think that the President ought to have the major responsibility in making policy while other people think that Congress ought to have the major responsibility. I'd like to ask you what you think?"

Louis Harris and Associates, Study #1900, under contract to Roger H. Davidson, and financed by the Social Science Research Council. Reprinted by permission of Professor Davidson.

A president has far less chance of recruiting his first choice for top posts after the first year of a new administration. In addition, press criticism invariably becomes more cutting and personally critical after the first year.

The frequency and duration of these ebbs and flows of approval between the president and the public are not well understood. Although presidents lose popularity during congressional elections and most presidents' popularity declines considerably in the public opinion polls over time, Eisenhower was apparently immune to this cyclic factor. Legislative activists like Truman and Johnson have suffered most in the polls, while Eisenhower and Nixon, until Watergate, enjoyed more stable support. Is more expected of Democrats? Johnson had enjoyed a comfortable margin of American trust for at least two-and-a-half years, then suddenly it was irretrievably gone.

Apparently, legislative activists such as Truman and Johnson suffered great declines in public approval in part because they were outspoken on domestic issues. Perhaps the expectations generated by these administrations were more difficult to fulfill, while the greater heterogeneity of the Democratic party made opponents more likely for any presidential action. Each time a president is forced to act on such controversial domestic issues as racial integration or the separation of church and state, he risks losing the support of intense minorities.[33] How to please both conservative southerners and blacks, both Baptists and Catholics, both farmers and housewives? The temptation to become the people's source of inspiration for every worthy policy can overcommit the political resources, as well as the institutional prestige, of the presidency.

The public's rhythmic "issue-attention cycle" also tends to restrict the president's leeway in maneuvering to seek solutions to the nation's domestic problems. Economist Anthony Downs persuasively argues that "American public attention rarely remains sharply focused upon any domestic issue for very long — even if it involves a continuing problem of crucial importance to society. . . . Each of these problems suddenly leaps into prominence, remains there for a short time and then, though still largely unresolved, gradually fades from the center of public attention." [34] But the main problem is that when a president is forced to act on a controversial issue, he is likely to create intense and often unforgiving opponents among his former supporters. Even without taking action, a president is likely to come under attack from those who voted for him but find themselves neglected in the distribution of federal patronage or contracts or otherwise disappointed by their inability to influence future presidential policies. Because modern press and television coverage gives so much emphasis to the presidency, they serve to quicken and intensify these reactions. Precisely because a president can gain immediate publicity, he is expected to communicate his views quickly. Precisely because he is supposed to be a shaper of public opinion, he is expected to inspire the country to great causes.

That presidents are firmly hedged in by public opinion is particularly evident and frequently substantiated by presidential avoidance of politically

FIGURE 4–2 PRESIDENTIAL POPULARITY (assessed at 3–5 month intervals, June 1945–1975)
Question: "Do you approve of the way _____ is handling his job as president?"

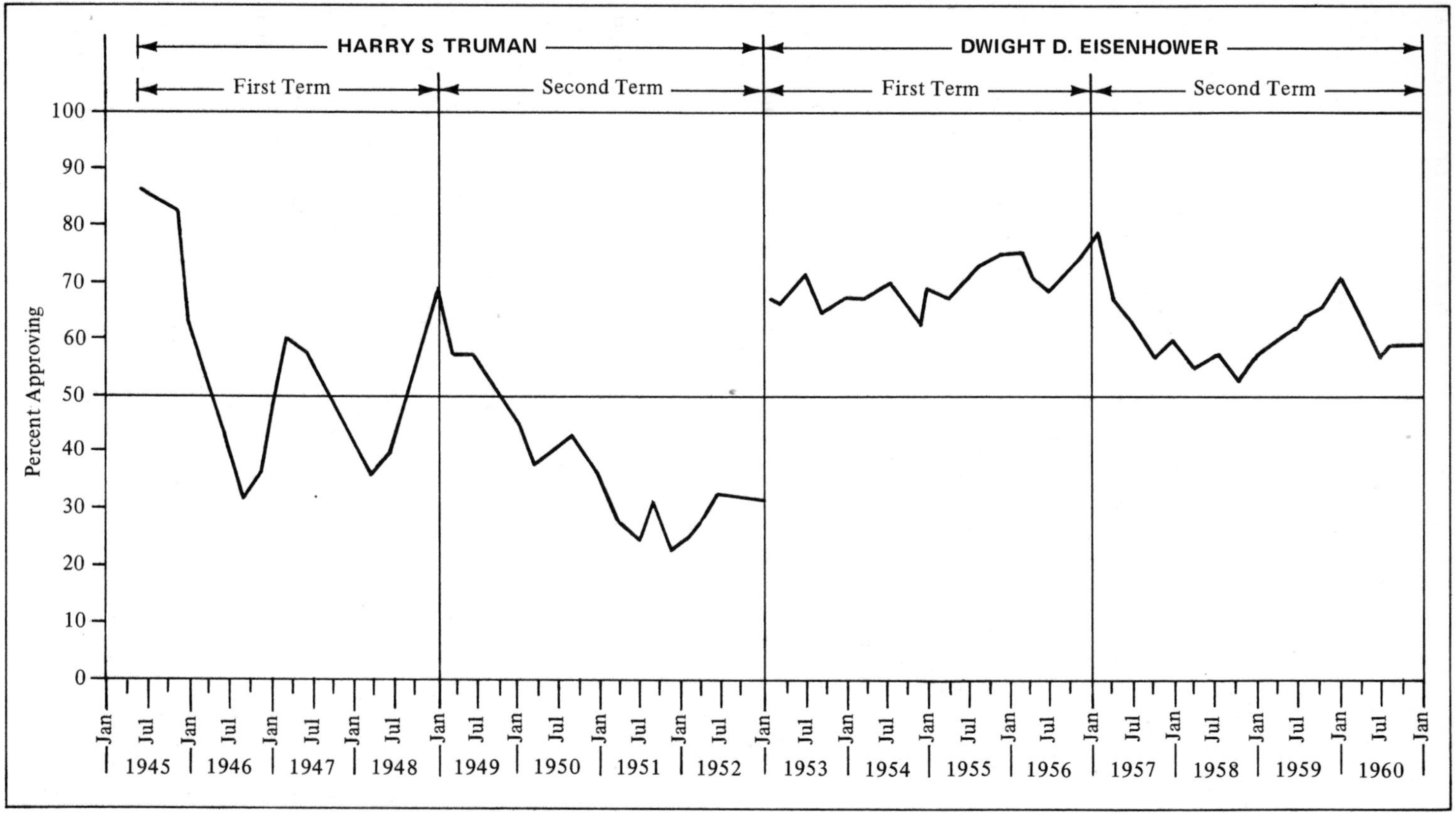

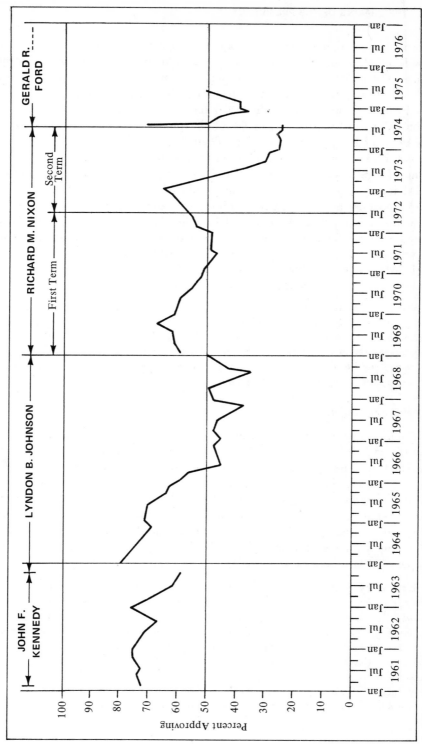

G. Gallup, Gallup Poll Index, 1935—1971 (Random House, 1972). Also, The Gallup Opinion Index, monthly reports.

sensitive issues that clearly lack majority support. The question of dispersing low-income housing throughout metropolitan areas is a prime example of such issues. The matter of civil rights, which most presidents have approached with timidity, is another. Recent presidents have shied away from progressive leadership in civil rights until either their hands were forced by intense minority protests or until sizeable majorities of the public at last became favorable to the goals of the policy in question. Then, too, the courts had taken the lead and had, in essence, imposed the need for leadership on a very reluctant president. If a president has been ineffectual in winning congressional approval of his domestic program, his failure may indicate no more than that a national consensus does not yet exist for his initiatives and that he has been unable or unwilling to educate and energize the public about the desirability of his proposed changes. Tax reform is one area in which presidents often enjoy substantial general support but are unable to win the specific support needed for controversial change. Former Nixon cabinet member George Romney assessed the impact of public opinion this way:

Even our most successful political leaders of recent times are limited in what they can do to what is politically possible. Congress, itself, enacts what it believes is politically possible. What determines what is politically possible? The level of understanding by the general public of the crucial issues at stake. The public's awareness or unawareness of the decisively important problems, the alternative political courses of action that are open to the nation, and the sacrifices and necessity for determination of priorities — the general public's awareness of all these things determines what is politically possible.[35]

Another factor mitigating against national leadership in behalf of social reform and redistribution has been the distinctively selfish mood of contemporary voters, many if not most of whom tire of purposive leaders calling for more sacrifice. Sacrifice translated into the language of the common man means higher taxes and, in return, a government which tells him far too much about what he can and cannot do. Is the performance of the American presidency largely a function of its constituency? And is that constituency now largely interested in the collective pursuit of noble goals that run counter to personal satisfactions? Andrew Hacker offers this gloomy prospect:

Much talk is heard, for example, of the need for purposive leadership. The argument runs that while the American people may be overly self-centered, this condition could be overcome by the emergence of leaders capable of inspiring citizenry to personal sacrifices for public ends. Yet the fact remains that there arrives a time in a nation's history when its people have lost the capacity for being led. Contemporary Americans simply do not want — and will not accept — political leadership that makes more than marginal demands on their emotions or energies. Thus, for all the eloquence about the need for leadership, Americans are temperamentally unsuited for even a partial merger of personality in pursuit of a common cause.[36]

The rapid shift from Johnson's altruistic Great Society to Nixon's self-reliant, do-it-yourself society may be part of a cyclical phenomenon. There have been other times when the public has grown tired of sacrifice, for example, during the periods from 1864 to 1885 and from 1918 to about 1930; such periods have alternated with others characterized by reform and redistribution, such as the Progressive era, the early New Deal, and generally from 1959 to 1966.

This cyclical fluctuation in the status of the presidency is not a recent discovery. Writing a generation ago, political analysts such as Corwin, Laski, and Herring emphasized a dynamic axiom of ebb and flow. In their view, the occasional supremacy of the presidency in American politics occurred at the expense of congressional initiative and discretion. In times of national emergency they observed that presidents become the beneficiaries of a supportive climate. Thus, during the early Franklin Roosevelt months, the presidency was granted greater discretionary authority in the hope that it could resolve the chaos of the depression. Once the pressure of crisis is lessened, however, the docility of Congress fades, as, recently, the gradual erosion of congressional support for the Gulf of Tonkin Resolution illustrates. Despite the ending of the Vietnam War and a landslide election victory, the Watergate revelations brought about a decline of more than 40 points in the public's approval of Nixon's presidential performance — the most precipitous drop yet recorded for a president. Laski also wrote of a longer-term shifting of support, arguing that the forces that operate against a continuity of activist presidential leadership are strong: "Though Lincoln and Woodrow Wilson both exercised, in the pressure of wartime conditions, an almost dictatorial power, it is, I think, true to say that each wielded it with uneasiness, and the exercise of that power was in each case followed by a strong reaction toward Congressional control of presidential action. It is not, I suggest, accident that for twenty years after Lincoln there was no strong president until Cleveland; and that the twelve years after Woodrow Wilson saw the effective leadership of American policy outside the White House." [37]

These tide theorists see a shifting current of support for activist presidential performance both within and over a series of presidential terms, with presidents affected by their immediate predecessor's degree of activism or aggressiveness. Strident concern about a proper balance of powers is aroused when presidential powers are used arbitrarily, or when powers assumed during an emergency are continued in more normal times. It is usually then that the nation is more critical of great concentrations of authority in the presidency. Thus great political tides appear to flow back and forth every few decades. The angry cry of presidential autocracy gradually is replaced with great fear that the power of the office, or the weakness of the incumbent, will prove unequal to the task of satisfying the expectations and of confronting the challenges visited on the president. These tides are as elusive as they are fascinating. Nearly every president is discredited in Congress before he retires. And, with some regularity, passive or go-slow presidents follow an activist one. However, passivity and going slow do not remain popular for very long, and the discontented seek an aggressive, dynamic, heroic standard-bearer once again. These same alternating and ambivalent moods of support and disapproval affect Congress, too, but less rapidly and less drastically.

People clearly support those institutions that they feel will act to further their personal values. If peace and prosperity and honest leadership are not attainable via the presidency, the nation turns to Congress. But if a period of congressional reassertion and congressional reform languishes without yielding much in the way of new and better policy developments, we look elsewhere, including back to the presidency. The public, then, with its biases, limited attention span, and alternating ebbs and flows of support, is a substantial check on presidents, especially in domestic policy. The processes by which it exercises its influence may seem haphazard and unsystematic, as doubtless they are. Nevertheless, the views and vagaries of the people do influence which problems the White House addresses and which go unattended. The politics of crisis and periods of extended sacrifice and confrontation build up public resentment, and these are usually followed by some form of return to normalcy or quiescence. No one understands these tidal fluctuations very well, but few would deny the existence of cycles and periodicity in American politics. Such factors contribute to a president's difficulties in drumming up widespread support.

To summarize the overall argument of this chapter: Congress, the bureaucracy, interest groups, the courts, and the public at large all represent checks and counterweights that can constrain presidential leadership. These brakes on the presidency should be remembered; but they certainly do not relieve a president of his responsibilities, nor should they in any way be so interpreted. These limits neither individually nor collectively do not determine all presidential behavior, all presidential choices, although what they can and do determine may be extensive indeed. A president still retains some leeway within which he can decide to pay attention to some issues over others; to choose as important officials people whose values he admires; and most important, to educate the public and Congress, to clarify the basic issues, and to widen the circle of discussion about them.

NOTES

1. Lyndon Johnson, quoted in Harry McPherson, *A Political Education* (Atlantic–Little, Brown, 1972), p. 268.
2. John F. Kennedy, television interview, 17 December 1962, *Public Papers of the Presidents,* U.S. Government Printing Office (1963), pp. 892, 894.
3. Alton Frye, "Congress: The Virtues of Its Vices," *Foreign Policy,* Summer 1971, p. 109.

4. See John Manley, *The Politics of Finance* (Little, Brown, 1970); Arnold Kanter, "Congress and the Defense Budget: 1960–1970," *American Political Science Review*, 66 (March 1972).
5. In general, see James Tobin, *The New Economics, One Decade Older* (Princeton University Press, 1974).
6. James L. Sundquist, *Politics and Policy* (The Brookings Institution, 1968), p. 415. On the degree to which platforms of the winning party become enacted, see Gerald M. Pomper, *Elections in America* (Dodd, Mead, 1968), chap. 8.
7. David E. Price, "Who Makes the Laws? The Legislative Roles of Three Senate Committees" (Ph.D. diss., Yale University, 1969), p. 490. See also David E. Price, *Who Makes the Laws?* (Schenken, 1972), chap. 8.
8. Nelson Polsby, "Policy Analysis and Congress," *Public Policy*, Fall 1969, p. 67.
9. Morris S. Ogul; "Legislative Oversight of Bureaucracy," in *Committee Organization in the House* (panel discussions before the House Select Committee on Committees, 93d Cong., 1st sess. [1973], 2, pt. 3:708).
10. For a variety of examples and views on this subject, see Frederic N. Cleaveland, ed., *Congress and Urban Problems* (The Brookings Institution, 1969); Martha Derthick, *New Towns In-Town* (The Urban Institute, 1972); Daniel P. Moynihan, *Maximum Feasible Misunderstanding* (Free Press, 1969); Gary Orfield, *The Reconstruction of Southern Education* (Wiley, 1969); and Jeffrey L. Pressman and Aaron B. Wildavsky, *Implementation* (University of California Press, 1973).
11. Harry Truman, quoted in Richard Neustadt, *Presidential Power* (Mentor, 1960), p. 22.
12. Arthur M. Schlesinger, Jr., *The Crisis of Confidence* (Houghton Mifflin, 1969), p. 291.
13. Morton Halperin, *Bureaucratic Politics & Foreign Policy* (The Brookings Institution, 1974), pp. 52–54.
14. Kermit Gordon, "Reflections on Spending," in J. D. Montgomery and A. Smithies, eds., *Public Policy*, vol. 15 (Harvard University Press, 1966), p. 13.
15. Douglass Cater, "The Power of the President," *The Center Magazine*, November–December 1970, p. 70. See also an earlier discussion of similar themes in Cater's *Power in Washington* (Random House, 1964), pp. 26–48; and J. Leiper Freeman, *The Political Process* (Random House, 1955).
16. Henry Fairlie, *The Kennedy Promise* (Doubleday, 1973), p. 169.
17. Joel D. Aberbach and Bert A. Rockman, "Clashing Beliefs Within the Executive Branch: Data on the Nixon Administration Bureaucracy" (Paper delivered at the 1974 Annual Meeting of the American Political Science Association, Chicago, Illinois, September 1, 1974), p. 29.
18. Peter Woll and Rochelle Jones, "The Bureaucracy As a Check Upon the President," *The Bureaucrat*, 3 (April 1974): 14–15.
19. *Ibid.*, p. 19.
20. Paul H. Douglas, *In the Fullness of Time* (Harcourt Brace Jovanovich, 1971), p. 235.
21. Richard Nixon, 30 April 1972, Floresville, Texas, *Weekly Compilation of Presidential Documents*, 8 (8 May 1972):814.
22. Arthur M. Okun, *The Political Economy of Prosperity* (The Brookings Institution, 1970), p. 9.
23. Alice M. Rivlin, "Dear Voter: Your Taxes Are Going Up (No Matter Who Wins Tuesday)," *New York Times Magazine*, 5 November 1972, p. 114.
24. Theodore Lowi, *The End of Liberalism* (Norton, 1969), p. 288.
25. Bert Cochran, *Harry Truman and The Crisis Presidency* (Funk and Wagnalls, 1973), p. 8.

26. Studs Terkel, "Jeb Magruder Reflects," *Harper's,* October 1973, p. 72. But see the debate on this general argument: Ben J. Wattenberg, *The Real America* (Doubleday, 1974); James Tobin, *The New Economics, One Decade Older* (Princeton University Press, 1974); and Philip Stern, *The Rape of the Taxpayer* (Vintage, 1974).

27. See Martin Shapiro, *Law and Politics in the Supreme Court* (Free Press, 1964), especially chaps. 1 and 2.

28. C. Herman Pritchett, *The Roosevelt Court* (Macmillan, 1948; reprint ed., Octagon Books, 1963), p. 7.

29. Jim Bishop, *A Day in the Life of President Johnson* (Random House, 1967), p. 271.

30. Data cited here comes from a national survey of adult Americans sponsored by the Department of Political Science, the University of North Carolina, March 1969. Field data was gathered by Harris Associates.

31. Sam Kernell, Peter W. Sperlich, and Aaron Wildavsky, *Public Support for Presidents* (University of California, November 1972; processed), p. 30.

32. Lyndon Johnson, *The Vantage Point* (Holt, Rinehart, & Winston), p. 433.

33. For a useful discussion of factors involved in presidential support, see John Mueller, *War, Presidents and Public Opinion* (Wiley, 1973), pp. 196–250.

34. Anthony Downs, "Up and Down with Ecology — The Issue-Attention Cycle," *The Public Interest,* September 1972, p. 38.

35. George W. Romney, "The Concerned Citizen's Movement" (Paper presented at the Center for the Study of Democratic Institutions, Santa Barbara, Calif.), 2 February 1973, p. 3.

36. Andrew Hacker, *The End of The American Era* (Atheneum, 1970), pp. 142–43.

37. Harold J. Laski, *The American Presidency* (Grosset and Dunlap, 1940), pp. 12–13. See also Pendleton Herring, *Presidential Leadership* (Farrar and Rinehart, 1940).

CHAPTER 5

THE SWELLING
OF THE PRESIDENCY

The President needs help. His immediate staff assistance is entirely inadequate. He should be given a small number of executive assistants who would be his direct aides in dealing with the managerial agencies and administrative departments.... These aides would have no power to make decisions or issue instructions in their own right. They would not be interposed between the President and the heads of his departments. They would not be assistant Presidents in any sense.... Their effectiveness in assisting the President will, we think, be directly proportional to their ability to discharge their functions with restraint. They would remain in the background, issue no orders, make no decisions, emit no public statements.

— *The President's Committee on Administrative Management,*
   Report of the Committee, *U. S. Government Printing Office,*
   1937, p. 5.

A wonderful variety of men has made its way to the White House staff in recent years. There have been men of extraordinary ability, clowns, scoundrels, ruthless sons-of-bitches, men of rare sensitivity, even a hero or two. The one factor almost all of them have shared is uncommon ambition, a thirst for power and glory, even reflected power and glory, and a willingness to sacrifice friends, family, and personal health, often to suffer personal and political humiliation in order to satisfy their ambitions.

— *Patrick Anderson,* The Presidents' Men
   (Doubleday, 1968), p. 3.

Franklin Roosevelt established the Executive Office of the President by issuing Executive Order 8248 in 1939. Roosevelt had pleaded for help. He needed, he said, some staff in order to serve more effectively in his chief executive and managerial roles. He also needed to be rescued from a great mass of detail which threatened to overwhelm and paralyze the political and constitutional obligations of the presidency. Presidents before him had managed to get along with merely a handful of secretaries. George Washington paid his nephew out of his own pocket to serve as his only full-time aide. Only in 1857 did the Congress appropriate money for a presidential clerk. Lincoln's staff grew to four, although he often opened and answered all his daily mail by himself. President Cleveland personally answered the White House telephone. Woodrow Wilson typed many of his own speeches.

But the verdict in 1939 was that the presidency needed staff assistance and some institutionalized resources. The Bureau of the Budget — then employing a total of only forty-five — was transferred from the Treasury to the executive office, and six administrative assistants were added to the White House office. Three other units were also created in 1939: the National Resources Planning Board, the Liaison Office for Personnel Management, and the Office of Government Reports.

The Executive Office of the President is now more than thirty-five years old. In recent years it has housed a White House staff of nearly six hundred and an overall executive office staff of up to five thousand employees (see Figure 5-1). But the presumption that a president needs all the help he can get is now being reappraised. Today, the president needs help merely to manage his help. The swelling and continuous expansion of the presidency have reached such proportions that the president's ability to manage has been *weakened* rather than strengthened. Bigger has not been better. The effectiveness of presidential leadership has not been enhanced by a bloated White House staff and a swollen executive office, and certainly not by that elaborate machinery for presidential press-agentry which in many ways has served to undermine the institutional credibility of the presidency. Perhaps it is not so much a matter of how big the presidential staffs are as it is a matter of for what purposes they are used. But size still plays a role.

A large executive entourage may indeed furnish a president with the kind of help that will make him an able manager and a responsive democratic leader. Thus, a president does need staffs that can help him identify and appreciate the major issues that cut across departmental jurisdictions. If a president has a respect for the democratic process, likes politics, and has a keen desire to run an open, free-flowing administration in which fresh ideas and criticism are encouraged and come from many diverse sources, then the executive office, properly staffed, could be a very valuable presidential and national resource, almost regardless of size. But if a president is an inept manager and is personally and politically insecure as well, the executive office will probably operate in such a way as to abuse power and impede the creative implementation of the laws Congress enacts. Nixon aide Jeb Magruder put it this way: "A President sets the tone for his Administration. If President Nixon had said, 'I want each of you to do his job, to obey the laws and not to worry about our critics,' there would have been no Watergate. Instead, the President's insecurities . . . led to an atmosphere in the White House that could create the plumbers, the enemies list, and Watergate. . . ." [1]

Thus, another paradox of the American presidency is that a large executive establishment can serve a president and the nation with great distinction, or it can be a breeding ground for chaos and the abuse of power and can grievously impair a president's contact with reality. A strong presidency needs a strong and competent staff, but a strong and able leader in the White House would keep

FIGURE 5–1 GROWTH OF THE WHITE HOUSE STAFF, 1938–1975 [a]

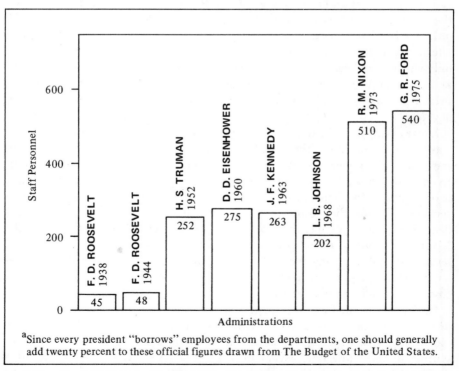

[a]Since every president "borrows" employees from the departments, one should generally add twenty percent to these official figures drawn from The Budget of the United States.

Adapted from Howard E. McCurdy, "The Physical Manifestations of an Expanded Presidency," paper delivered at the 1974 Annual Meeting of the American Political Science Association, Chicago, Illinois, September 1, 1974. Reprinted by permission.

the executive office staff to a minimum and make sure that his staff people have clearly defined and accountable responsibilities. Plainly, however, the presidency has become a large, complex bureaucracy itself and is rapidly acquiring many of the dubious characteristics of large bureaucracies: layering, overspecialization, communication gaps, inadequate coordination, and an impulse to become consumed with short-term operational concerns at the expense of systematic thinking about the consequences of various policies and priorities and important long-range problems.

What should be done? How can the presidency be rethought and recast into a more effective *and* more democratic institution? Our first two steps should be to try to understand (1) how the presidency works, and (2) how the internal workings of the institution have affected presidential leadership and public policy developments. This and the following chapter attempt to describe and dissect recent presidencies to shed more light on these questions.

The growth of the presidential establishment has made the traditional picture of the executive branch nearly obsolete. No longer is it more or less neatly divided into cabinet departments and their secretaries, agencies and their heads, and the president surrounded by a few prominent generalists as aides. Staff and cabinet specialization has long since set in. Presidents have been threatened, on the one hand, by a continuous succession of crises and rising expectations; and, on the other hand, by the increasingly elaborate relationships existing among alternative national institutions such as Congress, interest groups, and career military and civil servants. In an attempt to strengthen their bargaining hand and to acquire and distill vast amounts of policy and political intelligence, presidents have expanded their personal and ancillary staffs and established new ones.

Shortly before the Watergate investigations, former president Nixon said he was taking action to cut the presidential work force in half and to reduce substantially the number of organizations that now come under the White House. Even Nixon conceded that the presidency had grown like Topsy and needed to be pared back. This was, of course, far easier said than done, though a certain reduction did occur. Ironically, although the expansion of the presidential establishment has been by no means a phenomenon confined to the Nixon years, one of the largest expansions ever, in both relative and absolute terms, took place during the first term of this conservative, allegedly management-minded president who often had objected to the expansions of the federal government and its bureaucracy.

Under Nixon, in fact, an almost systematic bureaucratization of the presidential establishment occurred, in which more new councils and offices were established, more specialization and division of labor and added layers of staffing, than at any time except during World War II. From 1968 to 1972 the number of people employed directly under the president increased by 20 percent, to the point that the presidential establishment became only slightly smaller than the State Department's sprawling domestic bureaucracy. Among the major Nixonian additions were the Council on Economic Policy, the Council on Environmental Quality, the Council on International Economic Policy, the Domestic Council, the Office of Consumer Affairs, and, for a while, a special czar and staff for energy policy.

THE "WHY" OF THE SWELLING PRESIDENCY

The most significant factor in the swelling of the presidential establishment has been the accretion of new presidential roles during national emergencies, when Congress and the public have looked to the president for decisive responses. The Constitution neither authorized presidents to meet emergencies nor did it forbid them to do so. All strong presidents have taken advantage of this omission. The Great Depression and World War II in particular caused sizable increases in presidential staffs. After the Russians orbited Sputnik in 1957, President Eisenhower added science advisers; and after the Bay of Pigs in 1961, President Kennedy enlarged his national security staff. The cold war commitments as President Kennedy enumerated them in his Inaugural Address, to "pay any price, bear any burden, meet any hardship, support any friend, oppose any foe," and the presence of nuclear weapons fostered the argument that only presidents could move with sufficient quickness and intelligence in national security matters.

Much of the growth, especially since World War II, has been brought about by the belief that critical societal problems require that wise men be assigned to the White House to advise the president on appropriate solutions and to serve as the agents for implementing them. Congress has often acted on the basis of this belief; it has approved legislation creating the National Security Council, the Council of Economic Advisers, and the Council on Environmental Quality. Congress has also increased the president's chores by giving him statutory responsibility to prepare more and more reports on what are regarded as critical social areas, for example, annual economic and manpower reports and a biennial report on national growth.

Congress, although now critical of presidential aggrandizement, has in recent decades appeared either ill-equipped or simply disinclined to make some of the nation's most difficult political decisions, thereby abdicating authority to the presidency. President Nixon's order for massive bombing of North Vietnam in late 1972 and President Ford's order for bombing a Cambodian airport during the 1975 Mayaguez affair, both with little pretense of consultation, raised serious doubts about what remained of Congress's war-making authority. Another instance of disinclination to take the initiative was the passage by the House (although not by the Senate) of a bill in late 1972 that would have given the president the right to determine which congressionally authorized and funded programs would be trimmed back whenever the budget went beyond a ceiling of $250 billion. This bill in effect would have surrendered to the presidency some of the power of the purse long cherished by Congress. Such congressional actions increase presidential responsibilities and usually generate a need for more staff in the executive office. Thus by late 1973 Hubert Humphrey, half joking but half despondent, could say: "Ours is a system of checks and balances; Congress writes the checks and the Executive Office keeps the balances."

Former president Nixon responded to several problems that defy easy relegation to any one department — problems such as international trade, drug abuse, and the fuel shortages — by setting up special offices with sweeping authority and sizable staffs. Once established, such units rarely are dislodged and an era of apparently permanent domestic crisis insures their continuing proliferation. Often, when new federal programs involve more than one existing agency, it seems reasonable that someone at a higher level should fashion a consistent policy and reconcile conflicts. White House aides have claimed repeatedly that the presidency is the only place in government in which national priorities can be set and coordinated. This job is not done in Congress, they say, and it should not be left to the departments. Attempts by cabinet members to solve sensitive jurisdictional questions among themselves often produce bitter squabbles, and at times they recommend themselves that such multidepartmental issues be settled by the White House. Also, some new presidential appointees have insisted that offices be established for program coordination directly under the president.

Another reason for the growth of the presidential establishment is that occupants of the White House often distrust the permanent government. Nixon aides, for example, regarded most civil servants not only as Democratic but also as wholly unsympathetic to such Nixon objectives as decentralization, revenue sharing, and curtailment of several Great Society programs. The White House regards departmental bureaucracies as independent, unresponsive, unfamiliar, and inaccessible. They are suspected of repeatedly placing their own, congressional, or special-interest priorities ahead of those communicated to them from the White House. Even the president's own cabinet members come to be seen in the same light.

Presidents invariably become concerned about the possibility that sensitive administration secrets may be leaked out through the bureaucracies, and thus they rely on small staff teams of insiders and on their personal and often secret task forces and advisory commissions. The Senate Watergate hearings of 1973 revealed the extent of this insecurity and overreaction. Said one Nixon aide as he reflected on the Nixon first term, "No one who had been in the White House could help but feel he was in a state of siege. They were dumping on you from all sides." Indeed, the President and his top lieutenants, suspecting the loyalty of other White House aides, tapped the telephones of many of these White House aides, along with those of former aides, the president's brother, and noted Washington journalists.

An important reason for the swelling of the presidency is the addition of interest-group brokerage to the more traditional staff activities of counseling and administration. During the late 1960s and early 1970s a large number of special assistantships or semi-institutionalized offices were set up explicitly to serve as brokerages or clearing-houses to provide greater access to presidential attention for professional, demographic, or specialized organizations. The interests thus provided for comprise a veritable index of middle- and upper-middle-class American society. Even a partial listing (see Table 5-1) seems to suggest that presidents have appointed either an aide or an office for every American dilemma.

Interest groups and professions no longer seemed to settle for lobbying Congress; for influencing congressional aides engaged in casework or managing constituency relations to advance the interests of businessmen, veterans, labor officials, minorities, and so on; or for having one of their number appointed to departmental advisory boards or subcabinet positions. Although it now appears essential to interest groups to have their own man (or woman) right there in the White House, the White House itself seems to have seen the reciprocal political potentialities of the arrangement. Once their foothold is established, interest groups are certainly more able to transmit to the president their urgent priorities and play upon the potential political backlash that could arise should

TABLE 5–1   THE MODERN PRESIDENTIAL ENTOURAGE

Offices	Special Assistants	Ad Hoc Portfolios
National security	Military affairs	Regulatory agencies and
National goals	Disarmament	related industries
Intergovernmental	Foreign trade and	Wall Street
relations	tariffs	State party chairmen
International economics	Energy policy	Governors
Domestic policy	District of Columbia	Mayors
Management and budget	Civil rights	Intellectuals
Congressional matters	Labor relations	Women
Economics	Cultural affairs	Blacks
Energy	Education	Latinos
Science and technology	The aged	Ethnics
Telecommunications	Health and nutrition	"The Jewish community"
Environment	Physical fitness	Youth
Consumers	Volunteerism	
Drug-abuse prevention		

their representation be discontinued. At the same time, many of these operations were set up with a calculating eye on coming elections, and their primary reason for existing became to make the president and the administration more politically respectable among their various clientele. No matter that many of these offices may be underemployed and constantly trying to drum up new business to justify their continuation, business that too often belongs at the bureau level of government, or perhaps, as Peter Drucker suggests, belongs nowhere at all: "The staff people have no job and every job. They have the fullness of their chief's power, yet are not accountable. They are totally insecure, having no grounds of support except the boss' favor. And so, in the end, they always act irresponsibly, immorally, and with at least a touch of paranoia. For their basic position is irresponsibility and in the last analysis immoral — as power without responsibility always becomes." [2]

THE DIFFERENTIATED WHITE HOUSE STAFF

As the presidential establishment became swollen, it was compartmentalized by substance and function. Central staff activities are categorized by substantive policy areas — (1) domestic policy, (2) economic policy, and (3) national security — or by procedural functions — (4) administration, (5) congressional relations, and (6) public relations. The differentiated White House staff and its diverse avenues of activity are shown schematically in Figure 5-2. Much of the public relations work promotes greater public expectations of the presidency, and, at the same time, it disguises actual malfunctions of the presidency. The selling and reselling of presidents has become part of the very fabric of the institution and, as such, intimately related to the swelling of the presidency.

DOMESTIC-POLICY AND LEGISLATIVE-PROGRAM STAFF. Presidents once relied heavily upon department heads or the old Bureau of the Budget to generate a legislative program. Recent presidents, however, have wrested policy formation from the departments and placed it in closer and seemingly more loyal hands. Other developments that have increased the need for a larger and more professional staff for domestic policy and legislative programs include the growth in number and scope of federal domestic programs; the vast increase in the number of jurisdictional questions that are raised by multidepartmental programs; and the expectations of Congress that the president will set the budget and formulate legislation. Between 1961 and 1973 the White House staff for domestic policy and program development grew from about half a dozen persons to about seventy-five professionals.

Most Kennedy and Johnson members of the domestic policy staff were lawyers with previous and sometimes extensive Washington experience. The Kennedy aides came directly from the 1960 campaign and from Capitol Hill staff positions; the Johnson aides came mainly from within the executive departments, although many also had legislative experience. Both presidents used this staff to analyze departmental proposals, refine conflicting views, and define issues deserving presidential attention. Few of the Nixon domestic staff had prior Washington experience, although they soon acquired work habits and job orientations similar to those of their predecessors. These aides have been particularly sensitive to helping the president make decisions based on the full range of *"his* considerations and constituencies, which no Cabinet member

FIGURE 5–2 WHITE HOUSE STAFF AND CONSTITUENCIES

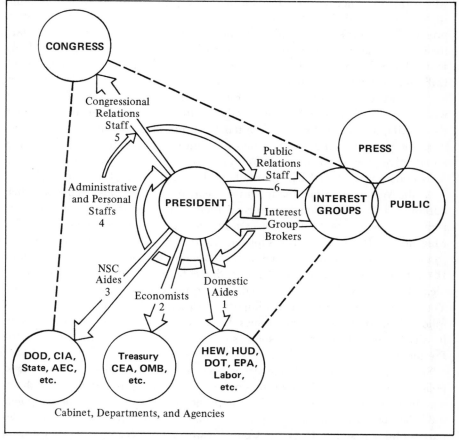

James MacGregor Burns, J. W. Peltason, Thomas E. Cronin, *Government by the People,* ninth edition (Englewood Cliffs, N. J.: Prentice-Hall, 1975), p. 453.

shared." [3] They usually see their work in terms of getting things started, getting bills to Capitol Hill, and, later, if programs are enacted, making things work.

More often than any other group within the White House, domestic policy aides tend to fashion a distinctly adversary relationship with their counterparts in the domestic executive departments. Priding themselves on possessing both a superior capacity to think analytically and the insight and foresight of that mysterious element called the presidential perspective, these domestic policy lawyers often see themselves as catalysts necessary and indispensable to bringing the departments into compliance with presidential intentions. They desire speed and results and have seen their disillusioned boss angered by his inability to bend departmental bureaucracies to his policy priorities. The domestic policy aides have tended to be younger than the cabinet and senior civil servants with whom they conduct most of their business; and, since they often tend to interrogate or prod their departmental adversaries in much the same spirit as prosecuting attorneys and with the same tutored and dispassionate disregard for niceties, they soon earn the dissapprobation of departmental officials. Thus, some domestic cabinet officers regarded the office of Johnson aide Joseph Califano, to whom they had to argue their department's case, often in vain, as "the sweatshop." Not a few domestic cabinet members resented having to wait outside Califano's office for meetings with a staff member and suspected that Califano magnified rather than tempered presidential whim. He and other domestic program aides were not above inventing presidential deadlines, surely an effective ploy in getting the jobs done. Nobody was in a position to find out independently whether LBJ had really said, "Get it to me by 9:00 A.M.!"

As the Watergate affair made all too clear, Nixon aides also expanded their authority and in addition transgressed their own personal sense of what was right in order to make themselves and their president look good. Said Jeb Magruder: "It's a question of slippage. I sort of slipped right into it. Each act you take leads you to the next act, and eventually you end up with a Watergate. It's very typical in large corporations. Someone else is influential. He has an idea and he gets the idea approved. You're the one who has to carry it out. You don't agree with it, but it's important to satisfy the group consensus. . . . I followed instructions and did things I did not agree with because I thought it was important for my personal success — and also for the good of the President." [4]

Since 1970 a Domestic Council has been in operation, presumably to assist policy formulation and program coordination among the domestic cabinet members. There is little doubt that a president does need a domestic policy staff that possesses the skills that could help him understand critical interdepartmental issues. The Domestic Council came about because it was felt that a counterpart to the National Security Council was needed. This was a view widely shared by Kennedy, Johnson, and Nixon aides. Originally, the Nixon

Domestic Council was to serve as a staff for the domestic cabinet members, to assist them in setting the agenda for their meetings and to staff various sub-committees created on specific problem areas.

In practice, the Domestic Council staff at the White House became, at least under Nixon, a kind of operating center. Matters of urgency were centralized there and the staff spent more of its time informing domestic departmental officials of what was to be done rather than consulting them about what should be done. Some of the Domestic Council staff soon became more prominent in policy decisions than the members of the council — the cabinet officials — whom they were supposed to assist. As one former domestic counselor put it, a little wryly, "Never underestimate the advantages of proximity." Moreover, meetings of the Domestic Council seldom took place; it met only twice in 1973, according to one report.

The Domestic Council was in part a casualty of Watergate. Several of its staff as well as some of its former consultants were indicted and convicted as participants in the Ellsberg affair, for tax fraud or campaign finance problems, or in the Watergate coverup case itself. The Domestic Council under John Ehrlichman never really succeeded in implementing the intent of Reorganization Plan #2 of 1970. Still, the idea of a small, well-staffed, well-run Domestic Council makes some sense, especially if it can decentralize operational responsibilities and encourage an active and vigorous White House role for domestic cabinet members. The Domestic Council remained relatively inactive during most of President Ford's first year in office. This occurred in part because of a struggle that developed over who was to control it. Certain of Ford's top White House assistants resisted a move by Nelson Rockefeller to gain control over the top staff positions and thereby over the operations of the Domestic Council. Eventually Ford appointed Rockfeller's people and asked Rockefeller to oversee the work of the Council, but not before office politics had further undercut the mission of the Domestic Council.

In reaffirming an interest in the Domestic Council, President Ford said he wanted it:

To assist in carrying out my responsibilities for domestic policy formulation within a broad conceptual framework, I want the Domestic Council to undertake the following responsibilities in domestic policy areas:

— *Assessing national needs and identifying alternative ways of meeting them.*
— *Providing rapid response to Presidential needs for policy advice.*
— *Coordinating the establishment of national priorities for the allocation of available resources.*
— *Maintaining a continuous policy review of on-going programs.*
— *Proposing reforms as needed.*[5]

In addition, Ford enlarged the membership of the Domestic Council to include the director of OMB, the chairman of the Council of Economic Advisers, the chairman of the Council on Environmental Quality, the administrators of the Environmental Protection Agency and the Veterans Administration, the director of ACTION, and the executive directors of the president's Economic Policy Board and the Energy Resource Council. This brought the Council's formal membership to nineteen. Rockefeller and his new staff directors set out to try to refashion its operations and make it live up to the multiple missions, old and new, that had been visited on it.

ECONOMIC STAFF. At least since the New Deal, presidents have had economic counselors either on their staff or on call. The original Roosevelt brain trust was comprised mainly of economists. Because of the expanded governmental commitments that grew out of the New Deal and such later acts as the Employment Act of 1946 and subsequent housing legislation, presidents and their domestic policy aides, usually lawyers, needed increasingly sophisticated counsel on unemployment, tax policy, and inflation control. By the 1960s several members of the Council of Economic Advisers and of the Budget Bureau directorate functioned as full-fledged members of the White House staff. Although dozens of economists already worked in posts throughout the executive office, the early 1970s saw a new and substantial proliferation of economic advisory staff. Advice on fiscal policy comes from both the old Budget Bureau and the Council of Economic Advisers. Advice on trade policy comes from so many governmental departments and executive office staffs that a Council on International Economic Policy was set up to coordinate diverse policies and program development. In addition, an Office of the Special Representation for Trade Negotiations functions as a negotiating agent. Independent advice comes also, whether presidents like it or not, from the chairman of the Federal Reserve Board.

As the economic recession of the early seventies set in, both Nixon and, later, Ford set up still more economic policy units in or very near the White House. Nixon, by executive order, set up the Council of Economic Policy, headed up by his secretary of the treasury, George Shultz. The creation of this new council was an attempt by Nixon to fashion a National Security Council apparatus for aggregate economic matters; all of the existing economic advisory units — the CEA, the Council on International Economic Policy, components of the NSC and of OMB, as well as other minor units — had to work under Shultz's leadership. But it all seemed to be in vain. Economic conditions grew worse. Soon after Ford became president he responded to increasing economic woes by setting up additional economic councils and committees. Thus, in September 1974 he set up (1) an Economic Policy Board, (2) a White House Council on Wage and Price Stability, and (3) a White House Labor-Management Committee. Of this last group he said: "The objective of this committee is not only to serve as advisers to me on major economic policy but to help assure effective collective bargaining, promote sound wage and price policies, develop higher standards of living, boost productivity and establish more effective manpower policies." [6] It was as if about half of the traditional functions of the Treasury, Labor, and Commerce departments were suddenly transferred to the White House by the issuance of a single executive order.

The Nixon and Ford actions in the economic area seemed constantly to ignore the common-sense rule of thumb that central staff should not be placed between a chief executive and the key people in the departments who are responsible for managing on-going operations. As these executive office staffs became increasingly involved in White House and cabinet-level operations, the distinctions between presidential *staff* and executive-branch *management* became at best hazy — and often confusing. The reorganization efforts in 1970 that set up an Office of Management and Budget as well as a White House Domestic Council stemmed in part from some of these earlier confusions. However, in practice these new arrangements did not alleviate matters. The Office of Management and Budget represented in essence an enlargement of the bureau's managerial and coordinating efforts. Save for an increasing politicization of this central support agency, little change occurred. The number of budget examiners and managerial staff members increased from about 350 to 400 in the early 1960s to about 650 to 700 a decade later.

The role of these aides as cost-conscious intermediaries between the White House and the departments almost inevitably begets an adversary relation with the departments. They are expected to raise tough questions about program promise and performance such as why certain programs have taken so long to get off the ground, why certain ones cost so much, and whether departments have collaborated with each other on parts of programs. They are expected to identify any departmental inconsistencies or any program activities that run counter to the president's intentions.

Budget officials, even more than White House domestic policy aides, are accustomed to their role as the nay-sayers of the executive branch. Presidents often transmit some of their most unpleasant decisions for cabinet leaders through the OMB leadership. One former director points out that conflict between the departments and the budgeters and managers is not only inevitable but also useful and healthy. "How else can you ferret out all the problems and possibilities? Said another OMB leader: "There is actually an inverse relationship between a cabinet member's effectiveness for the administration and his popularity with the Budget Bureau." If a cabinet member or bureau chief is to be prized by the administration as a fighter and an eloquent advocate of fresh ideas and programs, such qualities can be sharpened through vigorous budgetary confrontation. Ironically, of course, the more malleable and agreeable department members are the ones who are usually viewed as loyal to the president, but they are neither doing what is natural for people in their positions nor are they keeping the White House informed about new possibilities and new problems.

In the brief Nixon second term, OMB became somewhat more divorced from economic policy formulation and was relegated more to program evaluation and management. The professional businessmen who took over its leadership from economists and public administration specialists concentrated on the Nixon priorities of decentralization, revenue sharing, and regionalization. Again, however, these activities necessarily brought OMB into direct confrontation with departments and agencies.

NATIONAL SECURITY AND FOREIGN POLICY STAFF. Recent presidents have held that national security and foreign affairs must be directly guided by presidential policy. Most presidents wanted, most of the time, to run the State Department from the White House; consequently, they did not appoint strong secretaries of state. Instead, presidents have come to rely on their national security staffs and have moved into the White House much of the formulation and direction of national security policy. To date, presidents have used NSC staffs to balance departmental disagreements and to offset departmental resistance; and future presidents probably will rely on such staffs to dominate much of the process of formulating and implementing national security policy.

John Kennedy was warned in 1961 by many advisers against a multilayered staff interposed between himself and his national security departments. He succeeded in cutting down the size of Eisenhower's complex formal staff, but he did not lessen their responsibility. After the Bay of Pigs embarrassment, he actually increased their responsibilities and functions. The Kennedy staff had several economists and foreign affairs specialists recruited from universities. Gradually, the NSC staffs of both McGeorge Bundy and Walt Rostow added experienced regional specialists from the State Department or the CIA. Kennedy was able to keep his own staff small partly because of the almost unique friendliness and cooperativeness of the support staffs of the Systems Analysis and International Security Affairs groups under Secretary of Defense Robert McNamara; he treated them as close allies and sometimes even as adjunct staff.

It seems almost as though McNamara elicited some agreement from Kennedy in 1961 that he and his staff would remain relatively immune from White House and executive office interference. It is equally plausible that McNamara got an early agreement from Kennedy that he could run his own department, then deftly precluded White House competition by satisfying the president. The deliberate and often painful adversary process that McNamara created between the military and civilian components of the Department of Defense appeared to White House aides as a more useful arrangement than anything they might do along the same line. Johnson continued and expanded the Kennedy system, although he was inclined to rely on Dean Rusk's judgment more than Kennedy had. These close relations became eroded, however, in the later 1960s. By 1973, the Nixon-Kissinger national security team had tripled in size, in part to perform for itself some of those systems analysis and long-range policy planning operations that previously had been performed at Defense. It came to include, also, military or defense policy specialists, as well as more people on loan from the agencies, which earlier had been poorly represented. Kissinger's appointment in 1973 as both secretary of state and chief national security adviser to the president further consolidated power and procedures around a presidential intimate.

Recent national security aides at the White House picture their work very much in the context of an adversary process in which they act as presidential agents trying to make national security policy performance more consistent and responsive to the president's intentions. Most of those the author interviewed saw considerable conflict in departmental-White House relations, the exceptions being former departmental officials who felt that some of their colleagues exaggerated the extent of conflict. Those who have spent most of their careers working within government may find it easier to work with the departments and are generally more patient than those White House aides new to government.

One aide suggested that his job was much like "an espionage operation, digging out information from whatever source was available in anticipation of problems, and on the outlook for new ideas and problems." Another NSC aide said bluntly that the White House had to know how to "stir up the animals in the bureaucracy, know when to rap 'their' knuckles, fire them, create new agencies, make end runs around them, etc." A Johnson aide noted that the military and the CIA were particularly difficult to monitor because "their cables and reports are more about operations and hence either less available to us, or more difficult for us to reach and often both! Moreover, the military is such a vast machine that it is difficult to stop or affect it."

One Kennedy NSC aide complained sternly of relations with State, AID, the Treasury, and the military. In each case there seemed to be different reasons for strained relations. With Rusk at State the problem was: "on the whole our relations with Rusk were poor, he was quite a stuffy sort of guy; Bundy was a lot quicker and more forceful as an individual and hence Rusk was threatened by us." With AID the problem was: "Kennedy had difficulty getting people to do tough jobs. Thus with his AID head Kennedy felt that it was such a lousy job and the AID administrator was such a nice guy . . . he even said that it was not really fair to put this nice guy in such a lousy job." With Treasury: "Secretary Dillon resented White House staff intervention in his departmental matters and he would often go directly to Kennedy when he was irritated by us; this was partly due also to the fact he was older and had more conservative views than the NSC staff." With the military: "Kennedy used to get very uneasy about the way some of his top generals used to talk about strategic air deployment plans in case of nuclear attack. He used to be in disbelief — some of the military men were dumb — JFK would ask why a certain aspect was planned. Once a general answered, 'Because it's in the plan,' and Kennedy snapped back in disbelief and said, 'Yes, but *why* is it in the plan?'"

A senior White House counselor to President Nixon argued that dealing with the sprawling military and national security departments was by far the most difficult of their problems: "We have enormous difficulties with Defense, State and the military. I think we have gotten pretty much control over the domestic cabinet, but I think I can say in all candor that the foreign service and the military and all their rigidity are such that they perpetuate themselves even a lot more than is the case and than is done in the newer domestic departments. There are just enormous tensions and problems in getting the Defense and State departments to follow through and implement what the President wants done."

The National Security Council is noted more for the work of its staff and staff director (usually called an assistant or special assistant to the president for national security affairs) than for the work of NSC subcabinets or quasi-cabinet-level meetings. When he was participating in the first NSC meetings, Secretary of Defense James Forrestal noted in 1947 that his colleagues at the State Department feared that the new council would encroach on State Department prerogatives. He predicted that the State Department "would undoubtedly try to castrate [NSC's] effectiveness." [7] Recent interviews suggest that State is still trying but has been largely unsuccessful. As one former NSC staffer has concluded: "The need for a National Security Council seems logically inescapable in this age of nuclear weapons, interdependence of foreign and military affairs and deep U. S. international involvements. Yet what logic makes necessary, it does not necessarily make effective." [8] The NSC or its functional equivalent will most surely continue, although its utility and precise responsibilities will vary with the personal styles of presidents.

ADMINISTRATIVE STAFF.   Every president has had some kind of executive secretary, some executive assistants, usually an appointments secretary, and a band of clerks to handle the mail, the schedule, travel arrangements, and various other personal administrative chores. A president needs trusted aides to serve as watchdogs over his party's national committee and also to handle relations with important contributors, the members of the so-called president's clubs or their equivalents. Today, these aides often are referred to as the palace guard, the president's hatchet men, or as the gatekeepers. This type of staff is larger than ever, and it always reaches a peak as elections approach. Its exact number has always been a mystery, largely because of the long-established practice of detailing personnel to the White House from other departments, especially advance men, speechwriters, and political consultants on special assignment.

The growth of these administrative and personnel staffs has kept pace with the expanding job description of the presidency. Johnson and Nixon, in particular, became increasingly upset with the slowness. of cabinet and agency response to presidential requests. They also became overwhelmed with requests for appointments, memoranda to be read, and personal political errands. H. R. Haldeman, the former chief administrative assistant to President Nixon, noted that a president needs someone "to assist [him] in carrying out his job most effectively. . . . [Nixon's] view is that most of the things that come to the White House — in terms of quantity — can better be handled by someone other than the President. The key then is to manage the operation [so that] the President has the time, the access to information, and the background in order to handle those he needs to handle in the best way possible." [9]

Haldeman, who was Nixon's chief of staff for five years, became the personification of the president's palace guard. Together with five or six lieutenants, Haldeman viewed his job as keeping other people from getting closer than Nixon wanted them. He vigilantly protected a president who demanded solitude. Regarded as a courtier, he nevertheless instilled fear and resentment throughout the higher echelons of the Nixon administration. He became the person who said no to many people when they thought the answer should be yes. He was the person who often had to carry out orders requesting resignations. He was also the person who often conveyed the president's displeasure to cabinet members. From these functions come the labels "Mr. Bad News," "Hatchet Man," "Palace Intriguer," and "Swiss Guard." In retrospect, some fault Haldeman's single-minded zealotry in the cause of Nixon's reelection as a prime factor in helping to create the atmosphere of idolatry and overkill in which Watergate could happen.

However, administrative and personal staff aides to a president are often the least disposed of all aides to get into conflicts with the departments, except, of course, in personnel and patronage matters. These assistants deal most with the usually responsive offices of the cabinet secretaries or with their own carefully planted network of political aides. Requests for speech materials, for background papers on a potential presidential appointee, or for more material for a presidential press conference are accommodated more easily than requests for new policy initiatives, for a reorganization of a department, or for extensively documented briefing papers evaluating three or more alternative policy options.

Strictly speaking, none of the White House staff is far removed from policy matters, but in a relative sense, considerable variation exists in policy involvement. Ironically, those who are closest to a president, the administrative assistants, often have the least time or inclination to influence policy. The O'Donnells, Valentis, Watsons, Haldemans, and Rumsfelds by their very control of presidential access and information have certainly been involved in policy decisions; but as a former Nixon staffer suggests, most of these administrative assistants, most of the time, abhor substantive policy responsibilities:

They were not people who liked the play of ideas. When they assumed command, they didn't bring any ideas with them. [They were too busy electing and later re-electing presidents.] What, after all, is the difference between a Haldeman man or a Mitchell man? Was it issues like welfare or food stamps or starving people? If they had been fighting about something that was important they would have been anchored to something. The battles would have been on a different level. Instead, power became an end in itself. That's the troubling thing as you think about it. What the hell did they stand for? [10]

FIGURE 5–3 HALDEMAN: THE MAN WHO SAYS " NO "

Newsweek–Ranan R. Lurie

In notable departures from precedent, Nixon attempted several times to extend his own personal managerial influence. He bolstered the Office of Management and Budget's managerial staffs, and in 1973 he named two business managers to run the office. Hoping that OMB might become an extended personal administrative staff, he repeatedly urged reductions in staffs, dismantling of programs, and broad-scale consolidations of programs in the direction of revenue sharing. He also reassigned a host of loyal White House lieutenants to strategic subcabinet positions in departments and agencies. This dispersal was less an attempt at reducing the size of the White House staff than a setting up of White House outposts or command centers within the dozen or more organizations with which the White House had had trouble. Was this strategy to be a domestic pacification program? The creation of the so-called plumbers group to plug information leaks and uncover other disloyal activity marked another unprecedented presidential attempt to strengthen personal administrative control.

WHITE HOUSE CONGRESSIONAL RELATIONS STAFF. White House congressional relations aides are less concerned with policy formulation than with policy promotion. Their life styles are geared more to consensus building, bridge building, political accommodation, and compromise than to program generation. Whereas those White House aides having substantive policy portfolios spend their time winning support for a president's policies within the departments, congressional relations aides are busy seeking support for a president's programs within congressional committees, dealing generally with committee chairmen and the leadership of diverse factions within Congress. A former Kennedy-Johnson aide summed up his job this way: "We handled the agendas for the congressional committees, worked with leaders like Rayburn and Mansfield, took head counts. We had to hire congressional liaison people throughout the government, and we would have weekly meetings with them. Then, too, we also had to keep track of all the legislation — track it all down, keep big posters with all the relevant data. We had to work with some of the task force people telling them the mood of Congress. We always had to know what was possible. Our job was to keep LBJ and JFK informed about the Hill and keep their programs moving."

Because congressional relations aides are charged primarily with forging viable coalitions of support from one bill and one legislative session to the next, they seek to minimize conflict and maximize cohesion; they run a Dale Carnegie operation, winning friends and influencing votes. To suggest, however, that congressional relations staff merely runs an errand-boy operation underestimates the contribution of their perspective to the working of the White House staff as a whole. Program development aides and congressional liaison aides sometimes differ over the relative merits or feasibility of new ideas. Legislative aides, conscious of the ingredients of a bill that will pass or fail, tend to favor practical proposals; obviously, they don't want to be put in the position of having to sell programs that don't have a reasonable chance of passing.

Under recent Democratic and Republican administrations, congressional liaison aides often have mirrored the more conservative views of congressional committee chairmen in internal White House staff deliberations. And despite the more organized and even mechanical character of recent congressional relations activities, these alone have not assured successful presidential-congressional relations. Working majorities of the same party in both houses of Congress and high presidential prestige are factors that can easily overshadow the caliber of people or processes working in congressional relations. The White House domestic and budget staffs often are disappointed by the dearth of exciting ideas from the departments or by the hesitance of the president to back a controversial proposal; congressional relations aides, however, are more easily satisfied by modest projects and less inclined to encourage new or complicated ideas.

In marked contrast to the White House domestic and budget aides, congressional relations aides rarely have contact with nonpartisan civil servants or bureaucrats. During the 1960s, they enjoyed instead a close and cordial relationship with designated, compatible lieutenants within each major department. As Abraham Holtzman observed with regard to the Kennedy period:

> [Lawrence] O'Brien and his staff maintained close contact with departmental personnel on an informal basis. . . . There was a constant flow of telephone conversations, frequent meetings in the White House with specific departmental liaison officers and also with them and their superiors on particular bills, and occasional meetings with departmental liaison officers on the Hill or with lobbyists from interest groups associated with them in their legislative endeavors.
>
> White House lobbyists expected departmental lobbyists to occupy themselves principally with their committees, while the President's own unit assumed the greater role on the floor of Congress. . . . If departments cooperated on each other's legislation that had White House priority, the White House was prepared to intervene when departmental officers requested help.[11]

Most of these departmental congressional liaison officers were loyal partisans who owed allegiance almost equally to their cabinet members and to the White House congressional relations office, for the White House legislative liaison team had authority to remove departmental legislative relations aides. As a Nixon aide remarked: "This staff could work with like-minded staffs. Congressional relations people in the departments are usually political appointees and in the case of the Nixon administration, at least, Bryce Harlow had a major role in picking them just as Herb Klein had in picking departmental public relations people."

PUBLIC RELATIONS STAFF. One of the more disquieting aspects of the recent enlargement of the presidential establishment is the emergence of a huge public relations apparatus. Under Nixon more than one hundred presidential aides were engaged in various forms of packaging and selling the president and, at the same time, projecting imperial images of the office. This presidential press-agentry has not only expanded public expectations of the presidency but has also distorted the self-perceptions of persons within the presidential establishment; it is a kind of press-agentry that feeds on itself. Plainly, no president wants to look unconcerned or weak. The much-publicized flexing of presidential muscles, the continuous stream of messages to Congress, and the impressive presidential travels abroad seem occasioned in part because the public expects such displays of boldness and leadership. Soon a president can find himself having to pedal faster to stay in the same place — needing yet more speechwriters, jokesmiths, communications directors, and public information directors throughout the government, and now an activist Office of Telecommunications Policy as well.

Presidential aides concerned with public relations — press secretaries, speechwriters, media specialists, communications counselors, advertising executives, and advance men — continually debate alternative means of carrying out presidential tasks. Their means of gauging their success are the popularity polls, editorial opinions, substantial donations to reelection treasuries, congressional box scores, and more broadly, their president's reputation among the political and professional elite. Almost all of our recent presidents have had low resistance to the temptation of giving the appearance of doing more than actually was being done.

The most visible of the public relations staff members in the presidential entourage are those who serve in the press secretary's office. These staff people are the presidential spokesmen, the president's go-betweens with the press and the public. Press secretaries and their deputies generally are former newspaper or television people and usually have served other politicians or participated in presidential campaigns. The ranks of presidential speechwriters and other advisers on the media and communications have been swollen by scores of senior and secondary aides. Most of these people also are drawn from journalism, editorial work, television, and public relations.

Regardless of where they come from, public relations staff aides to a president soon realize that the relationship between the media and the president is and must be one of mutual manipulation. Policies seldom are argued on their merits alone, for the inside public relations staff nearly always views the Washington press corps as a herd of skeptics. The merits of their packaging becomes paramount, and often the prevailing view is that everyone and everything can be manipulated. But however a president's program gets sold, his public relations advisers are admonished constantly not to box their president into a corner from which there is no exit. James Hagerty tells of Eisenhower laying down the following law: "My boys, let me tell you this. Never close that backdoor! Don't prevent me or the other fellow from getting out." [12] Hence, public relations staff members are constantly caught between the often conflicting needs of being vigorous salesmen for their bosses and establishing trust and credibility in him. The ever-present tension between the two often makes life miserable for all concerned.

THE EFFECTS OF THE SWELLING
OF THE PRESIDENCY

The presidential establishment had become over the years a powerful inner sanctum of government isolated from the traditional constitutional checks and balances. Little-known, unelected, and unratified aides on occasion negotiate sensitive international commitments by means of executive agreements that are free from congressional oversight. With no semblance of public scrutiny other aides wield fiscal authority over billions of dollars that Congress may have appropriated but the president refuses to spend, or that Congress has assigned to one purpose but the administration directs to another. Such exercises of power pose an important question of governmental philosophy: should a political system that has made a virtue of periodic electoral accountability accord an ever-growing policy-making role to White House counselors who are neither confirmed by the U. S. Senate nor, because of powers inferred from the doctrine of executive privilege, subject to questioning by Congress?

Some members of Congress have insisted in vain that presidents obtain legislative authorization for all top-level White House officers. On most matters, Congress, lulled into a mindless compliance with what the White House wants, continues to let the White House do what it wishes with its staff and funds. The increasing influence of the presidential establishment has come at the expense of the traditional sources of executive power and policy making: the cabinet members and their departments. One former Kennedy-Johnson cabinet member reported that if he ever returned to government he would rather be a presidential assistant than a cabinet member, an increasingly familiar assessment of the relative influence of the two parts of the executive branch. In 1973 former Secretary of Defense Melvin Laird made precisely that transition. And in 1974 Donald Rumsfeld, Ford's White House chief of staff, also became a graduate of the cabinet. The presidential establishment has become, in effect, a new layer of government between the president and cabinet, and many of its members stand above most of the cabinet members in terms of influence with the president. The cabinet itself, as a council of government, has become somewhat of a relic. Continuous undercutting of the departments can cripple the capacity of cabinet officials to present policy alternatives and diminishes self-confidence and initiative within the bureaucracy. George Ball, a former undersecretary of state, noted the effects on the State Department: "Able men, with proper pride in their professional skills, will not long tolerate such votes of no-confidence, so it should be no surprise that they are leaving the career service, and making way for mediocrity with the result that, as time goes on, it may be hopelessly difficult to restore the Department." [13]

Ironically, the growth of the presidential establishment, which was intended, in part, to rescue the president from the communications and administrative overload so characteristic of post-New Deal government, has not increased his capabilities in like proportion; often, in fact, the liabilities seem to outweigh the gains. Presidential lieutenants often battle the executive departments or each other; they may misconceive or misrepresent their boss and isolate him from communication with others. White House and OMB officials vie with one another for liaison roles with departmental officials. Subsidiary aides in the executive office may be so removed from the president that their self-assumed assignment to inform departmental officialdom about presidential views is but an exercise in conjecture.

With the growth of the presidential entourage emerges a temptation to insist on blind loyalty, to guard reputations, and to seek concurrence at the expense of critical dialogue. The presidential establishment has become so large, disparate, and removed from close relations with the president that the president risks becoming a prisoner in his own house, a victim of his own over-specialized, overstuffed bureaucracy. Some observers see evidence in the presidential bureaucracy of those same constraining forces with which a president must contend elsewhere in the government: duplication; interoffice rivalries; inadequate coordination; and a tendency to become consumed with devising stopgap measures to meet urgent, short-term operational problems at the expense of systematic thinking about alternative policies that might better answer long-range problems. The presidential bureaucracy is becoming a miniaturization not only of important departments and agencies but also of politically important pressure groups and professions.

As White House aides assume more responsibility for the management of administrative operations, they inevitably begin to lose that objectivity essential for seeking out and evaluating fresh ideas. Can a lieutenant who is vigorously engaged in implementing a presidential program admit the possibility that what the president wants is wrong or just not working? Yet, a president such as Nixon depended increasingly on the judgment of these staff members alone. Even such a would-be Nixon counselor as Milton Eisenhower concluded that "President Nixon wanted to be isolated," that it was deliberate, and that Nixon "enjoyed it"; for, as Eisenhower put it, Nixon "maintained almost no direct contact with the press, avoided congressional leaders and distinguished citizens who might have given him points of view other than his own, and retreated in seclusion to Camp David or one of his other vacation homes at every opportunity." [14] To be afraid of outside advice, and to discourage contacts with diverse professionals and representatives of opposing points of view, is to weaken a president's capacity to learn, as well as his reputation. And this is precisely what happened. (See Figure 5-4.)

The role of devil's advocate, or the multiple-advocacy processes, apparently has been discouraged within the increasingly swollen presidential establishment. In the beginning of an administration each recent president seeks out genuinely new ideas, new blood, and the intellectual excitement of confrontations based on philosophical convictions. Each administration, however, has seemed to lose this commitment as its term has worn on, as the following retrospective commentary suggests:

> When [in 1969 and 1970] it became obvious that Burns and Moynihan were at odds over the most significant of the President's initiatives [the family assistance plan], [Nixon] turned immediately to a mediator, Secretary of Labor George Shultz, to work out a compromise.... In a matter of months, Moynihan was stripped of his staff and operational responsibilities and kicked upstairs to counsellor. [The value of a title depreciated as rapidly under Nixon as the dollar....] Burns, in the meantime, had departed for the Federal Reserve Board. The winners were Shultz... and John Ehrlichman, who became assistant to the President for domestic affairs. Ehrlichman and his staff of young lawyers with little political experience and no disposition for principled decisions guaranteed that the President would never again be bothered by the inconvenience of a substantive in-house disagreement over matters of public policy.[15]

As substantive conflicts are removed further from the president appearance is given top billing over substance by zealous presidential press-agentry. Image-making strategies, of course, are associated almost universally with public leadership. Machiavelli's *The Prince* includes a chapter entitled "How a Prince Must Act in Order to Gain Reputation." Contemporary presidential public relations practices have blurred the distinction between education and propaganda. Concern for a president's popularity and reelection often have been elevated to ends in themselves, quite apart from the purposes for which presidential powers were granted. These activities have become so integral to the contemporary presidency that they must be examined in greater detail.

HOW TO LOOK PRESIDENTIAL
WITHOUT REALLY BEING PRESIDENT

Perceived publicity imperatives have become a kind of director's script for the "acting president," or the "theatrical presidency." The placement of presidential activities is always downstage center; the star quality is looking presidential. If a president is to maintain a public following, to live up to public

FIGURE 5–4 MEMBERS OF THE NIXON ADMINISTRATION INDICTED, CONVICTED, OR PARDONED

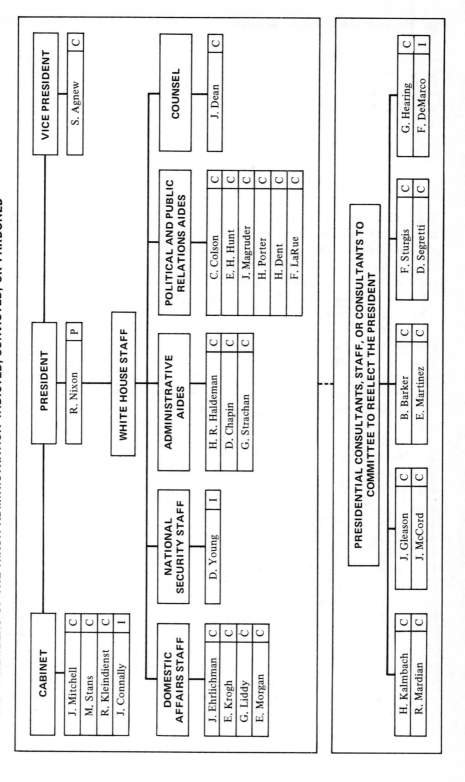

expectations, to compete for news coverage, he must be dramatic and exciting. So, time and again, policy decision and implementation become secondary to selling the appearance of leadership, selling themselves to become known, liked, and trusted. "Let's PR it through," was the way H. R. Haldeman often put it. The imperatives of the script may seem irreverent but they are wholly relevant to an understanding of public leadership in the United States today.

▶ *Don't Just Stand There; Do Something!*

More than any course of action, indecisiveness can hurt a president's popularity, or so White House people seem to believe. For many people nothing is more reassuring than a president who seems to know what to do and is willing to act, especially when others are confused. Declaring oneself is always more popular than remaining neutral, especially in the face of a threat to the status quo. The accepted PR technique is to be positive, seize the initiative, have plans — even secret plans if necessary — announce new programs, fly here and there, make new appointments. Above all, do not convey the impression that you are sitting on your hands, or worse yet, are asleep. Never, never, take a vacation. All vacations must be working vacations. This appearance of always being at work was perhaps carried to an extreme when Nixon observed in an interview: "The worst thing you can do in this job is to relax, to let up."

Logically, President Kennedy should have suffered a great loss of popularity after the Bay of Pigs failure, but his popularity actually rose by seven to ten points. Nixon's popularity dropped markedly when in his first term he failed to act decisively on inflation, and it dropped again dramatically in his second term when he failed to respond with dispatch to the Watergate revelations. George Gallup explains this phenomenon this way: "People tend to judge a man by his goals, by what he is trying to do, and not necessarily by what he accomplishes or by how well he succeeds. People used to tell us over and over again about all the things that [Franklin] Roosevelt did wrong and then they would say, 'I'm all for him, though, because his heart is in the right place; he is trying.' That's the most important thing in the world. . . ." [16]

Harry Truman aide Clark Clifford similarly recognized the public's hunger for novelty and image accentuating presidential activity. Clifford counseled: "A president who is also a candidate must resort to subterfuge. . . . He cannot sit silent; he must be in the limelight. . . . He must resort to the kind of trip Roosevelt made famous in the 1940 campaign — the 'inspection tour.' No matter how much the opposition and the press pointed out the political overtones of those trips, the people paid little attention, for what they saw was the Head of State performing his duties." [17] With guidance from this Clifford script and a little help from Thomas Dewey, Truman went on to win an upset victory in the 1948 elections.

The political incentives of the 1960s seemed to deflect energies away from rigorous policy experimentation and planning. The thinking seemed to be that it was better to act immediately and to worry about planning later. The curse of activism, regardless of its cost, seemed always at work. Presidents and congressional leaders were eager for quick results; they felt they were elected not to study policies but to make them and put them into operation. As one Kennedy-Johnson counselor recalled:

People were always wanting to turn pilot projects into full-scale programs all over the place before they knew the result or before they tested whether things would work. Often we would argue this brief before the President. But again and again between the presidential message and later when it was enmeshed in congressional committees, the departmental and lobbying interests had worked on it in such a way that the program idea would get expanded and markedly changed in scope. Political advisers would always say that to line up the right number of votes you had to spread the program around. So before you had a chance to debug a program it was being launched nationwide! The Budget Bureau lost any influence it might have had on many programs because they were set up so rapidly and thrown into the political processes too quickly — everybody wanted results right away. This was also in the character of President Johnson. He was impatient about problem-resolving programs; he wanted to do things right away and as fast as he could on a large scale.

▶ *Bend Over Backwards to Disprove Your Stereotypes!*

Most presidents seem to behave in such a way as to counteract the notable stereotypes people have of them — sometimes for the better, but often for the worse. The public feared that General Eisenhower might be swayed easily by his military advisers and that another war might result. Eisenhower not only disproved such fears but made large cuts in the military budgets. His military policies won little praise from the generals in the Pentagon. Indeed, once elected, he may have been the least popular modern president in the eyes of the military establishment.

John Kennedy constantly behaved as if he were trying to counteract his image as young, inexperienced, and not tough enough to deal with world leaders. As a result, he overcompensated, as in the Bay of Pigs humiliation, in the perilous if successful handling of the Russian missile sites in Cuba, and in the escalating involvement in Vietnam. And to still the people's fear of a Catholic president, Kennedy became so cautious about any commitments to the Church that his policies and practices have been characterized as perhaps the most anti-Catholic since those of Millard Fillmore.

Johnson, like Nixon, seemed determined to be a different kind of person as president than he had been previously. Aaron Wildavsky notes, for example, that "Johnson delighted in showing that he was not the canny politician everyone thought they had elected, the man who would always trim his sails so as to keep close to the people, but rather the statesman who would insist on doing right in Vietnam no matter what anyone thought." [18] Many people also doubtless thought of Lyndon Johnson as a parochial southerner who would be relatively weak on civil rights initiatives. Johnson himself recalled that while he was in Congress he had voted against six major civil rights bills, feeling that such legislation was written more to humiliate the South than to help the black people. "I represented a conservative constituency. One heroic stand and I'd be back home, defeated, unable to do any good for anyone, much less the blacks and underprivileged," he wrote.[19] But as his national responsibilities (and ambitions) grew, he sought to demonstrate that a southerner could rise above regional attitudes. In 1964 and 1965 Johnson seemed determined to prove once and for all that he should not be identified solely as a southerner and a compromiser who somehow would wriggle out of the controversy over civil rights. He later recalled in his memoirs how he tried to outdo the Kennedy commitment:

> When I sat in the Oval Office after President Kennedy died and reflected on civil rights, there was no question in my mind as to what I would do. I knew that, as President and as a man, I would use every ounce of strength I possessed to gain justice for the black American. My strength as President was then tenuous — I had no strong mandate from the people. I had not been elected to that office. . . . Even the strongest supporters of President Kennedy's civil rights bill in 1963 expected parts of it to be watered down in order to avert a Senate filibuster. . . . I had seen this "moderating" process at work for many years. I had seen it happen in 1957. I had seen it happen in 1960, I did not want to see it happen again. . . . I made my position unmistakably clear: We were not prepared to compromise in any way. . . . I wanted absolutely no room for bargaining. And I wanted everybody to know this, from the lowliest bureaucrat to the members of my cabinet, from the poorest black in the slums to the richest white man in the suburbs, from the staunchest Baptist in the South to the most devout Catholic in the North.[20]

President Nixon had numerous negative stereotypes to disprove, perhaps the most prominent of which was the "Tricky Dick" image of a devious dealer in used cars. Fortunately for him, his opponent in 1972 increasingly appeared to be a frequent buyer of used cars, thereby helping to offset Nixon's chief stylistic disadvantage. Nonetheless, Nixon continually attempted to posture as an open, candid leader, who wanted to make everything "perfectly clear," who was dedicated to law and order, and who was, according to him, guided by a lawyer's sense of probity and due process. Despite his giant public relations machine, however, he was never able to overcome the image of deviousness. When it became clear that his administration had nurtured the most widespread scandals and coverup of scandals the presidency had ever endured, he quickly became thoroughly distrusted and scorned.

► *Don't Be Soft: Appear Resolute and Dominant*
  and Accentuate the Sense of Crisis!

Machiavelli summed it up well when he said that "above all a prince must endeavor in every action to obtain fame for being great and excellent." [21] A president can appear more presidential if he can accentuate the nation's sense of being in a desperate predicament. This enlarges on the uncertainties and isolates the leader from the people, and even more from the sets of checks and balances that usually prevail. Therefore, because the important and critical problems are not necessarily those that people want to hear about, a self-enhancing technique is to place critical problems in an unreal light and pose illusory ones as if they were critical. When challenged for doing so, a president can condemn his critics as obstructionists on the one hand and as mindless romantics on the other. He can label them as radicals, Nervous Nellies, or vicious, myopic, ivory-tower intellectuals. A clever policy is to practice the politics of confrontation, to elevate external challenges to a call for a state of national emergency, and to know the value of keeping his subjects' minds uncertain and astonished, watching and waiting for his remedies.

John Kennedy sounded the clarion call on innumerable occasions; he always confronted problems as though they were dragons to be slain. The Kennedy sense of urgency is well illustrated in his anxious response to the Russian propaganda triumph with the first manned orbital flight in 1961. Said Kennedy to his staff: "Is there any place where we can catch them? What can we do? Can we go around the moon before them? Can we put a man on the moon before them? If somebody can just tell me how to catch up. Let's find somebody — anybody. I don't care if it's the janitor over there, if he knows. . . . There is nothing more important." [22] Kennedy's appeal to the nation to build fallout shelters during one of his early crises is another illustration of jolting the people and making them uncertain. Both Kennedy and Nixon publicly activated and put the Strategic Air Command and other nuclear air missions on alert — quite possibly as a means to excite the nation and create an aura of precariousness.

Another means of creating a sense of importance is to proclaim every new presidential action as a constitutional duty, as the nation's number-one priority, and as the right of every citizen. Whatever the content of his program and the direction of his commitments, the president can claim to be a reform leader dedicated to innovations and responsible change. Lyndon Johnson had a fondness that verged on a weakness for making nearly every novel social reform idea that came along his major priority — until, of course, so many things were top priority that the very term was reduced to near meaninglessness. Also, presidential opponents can be confronted with stern and irreconcilable dichotomies; they can, for example, love the country or leave it, have peace with honor or peace with dishonor, support either prudent fiscal policy or budget-wrecking activities. Such simplistic pronouncements insure good headlines, place the opposition on the defensive, and inhibit serious dialogue.

Also, a president can avoid dwelling on his mistakes — avoid any admission of them, if possible — and deny categorically that he ever was involved in any wrongdoing or mistaken endeavors. If necessary, he can shield himself behind national security and issue "no comment" statements rather than clarifications or further elaboration. A former administrative assistant to Franklin Roosevelt recalled an admonition by FDR to this then-young aide, who had suggested that some retraction or acknowledgment of error be released to the press: "My son, I've been involved in politics a very long time and I probably have made hundreds of mistakes, but I learned long ago *never* to talk about them!" [23] The lesson was clear: there is little incentive in politics to call attention to one's mistakes; whatever press space is available should be used to call attention to one's achievements.

President Nixon's response to the entire Watergate mess was an attempt to practice this Rooseveltian admonition. Time and again, he urged the nation to look forward, not backward. At the outset, he refused to acknowledge that Watergate had even occurred; then he called for all investigations to be downgraded or completed as soon as possible. Still, although he wanted the public to forget this seamy and tawdry aspect of his first term, he wanted extensive attention focused on his first-term accomplishments in Vietnam, China, and elsewhere.

▶ *Claim to Be a Consensus Leader when the Polls Are Favorable and a Profile-in-Courage Leader When They Are Not.*

Presidents can attempt to prolong the presidential honeymoon as long as possible; after all, a president must replace partisan politics with consensus politics, be the leader for the entire country, and unite all factions. When the popularity ratings drop, he can emphasize that although he is the president of all the people, he has a special responsibility to represent the underrepresented or the badly represented. This is a convenient strategy, particularly when he is faced by a majority opposition against part of his legislative program. He can say that he represents the silent majority, the next generation, the minorities, the young, or the ill-fed, and thereby become portrayed as a moral leader. He can claim that he is doing what is right rather than what is popular or easy.

The prerogative of claiming moral considerations in making an unpopular decision is a well-established presidential tradition. Consider President Nixon's explanation of why he sent U. S. troops to Cambodia in the spring of 1970:

*I have noted, for example, that a Republican Senator has said that this action I have
taken means that my party has lost all chances of winning the November elections, and
others are saying that this move against enemy sanctuaries will make me a one-term
President. . . . I would rather be a one-term President and do what I believe is right
than to be a two-term President at the cost of seeing America become a second-rate
power and to see this nation accept the first defeat in its proud 190-year history.*[24]

In the early years of his administration, Lyndon Johnson proudly walked
around with assorted favorable polls stuffed in his pocket; their results were
ever mentioned in his conversations to illustrate the virtues of his consensus
strategy. On one occasion Johnson told reporters with obvious delight, "This
paper has the latest Gallup figures and I now rate higher than John Kennedy
ever did." [25] As time wore on, public support and consensus politics diminished
measurably and so, understandably, did Johnson's high evaluation of the polls.
Later in his presidency Johnson took the tack that he was doing what was
right even if he was hurt significantly in the polls: "In this job a man must
set a standard to which he's working. In my case, it is what my grandchildren
think when I'm buried out there under the tree on the ranch. I think they
will be proud of two things. What I did for the Negro and seeing it through
in Vietnam for all of Asia. The Negro cost me 15 points in the polls and
Vietnam cost me 20." [26]

▶ *Travel Widely, Be a Statesman! Run for a Nobel Peace Prize,
and Be Your Own Secretary of State!*

Consensus is easier to achieve on national defense and international peace
aims than on the more divisive internal problems affecting the nation. Having
achieved celebrity-number-one status at home, every president since Theodore
Roosevelt has been mindful that no other prize is more cherished than a
Nobel Prize for peace. Lending one's name to a doctrine, as Monroe, Truman,
and Eisenhower did, is most presidential. Thus, to make history's list of great
presidents a president can first claim to be making the world safe for democracy and, second, making the American dollar safe for the world. He can
appear to be an architect for a lasting peace and for generations of peace,
as a statesman he can appear to be bipartisan and above politics. He can
concentrate on foreign affairs with trips, summits, treaties, negotiations, and
plans for generations of peace and still seem like an effective, or at least an
adequate, president. Ford became so caught up in the new excitement of
traveling here, there, and everywhere that party elder statesman Barry Goldwater had to admonish him by saying, "I think it would be a good thing for
the country if President Ford put Air Force One in the hangar for at least
eight months," implying that Ford should stay at home and begin realizing

the real problems we have here.[27] After all Nixon's travels, Ford's peregrinations caused people to see through this presidential ploy of staying 35,000 feet above their problems.

Finally, a president can refuse to relinquish to the secretary of state the personalized celebrity status that accrues from international travel and person-to-person diplomacy. That Nixon allowed Henry Kissinger to share or even steal the spotlight may be no more than the exception that proves the rule, although it could reflect as well his weakened position in his second term.

▶ *Don't Let the Vice-President or Any Other Member of the Cabinet or White House Staff Upstage or Outshine You!*

A president can avoid party responsibilities and fund-raising activities by delegating these to his vice-president, attorney general, or party officials. Highly partisan and divisive activities may be assigned routinely to the vice president to keep him busy, to ensure that his popularity does not outstrip the president's, and to demonstrate, by contrast, that he is above politics. Johnson's use of Humphrey and Nixon's use of Agnew in these ways are illustrative, as were Nixon's difficulties in retaining such strong-willed cabinet members as Hickel, Connally, Richardson, and Peterson.

The president can also accentuate his role as symbolic leader: he can cater to the American passion for a benevolent father image or superhero. The PR script may even require him to own dogs, preferably several, and to attend church fairly regularly even if he has not in the past. Ceremonial activities and close association with entertainment and sports superstars, astronauts, and winners in high-visibility professions are major priorities. Charisma, at least for a while, can be manufactured, borrowed, and staged. But attractive politicians are to be kept out of the cabinet, off your staff, and always at camera-arm's length. Unretired politicians make questionable cheerleaders.

▶ *Claim Credit When Things Go Right and Decentralize Blame! Choose Problems for Their Potential Credit Value!*

President Kennedy knew the value of expropriating credit when policies worked and decentralizing blame when they did not. At the conclusion of some White House discussions for handling a complex foreign policy problem, Kennedy cheerfully told some of the participants: "I hope this plan works. If it does, it will be another White House success. If it doesn't, it will be another State Department failure." [28] Nixon's classic statement in this regard was his assertion that he had the responsibility for Watergate but would not accept the blame.

Precisely because presidents prefer to be loved, not excoriated, their counselors are always under orders to find problems they can solve, or at least appear to solve. Presidents can urge their staffs to concentrate on those programs which can get passed, on what they can do well, on those matters for which credit is obtainable.

▶ *Proclaim an Open Presidency and an Open Administration*
But Practice Presidency-by-Secrecy, Manage the News,
and Circumvent the White House Press Corps!

Presidents can hold numerous news conferences during their honeymoons but afterwards appeal directly to the people by direct address over the heads of the Washington press, especially when unkept promises or unresolved scandals can make news conferences embarrassing. So distrustful was Nixon of the press and press conferences that he held fewer news conferences than any president in forty years. He gained extensive prime-time exposure, perhaps more than any other president, but only when he had well-crafted speeches, messages, or emergency announcements. These, of course, were the labor of many minds and skilled public relations counselors, not of a man standing alone before the uncertainties and hostile barbs of the prepared press. The news can be what the White House says it is. Presidents can generously say that press conferences will be held when they will serve the public interest, but the appropriate time for a press conference is always decided backstage by the White House public relations executives.

The phrase "compelling reasons of national security" can always serve as a cloak of justification. Reliance on secrecy, however, can tempt presidents and their aides to conceal grievous mistakes, deviousness, and a host of other activities to account for which would be embarrassing. Vietnam, Watergate, the Cambodian bombings, and similar events speak eloquently to the point.

Some presidents, it seems, have thought that the best policy toward the White House press corps was to make them comfortable and leave them ignorant and to keep them busy trekking to and from Camp David and other presidential retreats. It is true that presidents such as Harry Truman who were the most accessible and candid presidents also had the lowest popularity ratings. As one political scientist summed it up: "Like the movie star [the political star] is known primarily through pictures on screens and billboards, voices from loudspeakers, anecdotes in newspapers and magazines. These are appearances, and, as such, they are subject to certain kinds of manipulation. Like the movie star, the politician has the possibility of becoming a mythical character. In both cases, also, the myth can be a managed one." [29]

▶ *History and Historians Reward Him Who Protects
and Strengthens the Powers of the Presidency.*

According to this axiom, presidents should expand the executive powers and
the executive office, and leave the presidency a larger, more capable institution. They can always rationalize that even if such actions arouse controversy in
the short run, posterity almost always praises such enlargements. Then, too, presidents are criticized if they are too weak, conciliatory, or seem to lack machismo.
Lincoln, they may recall, is praised because he had the courage to violate one
clause of the Constitution to preserve the rest. Of course, a president can try
to defeat congressional measures that lessen presidential discretion. He can
decry such efforts as reactionary and contrary to the spirit of strict construction
of the Constitution. When doing so, he may recall that the Supreme Court invariably is more friendly to the presidency than to Congress.

▶ *If All Else Fails, Wage War on the Press, Impugn Its Objectivity,
Undermine Confidence in Its Fairness
and Integrity; Denationalize Networks, Pacify Public Broadcasting,
Investigate Reporters, and Intimidate Public Affairs
Video Journalism!*

According to this part of the PR script, being president means never having to
say you're sorry — or wrong. Any credibility problems are supposedly due to
the press, not to the presidency. In fact, the press may also be responsible for
hindering some projects that have not performed well or for sabotaging national security. Television, as "the" presidential medium, dramatizes the individual and can portray an individual's sense of stability and calm during
emotional events and his sense of moral certitude in times of great confusion.
When a president's popularity sags and when he is hedged in by Congress and
the Supreme Court, television provides an obvious platform from which to
dress up old platitudes in new slogans to proclaim bold initiatives. A dramatic
new video performance can almost always resuscitate some of his former supporters. Nixon's team especially tried to manage the press, although nearly
every president has tried to lessen its influence. According to his aides, Nixon
was constantly ordering his staff to get this or that opponent. "On one occasion, Nixon wanted somebody brought in 'full-time' to 'destroy' the press'
image, as if people like Colson and Buchanan were not doing enough of that
already" writes one ex-Nixon staffer.[30]

Another twist to this Hollywood script is the maneuver of exposing it and
campaigning — or seeming to campaign — against it. Fully understanding the
publicity imperatives that make up the script, the shrewdest of presidents
would write a profiles-in-courage kind of book to denigrate both the past uses

and misuses of it, and to denounce Machiavellianism and all its contemporary manifestations. But this presupposes not only that presidential candidates can appreciate fully all its implications but also that if elected they could cope with the burdens of office without resorting to it themselves.

The danger of this "how-to-look presidential" script lies in its misplacement of values; in the subordination of policy substance to presidential style, in the subordination of doing what is right but controversial to postponement, ducking, or coverup. A president, elected for reasons often unrelated to his leadership capabilities, can engineer a public reputation quite inconsistent with his substantive performance as a leader, at least for a while. The selling of the presidential administration and its image can be as devious, if not more so, as the original selling of the presidential candidate. A president is pressured on the one hand by exaggerated expectations of what he can accomplish and, on the other, by a large, restless, and often overzealous public relations machine. The resulting temptations to distort and exaggerate have the effect of creating presidents who are listened to — and who speak — as little more than shrewd public relations men. Too often, these script imperatives not only subordinate substance to style but also affect substance directly. The wrong people are hired for important White House counseling posts. The wrong people are asked for advice. Debates and multiple advocacy are thwarted. Telling the truth becomes dangerous. Manipulation becomes an end in itself, and a mindless confusion sets in about the proper relationship between ends and means.

NOTES

1. Jeb S. Magruder, "Jeb Magruder Unearths the Roots of Watergate," *Los Angeles Times*, 22 May 1974, sect. II, p. 7. On the expansion of the White House staff, see "The Development of the White House Staff," *Congressional Record*, 20 June 1972, 92nd Congress, 2nd session, p. H5819. Also see an earlier draft of these ideas, Thomas E. Cronin, "The Swelling of the Presidency," *Saturday Review of Society*, February 1973, pp. 30–36; and Howard E. McCurdy, "The Physical Manifestations of an Expanding Presidency" (Paper delivered at the 1974 Annual Meeting of the American Political Science Association, Chicago, Illinois, 1 September 1974).
2. Peter Drucker, "How to Make the Presidency Manageable," *Fortune*, Nov. 1974, p. 147. See also Jeb Stuart Magruder, *An American Life: One Man's Way to Watergate* (Atheneum, 1974).
3. Theodore Sorensen, *Kennedy* (Harper and Row, 1965), p. 289.
4. Studs Terkel, "Jeb Magruder Reflects," *Harper's*, October 1973, p. 67.
5. Gerald Ford, "Memorandum for Members of the Domestic Council," 13 February 1975, *Presidential Documents* (U.S. Government Printing Office, 17 February 1975), pp. 191–92. See also: John Kessel, *The Domestic Presidency* (Duxbury Press, 1975), and Ronald C. Moe, *The Domestic Council* (Washington, D.C., Congressional Research Service, 10 March 1975, processed.)
6. *Presidential Documents*, 7 October 1974, vol. 10: No. 40, p. 1210.
7. James Forrestal, in Walter Millis, ed., *The Forrestal Diaries* (Viking, 1951), pp. 315–16.

8. Robert H. Johnson, "The National Security Council: The Relevance of its Past to Its Future," *Orbis,* Fall 1969, p. 709.
9. H. R. Haldeman, quoted in *Newsweek,* 19 March 1973, p. 26.
10. Quoted anonymously in Lou Cannon, "The Siege Psychology and How It Grew," *Washington Post,* 29 July 1973, p. C4.
11. Abraham Holtzman, *Legislative Liaison: Executive Leadership in Congress* (Rand McNally, 1970), p. 263. See also Larry O'Brien, *No Final Victories: From John F. Kennedy to Watergate* (Doubleday, 1974).
12. Personal interview with James C. Hagerty.
13. George Ball, "Is This Trip Necessary?" *New York Times Magazine,* 13 February 1972, p. 55.
14. Milton Eisenhower, *The President Is Calling* (Doubleday, 1974), pp. 505–6.
15. Quoted anonymously in Lou Cannon, "The Siege Psychology," *op. cit.,* p. C1.
16. George Gallup, *Opinion Polls* (Center for the Study of Democratic Institutions, 1962), p. 35.
17. Clark M. Clifford, quoted in Joseph Goulden, *The Superlawyers* (Dell, 1973), p. 86.
18. Aaron Wildavsky, "The Presidency in the Political System," in Wildavsky, ed., *The Presidency,* 2d ed. (Little, Brown, 1975).
19. Lyndon B. Johnson, *The Vantage Point* (Holt, Rinehart and Winston, 1971), p. 155.
20. *Ibid.,* p. 157.
21. Niccolo Machiavelli, *The Prince and the Discourses* (Modern Library, 1950), pp. 81–82.
22. John F. Kennedy, quoted in Hugh Sidey, *John F. Kennedy, Portrait of a President* (Atheneum, 1964), pp. 122–23. See also his entire Chap. 8; and Hugh Young, Bryan Silcock, and Peter Dunn, "Why We Went to the Moon: From the Bay of Pigs to the Sea of Tranquility," *Washington Monthly,* April 1970, pp. 28–58.
23. Personal interview with James Rowe (October, 1973).
24. Richard Nixon, quoted in the *New York Times,* 1 May 1971.
25. Lyndon B. Johnson, quoted in Merriman Smith, *A White House Memoir* (Norton, 1971), p. 36.
26. David Wise, "The Twilight of a President," *New York Times Magazine,* 3 Nov. 1968, p. 131.
27. Quoted in an editorial, the *New York Times,* 14 December 1974.
28. John F. Kennedy, quoted in Harlan Cleveland, *The Future Executive* (Harper and Row, 1972), pp. 95–96.
29. Stanley Kelley, *Presidential Public Relations and Political Power* (Johns Hopkins Press, 1956), p. 221.
30. Douglas Hallett, "A low-level Memoir of the Nixon White House," *New York Times Magazine,* 20 October 1974, p. 56. For additional public relations techniques and how public officials use them, see the account by one of Spiro Agnew's press secretaries; Vic Gold, *I Don't Need You When I'm Right: The Confessions of a Washington PR Man* (Morrow, 1975).

CHAPTER 6

PALACE GUARD GOVERNMENT

PATTERNS OF WHITE HOUSE —DEPARTMENTAL RELATIONS

Everybody believes in democracy until he gets to the White House and then you begin to believe in dictatorship, because it's so hard to get things done. Everytime you turn around, people resist you and even resist their own job.

— *A Kennedy aide, 1970,*
   personal interview with author.

There are two main sources of power . . . in Washington. One is information. The other is access to the President. The White House staff now has information more quickly or just as quickly as the Secretary of State or the Secretary of Defense, and they certainly have physical access to the President more readily than the Cabinet Secretaries do. This tends to give the initiative to the White House staff operation.

— *Bill Moyers,*
   The Washington Monthly *(February, 1969), p. 4.*

There shouldn't be a lot of leeway in following the President's policies. It should be like a corporation, where the executive vice presidents (the cabinet officers) are tied closely to the chief executive, or to put in extreme terms, when he says jump, they [should] *only ask how high.*

— *John Ehrlichman,*
   The Washington Post, *24 August 1972.*

Every White House has problems with the departments and agencies that make up the bulk of the executive branch. It is difficult to overestimate the degree of frustration and resentment that White House aides develop about the seeming indifference of the permanent government toward presidential policy. This chapter and the next examine the contrasting perspectives during the Kennedy-Ford era of White House aides and their counterparts in departmental officialdom. This chapter focuses on the role of White House staffers as middlemen charged with winning departmental compliance. Chapter 7 focuses on the diverse roles of cabinet members as advocates and as advisers to the White House.

Earlier chapters have cited troubled relations between the White House staff and the executive departments as a factor in constraining the president's ability to implement policy and as a factor in promoting the swelling of the presidency. A rather vicious cycle develops as a result: a lack of shared attitudes reduces communications, which further widens the gap between the two perspectives. When the White House, for example, views the bureaucracy as "them" and the latest hostility between "us" and "them" flares up, the frequency and quality of communications deteriorate further. The consequences for information processing by either side are devastating.

The relationship between presidential staff and departmental officials has been shown to be almost inevitably adversary in character and conducive to considerable conflict. A president has only a few years to devise his priorities and set them in motion, whereas the federal bureaucracy is already well set in the routines of managing on-going programs, has well-established patterns of interest and interaction with Congress and groups outside government, and will outlive the new president and his particular directives. The primary loyalties of most career government officials are less to presidential lieutenants than to the professional norms and bureau activities to which they owe their livelihood and to which they have given years of work. Cabinet secretaries may be interest-group brokers from the beginning, and in any case they tend to become absorbed quickly by the relatively narrow objectives and politics of their particular fiefdoms. As department officials respond sluggishly to White House budget-cutting ideas or legislative strategies that may promote other interests at the expense of theirs, the president may perceive these weaknesses in his cabinet and reject the body as a continuing adviser in policy matters.

All of these tensions, all of the pulling and hauling, are a part of the informal but continuous power struggles within the executive branch. Presidential government is by no stretch of the imagination a pyramid-like structure with a single pinnacle. More characteristic, perhaps, are the triangular alliances that were shown in Figure 4-1.

PRESIDENTIALISTS VERSUS DEPARTMENTALISTS

Just as there are those who argue for a revitalized Congress that will reassert itself in presidential-legislative relations, so also there are some who urge that the cabinet and the departments need to be strengthened in relation to the White House staff. Liberal orthodoxy, even as late as a few years ago, held that the presidency should be the strongest partner in all executive branch relations. The reason behind the creation of the Executive Office of the President was to equip the presidency with the tools of management and with the authority commensurate with its responsibilities. What was needed, people thought, was a strong single executive to provide unity and direction on the one hand, and, on the other, to be held openly accountable for the administration of the national government.

The basic premise was that the requisite unity and energy for the political system could only come from a strong, well-staffed, vigorous presidency. This is the great office, the only truly national office in the whole system, say the textbooks. The presidency, the advocates of strength insisted, must be the central tower of strength and the articulator of the forward thrust in every sphere of policy, not because it was the ideal institution but because there was no alternative to it.

Opposed to the presidentialist view are departmentalists, who hold that the success or failure of federal programs rests almost entirely on the quality of the executive departments. Their underlying premise is that most federal laws deliberately allow discretion in many areas, and thus authority must be vested largely in departmental and bureau leaders. Appointed and career executives should have leeway to apply standards, modify regulations, and interpret legislative intent as they deem appropriate to fit specific situations. The involvement of the White House should be highly selective; moreover, Congress is as much a chief administrator as a president. After all, it creates the agencies and departments, it confirms the cabinet officers, it enacts the laws, and it also funds the programs. Certain departmental officials, for example, deplored the considerable White House involvement in clearing AID grants and in HUD model-city selections, HEW desegregation proceedings, and price supports for the dairy industry.

Presidentialists feel that only the presidency can provide the needed orchestration of complex, functionally interdependent federal programs. Only the president should have discretion over budget choices and the administration of federal policies. He is the one charged with faithfully executing the laws. These advocates assume that a strong presidency makes a major difference in the way government works, and that this difference will be in the direction of a more constructive (desirable) set of policy outcomes. They pledge allegiance to Alexander Hamilton: "A feeble Executive implies a feeble execution of the government. A feeble execution is but another phrase for a bad execution; and a government ill-executed, whatever it may be in theory, must be, in practice bad government." [1]

Presidentialists invariably argue that the presidency is not adequately staffed or funded. The presidency needs not just more help but a major infusion of skills, talent, tools, and loyalty if it is to gain control over the permanent federal departments. Implicitly, if not explicitly, their slogan is "more power to the White House!" Presidentialists argue that, because so many previous presidents have set up their own agencies in order to by-pass the bureaucracy, and because of the sheer size and diversity of the executive branch, the White House too often serves at the pleasure of the bureaucracy rather than vice versa. McGeorge Bundy spoke for many of this school of thought when he observed that the executive branch in many areas "more nearly resembles a collection of badly separated principalities than a single instrument of executive action." [2] What is needed, presidentialists imply, is more hierarchy: if a president is to be held accountable for program performance, he must have adequate control over the executive departments.

Ill-concealed within the presidentialist point of view is a contempt for the federal bureaucracy and a skepticism about the utility of the cabinet as an administrative tool. Presidentialists never completely trust civil servants; they frequently mistrust political appointees as well. Whatever of importance needs doing ought to be done directly from the White House; otherwise, the departmental people will temper or undermine the desired intentions of policy. As former Kennedy staffer Arthur Schlesinger, Jr., explained:

> At the start we all felt free to "meddle" when we thought we had a good idea or someone else a poor one. But, as the ice began to form again over the government, freewheeling became increasingly difficult and dangerous ... our real trouble was that we had capitulated too much to the existing bureaucracy. Wherever we have gone wrong ... has been because we have not had sufficient confidence in the New Frontier approach to impose it on the government. Every important mistake has been the consequence of excessive deference to the permanent government.... The problem of moving forward seemed in great part the problem of making the permanent government responsive to the policies of the presidential government.[3]

The presidency is a prime target of reform for presidentialists, who see it as lacking in adequate staff and resources for interdepartmental coordination and program evaluation, and who see presidents as the recipients of endless special-interest pleas and narrow-minded agitation, even from many of their own cabinet members. In its crudest form, their goal is *to presidentialize* the executive branch. Toward that end there are catalogues of reform proposals: "The strong Presidency will depend upon the Chief Executive's capacity to control and direct the vast bureaucracy of national administration. Ideally, the President should possess administrative powers comparable to those of business executives. What the President needs most can be simply formulated: a power over personnel policy, planning, accounting, and the administration of the executive branch that approaches his power over the executive budget." [4] Other variations on this theme call for better policy-evaluation and program-management staffs within the executive office. Presidentialists with a narrow policy interest are always asking that the formulation and administration of this particular interest be brought more intimately into the presidential orbit "much along the lines of the Council of Economic Advisers." Others would place within the presidential establishment field agents or expediters — federal domestic program "czars" — located in federal regional offices or large metro-politan areas to insure that presidential priorities are being carried out properly at the grassroots level.

THE DEPARTMENTAL LOYALISTS.   The departmentalist view has varying degrees of support among professional civil servants, many former cabinet officers, and even some former White House staff assistants. Often it is also supported by congressmen who disagree with presidential objectives. Moreover, an increasing number of skeptics have been persuaded that a larger presidency with greater resources or a greater institutionalization of the presidency is not a realistic answer to the problem of creating and then managing a more responsive federal government. Career public servants point to the abuses of White House powers in the events surrounding the 1972 election as evidence of how presidential aides can misuse their positions to influence officials of the IRS, CIA, FBI, and State and Justice departments.

Some departmentalists claim that in recent years the White House staff has become too much a center for operations management and less an overseer or chief executive institution. Presidents, they say, should be involved in broad policy questions, not in the nuts-and-bolts concerns of program operation. As David Truman has written:

> [The president] cannot take a position on every major controversy over administra-
> tive policy, not merely because his time and energies are limited, but equally because
> of the positive requirements of his position. He cannot take sides in any dispute without
> giving offense in some quarters. He may intervene where the unity of his supporters
> will be threatened by inaction; he may even, by full use of the resources of his office,
> so dramatize his action as to augment the influence he commands. But he cannot "go
> to the country" too often, lest the tactic become familiar and his public jaded. Rather
> than force an administrative issue, he may choose to save his resources for a legislative
> effort. . . . [For effectiveness he] must preserve some of the detachment of a constitu-
> tional monarch.[5]

But even if the president remains detached from the day-to-day operations of the federal government, communicating and delegating authority only indirectly through his close lieutenants, cabinet officials want both relative independence and a vote of confidence with which to carry on their work. They feel they should have the right of direct access to the president. They insist that the White House staff members should not have authority to issue directives independent of the president. And they feel rather strongly that the swelling of the White House staffs has caused an isolation as well as an obstacle to the free exchange and examination of ideas and alternatives.

The more the White House usurps responsibilities from their proper home in the departments, the more the White House undermines the goal of competent departmental management. A cabinet member ignored or by-passed by the president is made to look weak in front of relevant congressional and client support groups as well as his or her subordinates. Departmental officials who must fight hard to maintain access to, and rapport with, the White House have correspondingly less time and energy for internal departmental management. The takeover by White House staff of certain departmental functions also diminishes the capacity of the department to streamline these functions in the future. Imaginative professional people will not long remain in departmental positions if they are underused or misused consistently.

Departmentalists believe that White House meddling in department affairs is often disadvantageous for everyone involved — except perhaps for the White House aide who has to look busy. George Reedy noted that "there is, on the part of the White House assistants, a tendency to bring to the White House problems which should not properly be there, frequently to the disadvantage of the president." [6] His view is echoed loudly by a senior State Department official: "Part of the problem is endemic to the White House. It's Parkinsonian; unless the White House staff see problems, they'll become underemployed. So, naturally, they will see all sorts of problems. . . . White House staff have to find something to do, so they will see or even invent a need to modify this, or change that, intervene here, and so forth — otherwise there is no employment for them." Robert Wood, a professional urbanologist and former secretary of HUD, offered this sober evaluation:

The longer one examines the awesome burdens and limited resources of those who help the president from within his immediate circle, the more skeptical one becomes of a strategy for overseeing government by "running" it from 1600 Pennsylvania Avenue. The semiheroic, semihopeless posture has been captured many times in several administrations: dedicated men, of great intelligence and energy, working selflessly through weekends and holidays to master an endlessly increasing array of detail on complex subjects beyond their understanding on which decisions must be made "here" because a resolution elsewhere is not to be trusted. They persevere, taking their stand against "the bureaucrats," pushing programs through against sullen, hidden resistance from the departments. Committees are abolished, agencies rejuggled, staff reviews simplified, new reporting forms introduced, all in the effort to assure that more and more decisions are, or can be presidential. Yet, in the end, after thirty years, the effort to help the president in making government work has not succeeded.[7]

CONFLICTING PERSPECTIVES OF ROLES. A characteristic difference that distinguishes White House staff from department leaders often emerges from a difference in recruitment patterns. In its early months every administration makes an exhaustive effort to plant loyal friends in top departmental positions, but presidents and their chief patronage head-hunters often find that the number of their qualified as well as trusted acquaintances is far smaller than that of available department positions. An increasing number of presidential campaign aides are assigned to the White House — as, for example, were Kenneth O'Donnell, Lawrence O'Brien, Myer Feldman, Theodore Sorensen, Bill Moyers, George Reedy, Jack Valenti, H. R. Haldeman, John Ehrlichman, Ronald Zeigler, and Herbert Klein. On the other hand, most of the cabinet and more important subcabinet officers are recruited from among persons with previous governmental experience or from among the professional and business elite in the relevant subject area — as, for example, were Dean Rusk, Douglas Dillon, Robert McNamara, John Gardner, Alan Boyd, Clark Clifford, Elliot Richardson, John Connally, and Earl Butz. The selection of cabinet officials is also influenced by considerations of geography, ethnicity, religion, and party balance.

The White House aides generally reflect a concern for loyalty to the president, teamwork, interdepartmental coordination, follow-through on the president's priorities, and protection of the president's image. They see themselves as charged with keeping options open, with leaning against the wind rather than advocating fixed positions, and yet being able to end discussions and act when decisions can no longer wait. They seldom trust departmental aides enough to delegate such tasks. White House aides spend much of their time engaged in building alliances within the executive branch. They are concerned with how best to communicate what the president wants done; how to give the departmental leaders a sense of involvement in presidential decisions; how politely but firmly to tell them of the president's dissatisfaction with department performance; how to motivate them to give added energy to get presidential programs moving; how to extricate the operation of a program from what the aides consider to be a nearly impossible group of people.

Senior departmental officials such as assistant secretaries, bureau chiefs, and the like, are no less involved in exchanges with the presidential staff. Some are temporary political appointees; many are career civil servants with long experience in dealing with the presidency, especially with the budget officials in the executive office. Although wanting to cooperate with the objectives of the current presidential team, they are concerned at the same time with attending to departmental priorities and integrity. White House requests usually are honored; pressures and arrogant communications always are resented. Their day-today concerns are how to get White House endorsement and increased budget approvals for departmental initiatives; how to get the White House to side with them in a jurisdictional matter; how to make an end run around an unsympathetic and amateur White House aide and make sure the president hears about a new idea; when, if at all, they should notify the White House of some emerging and potentially embarrassing outside advisory report; whether they should supply a potentially credit-winning news announcement to the White House or use it to gain publicity for their own cabinet officer and department; in short, how to deal with the White House when it can help them, but otherwise preserve their autonomy.

More contention exists within the executive branch over the priorities and tempo of federal activity than over the basic ends or legitimacy of the government. In this sense the executive branch operates much like a trading arena in which different participants hope that their preferences will prevail. Few on either side of the White House-departmental exchange are easily pleased. Both sides have needs and expectations and often even illusions about what the other will give. White House aides usually come in expecting that people in the departments will do what they are told, whether out of respect, fear, or ambition. As one Johnson aide reported: "The president, and vicariously his staff, were thought to vibrate power. . . . The enormous panoply of office that surrounded us — the jets and helicopters, the limousines, the communications system, the ubiquitous guards, the train of press — all contributed to the idea. It was exaggerated. I never tested presidential power and authority over others without discovering that anew." [8]

One of the realities in Washington, however, is that the government needs a sense of purpose, a sense of leadership, and a sense of coherence; and often it needs to be told which way to go. Hence, the president and the White House aides must go about their job of asking tough questions, making hard decisions, and prodding people to do a better job. Shaping the issues, and shaping them in such a way that they can be resolved, becomes critically important. But such tasks, especially if performed rigorously, breed tension. Some of the relationships within the White House-departmental exchange system are sketched briefly in Richard Neustadt's comment: "Agencies need decisions, delegations, and support, along with bargaining arenas and a court of last resort, so organized as to assure that their advice is always heard and often taken. A president needs timely information, early warning, close surveillance, organized to yield him the controlling judgment, with his options open, his intent enforced. In practice these two sets of needs have proved quite incompatible; presidential organizations rarely serve one well without disservice to the other." [9]

Whether the tension inherent in these relationships will be constructive and tolerable depends on many factors, the most important of which is the attitude of the participants. If an aide such as Henry Kissinger (before he became secretary of state) goes around saying, "First of all, you have to weaken the bureaucracy! . . . They all want to do what I'm doing! So the problem becomes: how do you get them to push paper around, spin their wheels, so that you can get your work done," [10] a hostile relationship inevitably will evolve. Predictably, such acid attitudes toward the permanent government are countered by the evaluation of most White House aides as amateurish, arrogant, and ill-informed nuisances who serve the presidency poorly. By extension, it becomes conventional wisdom among veteran officials in the departments that the presidency actually needs to be protected against these presidential aides, who are only temporarily in residence and who are serving their own short-term interests at the expense of both the presidency and the nation.

Perhaps the most compelling concern is that the swelling of the presidency and the White House usurpation of operational responsibilities normally belonging in the departments might undermine what Aaron Wildavsky saw as "the one quality above all others which the White House staff must have if it is directly and dispassionately to serve the chief executive: the ability to view problems from the broad perspective of the presidency. . . ." [11]

CONFLICT AS PERCEIVED BY THE WHITE HOUSE STAFF

The fifty aides and former aides the author interviewed during 1970–1972 were asked whether they experienced major difficulties in working with the executive departments: "Can you give your view of this? Is this really a problem?" Conflict was widely acknowledged: 66 percent felt considerable conflict in White House-departmental exchanges; 26 percent, only moderate conflict; and only 8 percent, an insignificant amount. Some aides talked of conflicts within the executive branch as the single greatest problem in contemporary government. One man who had worked for both presidents Kennedy and Johnson said that "it was an absolutely terrible problem. . . . There are major problems with cabinet members and civil servants alike. Even the great members like Mc-Namara and Secretary of Agriculture Orville Freeman were terrible in evading their share of many of our efforts." A senior Johnson-administration counselor observed that "the separation of governments is not so great between Congress and the president as between a president and those people like subcabinet and bureau officials who become locked into their own special subsystem of self-interested policy concerns." Others talked about the increasing defiance of department personnel toward the White House:

It's a terrible problem and it's getting worse, particularly with the State Department. The major problem is the lack of any identification [on their part] with the president's program priorities. At State they try to humor the president but hope he will not interfere in their complex matters and responsibilities. It is equally a problem with civil servants and cabinet types. It is amazing how soon the cabinet people get captured by the permanent staffs. Secretary —— under Nixon, for example, was captured within days ... and Nixon's staff didn't even try to improve things. They just assumed there was a great problem. Personally, I think you can't expect too much from the bureaucracy. It is too much to expect that they will see things the president's way.

Some aides noted that conflicts varied with different departments and with different cabinet members: for example, "Yes, there are certainly many problems, but it differs from area to area and from president to president. I think the amount of friction is related to the role of the White House staff and what they undertake and what presidents let them do." A more tempered assessment of the existence of conflict comes from a congressional relations aide in the Kennedy-Johnson White House: "Oh, yes, there are problems to an extent. There is deep suspicion around the whole government toward the new president when he comes into power. . . . But the fights you get in are different all around town. . . . We had some excellent men around town, and some boobs. The important thing for a president to do is to get good men and then decentralize the responsibility. Let the department people do their job and don't let your [White House] staff interfere too much."

A few aides who had less involvement with the departments acknowledged little if any serious conflict. One speechwriter observed that "on my level this really isn't a problem. You have to remember that I wasn't in a straight policy role. When I had contact with department people, it was mainly to get facts and statistics for speeches, etc. . . . and I always had plenty of help. . . . 'They' would even stay after 5 o'clock if you emphasized that this stuff was for the president."

Conflicts in White House-departmental relations can be attributed to both *subjective* factors, such as differing allegiances, differing definitions of priorities and roles, personality clashes, or personal ambitions, and to *objective* factors, such as the size of the federal effort, time and communications restrictions, budget limitations, knowledge gaps, and the centrifugal pulls inherent in federalism and in the functionally independent department. White House staff members stressed as sources of conflict the subjective differences and the ill effects of the disjunction of presidential and departmental perspectives. Their responses are summarized in Table 6-1.

WHITE HOUSE SOURCES OF CONFLICT. White House staffers suggested that their own definition of their roles and the pressures under which they had to work often exacerbated relations with cabinet and department officials. Presidents and their staffs arrive at the White House charged up to produce results, to make good on the pledges of their campaign. The post-election euphoria and the simplification of issues during the campaign contribute to overextended and insensitive strategies:

Well, a Kennedy staff hallmark was to seize power from around town. In retrospect I think they often were insensitive to the channels of the existing government. They came in after the campaign with a pretentious "know-it-all" attitude, and they hurt their case by this stance. For example, I think the White House staffers often called people low in the departments and deliberately undercut cabinet people too much in the early years. . . . In retrospect, I don't think you can coordinate much from the White House. You just can't evaluate all that much [not to mention managing it].

No etiquette manual is available to help White House aides avoid antagonizing department officials; for newly appointed aides, the pressure-cooker, goldfish-bowl atmosphere is an invitation to problems. Hatchet men for the opposition party abound, as do columnists in search of conflicts of interest. Often, White House aides feel that as they try desperately to get faster results

TABLE 6–1   PRESIDENTIAL STAFF PERSPECTIVES
ON THE SOURCES OF CONFLICT AND STRAIN
IN WHITE HOUSE–EXECUTIVE DEPARTMENT RELATIONS

Types and Sources of Conflict	Percentage Acknowledging as a Source
White House sources:	
WH staff insensitivity toward department officials	49
WH staff and president communications failures	42
WH staff usurpation of departmental roles and/or excessive interference in departmental affairs	35
WH "tried to do too much too quickly"	30
Departmental sources:	
Civil servant and bureaucratic parochialism	50
Departmental leaders captured by narrow special interests	49
Cabinet leadership too weak or unimaginative	44
Red tape and inept staff work	32
Departments unable to work together	23
Complexity–diversity factors as sources:	
Sheer size and complexity of federal efforts	38
Lack of time for the needed follow-through, coordination, and implementation	32
Substantive and ideological differences about policy choices within the federal system	25

Personal interviews conducted by the author with forty-eight members of the presidential staff who served at the White House between 1961 and 1972. Because respondents could give more than one reply, percentages total more than 100 percent.

for their president from securely tenured department officials, they are either damned for becoming arrogant or rendered superfluous to the president. One Kennedy lieutenant concluded that "part of our problem was that we were too arrogant, and really for the most part we were all amateurs too." According to another former aide, many eager staffers "if they had the option between (1) giving an order to the bureaucracy or (2) trying to win their cooperation, would always settle quickly for issuing orders."

Many White House aides were ambivalent about staff insensitivity. They talked somewhat contemptuously of the need for more care and feeding of cabinet members, as though some of the cabinet were merely symbols, kept simply for window dressing, but they also insisted that they had to be aggressive to get anything accomplished. For example:

> *I think most of the problem lies in the disregard of some White House aides of the rank, and age, and positional dignity or status of cabinet members and agency heads. Three little words can give a White House aide a lot of power, "the President wants." You need to combine a proper sense of firmness with deference . . . but you have to know the danger traps and the mine fields and always have to keep in mind the question, "How can I serve the President?"*
>
> *I'll tell you exactly how to deal with this problem: you use two plans. Plan A: get in touch with the cabinet or department head and say "the President is anxious to have your judgment on X matter." If they squirm or delay or fail to comply, then you use Plan B: "Damn it, Mr. Secretary, the President wants it by 3 this afternoon!" You have to be tough in this business.*

Yet insensitivity may also be a direct product of personal arrogance, as reported by a former assistant to an HEW secretary about his first encounter with Daniel P. Moynihan:

> *"This report you sent me . . ." [Moynihan] said, interrupting. "It's a hell of a lot better than the usual junk I get from those goddam educators at the Office of Education."*
>
> *I must have beamed.*
>
> *"But it's barely good enough, goddamit! And good enough won't do. Don't forget, Moffett. You're not writing for some newspaper." He looked me straight in the eye and pointed a finger toward my face. "You're writing for smart people. Like me, Moffett."* [12]

Some of the aides' most instructive commentary concerned communications within the executive branch. Numerous aides mentioned that the basic reason for conflict was the lack of communications. Often, the problem is not that department officials fail to respond to White House policy directives, but rather that those directives are too hazy and inadequately communicated — or that the president and his aides really have not made up their minds. Sometimes different White House aides send out contradictory messages: for example, the domestic program and legislative development staff might press department officials for new ideas at the same time the budget director and his staff are warning the same officials of the need to reduce activities. Moynihan, in a pep talk to the Nixon cabinet, said:

> It is necessary for members of the Administration to be far more attentive to what it is the President has said and proposed. Time and again the President has said things of startling insight, taken positions of great political courage and intellectual daring, only to be greeted with silence or incomprehension within our own ranks. . . . Nixon's initial thrusts have rarely been followed up with a sustained, reasoned, reliable second and third order of advocacy. Deliberately or no, the impression was allowed to arise with respect to the widest range of Presidential initiative that the President wasn't really behind them.[13]

Yet the capacity of the departments to understand what the president means and to believe that he really means it should never be taken for granted. The president may have multiple audiences in mind when preparing his remarks, which handicaps a forceful, direct communication of his views to the departments. Said one Kennedy aide: "Often people don't know what the president really wants. Words sound different depending on where you sit. Professional civil servants feel they must protect their rational objective interests from White House interference — they regard most White House influence upon their activity as very degrading. The presidential voice has to make itself clear, heard and understood throughout Washington."

The sheer size of the federal enterprise also affects communications. A former Johnson aide gave the analogy that the dinosaur became extinct partly because signals were not transmitted from brain to foot or from foot to brain rapidly or accurately enough to create a picture of reality on which the dinosaur could act. Another Johnson aide summed up many of that president's troubles in Vietnam in a similar but more direct manner: "Even if the Vietnam problem could have been managed by the President of the United States acting as the Vietnam Desk Officer, the system would soon have broken down from sheer lack of communication. It is one thing for Great Men to make policy, it is another to implement it, monitor it, coordinate it with existing policies and programs, and undertake the advance planning to meet foreseeable problems and possible contingencies." [14]

Some aides stressed that the always delicate distinction between staff or advisory roles at the White House and operational, administrative line responsibilities in the cabinet departments became blurred during the Kennedy, Johnson, and Nixon years. Too many of the staff came to give orders rather than transmit requests. One Kennedy staffer became jokingly referred to as the "Over-Secretary" of certain cabinet departments because of the way he would give orders to some cabinet members. "His problem was that he was just too directive oriented and also too brusque!"

Under Kennedy, Johnson, and Nixon, not only has the presidential establishment taken over many policy-making functions from the cabinet but it has also absorbed a multitude of concrete operational activities. Kennedy's postmaster general, J. Edward Day, has noted: "After the first two or three meetings, one had the distinct impression that the President felt that decisions on major matters were not made — or even influenced at Cabinet sessions, and that discussion there was a waste of time. . . . When members spoke up to suggest or to discuss major administration policy, the President would listen with thinly disguised impatience and then postpone or otherwise bypass the question." [15] A major Johnson aide said that "after awhile he [Johnson] never even bothered to sit down with most of the domestic cabinet members even to discuss their major problems and program possibilities." Because of the war and because he had grown used to leaning on his own staff so heavily, "Johnson became lazy and wound up using some of the staff as both line managers as well as staff and, I think in retrospect, *it frequently* didn't work out!" In 1971 Senator Ernest Hollings noted: "It used to be that if I had a problem with food stamps, I went to see the Secretary of Agriculture, whose department had jurisdiction over that problem. Not any more. Now, if I want to learn the policy, I must go to the White House to consult [a special assistant]. If I want the latest on textiles, I won't get it from the Secretary of Commerce, who has the authority and responsibility. No, I am forced to go to the White House and see Mr. Peter Flanigan. I shouldn't feel too badly. Secretary [of Commerce Maurice] Stans has to do the same thing." [16]

Nearly one-third of the White House aides felt that their administrations tried to do too much too fast. Even President Johnson was quoted to this effect in the last days of his presidential term. The Great Society programs were seldom ill-conceived, merely insufficiently planned or ill-managed. One veteran budget counselor to presidents explained his view of the conflict:

Too much was attempted under LBJ. We didn't ask ourselves enough questions about whether we could do these things. Expectations outran the capability to work things out. There were too many other demands or problems in the mid- and late 1960s, Vietnam, inadequately trained manpower at all levels of government, and the structure of intergovernmental relations was inadequate. The space and missile programs had the backing of the people, but public support was terribly splintered over the War on Poverty, etc. . . . It was like a Tower of Babel, with no one interested in the other people's programs.

Another aide said, "You soon forget about programs that were started earlier, even programs begun earlier by your own administration," and "The burden of the presidency is to get things started. The presidency is not an executive agency with clout to carry out the goals of a president. Perhaps it ought to have been, but we did not have time for it, we just didn't work that way." A veteran budget adviser put it a slightly different way: "By and large, the presidency is in the retail business when it comes to policy formulation. It reacts, responds, modifies, and tinkers with departmental policy in program suggestions, but it does not wholesale public policy in the sense of recasting priorities and evaluating the relationship of crude commitments to long-term goals." Several idealistic aides, convinced that their foremost priority was to fashion a sweeping legislative record, accepted the Johnson rationalization of spending the first term putting the laws on the books. His second elected term, they presumed, would be used to streamline the executive branch and make things work.

DEPARTMENTAL SOURCES OF CONFLICT.

DEPARTMENTAL SOURCES OF CONFLICT. Securing the cooperation of the departmental bureaucracies is never simple. But White House aides seem to differ on precisely what the source of the problem is. Some, as mentioned, felt it was as much a matter of how the White House conducted itself as what the bureaucrats or political executives in the departments did. Still, many White House aides held a sinister opinion of the bureaucrats. One Nixon aide reported that "there are many of my colleagues who, like General Al Haig, hold almost a conspiracy view of this problem. They actually believe people out there are malevolent towards White House requests." The more preceptive presidential staffers recognized that there were just a lot of intrinsic problems, structurally built in, that inhibited cordial and frank relations between the White House and the bureaucracy. A Nixon aide summed up this perspective:

We over here in the Executive Office of the President only have one constituent — the President. If the President makes a clear statement of his preferences, then we know what to do and where to go. But over in the bureaucracy — in the departments and agencies — they not only have the president as a constituent, but they also have Congress, their civil servants, outside pressure groups, etc. . . . The difference in constituency is important. The difference especially in relationship to Congress is very different and intrinsically different. Also, there is just the bureaucratic problem inherent in a large, complex organization. Over here we serve the President, but down the line, like the Secretary of HEW, he has to spend some of his political currency heeding the qualms and wishes of the bureaucracy.

About one-half of the White House aides mentioned a seeming inability of many government workers to adopt the presidential perspective. This capacious point of view, always ill-defined, seems to include concern for the public interest, responsiveness to the electorate, maturity of judgment, and all manner of other virtues and wisdom. Whatever it is, many White House policy assistants were convinced that department people either did not understand it or resisted it: "Mostly, the bureaucrats are unresponsive; they view themselves as 'the professionals' and see your [White House] impact as purely political. They don't fight you openly, but they don't cooperate if they can help it!" Said another, "We tried to have department officials over to the White House for drinks and give them pep talks about our programs . . . but it was a band-aid operation, and at best it retarded their loyalties away from the [opposite] direction they otherwise would have gone. After six to twelve months even the political appointees in the departments get captured and taken in by the agencies."

One aide explained, with satirical insight, that some subcabinet officials come into office with great energy and much promise. Soon after they arrive, however, the permanent department staffs convince them that they must go out into the field "to see our extensive field operations." The permanent staff also makes sure that its new boss is kept out of his office and on an exhausting circuit of out-of-town speaking engagements. Meanwhile, back in the agency or bureau, the permanent staffers busily reorganize the office to serve their own priorities and promote themselves, their friends, and, of course, their pet programs. The overworked, travel-weary political appointee has so little time to learn what is going on within his office that he becomes dependent on his subordinates in, for example, testimony before Congressional committees or in encounters with the departmental secretary and White House aides. This version of what happens may be an exaggeration, but it expresses the frustrations of being a White House staff aide — and of being a subcabinet officer.

Arthur Schlesinger, Jr., suggested the existence of an active, organized resistance to the president's priorities: "The presidential government, coming to Washington aglow with new ideas and a euphoric sense that it could do no wrong, promptly collided with the feudal barons of the permanent government, entrenched in their domains and fortified by their sense of proprietorship; and the permanent government, confronted by this invasion, began almost to function (with, of course, many notable individual exceptions) as a resistance movement." [17] Schlesinger's view has much in common with the traditional Republican and conservative fear that the expanding New Deal bureaucracy might bring about a social revolution. By Schlesinger's time the revolution already had taken place, but its guardians in the bureaucracy often seemed committed to resisting rather than facilitating change.

Another way White House aides explain departmental sources of conflict is by questioning the competence or loyalty of an individual cabinet member. A cabinet member is faulted for being too much of an individualist, too aloof, too stubborn, and sometimes for not being a take-charge type. The frequent complaint that cabinet members are captured by narrow special interests was to some the major problem. Said one person: "Often times we appointed weak cabinet people to start with. ———— at Commerce was very weak. And ———— chickened out after he came aboard and saw the mess which he was supposed to administer — so he merely presided over it temporarily while he began making plans to leave and run for a U. S. Senate seat." Another felt that: "It all comes down to people, some people do a great job, like ————. They really run their show and get great people to help them and don't need White House interference. Rusk and McNamara were talented and loyal, but ———— was very weak and had loyalties mainly to his department's interests. Even ———— became seduced by special interests much faster than anyone predicted. And

———— was terrible. He saw himself as Labor's representative to the president rather than as part of the president's cabinet. He even out-Meanyed George Meany a few times." And a Nixon staffer observed:

> *After a man is secretary in a department over an appreciable time, too often there is a tendency for him to act as though this is "my department," "my program," "my men." This takes about a year or so. . . . After a while he forgets he serves at the pleasure of the president. Working for Nixon, for example, I occasionally would come up against a man who said that the President had goofed terribly in this or that, or the President didn't understand what was going on, etc. . . . and I had to stress to these individuals that they had better rethink exactly what they were saying because they serve at the pleasure of the President and should know that it is the President's intentions and the President's program that count and not what some cabinet member or undersecretary thinks. So, occasionally a White House aide like myself has to readjust the compasses of political appointees.*

A significant factor in promoting conflict between the departments and the presidential staff is their different perspectives on time. A president and his staff think in terms of two- and four-year frames, at the most. They strive to fulfill campaign pledges and related priorities with a sense of urgency, seeking always to build a respectable image for forthcoming election campaigns. The haste with which the White House rushed the announcement of many Great Society programs, such as Model Cities, the Teacher Corps, and Neighborhood Service Centers, may well have damaged the chances for the effective design and launching of these programs. Similar initiatives, such as the Family Assistance Program and efforts to promote black capitalism, suffered in the same way during the Nixon presidency. The Whip Inflation Now (WIN) and fuel conservation efforts of the Ford administration followed the same pattern. Career civil servants, on the other hand, are around after the elections regardless of the outcome; and, more important, they usually feel very accountable to the General Accounting Office, the Office of Management and Budget, or to congressional investigating committees for the way federal programs are administered (and for any mistakes that might be made). The work incentives for most careerists are slanted toward doing a thorough, consistent, and even cautious job, rather than toward any hurried dancing to the current tunes of the White House staff. The time frames of subcabinet officials fall in between: some seek to impress the president; others, the agency's permanent interest groups, congressional committees, and department professionals.

Conflict and strain also arise because the departments often disagree. Most presidents are willing to leave departments alone as long as they are doing a reasonably good job. But the White House is inevitably drawn into departmental matters when two or more departments are feuding with one another. Or when departments are refusing to work with one another — an all too common problem. Indeed, the growth of the White House staff is in part a direct response to the increased number of intradepartmental controversies. Thus,

Eisenhower's White House chief of staff, Sherman Adams, allegedly told two cabinet members who could not resolve a matter of mutual concern: "Either make up your mind or else . . . I will do it [for you]. We must not bother the President with this. He is trying to keep the world from war." [18] Kennedy, Johnson, and Nixon all turned more and more to their White House staff for coordination and particularly for help in resolving jurisdictional disputes between executive agencies. One White House aide remarked that the real dilemma is that when there are basic differences in points of view — for example, as between State and Defense — a resolution made at the White House is only temporary:

> *Then new situations develop, new events take place, new data become available, and at this point differences begin to emerge again — people translate the new data, the new events in a different light, sometimes regressing to their earlier pre-White House interpretation, sometimes to some other point of view [or misapplication of the White House decision]. After a while it is quite noticeable that the different departments are out of pace, out of agreement with each other. At this point a White House staff aide, like myself, often has to get involved to work out some common point of view again — and, if necessary, call it to the president's attention for needed clarification or emphasis.*

CONFLICT FROM COMPLEXITY. Nearly all of the comments by White House aides on executive branch conflict could be traced to the size of government and the complexity of the problem being attacked. Eisenhower aide Emmet J. Hughes suggested: "The sheer size and intricacy of government conspire to taunt and to thwart all brisk pretensions to set sensationally new directions. The vast machinery of national leadership — the tens of thousands of levers and switches and gears — simply do not respond to the impatient jab of a finger or the angry pounding of a fist." [19]

President Johnson made an effort to improve civil rights opportunities for departmental personnel and within programs administered by the departments. Although the president made occasional references to this in cabinet meetings, he could not spend much time on the effort, so he designated an aide to carry it out. That aide soon found out that most of the cabinet members themselves lacked the time to think through a logical strategy for action; some even bluntly disagreed with the effort, denying its importance as a priority. Moreover, "many of them have great internal problems and actually have little leeway to get things done with their subordinates. You cannot assume a cabinet member is in good control over his department. Sometimes it is a matter of geography — his department is spread all over Washington and, perhaps in twelve or more regions around the country." Not surprisingly, the aide soon concluded that "you have to do their work for them; that is, you have to know their internal situation and be able to come up with the alternatives." This aide appeared to be decidedly pessimistic about his job:

You can't really be an administrator at the White House. You have to get top personnel to carry things out — and that is literally impossible to do with this venal Civil Service system. Frankly, I would abolish it and rather live with a spoils system. You need to be able to make far more appointees than you can now. Civil Service officials can play very tough politics with their senior friends in Congress, and they can resist the White House constantly.... Another thing is that departments are so big that it is difficult for anyone to get "the message" around even when they want to do something about it.

Conflict between the White House staff and the departments may arise from substantive or ideological differences, sometimes reflecting political party positions, but more often they arise from differences about the role of the federal government in solving local or international problems. A typical controversial goal is that of pushing the government to new levels of commitment and compassion, an aim enunciated during heated campaigns or in major policy addresses. Prime ingredients for confused communication with a large bureaucracy include the failure of the White House to choose among intense and competing values, the naive effort to make every problem the first order of attention, and the inability to distinguish between what the federal government can and cannot do. The continual need to reset priorities and rethink program objectives is separated from organizational and implementation decisions only at substantial cost.

REALITIES AND IMPERATIVES

White House aides often become arrogant and insensitive because they are asked to do too much in too short a time. They breathe down the necks of cabinet and department leaders because presidents become impatient for answers and results. Departments appear inert or unresponsive because they have difficulty in pulling together diverse specialists to work on complex questions. Cabinet members give the impression of being weak (and sometimes are) because they must preside over huge holding companies of diverse, functionally specialized enterprises. Departmentalism — the constant clamor by departmental spokesmen for more money, more presidential support, or more autonomy from other agencies or priorities — thrusts itself ceaselessly on a president. White House aides are disappointed by the lack of coordination both within and among departments. Communications problems exist because many people are involved in administering programs throughout the country and are working within an environment of constantly shifting priorities and circumstances.

And legislative or executive intent, or the GAO and Civil Service Commission rulebooks and regulations, even if they could be memorized, do not provide sufficient guidance to the relationship of one complex problem to another.

Listening to White House aides' views of these conflicts heightens appreciation for the responsibilities of the chief executive. The presidency has to act, even in the face of in-house uncertainties, complexity, and opposition. Eventually, the consequences of inaction may outweigh the results of even an ill-designed initiative. As the general public expects more and more of the presidency and from presidential performance, and as the responsibilities become greater, the institution finds itself in the midst of a disillusioning squeeze.

It is tempting for a president to rely on a small brigade of hand-picked and personally loyal White House aides. Often, however, he will find that such a strategy will only exacerbate his situation. As Irving Janis and others have suggested, a consensus orientation easily takes hold, an artificial sense of conviviality and team-player mentality can set in that encourages a mentality that can falsify reports, denigrate alternatives that deserve consideration and in general keep unfavorable information from reaching a president.[20] Every president sooner or later will find himself surrounded by unremitting problems of complexity, diversity, jurisdictional disputes, and bureaucratic recalcitrance. But the essence of presidential leadership is, in one sense, the capacity to deal with complexity and to manage conflict. The president must be able to ask the right questions, preside over compromises, and engage in the art of making the difficult possible.

That the constraints on directing an effective application of presidentially interpreted policies to problems are enormous does not mean that the presidency should be removed or elevated from bureaucratic or societal conflicts. Resolving conflicts is a strategic occasion for exercising leadership. Information and evaluation are the prime needs. An open presidency capable of listening as well as giving orders is imperative. An open presidency that holds a due regard for the positive aspects of conflict is needed as well.

Conflict and competition do not inevitably indicate weakness in an administration. Adversary relationships may provide a salutary jolt toward the adapting and renewal of systems. Lewis Coser's suggestions are relevant: "Conflict prevents the ossification of social systems by exerting pressures for innovation and creativity; it prevents habitual accommodations from freezing into rigid molds and hence progressively impoverishing the ability to react creatively to novel circumstances." [21] Several former members of recent administrations have made the case that certain policies and practices with which they were involved suffered not from too much conflict, but from too little.[22] And certainly the history of the illegal plans and activities of the Watergate conspiracies of 1971–1974 illustrate a series of episodes that might have been halted or avoided had more competitive and adversary deliberations taken place.

Conflict and heated argument do not necessarily upset every president, although most presidents generally grow to dislike it. John F. Kennedy, for example, once made the point, to two aides in the midst of a heated debate that, "the last thing I want around here is a mutual admiration society. . . . When you people stop arguing, I'll start worrying." [23] Yet, Kennedy himself was criticized by a shrewd if caustic British observer, Henry Fairlie, who cautioned appropriately that

> . . . to the end of his days of power, the politician must believe that he has defective eyesight. He must seek the help, witting and unwitting, not only of a thousand pairs of eyes, but of eyes which see in a thousand different ways, eyes that flash at him, eyes that are suspicious, eyes that seem to sleep, eyes that are open, eyes that tell him nothing and, in doing so, tell him all which he needs to know. John Kennedy had the same object as Franklin Roosevelt, the accumulation of power to the Presidency; he had genuine political ability, as did many of those around him; but he and they saw, with few exceptions, with a single pair of eyes; that was how he wished it." [24]

Breathing and thinking space must be guaranteed by careful staffing, delegation, and use of presidential time; not by isolation, arrogance, or palace guards permitted to become egregiously antagonistic toward the permanent government and cabinet. Both sides — presidential staff and the bureaucracy — are needed to perform the functions of the executive branch; each wants certain types of help from the other; each usually seeks to avoid overt antagonism toward the other. Although White House staff members can be the creative connective tissue linking a president with the complex network of administration officials, bringing in the necessary information, and sending out word of presidential intentions, it is clear that operational and managerial activities should be delegated beyond his immediate entourage.

Presidents and most of their staff usually are aware that cooperation from the permanent federal departments must be earned rather than taken for granted. Loyalty and support, as well as crucially needed expertise, usually are eagerly sought from the departments; for a basic premise in White House-departmental relations is that department officials, especially civil servants, play — or can play — an all-important role in effecting (or subverting) presidential goals. But how to arrange proper administrative leadership remains a question. Can the cabinet be vivified and recast to do the job? Could a strengthened cabinet of counselors who are strong administrators be delegated authority to perform the managerial duties that people are constantly visiting on presidents? Can the presidency and the cabinet be strengthened at the same time?

To summarize, most presidents want an easy exchange of information. They want objective, neutral analysis as opposed to special pleading. Invariably, half the cabinet, or more, become staunch advocates of fairly fixed viewpoints and hence, in the president's eyes, they become special pleaders. It is clear that many of the cabinet posts have lost authority, usually to a more centralized and personalized White House staff. Nearly every recent president has tried to enhance the role and status of their cabinet members, frequently pledging, too, that they will hold regular cabinet meetings and use the collective wisdom of their cabinet. In practice, however, the cabinet has become a pallid and embarrassing institution. Outstanding individuals now regularly reject cabinet appointment. Cabinet members in many of the departments, especially HEW, Treasury, and Justice, seem to stay for only two years.

Richard Neustadt cautions that our equivalent to the British cabinet is not our formal cabinet but rather "an informal, shifting aggregation of key individuals — the influentials at both ends of Pennsylvania Avenue. Some of them may sit in what we call the cabinet as department heads; others sit in back rows there as senior White House aides; still others have no place there. Collectively these men share no responsibility nor any meeting ground. Individually, however, each is linked to all the others through the person of the president. . . ." [25] Thus, the whole notion of what a cabinet is needs rethinking. We have built up a counterpart to the British cabinet, but it is only in part drawn from our cabinet. We rely heavily, as Neustadt has demonstrated, on "in-and-outers." People like Clark Clifford, David Rockefeller, McGeorge Bundy, Averell Harriman, Dean Acheson, and George Meany, despite their absence from the formal cabinet, are often far more influential in shaping presidential policy decisions than cabinet officers. Sometimes members of Congress or even members of the press serve a president in the role of policy counselor. These developments have occurred, or so it has seemed, at the expense of securing talented cabinet officers.

Benjamin Cohen, the wise New Dealer, recently outlined the problem this way:

> In recent times it has not been unusual for cabinet members to be directed rather than consulted even in regard to policies within their own departments. There has been a growing tendency for the president to gather about himself a small elite group of advisers and assistants, generally with little political experience or standing in their own right, personally devoted to the president, eager to help him but reluctant to press their objections to a suggested course of action once they sense that the president is favorably inclined towards it. This elite group is not subject to confirmation but is chosen because of their aptitude to work easily and on the same wave length with the president.[26]

At the same time, however, a president needs able cabinet officers and, indeed, presidents should value the diversity of their views and the fact that certain information perhaps can only come from the cabinet officer, who reflects such organized interests as agriculture, the transportation industry, health professionals, and labor. To be sure, most cabinet officers after a while become more parochial and narrow-gauged than in the White House view. But a president who is to offer national leadership needs to be able to listen and weld together the myriad of contending factions, both the organized and unorganized.

Obviously, then, the contemporary cabinet needs systematic rethinking. How should it function? Should it be larger or smaller? Should it act under certain conditions as a collective council for policy formulation and program coordination? Should there be a cabinet secretariat at the White House? What should be the relationship of the cabinet to the congressional leadership? Who should be selected as cabinet officers? And what can be done to improve White House-department secretary relations?

NOTES

1. Alexander Hamilton, *The Federalist,* paper no. 70 (Modern Library, 1937), p. 455.
2. McGeorge Bundy, *The Strength of Government* (Harvard University Press, 1968), p. 37. See also his entire Chap. 2.
3. Arthur M. Schlesinger, Jr., *A Thousand Days* (Houghton Mifflin, 1965), p. 683.
4. Louis W. Koenig, *The Chief Executive* (Harcourt, Brace and World, 1968), p. 417.
5. David Truman, *The Governmental Process* (Knopf, 1951), pp. 407–8.
6. George Reedy, *The Twilight of the Presidency* (World, 1970), p. 94.
7. Robert C. Wood, "When Government Works," *The Public Interest,* Winter 1970, p. 45.
8. Harry C. McPherson, *A Political Education* (Atlantic–Little Brown, 1972), p. 286.
9. Richard E. Neustadt, "Politicians and Bureaucrats," in David Truman, ed., *The Congress and America's Future* (Prentice-Hall, 1965), p. 113.
10. Henry Kissinger, quoted in *Newsweek,* 21 August 1972, p. 19.
11. Aaron Wildavsky, "Salvation by Staff: Reform of the Presidential Office," Aaron Wildavsky, ed., *The Presidency* (Little, Brown, 1969), p. 697.
12. Toby Moffett, *The Participation Put-On* (Delta, 1971), p. 201.
13. Moynihan, farewell comments, 21 December 1970.
14. Chester Cooper, *The Lost Crusade* (Dodd, Mead, 1970), p. 414.
15. J. Edward Day, *My Appointed Rounds; 929 Days as Postmaster General* (Holt, Rinehart and Winston, 1965), p. 98.
16. Quoted in Dom Bonafede, "Ehrlichman Acts as Policy Broker in Nixon's Formalized Domestic Council," *National Journal,* 12 June 1971, p. 1240.
17. Schlesinger, *A Thousand Days,* p. 681.
18. Sherman Adams, quoted in Robert J. Donovan, *Eisenhower: The Inside Story* (Harper and Bros., 1956), p. 71.
19. Emmet J. Hughes, *The Ordeal of Power* (Dell, 1962), pp. 53–55.
20. Irving Janis, *Victims of Groupthink* (Houghton Mifflin, 1972). See also Alexander L. George, "The Case for Multiple Advocacy in Making Foreign Policy," *American Political Science Review,* Sept. 1972, pp. 751–85.
21. Lewis A. Coser, "Conflict — Sociological Aspects," in David Sills, ed., *International Encyclopedia of Social Sciences* (Free Press–Macmillan, 1968), p. 235.
22. This case is made by, among others, Charles Frankel, *High on Foggy Bottom* (Harper and Row, 1968); Roger Hilsman, *To Move a Nation* (Doubleday, 1967); Daniel P. Moynihan, *Maximum Feasible Misunderstanding* (Free Press, 1969); and George Reedy, *The Twilight of the Presidency* (World, 1970).
23. John Kennedy, quoted in Pierre Salinger, *With Kennedy* (Doubleday, 1966), p. 64.
24. Henry Fairlie, *The Kennedy Promise* (Doubleday, 1973), p. 159.
25. Richard Neustadt, "White House and Whitehall," *The Public Interest,* Winter 1966, pp. 65–66.
26. Benjamin Cohen, "Presidential Responsibility and American Democracy" (A Royer Lecture delivered at the University of California, Berkeley, processed 23 May 1974), pp. 7–8.

CHAPTER 7

THE CABINET IN PRESIDENTIAL GOVERNMENT

*Every one of these men I've introduced to you is an independent
thinker, I can assure you. I haven't found any one of them who
agrees with me completely on everything that I believe about what
ought to be done in this country.*

*But that's all to the good. I don't want a cabinet of "yes men."
Every man in this cabinet will be urged to speak out in the cabinet
and within the administration on all the great issues so that the
decisions we make will be the best decisions we could possibly reach.*

— *President-elect Richard M. Nixon,*
    New York Times *(12 December 1968), p. 37.*

*Permit me to suggest that you [President Nixon] consider meeting,
on an individual and conversational basis, with members of your
Cabinet. Perhaps through such conversations we can gain greater
insight into the problems confronting us all, and most important,
into solutions of these problems.*

— *Secretary of the Interior Walter J Hickel to President Nixon,
    6 May 1970,* New York Times *(7 May 1970), p. 18c.*

*It is inevitable when an individual has been in a Cabinet position
or, for that matter, holds any position in government, after a certain
length of time he becomes an advocate of the status quo; rather
than running the bureaucracy, the bureaucracy runs him.*

— *President Richard M. Nixon, 27 November 1972,*
    New York Times *(28 November 1972), p. 40c.*

Since 1790 most presidents have wanted to use their cabinets as a committee of key advisers. Always recognizing that a president is neither bound to consult nor to accept the advice he receives, they generally have started out meeting with them regularly, even wanting to listen to their private doubts and counsel. In practice, however, the notion of a cabinet as a collective agency, one in which its members transcend the tasks and ambitions involved in administering their respective departments, has failed.

The Constitution makes no specific provision for a cabinet. Indeed, the term is nowhere specifically used in that document. Newspapermen coined the term during the Washington presidency, probably sometime in the mid-1790s. Heads of departments had actually existed under the Articles of Confederation and in essence Washington's cabinet merely evolved out of the pattern established in the 1780s. Washington's biographer notes: "Whether what was defined as 'the heads of the great departments' were to be under the jurisdiction of the President was not stated: the President was merely empowered to require their opinions relating to their duties." [1]

However, both Washington and his successor, John Adams, rather naturally developed the practice of consulting with their department heads, collectively as well as individually. "It was not long before matters of state came to Washington's desk for decision which concerned more than one department or were of such importance that he was unwilling to rely merely on the advice of the Secretary who was most directly involved." [2] Washington did not seek to have his department heads — State, Treasury, War, and a part-time Attorney General — function as a policy-making and program-coordinating body, so much as he hoped they could consult and work with one another harmoniously when matters were interdepartmental in character.

President Washington's hopes were dashed very early on; for his secretary of state, Thomas Jefferson, and his secretary of the treasury, Alexander Hamilton, hated each other personally and differed with each other on a wide range of significant policy controversies. They feuded continually. Washington tried desperately to get them to work together amicably, but he failed. Jefferson resigned in the summer of 1793. Hamilton left the cabinet soon thereafter. Washington then chose men of lesser talents, individuals whom he privately distrusted, and the idea of a body of collective responsibility evaporated almost entirely. "Unlike their predecessors [Hamilton, Jefferson, Knox and Randolph] they were not consulted concerning executive decisions; they were limited to the routines of their departments." [3] It sounds familiar.

Adams, who retained most of Washington's cabinet, suffered even more painful disillusionment with his cabinet. Deep differences of opinion developed between Adams and his three key department heads. His cabinet members were decidedly more loyal to private citizen Alexander Hamilton, their party and personal leader, than to President Adams. In the end, Adams required his secretary of war to resign and he fired outright his secretary of state. Adams maintained that he was under no obligation to consult his department heads or suffer their insubordination. His discharged department heads, while not going so far as calling for the English cabinet system, insisted upon the duty of a president to consult on all important measures and the duty of department heads to try to persuade the president to their views. They were less concerned with unity and energy and responsibility in a central government than with the fear that Adams' actions would reduce the role of cabinet members to little more than mere clerks. They raised the questions that are still raised, indeed with mounting intensity, today: "Do not the heads of departments like him [Adams] hold high and responsible station in government? In offering advice to a President, do they not perform an incumbent duty. . . . [Adams should] conciliate his ministers by a conduct, which does not reduce them to ciphers in the government and, by this means, endeavor, at least, to restore mutual confidence and harmony of action." [4]

Presidents have never had a completely free hand in choosing their cabinet members. Thus a natural mistrust often developed because their cabinets were so often dictated by considerations of political expedience. Powerful and dangerous rivals had to be disarmed or placated. Regional and geographic considerations were always important. Abraham Lincoln's attorney general viewed the Lincoln cabinet as "departmentalized, each secretary keeping monastic-like in his own office, knowing little of what was going on in the others, not participating in the general concerns of the nation." [5] More generally, Burton Hendrick said of Lincoln's cabinet:

That the cabinet disintegrated in 1864 was not surprising; the really astonishing thing was that it had held together so long. No such uncongenial or contentious group had ever assembled beneath the White House roof. Lincoln's conception of a coalition was politically sound, but on the personal side it inevitably led to trouble. For the most part Lincoln's councilors were forceful men, with their own programs, their own ambitions, their own vanities, jealousies, obstinacies, and defects of temper. Each had his set of ideas and his personal following, and on few matters had any two agreed. The criticism constantly made that the cabinet was not a "unit"; that each of its members went his own way and lived by himself in a watertight compartment, was largely justified. [6]

HOW TO ORGANIZE AND EMPLOY A CABINET

Despite this legacy of mutual distrust and disappointment, substantial support still exists for strengthening the cabinet. That presidents should upgrade the cabinet was a major reform prescription in the wake of Watergate. Management consultants maintain that an effective president will encourage strength and ambition in his key department executives and insure continuity in key positions. Thus, Nixon was faulted because few of his appointees stayed in their cabinet posts long enough to be effective: "During his administration, the median length of service in cabinet jobs dropped to around eighteen months (versus a median of forty months for cabinet officials during 1933–65)." [7]

Plans to reform the cabinet span the whole range of structural possibilities. Senator Walter Mondale (D. Minn.) urged the passage of legislation to create a question and report period during which the U. S. Senate would be able to question cabinet officers about vital matters of public policy. Not only would Congress learn more this way, he felt, but a president might be forced to pick better people. He reasoned also that if cabinet members are going to have to defend their departmental policies on the floor of the Senate during televised sessions, they will surely insist on being involved in the formulation of the administration's policies.

Others ridicule the notion of a genuinely strong, resilient cabinet, either as a resource for creative policy planning or as a mechanism for keeping a president in contact with reality. George Reedy, for example, said that the cabinet is invariably filled with presidential servants and that in reality nothing can be done about it. In fact, as several former White House aides observe, a president is free to supervise and consult department heads any way he chooses. A president could be required to consult with a formal cabinet; but if he prefers not to, nothing can prevent him from going through the form of consulting them, but in practice disregarding their views and advice. This has led a few people, very few at this writing, to conclude that the only other practical recourse would be the creation of an executive council of not less than five or more than eight persons to be nominated by a president and confirmed by the Senate. This council, suggested ex-New Dealer Benjamin Cohen, would constitute a small supercabinet with authority to participate in the decision making *before* important or potentially important presidential plans, programs, and policies were made final. We will treat this proposal in more detail in Chapter 9; but in essence it would doubtless require a constitutional amendment, and in effect would be an attempt to constitutionalize the informal counselor arrangements that most presidents from Washington to FDR have relied on during more critical decision-making periods.

In short, nearly everyone who writes about the presidency these days says the cabinet deserves to be strengthened and that outstanding people should be recruited to the cabinet. They shouldn't be selected, these writers say, because of geography, ethnicity, or political patronage. We need, instead, a strong cabinet that will speak out and check a president when he abuses presidential powers. We need talented managers in the cabinet who can make the sprawling executive branch function efficiently, effectively, responsively. As one of Lyndon Johnson's former cabinet officers put it: "The cabinet is in a sorry state; the recent tradition is all wrong on this and we need to change it. We can't let this tradition of neglect and downgrading go on; we need another new tradition."

What is needed is a better understanding of the incentive systems that motivate and shape presidential relations with the cabinet as well as the incentives that shape cabinet performance. The contemporary cabinet needs systematic rethinking. Its many inherent limitations notwithstanding, it has been abused and misused. A strong presidency and a strong group of cabinet members could and should be able to act collaboratively and effectively. Surely we should ask whether it can act under certain conditions as a collective body, who should be selected as cabinet officers, and what can be done to improve the relations between cabinet members and the White House.

The idealization of an American cabinet that never was is in part encouraged by presidents themselves. Kennedy and Nixon, for example, emphasized the importance of their cabinets when they picked their original teams. Perhaps this is part of the post-election euphoria and one of the first manifestations of the presidential honeymoon. Similarly, Harry Truman said that "the cabinet is not merely a collection of executives administering different governmental functions. It is a body whose combined judgment the president uses to formulate the fundamental policies of the administration." But one of Truman's most objective biographers argues that "while President Truman claimed that he used his cabinet to formulate decisions, in practice, many important decisions were made by ad hoc groups containing cabinet officers and others. He did not wish to create a cabinet secretariat and to formalize the meetings." [8]

President Dwight Eisenhower was perhaps the most enthusiastic recent proponent of an upgraded cabinet. It was as though he didn't want to believe that by the well-established law of politics secretaries of the great executive departments must serve several masters simultaneously. He hoped that each cabinet member in his administration would be a broad-gauged adviser, taking into account the total national welfare, not merely the clientele or congressional committees to which their departments traditionally had been beholden. Milton Eisenhower, the president's brother and close confidant, sums up Eisenhower's hopes:

General Eisenhower was determined to have the Cabinet become a major policy and program force in his administration. . . . [He] felt it imperative that the men and women who headed the major executive establishments should be consulted constantly in policy formation, for then they would more intelligently and enthusiastically carry out the agreed-upon policies and programs. Further, he did not want cabinet meetings to become merely a compromise of the preconceptions of its members. He wanted policies and programs of consequence to be analyzed and discussed thoroughly and candidly, with evidence and views based on careful research, reserving to himself, of course, the making of final decisions.[9]

As it turned out, Eisenhower did take his cabinet fairly seriously. He had it meet regularly. He created a cabinet secretariat and charged it with the explicit duty not only of preparing for the cabinet meetings, often held on a weekly basis, but also of following up to insure that every decision was carried into action. Eisenhower also expanded the cabinet to include a handful of presidential assistants and directors of important government agencies whom he recognized as the equivalent of cabinet rank and status. The Eisenhower cabinet, then, often numbered twenty or more, including the ambassador to the U. N., the budget bureau director, the director of defense mobilization, the director of mutual security, the national security affairs assistant, and assorted top White House aides. Sherman Adams, the ranking White House assistant, reports that "as Eisenhower explained it, these officials held positions in the government equal, in his opinion, to those of Cabinet Secretaries in responsibility and importance, but in previous administrations their lack of rank forced them to deal with Cabinet departments at almost a clerical level. Eisenhower aimed to raise their posts to the same rank as Secretaries so that they could work among the top-level officers of the government where they properly belonged." [10]

From every indication, Eisenhower did try to make the cabinet work as something more than just a body of advisers to the president. Issues of great diversity and often of great importance were on the cabinet agenda. He did not, as Woodrow Wilson had done, treat his cabinet members like office boys. And he did, within certain limits, encourage his cabinet members to take an independent line of their own and argue it out within the cabinet session. Eisenhower fully appreciated the limits of a cabinet system but seemed motivated to use the cabinet sessions both as a means to keep himself informed and as a way to prevent the personality conflicts, throat-cutting, and end-running that had characterized the history of past administrations.

The Eisenhower cabinet did not, however, decide policy nor did it really formulate policy, but it came about as close to the ideal of an upgraded or European-style cabinet as we have witnessed in the United States. Harold Laski's description of what a good cabinet should be is doubtless one of the best available:

A good cabinet ought to be a place where the large outlines of policy can be hammered out in common, where the essential strategy is decided upon, where the president knows that he will hear, both in affirmation and in doubt, even in negation, most of what can be said about the direction he proposes to follow. The evidence, I think, makes it clear that few American cabinets have been of this quality; they have not been a team of first-rate minds pooling their ideas in common. And until they become, by deliberate construction, as near such a team as it is possible for a president to make, he will not have at his disposal the basic human resources he needs to grapple with his formidable task.[11]

By Laski's criteria, the Eisenhower cabinet would be ranked deficient. Yet the fact is that Eisenhower did at least hold cabinet meetings, often for three hours, and critical issues were discussed there. One can only speculate about why Eisenhower chose to treat the cabinet in this atypical way. Perhaps in his career as a military and Pentagon official he simply had acquired a patience and a high tolerance of staff and mangement meetings. It is probable, too, that Eisenhower, perhaps in common with Franklin Roosevelt, was more secure, politically and personally, and thus more permissive of free interchange from stronger cabinet members. Still another factor may have been his notion of policy leadership, which, in short, was to move slowly, cautiously, and only after public opinion, Congress, or the courts had already taken a stand. In this sense, Eisenhower viewed himself as more of a manager and a moral leader than as a catalyst for initiating progressive change.

If the Eisenhower use of the cabinet was an exception to the general practice, it is nonetheless still true that even in his administration congeries of functional cabinets with reduced and appropriate membership were often relied on. By all odds Eisenhower's favorite policy-review group was the National Security Council. The NSC meetings were much smaller and the issues were of more personal interest to him. "More and more, we find that the central body in making policy is the N.S.C. Its sessions are long, bitter and tough. Out of that sort of discussion we're trying to hammer policy." [12] Moreover, close observers concluded that Eisenhower was bored more often than not with non-national security matters, especially with the business of the departments of Agriculture, Commerce, Labor, and Health, Education and Welfare.

CABINET USE AND DISUSE

A consistent pattern seems to characterize White House-cabinet relations over time. Just as a president enjoys a distinctive honeymoon with the press and partisan critics, so also White House-department ties usually are the most cordial and cooperative during the first year of an administration. The newly staffed executive branch, busy recasting the federal policy agenda, seems to bubble over with new possibilities, daring ideas, and imminent breakthroughs. White House ceremonies feature the installation and self-congratulatory ritual of welcoming in the recently annointed cabinet chieftains. Ironically, the White House staff, which soon will outstrip most of the cabinet in power and influence, receives less publicity at this time. In the post-inaugural months, the Washington political community, and the executive branch in particular, becomes a merry-go-round of cheerful open doors for the new team of leaders. One Kennedy cabinet member, recalling those early days, noted that Kennedy told his cabinet that frequent cabinet meetings would be held and that individual cabinet officers should telephone him or Vice President Lyndon Johnson about anything of importance; when in doubt, they should "err on the side of referring too much" on policy matters.[13] Even silly or trivial proposals by cabinet members were entertained at this time by a deferential White House staff and a happily-elected president.

Domestic crises and critical international developments, however, soon begin to monopolize the presidential schedule. As the president has less time for personal contacts, cabinet members become disinclined to exhaust their personal political credit with him. The president's program becomes fixed as priorities are set, and budget ceilings produce some new rules of the game. Ambitious, expansionist cabinet officers become painfully familiar with various refrains from executive office staff, usually to the effect that there just isn't any more money available for programs of that magnitude; or that budget projections for the next two or three years just can't absorb that type of increment; and, perhaps harshest of all, that a proposal is excellent but will just have to wait until the next term. The perspective of the president's aides was described this way by Charles Dawes, the first director of the Budget Bureau: "Cabinet members are vice presidents in charge of spending, and as such they are the natural enemies of the presidents." [14]

A high policy aide during Nixon's first term nicely captured the complex entanglements of time, presidential priorities, and interactions of people in the following passage:

Everything depends on what you do in program formulation during the first six or seven months. I have watched three presidencies and I am increasingly convinced of that. Time goes by so fast. During the first six months or so, the White House staff is not hated by the cabinet, there is a period of friendship and cooperation and excitement. There is some animal energy going for you in those first six to eight months, especially if people perceive things in the same light. If that exists and so long as that exists you can get a lot done. You only have a year at the most for new initiatives, a time when you can establish some programs as your own, in contrast to what has gone on before. After that, after priorities are set, and after a president finds he doesn't have time to talk with cabinet members, that's when the problems set in, and the White House aides close off access to cabinet members and others.

Jeb Stuart Magruder, a former Nixon aide, attested to the subsequent hostile White House treatment of the Nixon cabinet when he wrote: "From our perspective in the White House, the cabinet officials were useful spokesmen when we wanted to push a particular line — on Cambodia, on Carswell, or whatever. From their perspective, however, it was often a rude awakening to have Jeb Magruder or Chuck Colson calling up and announcing, 'Mr. Secretary, we're sending over this speech that we'd like you to deliver.' But that was how it was. Virtually all the cabinet members had to accept that they lacked access to the president and that their dealings would be with Haldeman and his various minions." [15]

A senior Kennedy staffer recalls an experience with one cabinet officer: "He kept calling and calling [for an appointment with the president], and so finally about the forty-third time — after I had told him over and over again that this wasn't the type of problem the president wanted to discuss with cabinet members — I finally relented and scheduled an appointment. Immediately after the secretary had completed his appointment and left, Kennedy stormed into my office and [in emphatic language] chewed me out for letting him in!" In his witty and somewhat bitter memoir, J. Edward Day, Kennedy's postmaster general, suggested that the president had neither the time nor the inclination to use the collective judgment of his cabinet. He also hinted that Kennedy hardly made use of several of the cabinet members even in their roles as departmental leaders.

> *President Kennedy had never had the experience of being an executive among lesser but by no means subservient executives; he had been served by a fanatically devoted band of men of his own creation. His Cabinet was a different run of shad. Each member was independent and quick to express his views, perhaps too much so to the President's taste....*
>
> *The atmosphere at Cabinet meetings should have been right for free-and-easy, frank discussion. At the outset it had been only natural to assume that such discussion would be encouraged.... The setting may have been right, but....*
>
> *The impression was created that the President preferred smaller meetings with those Cabinet members concerned with a specific problem.* But his absorption with politics, publicity, and foreign policy allowed him little time to be concerned about the domestic departments, *unless they had an immediate political aspect. For the domestic Cabinet,* personal meetings with the President became fewer and farther between, *and more than one member grew increasingly unhappy because it was so difficult to see the President.*[16] *(Emphasis added)*

President Kennedy regarded the idea of the cabinet as a collective consultative body largely as an anachronism and often told close friends of this view in blunt terms. He felt that the nature of a problem should determine the group with which he met. Time and again, he and his top aides noted that the historical status of the cabinet should carry with it no special claim on his time. He believed that there were few subjects that warranted bringing together, for example, the postmaster general, the secretary of agriculture, and the secretary of defense. As Kennedy aide Theodore Sorensen recalls:

> *[Kennedy] had appointed his Cabinet members because he regarded them as individuals capable of holding down very difficult positions of responsibility. He did not want to have them sit through lengthy cabinet sessions, listening to subjects which were not of interest to them, not of importance to them, at least not of an interest to their primary duties and their primary skills. So he called Cabinet meetings as infrequently*

as possible, he called them only because he was expected to call them — tradition, the press, and public opinion being what it is — and he preferred to call Cabinet members to smaller ad hoc meetings at the White House, where the subject under discussion involved their departments or on which he wanted their particular judgments.[17]

The tension between the presidency and the departmental secretaries on the one hand, and the Congress on the other, has been construed too often by presidents and their aides as a liability and a hindrance. But, on the contrary, it may create some of the most important of the creative confrontations that should be continuous in a democratic polity. What Henry Fairlie has written of Kennedy and his cabinet relations might easily be expanded to embrace most recent White House relations with cabinet officialdom:

The criticism is not so much of John Kennedy's unwillingness to use the Cabinet but of the reasons he gave for not using it. He does not appear to have understood the qualities which are even more valuable than intelligence and competence: that political judgment — at its highest, political wisdom — is often to be found where one would least be inclined to look for it, in men who digress, or who are slow, or who have no ready point to make, but who are feeling their way to an unformed doubt in their minds. Above all, he appears to have been trapped by his beliefs that he needed the advice only of those who were directly concerned with the problem. But those who are handling a problem, however much they differ, have to establish very early a frame of reference within which they can contain their differences, and that frame of reference then becomes fixed, and those acting within it find it hard to escape.[18]

The point is that most of the recent presidents have found it neither comfortable nor efficient to meet frequently with their cabinets as a whole. When they have, it seems to have been as much for purposes of publicity, symbolic reassurance, or appearance of activity as for substantive debate or learning. In the words of one Johnson White House lieutenant: "The cabinet became a joke; it was never used for anything near what could be called presidential listening or consultation." A Johnson cabinet officer complained that "cabinet meetings under L.B.J. were really perfunctory. They served two purposes: to let Dean Rusk brief us on the state of foreign affairs and let the President give us some occasional new political or personnel marching orders."

Cabinet members who went to President Johnson with requests often were asked to do favors in return, an added factor that kept some of them at a distance. One cabinet member noted that most domestic department heads tried not to bother the president because of his Vietnam war burdens: "But even at that, it was known that the president would welcome visits by domestic cabinet members on Saturday mornings. In retrospect, several of us regret that we did not make greater and better use of those opportunities. But part of the reason we didn't was because Johnson had an uncanny way of asking favors of you or giving you a number of political chores to do that you knew you didn't want and often couldn't carry out." This suggests, in part, that some cabinet members do not want too close a presidential relationship — surely an unconventional perspective, although in certain contexts understandable.

By the time of mid-term elections, the White House expects cabinet members to campaign for the administration, celebrating the administrative and legislative record of the past two years. Cabinet members come to be judged by the White House on their capacity to generate favorable publicity and to proclaim the virtues of the recent White House achievements. Strong-willed men of independence — ones who might be praised as "men of distinguished excellence in an open administration" — can hardly be expected to be enthusiastic about performing public relations tasks assigned to them by White House political counselors.

When in the course of an administration cabinet members grow bitter about being left out of White House decisions, they seldom make their opinions public.[19] Some exceptions exist, of course, and many cabinet officers will talk about the problem privately. The case of Interior secretary Walter Hickel, who had had only two or three private meetings with his president in the two years before his public protest and subsequent firing, is perhaps extreme. Most cabinet officers have more frequent contact with their president, but few of the domestic cabinet members have been wholly pleased by the quantity or quality of these meetings. Lyndon Johnson's memoirs confirm what many of his aides and cabinet members said privately: that he seldom sat down for substantive policy discussions with his domestic cabinet but spent vast amounts of time with his national security cabinet heads. In his book foreign policy matters occupy six or seven times as much space as domestic policy; and whereas only passing reference is made to most domestic department heads, more than one hundred references are made to Dean Rusk. One member of the Johnson cabinet said resignedly, "I just don't know what you can do. You just have to realize that his day is the same length as yours and become resigned to the reality that he just can't afford to spend much time with most of us, especially with that war going on."

Nixon's increasing centralization of power in the White House was an apparent vote of no confidence in his cabinet members, especially those in the domestic departments. In naming his original cabinet in December 1968, Nixon claimed to have appointed men who had the potential for great leadership, men with "an extra dimension which is the difference between good leadership and superior or even great leadership." Five years later he had a totally new cabinet. Nixon ran through cabinet members faster than any president in recent history. During one period of about eighteen months he had five attorneys general. After the Watergate revelations Nixon promised to deal more directly and meet more often with his cabinet members, but this was neither his habit nor to his liking and it was not to happen. His second director of the Domestic Council noted a temporary shift in Nixon's habits in 1973, but his obvious distaste for openness was readily apparent.

> *The President looked in great measure to his staff to communicate his wishes to the cabinet on the basis that there are only 24 hours in a day, that there are some problems that only he could deal with, and that he had to have a staff system that would allow him to deal with those problems and at the same time get the other jobs that the government had to do, done.*
>
> *So he didn't have a whole lot of time to spend with people and by spending 10 minutes with me it can translate into hours with the Cabinet, hours with them that he doesn't have to spend. . . . So he tended to work that way. . . . He realizes that you play the ball where it lies and with that set of conditions he's got to take more of his time from study and thought and spend it in contact with people. Consequently [as of late 1973], he's doing that. But he's still telling these people the same thing that he would be telling us or that we would be telling them under the old system.*[20]

A CABINET OF UNEQUALS

Cabinet roles and influence with the White House differ markedly according to personalities, the department, and the times. Each cabinet usually has one or two members who become the dominant personalities. Herbert Hoover's performance as secretary of commerce under Harding was of this type. George Marshall's performance in both State and Defense under Truman was similar. George Humphrey of the Treasury and John Foster Dulles of State clearly towered over others in the Eisenhower cabinet. Robert McNamara enjoyed especially close ties with both Kennedy and Johnson. His reputation as manager of a large, complex organization and his performance in a similar capacity at Defense virtually mesmerized both presidents and most of the White House staff, few of whom had ever managed any organization except temporary campaign staffs. Both Kennedy and Johnson repeatedly pointed to McNamara and the Defense Department as models for other departments to imitate, conspicuously congratulating their Planning, Programming and Budgeting System (PPBS), cost reduction, and cost-effectiveness operations. McNamara's capacity to present his own case before the presidents seemingly made it unnecessary for White House aides to serve as intermediaries; for example, he personally carried his annual budgetary requests directly to the president, and the president granted the budget director the opportunity for selective appeals or disagreements. George Shultz's early influence with President Nixon substantially exceeded the power inherent in the Labor Department, leading to his reassignment first as director of the Office of Management and Budget, then as secretary of the Treasury.

Certain departments and their secretaries gained prominence in recent decades because every president has been deeply involved with their priorities and missions — Defense and State in the cold war years, for example. The Acheson-Dulles-Rusk tradition of close and cordial ties with their presidents was founded in an era of continuous international tension during which diplomatic and alliance startegy loomed large. Other departments may become important temporarily in the president's eyes, sometimes because of a prominent cabinet secretary who is working in an area in which the president wants to effect breakthroughs: for example, John Kennedy's Justice Department headed by his brother Robert. HEW sometimes was thought to be developing into a presidential department during the mid-1960s when under John W. Gardner it was growing rapidly in order to manage Johnson's major educational and health programs. When the Vietnam War began overshadowing all else, however, Gardner's White House access and support became less privileged.

The new popularity of an issue relevant to a department's activities occasionally can work to the detriment of relations between the White House and that department. The law-and-order issue in the late 1960s elicited cutting partisan attacks against Johnson's attorney general, Ramsey Clark. Clark resisted acting in a retaliatory or repressive manner, but the president felt he was too dispassionate and tolerant. Secretary of the Interior Walter Hickel was a cabinet member who apparently decided to champion several issues unpopular with Nixon. Of course, presidents and their staffs may deliberately choose to have cool relations with a cabinet member. A president may lack interest in a department's domain, or ill will may exist between a strong president and a strong and perhaps quite stubborn cabinet member. Sometimes issues arise that are politically not discussable or at least unpopular, and a president may not want to associate himself with them and will surely avoid placing them in the public arena for discussion.

Much White House-cabinet estrangement undoubtedly arises because presidents simply lack the time to spend with all cabinet officers, let alone the leaders of independent agencies or major bureau chiefs. Most of a president's schedule is consumed with national security and foreign policy matters. One recent cabinet member complained: "In retrospect, all of the past three presidents have spent too much time on foreign affairs. They all felt that's where the action is and that's how they would be judged in the history books!"

Vast differences exist in the scope and importance of cabinet-level departments. The nearly four-million-person Defense Department and the ten-thousand-person departments of Labor or Housing and Urban Development are not similar collectives. Certain agencies not of cabinet rank — the Central Intelligence Agency, the National Space and Aeronautics Administration, the Veterans Administration, the Federal Energy Administration, and the Federal Reserve Board — may be more important, at least for certain periods of time, than cabinet-level departments. Conventional rankings of the departments are based on their longevity, annual expenditures, and number of personnel. Rankings according to these indicators can be seen in the first three columns of

TABLE 7–1   WAYS OF LOOKING AT THE EXECUTIVE DEPARTMENTS

A. BY RANK-ORDER

Seniority	Expenditures	Personnel	Real Political Power and Impact (Alsop's assessment)
1. State	1. HEW	1. Defense	1. Defense
2. Treasury	2. Defense	2. HEW	2. State
3. War/Defense	3. Treasury	3. Treasury	3. Treasury
4. Interior	4. Labor	4. Agriculture	4. Justice
5. Justice	5. Agriculture	5. Transportation	5. Interior
6. Agriculture	6. Transportation	6. Interior	6. HEW
7. Commerce	7. HUD	7. Justice	7. Labor
8. Labor	8. Interior	8. Commerce	8. Agriculture
9. HEW	9. Justice	9. State	9. Commerce
10. HUD	10. Commerce	10. HUD	10. HUD
11. Transportation	11. State	11. Labor	11. Transportation

B. BY ORGANIZATION

Inner and Outer Clusterings[a]	Nixon's 1971 Proposals	Supercabinet Plan A[b]	Supercabinet Plan B[c]
Inner:	State	National security	Foreign affairs
State	Defense	Economic stability	Economic affairs
Defense	Treasury	and growth	Natural resources
Treasury	Justice	Domestic policy	Science and
Justice	Human resources		technology
Outer:	Natural resources		Social services and
Agriculture	Economic		justice
Interior	development		
Transportation	Community		
HEW	development		
HUD			
Labor			
Commerce			

[a] Generic clustering is made according to counseling-advocacy dimensions.

[b] The way some White House aides view aggregate departmental concerns, and the apparent priority of these concerns as viewed by recent presidents.

[c] An example of cabinet consolidation that is one of many plausible by politically unlikely reforms.

Expenditures from estimated budget outlays of the executive departments in 1975; personnel from *The Budget of the United States Government, Fiscal Year 1975*, p. 506; Alsop's assessment from Stewart Alsop, *The Center* (Harper & Row, 1968), p. 254; Nixon's proposals from the State of the Union Message, January 22, 1971.

Table 7-1. Even a casual comparison of these columns reveals unexpected characteristics. Thus, although the State Department is about 175 years older than some of the new departments, its expenditures are the lowest of all. On the other hand, the Department of Health, Education and Welfare, formally only twenty-three years old, ranks first in expenditures and second only to Defense in personnel.

Other significant points of view toward classifying the departments include Stewart Alsop's journalistic appraisal of real political "power and impact," as of 1967.[21] Alsop's ranking takes into account the attitudes of the Washington press corps, other government officials, and the White House staff toward the status of contemporary cabinet members and departmental activities. His listing acknowledges the higher budget allocations of Defense and HEW as well as the personal celebrity status of Robert McNamara and John Gardner in the capital. Emmet J. Hughes, looking at the Eisenhower period, saw a convergence of raw strength of personality and leadership in the defense, treasury, and state cabinet posts.[22] Theodore Sorensen wrote that it was the "nature of their responsibilities and the competence with which they did their jobs" that brought six cabinet secretaries particularly close to John Kennedy, apparently in the following order: defense secretary Robert McNamara, attorney general Robert Kennedy, secretary of state Dean Rusk, treasury secretary Douglas Dillon, and, in varying ways, labor secretary Arthur Goldberg and Vice President Lyndon Johnson.[23] Furthermore, Rusk and McNamara continued to hold superordinate status in the Johnson cabinet in relation to their cabinet colleagues.

The contemporary cabinet can be differentiated also into inner and outer cabinets, as shown also in Table 7-1. This classification, derived from extensive interviews, indicates how White House aides view the departments and their secretaries. The inner cabinet has comprised the secretaries of state, defense, and treasury and the attorney general. The occupants of these cabinet positions generally have maintained a role as counselor to the president; the departments all include broad-ranging, multiple interests. The explicitly domestic policy departments, with the exception of justice, have made up the outer cabinet. By custom, if not by designation, these cabinet officers assume a relatively straightforward advocacy orientation that overshadows their counseling role.

THE INNER CABINET. A pattern in the past few administrations suggests strongly that the inner, or counseling, cabinet positions are vested with high-priority responsibilities that bring their occupants into close and collaborative relationships with presidents and their top staff. Certain White House staff counselors also have been included in the inner cabinet with increasing frequency. The secretary of defense was one of the most prominent cabinet officers during all recent administrations, for each president recognized the priority of national security issues. Then too, the defense budget and the DOD personnel, the latter ranging from 3.5 to 4.5 million (including military), makes it impossible for a president to ignore a secretary of defense for very long. Despite the inclination of recent presidents to serve as "their own secretary of state," this cabinet secretary has had a direct and continuous relationship with contemporary presidents. Recent treasury secretaries — Fred Vinson, George Humphrey, Robert Anderson, Douglas Dillon, John Connally, George Shultz, and William Simon — also have played impressive roles in presidential deliberations on financial, business, and economic policy. The position of attorney general often, though not always, has been one of the most influential in the cabinet.

The inner cabinet, as classified here, corresponds to George Washington's original foursome, to Stewart Alsop's journalistic appraisal, and to most memoirs of the Eisenhower through Ford period. Moreover, these inner-cabinet departments alone were immune to President Nixon's proposed overhaul of the executive branch in 1971; all others were nominated for abolition. The status accorded these cabinet roles is, of course, subject to ebb and flow, for the status is rooted in performance and the fashions of the day as well as in reputation.

A NATIONAL SECURITY CABINET.

The seemingly endless series of recent international crises — Berlin, Cuba, the Congo, the Dominican Republic, Vietnam, and the Middle East — have made it mandatory for recent presidents to maintain close relations with the two national security cabinet heads. Just as George Washington had met almost every day with his four cabinet members during the French crisis of 1793, so also John Kennedy and Lyndon Johnson were likely to meet at least weekly and be in daily telephone communication with their inner cabinet of national security advisers. One Johnson aide said it was his belief that President Johnson personally trusted only two of his cabinet, Rusk and McNamara. A Kennedy subcabinet officer quotes the president to the effect that his "regional assistant secretaries of state were more important officers of the government than most of the cabinet." [24]

Throughout recent administrations, more than a little disquiet has been engendered in the White House by the operational lethargy of the State Department. Although the secretary of state customarily is considered by White House staff to be a member of the president's inner cabinet, the department itself was regarded as one of the most difficult to deal with. More than 25 percent of the White House staff interviewed cited the State Department to illustrate White House-department conflicts. They scorned the narrowness and timidity of the encrusted foreign service and complained of the custodial conservatism reflected in State Department working papers. And even secretary of state William Rogers pointed out that the White House no longer believed the department could act in confidence: "One problem that stands between Presidents and the Department of State has to do with leaking information. Both John F. Kennedy and Lyndon Johnson often expressed doubts about the department's reliability. The trouble I've found is that the more we appear to lack the President's confidence in deliberations, the more likely information is to leak. I think I have improved that situation and increased confidence within the ranks. Yet to safeguard our secrets, I've often had to keep a great deal to myself." [25]

Some of State's problems may stem from the threats of the McCarthy era of the early 1950s, which intimidated State Department careerists into holding only the most puristic interpretations of the received policies of the day and inhibited imaginative and inventive policy. In State, more than in the other departments, the method and style of personnel, the special selection and promotion processes, and the protocol consciousness all seemed farther removed from the political thinking at the White House. Although they often may be gifted and cultured, State's personnel invariably become stereotyped by White House aides as parochial, cautious, and tradition bound.

Another source of the department's problems is the way in which recent secretaries, especially John Foster Dulles, Dean Rusk, and Henry Kissinger, have defined their job. Thus the demands on Rusk personally were such that departmental management was hardly his major priority. John Leacacos has surmised that the priorities appeared to have been: "First, the President and his immediate desires; second, the top operations problems of the current crisis; third, public opinion as reflected in the press, radio and TV and in the vast inflow of letters from the public; fourth, Congressional opinion; fifth, Rusk's need to be aware, at least, of everything that was going on in the world; and only sixth and last, the routine of the State Department itself." [26] That the secretary of state so often serves as the president's representative abroad or before Congress is another reason so few secretaries have had the time or energy necessary for managing the department's widely scattered staff. Moreover, more than fifty federal departments, agencies, and committees are involved in some way in the administration or evaluation of U. S. foreign policy.

Recent presidents have vested increasing amounts of authority in their National Security Council staff. Under McGeorge Bundy this staff was dubbed "Bundy's little state department" by the press. In another step to centralize and coordinate international economic policy, Nixon instituted a White House-level Council on International Economic Policy with broad authorities and later subsumed it under the even broader and more hierarchical Council on Economic Policy. During the early 1970s the NSC staff grew in importance, and Henry Kissinger acquired considerably more authority and operational responsibility than his predecessors. In marked contrast to nearly all other White House policy counselors, Kissinger had consciously prepared for his role for fifteen years. Although teaching at Harvard University for most of this' time, he had served as an adviser to New York Governor Nelson Rockefeller, long a presidential aspirant, and as a consultant to the Council on Foreign Relations, the national security agencies, the RAND Corporation, and the Kennedy and Johnson White Houses. Gradually, he developed a world view and a vision of a balance of power that he believed would be appropriate to the times. Eventually, he served both as tutor to presidents and as oversecretary of foreign policy — almost as deputy president for foreign policy. In 1973, when he was appointed secretary of state while continuing as the chief White House aide on foreign policy, the authority and centrality of the two positions were merged. Although most secretaries of state have enjoyed a far greater intimacy with presidents than have members of the domestic cabinet, the Nixon-Ford experience posed special problems. One man, Henry Kissinger, whether in the White House or at State, was the dominant counseling influence on the president. Overreliance on one person, however, incurs innumerable risks, especially when this person is primarily at the White House.[27]

LEGAL AND ECONOMIC COUNSEL.   The Justice Department often is identified as a counseling department, and its chiefs usually are associated with the inner circle of presidential advisers. That both Kennedy and Nixon appointed their most trusted campaign managers to be attorneys general indicates the importance of this position, although extensive politicization of the department goes far back. The Justice Department traditionally serves as the president's attorney and law office, a special obligation that brings about continuous and close professional relations between White House domestic policy lawyers and Justice Department lawyers. The White House depends heavily and constantly on the department's lawyers for counsel on civil rights developments, presidential veto procedures, tax prosecutions, antitrust controversies, routine presidential pardons, and the overseeing of regulatory agencies and for a continuous overview of the congressional judiciary committees. That these exchanges involve lawyers working with lawyers may explain in some measure why White House aides generally are more satisfied with transactions with Justice than with other departments. Close and frequent White House-Justice Department professional collaboration continued even during the height of the Agnew and Nixon scandals of 1973 and 1974.

The secretary of the treasury continues to be a critical presidential adviser on both domestic and international fiscal and monetary policy, but he also plays somewhat of an advocate's role as an interpreter of the nation's leading financial interests. At one time the Bureau of the Budget was a part of Treasury, but with the budget staff and the numerous economists, particularly within the Council of Economic Advisers, now attached to the White House itself, Treasury's monopoly of economic counsel has been broken. But Treasury is a department with major institutional authority and responsibility for income and corporate tax administration, currency control, public borrowing, and counseling of the president on questions of the price of gold and the balance of payments, the federal debt, and international trade, development, and monetary matters. In addition, Treasury's special clientele of major and central bankers has unusual influence. Although the Council of Economic Advisers and the Federal Reserve Board may enjoy greater prestige in certain economic deliberations, they are less effective as counterweights in international commerce and currency issues, in which Treasury participation is most important. The latter connection helps to draw the department's secretary into the inner circle of foreign policy counselors to the president. Thus, C. Douglas Dillon played a significant role in policy determinations during Kennedy's Cuban missile crisis, and under President Nixon, John Connally sat in on national security deliberations for a year or more; and William Simon was often a central figure in the Ford administration.

The importance of the treasury secretary as a presidential counselor derives in part from the intelligence and personality of the incumbent. Dillon and Connally, for example, were influential in great part because of their self-assuredness and personal magnetism. President Eisenhower had found himself responding in a similar manner to George M. Humphrey: "In Cabinet meetings, I always wait for George Humphrey to speak. I sit back and listen to the others talk while he doesn't say anything. But I know that when he speaks, he will say just what I was thinking." [28] Leonard Silk has suggested, however: "Formally, the Treasury Secretary had a mystique and power potential fully comparable to those of the Chancellor of the Exchequer in Britain or the Minister of Finance in France. The mystique may not be all that mysterious to explain; it derives from money. Power over money, in the hands of the right man, can enable a Secretary of the Treasury to move into every definite action of government — in military and foreign affairs as well as in domestic economic and social affairs." [29]

President Johnson's second treasury secretary, Henry H. Fowler, described his cabinet role this way:

> *I am particularly concerned with the means chosen to implement these goals [an adequate rate of economic growth, price stability, a balance in our international payments, and maximum employment]. I am concerned with selecting means that have a good chance of being realized in Congress. A set of policy prescriptions are no good if they can't be implemented, and in deciding on the mix of tax policies, debt management policies, and expenditures in the budget, on the annual delineations of the government's fiscal program, I want to be sure that they can be implemented and*

that they work. A second concern of mine has been that fiscal policy be fully co-ordinated with monetary policy, that fiscal policy bear its share of the job of reaching our economic objective.[30]

As Justice Department lawyers interact with White House lawyers, so also economists and financial specialists at Treasury and their opposite numbers on the White House staff are linked by a common professional bond.

INNER CIRCLES. The inner-circle cabinet members have been noticeably more interchangeable than those of the outer-circle cabinet. Henry Stimson, for example, alternated from Taft's secretary of war to Hoover's secretary of state and then back once more to war under FDR. Dean Acheson was undersecretary of the treasury for FDR and later secretary of state for Truman. Dillon reversed this pattern by being an Eisenhower undersecretary of state and later a Kennedy secretary of the treasury. When Kennedy was trying to lure Mc-Namara to his new cabinet, he offered him his choice between Defense and Treasury. Attorney general Nicholas Katzenbach left Justice to become an undersecretary of state; Eisenhower's attorney general William Rogers became Nixon's first secretary of state; and John Connally, once a secretary of the Navy under Kennedy, became Nixon's secretary of the treasury. Within a mere four-and-a-half years, Elliot Richardson moved from undersecretary of state to HEW secretary to defense secretary to attorney general. He became, his unexpectedly short tenure notwithstanding, the fourteenth head of the Justice Department to have served also in another inner-cabinet position. Occasional shifts have occurred from inner to outer cabinet, but these have been exceptions to the general pattern.

This interchangeability may result from the broad-ranging interests of the inner-cabinet positions; from the counseling style and relationship that develop in the course of an inner-cabinet secretary's tenure; or from the already close personal friendship that often has existed with the president. It may be easier for inner-cabinet than for outer-cabinet secretaries to maintain the presidential perspective; presidents certainly try to choose men they know and respect for these intimate positions.

In recent years several members of the White House staff have performed cabinet-level counselor roles. Eisenhower, for example, explicitly designated Sherman Adams to be a member of his cabinet ex officio. Kennedy looked upon Theodore Sorensen, McGeorge Bundy, and some of his economic advisers as perhaps even more vital to him than most of his cabinet members. Johnson and Nixon also have assigned many of their staff to cabinet-type counseling responsibilities. Quite reasonably, Nixon appropriated the term "White House counselor with cabinet rank" for several of his personal staff: Arthur Burns, Daniel P. Moynihan, Bryce Harlow, Robert Finch, Donald Rumsfeld, Melvin Laird, and Anne Armstrong. The dual role of Henry Kissinger already has been discussed.

The people to whom presidents turn for overview presentations to congressmen and cabinet gatherings are another indicator of inner-counselor status. When Kennedy wanted to have his cabinet briefed on his major priorities, typically he would ask Secretary Rusk to review foreign affairs, chairman of the Council of Economic Advisers Walter Heller to review questions about the economy, and Sorensen to give a status report on the domestic legislative program. In like manner, when Lyndon Johnson held special seminars for gatherings of congressmen and their staffs, he would invariably call upon the secretaries of State and Defense to explain national security matters and then ask his budget director and his chairman of the Council of Economic Advisers to comment upon economic, budgetary, and domestic program matters. Nixon usually called upon Henry Kissinger, the director of the Office of Management and Budget, and one of his chief White House domestic policy counselors to inform his assembled cabinet and subcabinet.

THE OUTSIDERS OR OUTER CABINET. The outer-cabinet positions deal with strongly organized and more particularistic clientele, an involvement that helps to produce an advocate or adversary relationship to the White House. Most White House aides cited five departments — HEW, HUD, Labor, Commerce, and Interior — as the ones with which they had the most difficult working relations. These departments, together with Agriculture and Transportation, make up the outer-cabinet departments. Because most of the president's controllable expenditures, with the exception of defense, lie in their jurisdictions, they take part in the most intensive and competitive exchanges with the White House and the Office of Management and Budget. These departments experience heavy and often conflicting pressures from clientele groups, from congressional interests, and from state and local governments, pressures that may run counter to presidential priorities. Whereas three of the four inner-cabinet departments preside over policies that usually, though often imprudently, are perceived to be largely nonpartisan or bipartisan — national security, foreign policy, and the economy — the domestic departments almost always are subject to intense crossfire between partisan and domestic interest groups. Public opinion is less permissive on domestic issues than on the broader, more complex issues, such as international monetary policy or on hard-to-comprehend executive agreements, even when the latter might have far-reaching and long-term consequences.

White House aides and inner-cabinet members may be selected primarily on the basis of personal loyalty to the president; outer-cabinet members often are selected to achieve a better political, geographical, ethnic, or racial balance. In addition to owing loyalty to their president, these people must develop loyalties to the congressional committees that approved them or those that finance their programs, to the laws and programs they administer, and to the clientele and career civil servants who serve as their most immediate jury. Johnson's HEW secretary Wilbur Cohen describes the cross-pressures vividly: "If you're the Secretary of HEW, you're responsible really in the end, to the Ways and Means Committee, and to the Interstate and Foreign Commerce Committee and the House Education and Labor Committee. And, boy, they can tell you in the White House, they can tell you in the Office of Management and Budget, and they can tell you everywhere, do this, that and the other thing. But if you come back next time to Capitol Hill, and you've violated what is their standard for their delivery system, you're not going to get what you're asking for." [31] The blunt advice of a former Nixon labor secretary to those who would come after him was that "nobody is going to appreciate what you do [and] you are going to get shafted from all sides." [32]

ADVOCACY CONFLICTS. Invariably, the White House staff suspects that outer-cabinet executives accentuate the interests of extragovernmental clientele over the priorities of the president. One of Franklin Roosevelt's commerce secretaries frankly acknowledged his representational and advocacy obligations when he explained: "If the Department of Commerce means anything, it means as I understand it the representation of business in the councils of the administrations, at the Cabinet table, and so forth." [33] Very few White House aides spoke of the virtue of having a cabinet member reflect his or her constituency and how this helps, or could help, educate a president. Most of the White House aides spoke of the cabinet as a burden and an ordeal for presidents rather than as a chance to forge coalitions and exercise leadership. Advocacy usually, though not always, was viewed in negative terms. No one seemed to ask, as someone in a different setting has: "If the President cannot weld together his Cabinet into a semblance of cohesive government, how can he weld together the nation which they represent?" [34]

Because presidents have less and less time to spend with the outer-cabinet members, however, the advocate role becomes less flexible and more narrowly defined. Unlike White House aides who enjoy greater access to the president, outer-cabinet members find they have little chance to discuss new policy ideas or administrative problems with the president. Because they must make the most of their limited meetings, they are tempted to perform a compromise rather than creative type of advocacy. A former subcabinet official summed up the problem persuasively:

One basic problem lies in the fact that domestic cabinet members are so rarely with the president that when they do have a chance to see him, they have to advocate and plug their departmental program in an almost emotional style, trying to make a plea for expanded appropriations or some new departmental proposal. But precisely at such times, the senior White House aide present can adopt or strike a pose as the more objective, rational statesman taking a non advocate and more "presidential" position — all of which leaves the domestic cabinet members appearing like a salesman or lobbyist rather than part of the president's team. But the cabinet member seldom has a chance to make his points or his case. The White House aide knows, on the other hand, that he can see the president later that day or the next, and so can afford to play a more reasonable and restrained role in such meetings. Such role-casting clearly favors the staff man while placing the cabinet member in a most uneasy position.

The interpretation of the advocate role by both the outer-cabinet member and the president may vary. It is much easier to listen to an advocate whose point of view fits with the White House philosophy than to one who continually transmits substantively different arguments or who encroaches upon other policy arenas. As departments have grown and their administration has become more exhausting, fewer of the department heads have had time to be well versed on problems beyond their domain. And as the last three columns in Table 7-1 suggest, White House aides and, to a lesser extent, recent presidents have come to feel that in many ways today's cabinet remains organized around problems of the past far more appropriately than the problems challenging the nation's present or future.

Interior secretary Walter Hickel complained that the performance of the adversary role alienated him from the president. Noting that President Nixon "repeatedly referred to me as an 'adversary,' " he continued:

Initially I considered that a compliment because, to me, an adversary within an organization is a valuable asset. It was only after the President had used the term many times and with a disapproving inflection that I realized he considered an adversary an enemy. I could not understand why he would consider me an enemy.

As I sensed that the conversation was about to end, I asked, "Mr. President, do you want me to leave the Administration?"

He jumped up from his chair, very hurried and agitated. He said, "That's one option we hadn't considered." He called in Ehrlichman and said: "John, I want you to handle this. Wally asked whether he should leave. That's one option we hadn't considered." [35]

Hickel's advocacy and style both differed from Nixon's and he was fired later that week. Such an occurrence is not inevitable, however: an outer-cabinet member's advocacy and adversary role can and often does fit perfectly with an administration's substantive philosophy.

OUTER-CABINET ISOLATION. As tension builds around whether or to what extent domestic policy leadership rests with the departments or with the Office of Management and Budget or the White House, and as staff and line distinctions become blurred, the estrangement between the domestic department heads and the White House staff deepens. White House aides believe they possess the more objective understanding of what the president wants to accomplish. At the same time it is the cabinet heads who, day in and day out, must live with the responsibilities for managing their programs, with the judgment of Congress, and with the multiple claims of interest groups. Outer-cabinet members have complained bitterly about the unmanageability of their departments and the many pressures on them. Robert Finch reacted to his liberation from the outer-cabinet into a quasi-inner-cabinet role as a White House cabinet-level political counselor by remarking: "It's great, just great, to be a Cabinet member without having to run a big department. [Here at the White House] I'm in on everything." [36] Relieved of the advocacy role, he had been graduated to a more congenial assignment.

Interviews with the domestic cabinet members yield abundant evidence that most of them felt removed from the White House.

From a Kennedy-Johnson cabinet member:

> *Kennedy had my policy area way down on his agenda. The White House people, especially the President, left me alone. It was a pleasant relationship, though his top aides were tough keepers of the door. So often was I kept away that when I wanted to see JFK, I would have to talk to him on the run ... or on a trip. There is a tendency on the inside to guard the president too much — they develop considerable power by tightening up the ring around the president. They all play on the fact that he hasn't any time for this or that, etc.*

From a Kennedy-Johnson cabinet-level administrator:

> *Recent presidents have let their White House political and personal aides go much too far in pressing administrators to do things they shouldn't. Too many of them are trying to make administrators squirm. There are too many aides at the White House who are just looking for a headline for the president. You have to guard against those types. There is just too much of it and presidents are guilty of letting it continue — they don't sufficiently realize that you have to have confidence in your department administrators. Perhaps it is due to the fact that they have never been administrators — they spent all their time in the Senate.*

From Nixon's first secretary of the interior:

> *There was an "isolation of thought" developing [in the Nixon presidency]. In early 1970, I was conscious of a deepening malaise inside the Administration — a sense of vague uneasiness. Others in the Cabinet shared my feelings that some of the White House staff were stepping up their efforts to filter contacts between the Cabinet and the President. It appeared that an effort was being made to centralize control of all executive branch activities of the government immediately within the White House, utilizing the various departments — represented by secretaries at the cabinet level — merely as clearing houses for White House policy, rather than as action agencies.*

Should a department — for example, Interior — develop policy for those activities under its control, submit those ideas to the White House for approval or disapproval, then follow through at the administrative level? Or, as some of the White House personnel seemed to want it, should a department wait only for marching orders to be issued by the Executive Mansion? [37]

The size of the bureaucracy, distrust, and a penchant for the convenience of secrecy have led presidents to rely more heavily on smaller groups of aides, usually White House staffers. The White House and executive office aides increasingly became involved not only in gathering legislative ideas but also in getting those ideas translated into laws and those laws into programs. Program coordination and supervision, although often ill-managed, also become more central White House interests. To an extent these additional responsibilities transform the White House into an action agency, if not exactly into a department unto itself.

President Johnson relied so heavily upon his top domestic staff and his budget directors that occasionally they were known facetiously as "oversecretaries" of the domestic departments. Nixon aides John Ehrlichman, George Shultz, Roy Ash, and Alexander Haig continued much in this same manner; indeed, the first two were regarded widely as supercabinet chieftains during their White House service. Outer-cabinet departments, understandably, began to lose the capacity to sharpen up their programs, and the department heads felt uneasy about the lack of close working relations with the president. This disillusionment was perhaps the greater because Nixon had pledged in the early days of his presidency, as mentioned, that he was going to upgrade the cabinet. Most of the Nixon domestic cabinet grew accustomed, however, to a substantially different type of presidential-cabinet officer relationship.

One of the difficulties of this tendency to pull things into the White House and exclude departmental officials is that often the excellent ideas or proposals that exist lower down in the bureaus of the permanent government seldom can get the attention they deserve because, according to the departmentalists, nobody asks them. As social psychologists have suggested, one group tends to develop stereotyped perspectives that not only dehumanize the outsiders but also cut off the very communications channels that might provide valuable and even vital information.

In the early 1960s Kennedy and his staff tried to get the domestic departments to come up with proposals for innovative legislation. But, according to White House aides, they usually came up with "interest-group types of claims, very parochial, more-of-the-same types of proposals." Rather than try to strengthen departmental capacities to come up with broader, more innovative proposals, White House aides, impatient for action, instead developed congeries of advisory committees, commissions, and secret task forces — indeed, a widespread extragovernmental presidential advisory system.[38]

WHITE HOUSE AIDES' PERSPECTIVES ON REDUCING CONFLICT

To establish the existence of White House frustration with department unresponsiveness and parochialism and of cabinet and department distress at the overtly political and abrasive behavior of the White House staff is not difficult. But to evaluate the varied prescriptions put forth as ways of improving White House-department relations is much less easy. As shown in the preceding chapter, White House aides perceive several sources of conflict between the White House and the executive departments; they also suggest a number of different remedies. The appropriateness of any suggested reform depends not only on the type of problem, but also on which staff functions at the White House and which departments are involved. Rather than calling uniformly for a strengthened presidency, as might have been expected, White House aides supported fully as much what might be called an integrative model. However, many also wanted to strengthen the cabinet departments. Table 7-2 shows the percentage of interviewees advocating particular solutions.

Most White House aides acknowledge, at least implicitly, that numerous remedial or regenerating efforts are needed within the White House as well as between the White House and the departments. Many former presidential aides began their discussion of reforms by pointing out that presidential styles, as well as policy preferences, differ, so "each president should organize his office more or less as he sees fit." And not a few aides recalled intentions of remedying bad habits at the White House that quickly evaporated:

> *Johnson would occasionally try to organize us into some better relationship to the cabinet and agencies. He would get memos on a certain day from two different White House people with two differing views or competing thoughts. He must have told me several times [after such occasions], and I know he told some of the others on the White House staff to "organize this place!! — organize it along more coherent lines so there won't be so much overlap." But this [when tried] wouldn't last for more than a few days, because the President himself wouldn't stick to it or honor it. In practice, the White House just does not lend itself very easily to that type of straight-line or box-like organization.*

Nearly 80 percent of the domestic and budget policy aides offered suggestions that would strengthen White House policy planning and management capabilities. Even those who complained about the arrogance of the White House staff often concluded that presidents must have tough and aggressive staff help. The following responses, suggested as remedies for reducing problems with the departments, provide some flavor of the strong presidentialist beliefs of many of these aides.

The presidency has to be the activist within the very conservative federal bureaucracy. The bureaucracy is the conservative agent or the custodian of old laws and old policies. They fight against anything new suggested by the White House, hence a president has to be the destabilizing factor in the system. The inability of department institutions to be creative or to take on new responsibilities is fantastic! In my view, the most important thing for a president is to know how to shake up *the bureaucracy! My own law is that for every new major priority you need to create a new agency — never give it to the existing department. You need a new agency to get the resources and the leadership to pull off anything that is a major departure — like getting a man to the moon.*

I think it is impossible to run the White House staff without having tough men to do the work of the president. Sorensen, Myer Feldman, and Ralph Dungan [Kennedy aides] were of this type. They could be very tough, abrasive, and uncompromising. But they had to be tough because if they were not the people in the agencies and departments just wouldn't respect the communications that came from the White House. I think it is a fundamental dilemma that people working for a president have to be

TABLE 7–2   PRESIDENTIAL STAFF PERSPECTIVES ON HOW TO IMPROVE COOPERATION AND REDUCE CONFLICT IN WHITE HOUSE–EXECUTIVE DEPARTMENT RELATIONS

Strategy Recommended	Percentage Recommending[a]
From the presidential perspective (68%)	
Stronger White House management-monitoring system	46
More aggressive White House sanctions and controls over executive departments	38
Stronger White House policy-determining capability	32
From the integrative perspective (66%)	
Make it more of a "two-way street"	42
More collaboration and departmental involvement in policy setting	40
More White House staff sensitivity and homework about intradepartmental concerns	38
From the departmental-cabinet perspective (42%)	
Strengthen cabinet secretaries and the cabinet-president linkage	28
Delegate more to departments, less White House interference and primacy, more trust and better communications	22

[a] Percentages here reflect multiple responses of the 50 persons interviewed.

Personal interviews of White House staff members who served during the period from 1961 to 1972.

arrogant, and almost be bastards, in order to get White House work done with the departments.

Although considerable overlap exists between those aides who supported the presidential and the integrative perspectives, the latter approach received relatively more support from among the administrative, public relations, and national security policy aides than from among the domestic and budgetary policy advisers. Integrative recommendations seemingly are based on the assumption that the White House is unlikely to have much effect on the implementation of federal programs unless it can win support and cooperation from the middle and upper echelons of the executive branch departments. For example:

I think the basic solution to the problem of dealing with the departments is to get one or two top staff people in the office of a cabinet member or department head and have these people work closely with the White House team. This helps a lot. It has to be a two-way street between the White House and the cabinet members. It is very important for White House aides to do favors for Cabinet members when they really want to get a promotion for somebody, or get some projects done. If you don't go along with them occasionally, and do this type of thing for them, they in turn are going to be difficult to deal with for yourself. It should be a bargaining, give and take, two-way relationship.

Keep them [department officials] involved and make sure you have some subcabinet people on your side whom you can trust and keep in touch with, and let you know what's happening. For example, I had an assistant secretary in the Commerce Department who knew our [White House] view, and was fighting with us against the State Department on textile tariff matters. He would go to the meetings and keep us posted if we needed to know more about anything.

Try to make them see the potential resources as well as the reason for the existence of a White House staff man assigned to their area (1) Frankly, they can't cut you off because every agency needs to know what the president thinks on matters pertaining to their agency. (2) The White House staff man can help a department or agency on internal matters and often does help a department official if he [the department official] knows how to use him wisely: for example, in regard to appointments, promotions, reorganizations, etc. (3) White House staff can be effectively used on interdepartmental problems, as in communicating something from one agency to another. Of course, there are always costs to these various usages, but in my experience the benefits outweigh those costs.

Forty-two percent of the former White House staff aides noted that even a strong presidency could succeed only with an executive branch characterized by a strong cabinet and departmental leadership. Many of these aides felt that Kennedy and Johnson and their senior staff had underestimated the importance of these factors in making the government work. One aide insisted that letting the domestic cabinet departments become so divorced from the White House was a major mistake: "One way to improve things is to have the president and the cabinet members, particularly in domestic areas, meet at least six or seven times a year and talk in great detail and in highly substantive terms about the major priorities of the administration. You have to have better communication. Basically you have to make the cabinet less insecure." Other aides criticized certain of their colleagues for having usurped operational responsibilities of the regular agencies, adding that if they accomplished anything, these aides enlarged their own importance more often than they expedited programs. Still other aides were less sure of remedies than they were convinced that past behavior by the White House is no longer adequate:

> *I think one major problem is the care and feeding of cabinet members. Most of these guys are people too, and the White House staff must be sensitive to that.* ———— *spent four most miserable years [as Secretary of Commerce] and* ———— *[Postmaster General] was also very discontented. They got the feeling that they were left out. As the White House gets more of the action and much larger, the cabinet people will resent it even more. Even if and when you are able to recruit good people to the cabinet, they are likely to let their jobs go and be less excited about the challenges of their work if they are continually kept at a distance from the White House.*

THE MERITS AND LIMITS
OF ADVERSARIAL RELATIONS

Inner-cabinet members may enjoy close ties with the White House, and outer-department heads may have to contend with centrifugal forces that tend to dissipate the counseling relationship. Other implications of this dichotomy, however, may be less immediately obvious. Rather than reforming the outer cabinet to approximate more closely the inner cabinet, both the White House and the inner cabinet might benefit from relating to each other in some of the ways that characterize the relationship between the White House and the outer cabinet.

The cordial and frequent contact between White House and Defense, Justice, Treasury, and the secretary of state actually may camouflage substantive problems that should be contended and issues that should be subject to the clashing of adversary views. The U. S. policy in Vietnam, the Bay of Pigs episode, a persistently inadequate tax structure, and the too casual concern for rigorous criminal prosecutions exemplified by the Watergate and related scandals are among the recent sorry by-products of the handling of inner-cabinet responsibilities. The inner departments may seem so congenial and professional in comparison with the overtly advocate departments that the White House may accept their judgments too readily, overlooking potentially divisive issues and neglecting to create an effective system for scrutinizing the substantive and operational aspects of these departments. Important debates may be foreclosed procedurally with reference to inner-cabinet policy choices. If this is so, then many of the more popular and conventional reforms — including much of what President Nixon proposed in his 1970 State of the Union message — misunderstand an important aspect of White House-executive department relations. Efforts could be made to increase certain kinds of conflicts, critical thinking, and adversary proceedings in order to maintain a strong awareness of the values inherent in alternative policy choices.

Presidents probably will not stop delegating the leadership and coordination of domestic policy matters to White House aides. But is it now enough to have a small band of staff lawyers or former public relations specialists manage the nation's domestic policy? Seldom have these White House aides had much experience in organizing or managing large complex bureaucracies, and White House aides too often mirror a presidential disposition to set up new White House councils, or to pass new bills, to the neglect of implementation or departmental management responsibilities. By doing so, the aides reinforce presidential learnings — and emotions and whims — rather than serving as an independent counterbalance. Peter Drucker, a presidential management critic, makes a good point: "The handling of foreign affairs, the economy, and social welfare *are* basic operations of government. Thus the President's counselors have jobs that parallel operating functions and, inevitably, they compete with and tend to undermine these functions. But no matter how he organizes his effort to get ideas, the chief executive will fail if he has a central operating staff. Anyone providing fresh ideas is, almost by definition, critical of the accepted wisdom and will therefore seem obviously disloyal. A central operating staff [in the White House] will always resent and fight him." [39]

Obviously, a president will have to have some aides to assist him in the White House. But they must, if they are to be helpful to the president, see themselves as part of the larger political system. They must appreciate that the department heads have to, both constitutionally and politically, serve more than one master. The White House aides of the recent past have too often refused to accept that cabinet heads quite naturally will have a different perspective, different incentives, and different rewards than those influencing a president.

Strength in cabinet members is not an unmixed blessing. Too much independence and too much feuding can paralyze. William Jennings Bryan and Henry Wallace both had to leave the cabinet, and, no doubt, this was proper. Overall, however, a weak cabinet member is more of a liability than a strong one. What needs to be continually understood at the White House is that a cabinet member's authority is constantly challenged by powerful legislators, muscular interest groups, and an admixture of personnel and program mandates of a distinctly centrifugal character. If a cabinet member is ever going to survive and stay a few years, he or she will need to have his or her hand strengthened by the president and the White House. Toward this end, a cabinet officer will almost always need help in developing and using high-caliber staff assistance for the tasks of budgeting, program planning and evaluation, and coordinating decentralized field operations. The strength and effectiveness of the presidency depends in no small measure on the quality of departmental leadership, especially on the effectiveness of learning through administrative feedback systems at that level.

"A good cabinet member — one who isn't just filling some political niche — can be a very excellent corrective to the White House 'hothouse' staff who are confined there and are virtually locked up fourteen hours a day. The President needs to hear from his cabinet. Presidents should occasionally sit down in a leisurely way with his cabinet members and listen and ask that important question: 'What do you think?' But this occurred very rarely with either President Kennedy or Johnson." This was the view of one Kennedy-Johnson cabinet member. Another stated that, without question, more cabinet meetings should have been called:

> There are two important things that should be done through the use of the cabinet meetings. First, meetings should be held to inform the cabinet members about major developments or new priorities. Second, the president should occasionally bring some major policy issue before the cabinet and open it up for detailed discussion. He should take advantage of the broad-gauged abilities of these very able men. For example, never once was there any discussion of whether we should send more troops to Vietnam. This type of policy matter was always confined to the national security council group — but they could have benefited from our views and ideas on this type of matter, for we had less personal involvement in the earlier decisions and might have been able to give valuable added perspective or fresh appraisals.

Regardless of how organization charts are drawn, future presidential use of the cabinet and White House staff probably will give greater weight to the realities of the differentiated roles and activities of the federal departments. The cabinet as a collectivity will move farther toward oblivion with the more complete emergence of (1) a national security cabinet, (2) an economics directorate, and (3) a domestic policy cabinet. Each of these will be presided over by some combination of presidential counselors, from the president's staff or from the executive departments. Cabinet advocates surely will still exist, but they may operate from posts within rather than atop the executive departments.

A redesigned and strengthened outer cabinet might enable the White House staff to abstain more often from the temptation to gather administrative responsibilities to itself. But reorganizational developments will not lessen the need for skillful and decisive executive branch mediators who, with the full confidence of the president, can preside over thorny and complex claims and counterclaims by competing domestic departments, and who also can know when important elements of a debate are being seriously neglected or misrepresented within cabinet-level negotiations. Unfortunately, White House aides seldom are chosen for these abilities.

To summarize, the American cabinet has had a strange and anomalous history. It has seldom operated as a policy-making body. And few presidents have used it as a collegium. No law or constitutional authority commands a president to consult with a collective cabinet or even to hold cabinet meetings. The job of the department head, especially in modern times, necessarily demands that department heads heed the concerns of Congress, bureaucracies, the Constitution, and various professional and ethical considerations *in addition to* the desires and demands of a president. Thus, even the most carefully chosen cabinet member will occasionally differ, if not clash, with certain presidential wishes.

It is a fact that a president will seldom be wholly satisfied with the loyalty of department heads. To be sure, most cabinet members will aspire to a president's intimacy, and many of his inner cabinet will indeed become long-term counselors and friends, but even some of these will often break with him, frequently without realizing how serious their differing perspectives have been. A president, however, must welcome advocacy from his cabinet officers. And although open and frank discussions in cabinet meetings will sometimes limit a president's discretion, a president will generally profit from using the cabinet as a consultative body.

Properly chosen and used, a cabinet can provide the very necessary on-the-job education and contact with political reality that is essential for effective presidential leadership. A collection of talented and strong cabinet members can be made to work together. This requires a president who has great self-confidence; is secure, personally and politically; and is willing to encourage advocacy, fresh thinking, and reappraisals of past commitments. For the cabinet to be used effectively, it would be helpful too if cabinet consolidation, and thus decreased size, were approved, and if the tradition were to begin again of appointing to the cabinet only people of extraordinarily high public standing, of indeed presidential caliber themselves. None of this is to suggest that we want or can fashion a cabinet having collective responsibility or that a collegial presidency is what is needed. What it does suggest is that a revitalized cabinet, organized by general purposes, rather than along the lines of the interests of existing clientele and special categories, could strengthen the presidency and make it more responsible.

NOTES

1. James Thomas Flexner, *Washington: The Indispensable Man* (Little, Brown, 1974), p. 220.
2. Leonard D. White, *The Federalists* (Macmillan, 1948), p. 38.
3. Flexner, *Washington,* p. 326.
4. Quoted in White, *The Federalists,* p. 45.
5. Burton J. Hendrick, *Lincoln's War Cabinet* (Little, Brown, 1946), p. 191.
6. *Ibid.,* p. 369.
7. Peter F. Drucker, "How to Make the Presidency Manageable," *Fortune,* November 1974, p. 234.
8. Harold Gosnell, *Harry S. Truman: Near Failure or Near Great?* (forthcoming).

9. Milton S. Eisenhower, *The President Is Calling* (Doubleday, 1974), p. 257.
10. Sherman Adams, *First-Hand Report: The Story of the Eisenhower Administration* (Harper, 1961), p. 61. See also, Dwight D. Eisenhower, *Mandate For Change: The White House Years* (Signet, 1963), chaps. 4 and 5, especially pp. 176–78.
11. Harold J. Laski, *The American Presidency* (Grosset & Dunlap, 1940), pp. 257–58. Laski's Chapter 2, "The President and His Cabinet," is a useful dissection of the cabinet problem in America. The best book on the same topic is Richard F. Fenno, *The President's Cabinet* (Vintage, 1959).
12. Quoted in Peter Lyon, *Eisenhower: Portrait of the Hero* (Little, Brown, 1974), pp. 503–4.
13. J. Edward Day, *My Appointed Round: 929 Days as Postmaster General* (Holt, Rinehart and Winston, 1965), p. 97.
14. Quoted in K. Gordon, "Reflections on Spending," in J. D. Montgomery and Arthur Smithies, eds., *Public Policy*, vol. 15 (Harvard University Press, 1966), p. 15.
15. Jeb Stuart Magruder, *An American Life: One Man's Road to Watergate* (Atheneum, 1974), p. 102.
16. Day, *My Appointed Round,* pp. 96–98. (Emphasis added.)
17. Theodore C. Sorensen (Transcript of a panel discussion at the Annual Meetings of the American Society for Public Administration, New York, 22 March 1972), p. 22. Reprinted as an article "Advising the President: A Panel," *The Bureaucrat,* April 1974, p. 33.
18. Henry Fairlie, *The Kennedy Promise* (Doubleday, 1973), p. 167.
19. One Kennedy-Johnson cabinet official told me that President Johnson had an uncanny ability to intimidate the occasional dissenter within his cabinet, especially when the going became rough during the peak of public anguish over involvement in Vietnam. Apparently, or so it seemed to this cabinet member, LBJ let it be known indirectly to several of his cabinet members that should they ever decide to resign in protest and make public their opposition to his war policies, they better well know that the FBI and IRS directors would be on their heels following them right out of office. To this particular cabinet member, it did not really matter whether Johnson actually would have done this — indeed, he felt that Johnson would say this sort of thing only in weaker moments over a drink or two with his closest aides — but the very fact that on occasion he would suggest such reprisal was intimidation enough.
20. Kenneth R. Cole, Jr., quoted in Dom Bonafede, "Nixon's Troubles Bring Enhanced Role for Cabinet, Better Working Relationships," *National Journal Reports,* 6 Oct. 1973, p. 1477.
21. Stewart Alsop, *The Center* (Harper and Row, 1968), chap. 9.
22. Emmet J. Hughes, *Ordeal of Power* (Dell, 1962), p. 61.
23. Theodore Sorensen, *Kennedy* (Bantam Books, 1966), p. 297, and chap. 10 in general.
24. Lincoln Gordon, "The Growth of American Representatives Overseas," in Vincent Barnett, ed., *The Representation of the United States Abroad* (Praeger, 1965), pp. 25–26.
25. William Rogers, quoted in Milton Viorst, "William Rogers Thinks like Richard Nixon," *New York Times Magazine,* 27 Feb. 1972.
26. John Leacacos, *Fires in the In-Basket* (World, 1968), p. 110.
27. I. M. Destler, "Can One Man Do?" *Foreign Policy,* Winter 1971–1972, pp. 28–40. A national security advisory system dominated by one person invites many perils, as several writers, including Destler, point out. Irving L. Janis, in *Victims of Groupthink* (Houghton Mifflin, 1972) sums up perhaps the most disquieting possibility when he writes that: "We know that most individuals become heartily involved in maintaining their commitment to any important decision for which they feel at least partly

responsible. Once a decision-maker has publicly announced the course of action he has selected, he is inclined to avoid looking at evidence of the unfavorable consequences. He tries to reinterpret setbacks as victories, to invent new arguments to convince himself and others that he made the right decision, clinging stubbornly to unsuccessful policies long after everyone else can see that a change is needed. Each policy-maker, whether he has made the crucial decisions by himself or as a member of a group, is thus motivated to perpetuate his past errors — provided, of course, that his nose is not rubbed in inescapable evidence" (p. 117). See also David Halberstam, *The Best and The Brightest* (Random House, 1972).

28. Quoted in Richard H. Rovere, "Eisenhower: A Trial Balance," *The Reporter,* 21 April 1955, pp. 19–20.
29. Leonard Silk, *Nixonomics* (Praeger, 1972), p. 81.
30. Quoted in Lawrence C. Pierce, *The Politics of Fiscal Policy Formation* (Goodyear, 1971), p. 100.
31. Wilbur Cohen, former secretary of HEW under Lyndon Johnson, quoted in *National Journal,* 16 Dec. 1972, p. 1921.
32. James Hodgson, former labor secretary in the Nixon administration, quoted in the *Wall Street Journal,* 13 Feb. 1973.
33. Jesse Jones, quoted in Richard Fenno, "President-Cabinet Relations and a Pattern and a Case Study," *American Political Science Review,* March 1958, p. 394.
34. Anonymous participant, Conference on the Institutional Presidency, sponsored by the National Academy of Public Administration, Warrenton, Virginia, April 1974.
35. Walter J. Hickel, *Who Owns America?* (Prentice-Hall, 1971), p. 259.
36. Robert Finch, quoted in *The New Republic,* 3 Oct. 1970, p. 14.
37. Hickel, *Who Owns America?,* pp. 221–22.
38. See Thomas E. Cronin and Sanford Greenberg, eds., *The Presidential Advisory System* (Harper & Row, 1969).
39. Drucker, "How to Make the Presidency Manageable," pp. 148–49.

CHAPTER 8

THE VICE-PRESIDENCY IN PRESIDENTIAL GOVERNMENT

Vice presidents were useless to the presidents on congressional relations matters. Both LBJ and HHH were ineffective when they were in the isolated vice presidency slot. I never even saw LBJ [when he was vice president]. I took Humphrey with me once when I went to Speaker John McCormack's office and McCormack was very upset. He said, looking at the Vice President, "You're a senator," as if to say that senators should "stay away from us" in the House.

— *A former Kennedy-Johnson aide,*
1970, personal interview with author.

The Vice President, it quickly turned out, was not his own man; no vice president is, but the vice president under Lyndon Johnson was doomed to be even less so. Lyndon Johnson had always viewed Hubert Humphrey as something of a convenience, to be used at times for his own and the country's good.... Rarely would a high public official undergo the humiliation and virtual emasculation that Humphrey underwent as vice president....

— *David Halberstam,* The Best and the Brightest
(Random House, 1972), p. 533.

I am not in a leadership position.... The President has the responsibility and the power.... The Vice President has no responsibility and no power.

— *Vice President Nelson Rockefeller,*
Time *Magazine (20 January 1975), p. 23.*

A stranger, more baffling office is hard to imagine. To the Founding Fathers it was pretty much an afterthought. To many historians and constitutional scholars it is one of our most conspicuous constitutional mistakes. To vice presidents it is usually a humiliating, confusing experience. To presidents it appears to be more of a headache than an asset.

The office is often condemned as a superfluous nonjob. And it is very clear that any serious duties or prerogatives a vice president has come only at the pleasure of the president. Still, many people are puzzled as to why vice presidents do not do more to help presidents, to ease the burden and the ordeal of the presidency, to assist in congressional relations, to serve as a kind of deputy president. If nothing else, cannot a vice president relieve a president of onerous ceremonial obligations?

Some vice presidents doubtless have served their presidents and their nation well. But, in general, the obstacles, both political and psychological, that stand in the way of constructive use of vice presidents are considerable. This office, which in theory could make the presidency more manageable and presidents more effective political leaders, seldom works that way. Our system for selecting vice presidents and the tradition of ridicule and misuse of them once they "win" office, are both perverted. Suggestions that the office should be abolished have been made for 180 years. These suggestions merit serious consideration today. Historian Arthur Schlesinger, Jr., who called it a "doomed office," concluded that it is not only a meaningless office but "a hopeless office." If one appreciates the singular emptiness of that office, said Schlesinger, a belief in democracy surely suggests its abolition and that a special election be arranged when the presidency falls vacant.

American political tradition at least since Jefferson's day decrees that the vice-presidency and vice presidents are not to be taken seriously. No office has been so disdained and lampooned. Our first vice president wrote to his wife in December 1793 that: "My country has in its wisdom contrived for me the most insignificant office that ever the invention of man contrived or his imagination conceived." John Nance Garner, vice president during FDR's first two terms, concluded that the job, "isn't worth a pitcher of warm spit." He also called it a "spare tire on the automobile of government." Daniel Webster remarked in 1848 when he turned down the vice-presidential nomination: "I do not propose to be buried until I am dead."

Theodore White contended that of all the absurdities of American politics, none is more absurd than the choosing of a vice president. Theodore Sorensen, former aide to John Kennedy, noted that the process of picking a vice president invariably begins with a search for someone who will strengthen the presidential ticket but invariably ends with a search for someone who will not weaken it.

And scholars and citizens alike recognize that our practice of leaving the vital choice of future national leadership to the discretion of a single individual — the presidential candidate or the president — is unacceptable in a nation that professes to be democratic.

PRESIDENT OF THE SENATE
OR PRESIDENTIAL AMBASSADOR?

What should a vice president do? Until recently most presidents viewed it almost exclusively as a legislative job and outside the presidential orbit. Vice presidents were to serve as president of the Senate, presiding there and casting an occasional tie-breaking vote. But in recent times this Senate post is widely viewed as a ridiculous chore and is increasingly neglected. Vice President Spiro Agnew set a record for nonperformance as the Senate's presiding officer. During the first eight months of 1973 he wielded the gavel for 2 hours and 26 minutes out of some 670 hours the Senate had been in session. On the average, a vice president gets to cast a tie-breaking vote less than once a year. This prompted a *New York Times* reporter to conclude that the "single job conferred on a Vice President by the Constitution — presiding over the meetings of the United States Senate — can be performed by any six year old. The presiding officer need do no more than sit there like an elegant dunce, and repeat aloud whatever the parliamentarian stage-whispers to him. It is about as challenging as having your hair cut. . . ." [1]

Is the job of presiding over the Senate a thankless one without any real power? Assuredly this is now the case. Vice President Calvin Coolidge, of all persons, had a somewhat pre-emptory manner of presiding and once even claimed that the vice president was the person to decide what business is to be taken up and who is to have the floor at a specific time. But that was an exception to the general custom. Even Aaron Burr strove to be a conscientious and impartial president of the Senate, generally taking his duties seriously (save for the time he took off to duel and kill Alexander Hamilton).

Technically a vice president could become arbitrary and domineering in the Senate. In practice they do not. Especially in recent times, the members of Congress look upon a vice president as a member of the executive branch. They are jealous of their prerogative and seldom welcome vice presidents as "insiders." Lyndon Johnson, upon election as vice president, for example, sought to retain a certain measure of the control over Democrats he enjoyed as majority leader. He apparently talked Senator Mike Mansfield into inviting him to preside over Democratic caucus meetings, even though he was about to become vice president.

The proposal that LBJ as vice president serve as presiding officer of all the Senate Democrats whenever they met in a formal conference was opposed not only by several of his liberal antagonists but also by members of his own so-called "Johnson Network." The liberals, of course, wanted revenge for his having ridden roughshod over them too long. One rational argument they put forth was that it was an unnatural mixing of the separate branches: "We might as well ask Jack Kennedy to come back up to the Senate and take his turn at presiding," snapped Senator Albert Gore.[2] More telling was the opposition of Senator Clinton Anderson, a long-time Johnson intimate. Reporters Evans and Novak recall:

Anderson specifically noted his support at Los Angeles and the debt all Democratic Senators owed Johnson for his leadership in the Senate the past eight years. But the office of the Vice President, said Anderson, was more a creature of the executive branch than the legislative branch. Therefore, quite apart from the fact that the Senate Democrats would look ridiculous electing a non-Senator to preside over them, to do so would violate the spirit of separation of powers.

The debate continued in a mood of embarrassment. Johnson was present. . . .[3]

Johnson understood the message and seldom again did he try as vice president to influence Senate proceedings. Indeed, much of his vice-presidency was marked by a subdued deference to the Congress and a disinclination to serve as a lobbyist for Kennedy's New Frontier legislation. Some people claim Johnson was not asked to do so. Others conclude that he just lost interest in trying to win friends and influence votes, especially in light of the Senate's humiliating rebuff. He became, at best, a reluctant liaison with Congress. He would do so when specifically asked by the president, but rarely otherwise. "Johnson also was asked to help round up votes on crucial issues, but so many times he found excuses not to do so that eventually he was no longer asked. Nor did he usually take part in the discussions leading to the development of legislative proposals. He was present at these discussions, but he did not participate."[4]

Vice presidents rarely are used effectively in congressional liaison work. This is often because they are not properly prepared by their president. Harry Truman, in his very brief tenure as a vice president, wanted to become an outstanding link between Congress and the White House. But this depended on close contact with FDR, which was virtually nonexistent. Lyndon Johnson's brother claims that LBJ was similarly underused and kept at arm's length. "The Kennedys," he writes, "had easy access to the greatest legislative strategist of this century — Lyndon Johnson — but they refused to use him. Instead there was a swarm of young, conceited New Frontiersmen running around Capitol Hill trying to tell elderly congressmen, 'this is the way it's got to be,' and to impress on Senator X or Congressman Y that they were speaking for the White House."[5] If Johnson's brother can be believed, then Johnson was simultaneously rebuffed by both the Congress and the White House. Caught both coming and going, he retreated into a nearly three-year sulk.

Roosevelt's troubles with John Nance Garner were altogether different. Garner was an important figure in the Congress and he skillfully assisted the passage of a number of New Deal measures in FDR's first term. But he grew upset with the pace and scope of later New Deal measures and became outspoken in his opposition to several of them. He opposed Roosevelt's scheme for packing the Supreme Court. He opposed FDR's bid for a third term. By the end of his second term, Roosevelt avoided Garner whom he considered an impossible person.

The limits of vice-presidential influence in the Senate are illustrated by one of Spiro Agnew's not uncommon transgressions of political convention. Early in his tenure as president of the Senate, Agnew tried to interest himself in mastering Senate rules as well as learning the Senate's informal folkways: "But he violated protocol by lobbying on the Senate floor in behalf of the tax surcharge extension supported by the administration. 'Do we have your vote?' he asked Senator Len Jordan of Idaho, a Republican. The Senator replied, 'You did have until now.' Thus, was established Jordan's rule: When the Vice President lobbies on the Senate floor for a bill, vote the other way." [6] Thereafter, Agnew seemed to lose interest in trying to become a major presidential emissary on Capitol Hill. And, in any event, Agnew was pretty much frozen out by Nixon's White House staff. He seldom was involved in policy or program development, excepting perhaps the promotional role he performed in trying to sell revenue-sharing legislation.

Vice President Hubert Humphrey had served in the Senate for sixteen years prior to becoming vice president. He was fully aware that as presiding officer in the Senate he was to be seen but not heard, except for procedural matters. This was a difficult adjustment for the loquacious Humphrey. Custom, folkways, and good manners pretty much dictated his behavior as Senate president:

You recognize the majority leader whenever he seeks recognition. You recognize the minority leaders following the majority leader. You try to recognize a Democrat and then a Republican, that is on ordinary matters. When you get into a hot debate, when the issues are difficult, you recognize on the basis of who is up first — whether the Vice President's eye catches a particular person. Now, of course, you can occasionally blink. But I think that most Vice Presidents try to play it pretty fair, and, as we say, on the level.[7]

SHOULD THE VICE PRESIDENT SERVE AS SENATE PRESIDENT?

Neither presidents nor vice presidents are now well served by having vice presidents preside over the Senate. Initially, the Senate was a small handful of prominent elder statesmen, twenty-six men plus the vice president. Tie votes were more frequent then: John Adams cast twenty-nine tie-breaking votes. Since Adams, however, mainly because the Senate has grown to one hundred members, tie votes occur less than once a year.

The Senate as originally designed was in many ways an ideal place for a vice president to learn the business of government and serve an apprenticeship. The Senate was intended to pass laws, confirm major presidential appointees, oversee treaties, and, more generally, to advise and counsel presidents. Over time, as it grew and also delegated vast discretion to the executive branch, the Senate has become decidedly neither a council of state nor a presidential counselor. Today, the job of presiding over the Senate offers little training for the position of chief executive; and, the Senate views all vice presidents as semi-intruders, certainly not as providers of leadership or instructions.

As matters now stand, a vice president is a full member of neither branch. The office, because of the duties as presiding officer of the Senate, is clearly a constitutional hybrid, limiting somewhat the use a president can make of a vice president. Thus, President Eisenhower "asserted repeatedly in his memoirs that the vice president 'is not legally a part of the Executive Branch and is not subject to direction by the President.' In Eisenhower's view, any performance of executive functions by the vice president was voluntary and by his request." [8]

There is good reason today to drop the vice president from his presiding role in the Senate quite apart from whether he takes on more work elsewhere. But there are some who feel that if we are to have a vice president, he should be relieved of his traditional Senate functions and freed to participate much more directly in cabinet and executive office responsibilities. The late James F. Byrnes of South Carolina, a former senator, governor, associate justice of the Supreme Court as well as secretary of state, offered this perspective:

If a motion (in the Senate) does not receive a majority vote, it should be considered lost. It is not wise that the Vice President, a representative of the executive branch of government, should affect the will of the legislators by casting a decisive vote. In short, participation by the Vice President in Senate voting, either in support of his own views or the President's, constitutes a violation of the spirit of the fundamental provision of the Constitution that the three branches of our government shall forever be separated. [9]

Byrnes proceeded, as a few scholars have also argued, to suggest that we adopt a constitutional amendment to effect this change.

Constitutional scholar Joseph Kallenbach also favored this change, contending that the vice president could then become a sort of "minister without portfolio," subject to executive assignments as a president may direct. "This would not only insure that he would function in a subordinate administrative capacity to the President and not be tempted to become a rival; it would also make possible an adjustment of his duties to his particular talents. A series of different assignments over a period of time would enable him to acquire a wider knowledge of the operations of government as a whole." "In this way," adds

Kallenbach, "he could be given a better opportunity than at present to prepare himself for the responsibility of serving as chief executive in case fate should thrust the role upon him." [10]

Kallenbach's reasoning may strike some people as naïvely rational, ignoring both the political reasons for selecting vice presidents and the seemingly inevitable strained relations between president and vice president. We shall treat this second phenomenon in a moment. But first, it is useful to consider whether abler or more outstanding individuals would seek the vice-presidency if the job held promise as a challenging and explicitly defined executive post.

Dozens of able people have rejected invitations to the vice-presidential nomination. Increasingly, however, there are some signs that able individuals have sought out the job, with all its underdefined and hybrid qualities. In 1920 Franklin Roosevelt ran for the vice-presidential nomination and won it, only to see the Democratic ticket go down to defeat. In 1956 John F. Kennedy made a vigorous effort to capture his party's vice-presidential nomination and nearly won it. Hubert H. Humphrey and Nelson Rockefeller waged quiet but concentrated campaigns for selection as vice president. Since FDR, Eisenhower has been the only president who had no connection with the vice-presidency as far as his own career was concerned. Doubtless several have sought out the post because the post does now carry added responsibilities and because everyone is more aware of the likelihood of vice presidents becoming president. The post may also be sought out because thirteen vice presidents have become president and the office has strategic political visibility. Moreover, in the twentieth century all of the so-called accidental presidents later were elected president in their own right.

Suppose that in addition to knowing that the vice president would not have ex-officio Senate duties, a vice-presidential nominee and everyone else concerned knew that he would hold a cabinet post — State, Defense, Treasury, or perhaps chairman of the Domestic Council or director of the Office of Management and Budget. This need not be a constitutional assignment, but rather one that would be understood to be held at the pleasure of the president. Wouldn't the vice-presidency then be more attractive and important? Should a future president put into effect former president Nixon's cabinet consolidation reform (decreasing the number of cabinet posts), the attractiveness of the vice-presidency would be enhanced even further. A vice president might serve, should he be reelected with his president for a second term (as eight have been), in one cabinet post one term and another during the next. Or certain emergencies might warrant his being shifted to a different department in mid-term.

Some observers argue that a vice president would surely be compromised by the narrow concerns of the clientele and constituencies of any single department. Surely this could occur, but the larger counseling departments and their corresponding central review staffs in the executive office, which usually make up the inner cabinet, seldom have suffered from that affliction compared to the labor, agriculture, commerce, and transportation agencies. Former secretary of state James Byrnes believed that "a vice president who has been elected by the people would be assured of a degree of cooperation from department officials and members of Congress that would not be accorded an appointed official. The people and the politicians will realize that he may at any time become President." [11]

However, this arrangement might affect a president's selection of a vice president. He might pick, for example, someone who would run a department well but was not well known to the public-at-large, or who was without broad political experience. Would this kind of risk be good to take with a potential successor? Some students of the presidency advise against putting an elected running mate anywhere near a major department. They reason this way: it is already difficult to make cabinet members responsive. As an elected department head, a vice president would be even tougher to make accountable or even to fire.

There are two other problems with this proposal. First, it is not wholly evident that a departmental secretary position provides presidential training. Under some circumstances it might, under others it clearly would not. How many recent department heads come readily to mind as especially promising presidential candidates? To be sure, Jefferson and Madison served as cabinet members prior to their presidencies, but so too did James Buchanan and Herbert Hoover. Second, nearly all members of a president's team either depend on him entirely for their status (i.e., the White House staff) or are national politicians seeking his job (i.e., some cabinet members) and already ensconced in a bureaucratic setting. A vice president has the disadvantages of both the cabinet members and White House aides with the advantages of neither. That is his basic problem and doubtless the reason this proposal is not given more reasoned consideration.

THE "THROTTLEBOTTOM COMPLEX"

Alexander Throttlebottom was a character in the successful 1930s Broadway play *Of Thee I Sing* by George S. Kaufman and Morrie Ryskind. Throttlebottom was a stumbling, mumbling caricature of an unemployed vice president. Neglected by his president, John P. Wintergreen, Throttlebottom is artfully drawn as an unknown, an unwanted, and an improbable national leader. Not only did he not want to be vice president or know what was expected of him, but he was even refused the right to resign. The character of Throttlebottom provided for splendid satire and comic relief, but the mocking portrait lives on and the name has become a familiar term for the real plight of contemporary vice presidents.

The estrangement of vice presidents from presidents began with Adams and

Washington. Washington's biographers tell us that relations between the two were civil but scarcely friendly. During his tenure as vice president, Thomas Jefferson refused diplomatic assignments from Adams. And Jefferson said of Aaron Burr, his first vice president, that he was a "crooked gun whose aim or shot you could never be sure of." Time and again relations between presidents and vice presidents are strained, abrasive, and cold to the point of open hostility. A few examples drawn from the accounts of observers underscore the unusual and mutual frustration.

Roosevelt and John Nance Garner:

The once cordial relations between the two men had long since turned sour. They had little contact except at cabinet meetings, where Garner, red and glowering, occasionally took issue with the President in a truculent manner. Roosevelt hinted he would desert the Democratic cause before he would vote for the Texan for President (in 1940). By early 1940 even official relations between the two men had almost ceased; Roosevelt was hoping that the Vice President would not show up for cabinet meetings. The President was gleeful about Garner's tribulations as a presidential candidate....[12]

Eisenhower and Nixon:

It seems clear that President Eisenhower was neither close to nor fond of Richard Nixon. He accepted him on his 1952 ticket on the advice of several political advisers but as much because he (Eisenhower) was tired and Nixon came from California as any other reason. However, Eisenhower tried to relieve himself of Nixon on at least three occasions, 1952, 1956, and 1960. After revelations about the "Nixon Fund" in 1952, Ike was for getting Nixon off the ticket. In 1956 Eisenhower continually suggested that Nixon move out of the vice presidency post and into the cabinet. Nixon recalled: "The impression I got was that he was really trying to tell me that he wanted me off the ticket." And in 1960, of course, the President had several other people he preferred over Nixon — most notably his Secretary of the Treasury Robert Anderson.

John F. Kennedy and Lyndon B. Johnson:

They made his stay in the Vice Presidency the most miserable three years of his life. He wasn't the number two man in that administration; he was the lowest man on the totem pole. Though he has never said this to anyone (perhaps because his pride would never let him admit it) I know him well enough to know he felt humiliated time and time again, that he was openly snubbed by second-echelon White House staffers who snickered at him behind his back and called him "Uncle Cornpone." [13]

Richard M. Nixon and Spiro Agnew:

Nixon barely knew Agnew when he selected him in Miami Beach in 1968. Nixon, himself, had been humiliated in the vice-presidential job, a job he called, a hollow shell — the most ill conceived and poorly defined position in the American political system. He proceeded nonetheless to visit an even greater humiliation on Agnew. By most accounts Agnew was scorned by the White House staff. He was assigned nothing of importance and only his attacks on the media — the initiative was actually his own — will ever be remembered.

Agnew himself viewed the vice-presidency as a "damned peculiar situation to be in, to have authority and a title and responsibility with no real power to do anything." His distance from Nixon and the White House was such that during the height of the Watergate coverup Barry Goldwater could contend, "If there is one thing the Vice President can back up it's that he doesn't know what the hell is going on at the White House." [14]

Some of Agnew's staff contend he was lazy and quite bored with policy matters. Some White House staff sources remember that Agnew even considered resigning before his first term was completed. Apparently he was very unhappy in the office. In any event, his experience was truly an instance of the White House feeling that it owned the office. His experience also fits Arthur Schlesinger's generalization that the vice-presidency is less a *making* than a *maiming* experience. Asked by reporters in his fifth year as vice president what his role was, Agnew answered: "Quite candidly the President hasn't defined my role yet." Asked again two weeks later he had to respond: "I'm still waiting for the President to think through that situation." Meanwhile his staff had been cut back 30 percent.[15]

Why does the "Throttlebottom Complex" persist? Is there something congenitally or structurally deficient in the relationship between the presidency and the vice-presidency? Does the relationship always have to be hollow, hostile, and counterproductive? "Mistrust is inherent in the relationship," writes Arthur Schlesinger. Vice Presidents are "intolerable reminders of their president's own mortality." [16] This mistrust is also not without historical foundation. Previous vice presidents have turned against their presidents, mobilizing opposition in the Congress, proposing alternative legislative programs, and preparing to run for the presidency itself against the president they were then serving. Calhoun became so disenchanted that he simply resigned the office. Coolidge's Charles Dawes refused to honor his president's request to attend cabinet meetings.

For at least our first 150 years, presidents viewed vice presidents as more an official of the legislative branch than a member of the executive branch. Their offices were on Capitol Hill, their most explicit constitutional job to preside over the Senate. Lyndon Johnson was the first vice president to be given a suite of offices in the Executive Office Building next to the west wing of the White House. Still, the job description for the vice-presidency is cloudy and undefined. To be sure, almost every president pledges at the outset that he is going to upgrade the office, make it more meaningful, and insure that his vice president will be the best informed in history.

Although some progress has been made, a psychological barrier, an intangible distance, still seems to mitigate against a significant delegation of power to a vice president. Schlesinger is no doubt correct that vice presidents do remind a president of their mortality. Doubtless most presidents are in constant fear of being upstaged. The vice president is the only other nationally elected politician, and it is no matter that voters do not really vote for the vice president, that whether a person becomes vice president depends almost entirely upon the relative popularity of the candidate for president.

Even so, if the presidential job is now so swollen and burdensome, why wouldn't a president welcome a major contribution from vice presidents? This, in fact, has seldom been the case. Indeed, there is reason to believe that most presidents consciously assign jobs that are unpresidential in character. Thus, Alan Otten, the *Wall Street Journal* political analyst, can write: "The very fact that a problem is turned over to the Vice President argues that it's not very important, or that the Vice President actually is going to play a far less critical role in solving it than announced, or that the President recognizes the impossibility of solving the problem and therefore wants to stay as far away from the whole thing as possible." [17]

Some vice presidents refuse to accept demeaning jobs. Lyndon Johnson, for example, just went into a retreat or eclipse. Others willingly become partisan "hit-men," straight-arming the press, slashing back at presidential opponents, and stumping endlessly for the reelection of friendly members of Congress. Thus, Spiro Agnew was used as a mouthpiece and as a surrogate presidential speaker at partisan events. Nixon told Theodore White in 1972 that Agnew, not Nixon, would circulate to support congressional candidates: "That's his job, that's a Vice President's job. I did it in 1956...." [18]

Often, it is as if a vice president is entirely unacceptable and unwanted unless he is willing to merge his identity completely with that of the president. The following passages from a televised "Conversation with Vice President Hubert H. Humphrey" illustrate how one recent vice president seemingly cast his own personal ambitions to the wind and vowed nearly feudal homage to his president:

I did not become Vice President with President Johnson to cause him trouble. I feel a deep sense of loyalty and fidelity. I believe that if you can't have that you have no right to accept the office. Because today it is so important that a President and his Vice President be on the same wave length....

I'd hate to have the President be worried about me, that I may do something that would cause him embarrassment or that would injure his Administration....

There are no Humphrey people, there are no Humphrey policies, there are no Humphrey programs. Whatever we have we should try to contribute, if it's wanted, to the President and his Administration. You can't have two leaders of the Executive Branch at one time.... [19]

In spite of this pious, subservient bending of himself "to lean over backwards," Humphrey was never really trusted by LBJ. One of his former aides told the author: "Humphrey was the victim of the White House and especially of domestic aide Joe Califano time and time again. Humphrey frequently sought more substantive assignments but only to be shot down. Overall his work boiled down mainly to 'politicking' on behalf of the President and the party — work that a good National Committee chairman could have done just as well." Johnson would simply exclude Humphrey from his team of insiders whenever the vice president sought independence or tried to develop his own line of thinking. This was especially true in the case of occasional policy differences he had with Johnson over the Vietnam war. To get on the good side of LBJ and back on the team again Humphrey had to yield. "The way to come on board would be to sell the war to his liberal constituents, or failing that, at least to fend them off, to neutralize their liberal voices with his liberal voice." [20]

When is loyalty to a president carried too far? Vice Presidents Humphrey, Agnew, and Ford became such apologists for their administrations that they could not help but diminish their credibility, perhaps undermining their own future capacity to provide serious leadership. Is the problem simply one of selecting better people to run for the office? "There is nothing wrong with the vice presidency that honorable, talented men cannot overcome" writes Irving Williams, who has written two books on the office. Williams seems to be saying that if we have better vice presidents we would have a better vice-presidency. If only a president likes and trusts his vice president, then all would be well; he could "be busy in a variety of ways: as another pair of eyes and ears at home and abroad, he can lighten the President's load by taking on ceremonial assignments; he can be an effective liaison with Congress — especially with the Senate; he may even have administrative work assigned him." [21]

Recent experience suggests, however, that not only will presidents not trust their vice presidents but the relationship in terms of real assignments will be a limited one. Can a vice president — even an outstanding one — become a significant force in the presidential establishment? Or was John Nance Garner correct when he reasoned that a great person may be vice president but can't be a great vice president because the office in itself is unimportant. Perhaps Nelson Rockefeller will be a test case, although people clearly differ as to whether he is a "great man." (Even if Rockefeller succeeds in this office, it may well be due more to the character of the Ford presidency and his unique rise to the office of the president than to Rockefeller's competence or the usefulness of the vice-presidency.) In any event, it may turn out to be next to impossible to relate a vice president's performance to the results of an administration's policy. In the past, however, we could say with some confidence that how the vice-presidency works and the behavior of vice presidents had negligible significance on the policies of the government.

VICE PRESIDENTS AS CABINET COUNSELLORS
AND "ASSISTANT PRESIDENTS"

Corporate officials are often baffled with the way presidents seldom make serious use of their vice presidents. The trend in top management circles in the private sector, particularly in recent years, has been to form corporate managerial teams. The chief executive officer usually relies quite heavily on an executive vice president and a vice president for finance, a vice president for marketing, and often a series of group vice presidents heading up major divisions or subsidiary companies. Collegial leadership, although not always a success in practice, is a celebrated ideal in business communities. The talented chief executive in the private sector delegates well and delegates often. Nurturing up-and-coming executive talent is widely applauded.

Why, then, do we find such a contrary phenomenon in the Executive Office of the President? (Of course, presidents do delegate some of their responsibilities — but seldom to vice presidents, who are considered outsiders. Rather, they delegate to their own insiders, such as Harry Hopkins, Joseph Califano, and H. R. Haldeman.) Have presidents tried to nurture their vice presidents, assigning them important executive apprenticeship experiences? Have vice presidents been called upon to serve as cabinet counsellors, policy advisers, and "assistant presidents"? Rarely.

The cabinet is as nebulous an entity as the vice-presidency. But a brief examination of vice-presidential involvement in the cabinet helps to illustrate the changing, if still limited, vice-presidential executive portfolio.

George Washington conferred on occasion with vice president John Adams, but Adams only acted in his official executive capacity one time, when he attended a cabinet meeting in 1791. Washington was away and wanted his department heads to get together in his absence, and he requested Adams to join them. It was the last time, so many reports have it, that a vice president was to attend an official cabinet meeting until Woodrow Wilson's Thomas R. Marshall substituted for his boss when the latter was in Europe in December 1918.

Jefferson declined President Adam's invitation to attend cabinet meetings. Other vice presidents for the next 120 years stayed away from the cabinet sessions — either by personal or presidential desire, usually both. However, President Warren Harding invited his vice president, Calvin Coolidge, to come to cabinet meetings, thus reviving the practice George Washington had begun. FDR's second vice president, Henry Wallace, who had already served two terms as secretary of Agriculture, was the first vice president to be assigned major administrative duties. Roosevelt made Wallace chairman, successively, of the Economic Defense Board, the Supply Priorities and Allocations Board, the War Productions Board, and the Board of Economic Warfare. In the latter post Wallace became an aggressive administrator and an outspoken advocate. "Wallace was restless with the failure of the American government to set forth in clear detail a plan for the future that would lift the spirits and galvanize the wills of men everywhere. He fretted not the least because the relative silence from the White House permitted other voices to seem louder and more persuasive than in his opinion they should have." [22]

Henry Wallace was idealistic, stubborn, and outspoken. He cherished the idea of succeeding Roosevelt as president, but he was always loyal. Roosevelt delegated considerable authority to Wallace — authority to oversee much of the domestic economy — strategic imports, exports, shipping, foreign exchange, and related matters. But his political base as vice president and the authority delegated to him proved inadequate to his responsibilities. Wallace fast became embroiled in a massive collision with the departments of State and Commerce, and with secretaries Cordell Hull and Jesse H. Jones, in particular. Both men vigorously defended their departments from nearly every Wallace intrusion. Both men attacked Wallace viciously, Jones often in public.

To perform his executive assignments Wallace had to secure State's and Commerce's approval with some frequency, but his efforts were in vain. He sought Roosevelt's approval for enlarging his authority to correspond with his duties, but Roosevelt yielded only a little. For a year-and-a-half — 1942 to June of 1943 — Wallace sought to make a go of it; but after several public skirmishes and open warfare between the vice president and the secretary of commerce, Roosevelt abolished Wallace's board. "He transferred its functions to a new superagency, the Office of Economic Warfare," and appointed a chairman quite unlike Wallace "whose ability to flatter the President and to placate Congress considerably exceeded his taste for reform or his personal probity." [23] So ended a year-and-a-half experiment of having a vice president serve as an administrator. By most standards it was an experiment that failed, although factors other than the office of the vice-presidency were involved. Thus, some people would claim that this failure was primarily due to Wallace's stubborn and apolitical temperament. Others might contend, perhaps correctly, that Roosevelt never gave Wallace adequate authority with which to do the job assigned him. In any event, the Wallace example stands out as the sole instance up to the present of serious administrative responsibilities being delegated to a vice president.

Since 1943 vice presidents have, however, been invited to cabinet meetings and related policy councils with some regularity. By a 1949 amendment to the National Security Act of 1947, the vice president now sits as a regular member of the National Security Council. Since the Eisenhower presidency, the vice president has been made the cabinet's acting chairman in the president's absence. Nixon chaired several cabinet sessions during Eisenhower's several illnesses. LBJ and Humphrey chaired several presidential-level councils and commissions, and, like Wallace and Nixon before them, they travelled widely as goodwill ambassadors as well as on some sensitive policy missions. FDR actually began the tradition of sending vice presidents abroad; John N. Garner was FDR's representative at the installation of a Philippine president in 1935 and Henry Wallace as vice president traveled to Latin America as well as to China and Siberia. Nixon traveled to 54 countries, LBJ to more than 30. Humphrey and Agnew were often sent to visit Asia. By executive order the vice president has been a member of the Domestic Council since 1970. And both Hubert Humphrey and Spiro Agnew were asked to serve as a liaison with mayors and governors. Agnew headed the Intergovernmental Relations Council until December 1972, when it was phased out and its duties transferred to the Domestic Council.

Nearly every vice president in recent times has found it difficult to impose on cabinet members. The departmental secretaries preside over congressionally authorized departments; hence, a vice president is very much an intruder unless a problem arises which is definitely interdepartmental. Even then, what is an interdepartmental matter to some may not be to others. Spiro Agnew described the problem:

I don't really see that a Vice President can be given a direct line assignment. Suppose the President handed me an assignment in a field that conflicts with a Cabinet Officer's direct responsibility? That would be automatic trouble because I'd be stepping on his toes. So usually what the Vice President is given to do cuts across Cabinet lines, like dealing with revenue sharing. I think President Nixon views the Vice President as a spokesman for Administration policy. He is not dealing with conflicting interests within the government. He is dealing more with expressing established policy to opinion leaders throughout the country.[24]

Vice President Humphrey, for a somewhat different set of reasons, learned that being vice president was sometimes more a liability than an asset in collaborating with cabinet officials. Halberstam reports, for example, that the administration's key Vietnam War policy-making officials for a time became wary of being seen with the vice president: "he had become a cripple and everyone knew it" and to keep on the right side of LBJ they shied away from HHH. "When Humphrey's people heard in the early months of 1965 that George Ball was making a major stand against the war, they had thought it might be a good idea if Ball and Humphrey got together, since they were both working in the same general area." But soon after a Humphrey aide approached a Ball aide it became clear, "that the Ball people did not want Humphrey involved; his assistance was not, so to speak, an asset. And Humphrey remained cut off and isolated." [25]

Nixon under Eisenhower had also learned that being a vice president was something altogether different than being a cabinet secretary with administrative responsibilities. Eisenhower had encouraged Nixon on several occasions to take a cabinet post in the second term. "You should," Eisenhower told

Nixon, "make a searching survey of the probable advantages and disadvantages to yourself and to the party before you give me an answer." [26] But the insecure Nixon refused to consider taking himself off the ticket, feeling, doubtless correctly, that politicians and the press would interpret his removal from the ticket as a demotion, or even a political dumping. In the vice-presidency he had a four-year incumbency with a fair possibility of becoming president if anything happened to Eisenhower. As a cabinet official he would have had more responsibilities but he would serve at the pleasure of the president; and if he did poorly or was made to look as if he were doing poorly, he could be readily eased out.

Thus Nixon held on dearly to the vice-presidency. There, with a staff of less than twenty, he launched his campaign for the presidency, making highly publicized overseas trips and shouldering some of the routine Republican party chores that Eisenhower liked to avoid. Still, the job of the vice president remained very ad hoc and lacked coherence. After nearly eight years of occupying the post, Nixon had not apparently been able to contribute much, if anything, to the administration's public policy. Thus the following exchange between a reporter and Eisenhower on 24 August 1960:

Q. *We understand that the power of decision is entirely yours, Mr. President. I just wondered if you could give us an example of a major idea of his (Nixon's) that you had adopted in that role, as the decider and final....*
President Eisenhower: *If you give me a week, I might think of one. I don't remember.*[27]

Both Presidents Hoover and Eisenhower recommended the creation of an additional appointed vice-presidental post. Hoover advocated an administrative vice president; Eisenhower a "first secretary of government" for foreign affairs. Neither proposal received much attention. More recently, Milton Eisenhower urged the creation of two executive vice presidents, to be appointed by the president — one to deal with domestic policy, the other with international affairs, but both to work "in close collaboration with the President." Milton Eisenhower claims that the elected vice president cannot hope to do what appointed vice presidents could. First, he says, echoing his older brother, the elected vice president is not a member of the executive branch. Second:

Even though he normally is suggested to a convention by the presidential nominee as a running mate, there is no guarantee that he will be in agreement with the President; there is no legal bar to his openly disagreeing with the President. Vice Presidents have often disagreed with Chief Executives. Vice President Dawes frequently and openly advocated the passage of legislation which President Coolidge denounced and vetoed. Most important of all, the President cannot discharge the elected Vice President. This point is critical. In any organization delegation of authority is workable only if the chief executive has absolute confidence in the individual to whom he del-

egates some of his own duties, and this confidence exists only if there is mutual trust, a shared philosophy, and a recognition by the subordinate that final authority always rests with the chief; should directives of the President be unacceptable to the appointed Executive Vice President, and he felt that he could not loyally do what was expected of him, he would have to resign or be removed by the President.[28]

This reform suggestion of Eisenhower's seems based on the premise that from a president's point of view, it is easier to take an assistant president from his staff and make him vice president than it is to take a vice president and make him an assistant president.

This proposal of Eisenhower's raises the much debated question of whether we need an elected vice president. If, as seems the case, we neither elect vice presidents anyway — that they come as part of a package deal — nor use them intelligently, then Arthur Schlesinger's argument makes sense:

> *There is no escape . . . from the conclusion that the Vice Presidency is not only a pointless but even a dangerous office. A politician is nominated for Vice President for reasons unconnected with his presidential qualities and elected to the Vice Presidency as part of a tie-in sale. Once carried to the Vice Presidency not on his own but as second rider on the presidential horse, where is he? If he is a first-rate man, his nerve and confidence will be shaken, his talents wasted and soured, even as his publicity urges him on toward the ultimate office for which, the longer he serves in the second place, the less ready he may be. If he is not a first-rate man he should not be in a position to inherit or claim the Presidency. Why not therefore abolish this mischievous office and work out a more sensible mode of succession?* [29]

SHOULD WE ABOLISH THE VICE-PRESIDENCY?

Most students of the vice-presidency have wanted to reform it, not abolish it. Some have suggested, as discussed earlier, that the office should be moved from the legislative branch to the executive branch. "Surely we should raise the status of the Vice President and legally amplify the duties and responsibilities of that office in order that the Chief Executive is given all possible help in carrying his crippling load," wrote James F. Byrnes.[30] His view seemed to be supported by public opinion data. The Gallup organization asked in May of 1948 whether the vice-presidency should be given more duties, and the vast majority responded affirmatively.[31]

Q. *"It has been suggested that the Vice President should help the President with administrative problems so that the President would have more time to deal with matters of policy. Do you agree or disagree with this idea?"*

A. *Agree*   *80%*

   Disagree   *8*

   No opinion   *12*
   ———
   Total   *100%*

Most politicians and scholars have also held that the vice-presidency is needed to provide continuity in case of death, disability, resignation, or removal of a president. Such occasions are traumatic and destabilizing for the nation. "It is my judgment that we need some prompt means of presidential succession, so that government can proceed in an orderly manner and the inevitable confusion and possible chaos that could come from any prolonged delay in filling the presidential office can be avoided," writes former vice president Hubert Humphrey.[32] Senator Birch Bayh contends that "the nation longs for stability, for a heightened sense of continuity with an understood heritage. Improbable as it may seem, given the very recent history of the vice presidency, that office may now turn out to be just that sort of stabilizing, reassuring force." [33]

Let's reform it, not abolish it, has been the response from the two major parties as well. In short, they have taken the stand that it would not be too difficult to alter the selection process and upgrade the functions of the office to make it vital and useful — one that could attract high-caliber people and prepare them for the responsibilities of the presidency. It is suggested, too, that no job can fully train or prepare people for the presidency, but that the vice-presidency can be refashioned to do that job as well as any other post. Certainly a vice president has a lot of time on his hands to serve as an understudy.

Both parties have investigated improvements in the nominations and selection process. Senator Eagleton suggested that presidential candidates should pick running mates before the primaries and run with them as a team. Senator Humphrey urged that in order to evaluate systematically vice-presidential candidates, the conventions should allow a presidential nominee either an extra day or, if necessary, a period of three weeks to select a running mate.

Then there are those who argue that the choice of a vice-presidential nominee ought to be thrown open to the convention, making the selection more democratic. Several names could be offered to the delegates, either by the presidential nominee or by some other appointed screening committee, and the delegates could be the final judges, as in the 1956 Democratic Convention. Still others, in both parties, propose that candidates for both president and vice president campaign and be elected separately, not as a team or package deal as is the case now. The advocates of this plan are apparently willing to accept the possibility of having occasionally a president from one party and a vice president from another. They point out that we already often have a president from one party and a Congress from another. Reformers have suggested, too, that perhaps the nomination for the vice-presidency should precede the nomination for president. Eugene McCarthy has suggested, tongue-in-cheek presumably, that we nominate the vice president and then let him choose the presidential candidate. (That's one way to resolve the Throttlebottom problems.)

More radical is Michael Novak's proposal that what we really need to do is to separate the presidency into two functions: the head of state and the chief executive. "What we can do, perhaps, is establish a head of state to greet foreign dignitaries and to visit them abroad, to officiate on occasions when a personification of the nation is required, to become the central figure even at the inauguration of the chief executives, and to live at the White House. The chief executive who would be elevated every four years as at present, would live as cabinet members live." [34]

Novak contends that our deep-seated need for symbolic and ceremonial leadership requires this separation. Perhaps another way to say it is that our needs point toward a symbolic, ceremonial leader, but good government requires that this be separated from the actual head of government. Human beings, he claims, are symbolic animals and thus it is idle to think we can somehow ignore or wish away the symbolic power of the national leader. As things now stand, he notes, we cannot help responding to presidents with all the extra affect of an appropriate response to a head of state. Hence Novak suggests:

> A president may hold all the powers and responsibilities for foreign affairs and domestic management now in his possession, while being stripped of his role as personifier of the national identity, and be greatly liberated, not impeded, in his performance of his daily duties. It is true that he would lose some of the magic and mysticism surrounding his present office. It is true that living outside the White House and working in closer proximity to the working offices of the Senate and the House, he would not be held in quite the awe his present eminence now affords him. But his actual administrative authority would remain clear and untrammeled. . . .
>
> A chief of state, meanwhile, would be elected at the beginning of each decade. By his prior career and his personality he would furnish to that decade part of its symbolic character. He would be charged with reinforcing ceremonially all those qualities among citizens that make a nation civilized, accomplished and creative.[35]

Novak does not specify how his proposal could be implemented nor does he relate his recommendation to the existing vice-presidential office. In any event, beguiling and perhaps prescient as the Novak innovation might be, it isn't likely that it will be seriously considered, let alone be heeded in this country.

Is there really a satisfactory way of selecting a vice president? Most careful students of this office are coming to the conclusion, many of them reluctantly, that both the traditional means of selection and the more recently posed alternatives have grievous flaws. All of this took on added weight in the mid-1970s, when neither the president nor the vice president were popularly elected.

One suggested intermediate step, one that could partially solve the undesirable aspects of the Twenty-fifth Amendment, is the idea of a special election for a vice president if that office is vacated. Ex-governor Endicott Peabody, among others, has proposed this remedy. In 1952 the Gallup Poll organization put a somewhat modified version before the public.[36]

Q. *"It has been suggested that if a President dies while in office, the Vice President should then serve as President only until the next general election or a maximum of two years. Do you approve or disapprove of such a law?"*

A. *Approve*   *61%*

   Disapprove   *30*

   No opinion   *9*

     Total   *100%*

If the idea of a special election for vice president makes sense and is also more democratic than our current practice, why not go one step further and hold a special election for president in case of death, disability, resignation, or removal? Why not, in the case of such a need, have a caretaker government presided over by a designated cabinet member (e.g., the secretary of state, defense, or treasury)? At the end of a ninety-day period we could have a special election to fill the presidency until the next regularly scheduled quadrennial election. The designated cabinet officer would become acting president instantly upon death, disability, or removal. He would not be subject to congressional inquiry or congressional confirmation. "If the person who succeeds to the presidency is to be considered legitimate the plan for determining who he will be should be as stable as possible so that it can gather force from longevity and tradition. Stability is a desirable standard because it gives the greatest assurance that the plan will be known by the largest number of citizens." [37]

Will the person who is acting president for ninety days be effective enough to handle the job? Much can happen in ninety days — especially if the nation lacks confidence in the acting president. Aaron Wildavsky warned, for example:

A man who is in office for only a short period of time, and who must soon give way to another person, can hardly be expected to act with confidence, vigor, and dispatch. At best, he could undertake holding actions because he could not commit the executive branch to any policy that lasted beyond a few months. Weakness, indecision, futility, even challenges of the right of a temporary occupant to act like a President would be the most likely consequences of failing to allow a successor to serve until the end of the established presidential term." [38]

If the vice-presidency, with all its failings, at least provides for a reasonable and psychologically secure transition, then any alternative plan would seem to have to do as well. These are real concerns, although the advantages of stability and continuity may be overestimated and the equal if not more important need of securing democratically elected presidents and skilled national political leaders favors overhauling the present arrangement.

The multiple problems of selection and usage that now cripple or depreciate the vice-presidency could simply be eliminated by eliminating the office itself.

The Throttlebottom complex would be solved. We would stop elevating to the presidency individuals who have not really won election. Presidents could appoint one or more vice presidents along the lines suggested by Milton Eisenhower. "If the principle be accepted — the principle that if a President vanishes, it is better for the people to elect a new president than endure a Vice President who was never voted for that office, who became Vice President for reasons other than his presidential qualifications and who may very well have been badly damaged by his vice presidential experience — the problem is one of working out the mechanics of the intermediate election. This is not easy but far from impossible." [39]

At the heart of the matter is whether we want to be a government of and by the people. It is widely acknowledged that we choose vice presidents for the wrong reasons. It is equally clear, however, that today the vice-presidency has become a major steppingstone either to the presidency directly or at least to presidential nomination. Twenty-five percent of our presidents did not serve out the terms they were serving. Thirteen vice presidents have become president, nine accidentally (see Table 8.1). Twenty-eight percent of our presidents have been vice presidents; in this century, six out of thirteen.

To be sure, many will say that the nation could not afford a special election after a presidential death, as in 1945 or in 1963; but many other Western nations do so regularly. Others argue that intermediate elections violate the tradition of quadrennial elections. But what is so compelling or virtuous about waiting until that fourth year if what is at question is the quality and character of the nation's leadership? Moreover, the special election would merely be to fill out the remainder of the departed president's term. Would this new arrangement be a departure from the intent and spirit of the Founding Fathers? With Arthur Schlesinger, the author is persuaded that it would not: "Quite the contrary: we would be reaffirming their view — and what view could be more sensible for a self-governing democracy? — that the Chief Magistrate of the United States must, except for the briefest periods, be a person elected to that office by the people." [40]

To summarize: The vice-presidency has had a mixed history at best, and basically serves the nation poorly. We now have had nine examples of what happens when a vice president is forced by necessity to become president. These instances have not been our finest hour, although a few of them have produced adequate presidents. What is more disturbing, however, is that an assessment of those who have mercifully not become president, from Aaron Burr to Spiro Agnew, is not in the least reassuring. As one writer aptly put it, "If the presidential nominee or some body of politicians selects the VP, there is enormous pressure to subordinate considerations of presidential ability to those of vote-getting power. If the voters are to make the decision in some kind of primary system, one wonders whether people of presidential caliber will seek an office whose duties are so limited." [41]

TABLE 8–1 VICE PRESIDENTS AND THEIR TERMS

Vice President	Term	President
1. John Adams	1789–97	Washington
2. Thomas Jefferson	1797–1801	J. Adams
3. Aaron Burr	1801–05	Jefferson
4. George Clinton	1805–09	Jefferson
George Clinton[a]	1809–12	Madison
5. Elbridge Gerry[a]	1813–14	Madison
6. Daniel D. Thompkins	1817–25	Monroe
7. John C. Calhoun	1825–29	J. Q. Adams
John C. Calhoun[b]	1829–32	Jackson
8. Martin Van Buren	1833–37	Jackson
9. Richard M. Johnson	1837–41	Van Buren
10. John Tyler[c]	1841	W. H. Harrison
11. George M. Dallas	1845–49	Polk
12. Millard Fillmore[c]	1849–50	Taylor
13. William R. D. King[a]	1853	Pierce
14. John C. Breckinridge	1857–61	Buchanan
15. Hannibal Hamlin	1861–65	Lincoln
16. Andrew Johnson[c]	1865	Lincoln
17. Schuyler Colfax	1869–73	Grant
18. Henry Wilson[a]	1873–75	Grant
19. William A. Wheeler	1877–81	Hayes
20. Chester A. Arthur[c]	1881	Garfield
21. Thomas A. Hendricks[a]	1885	Cleveland

The verdict of history is harsh on the vice-presidency. The office has done only one thing well, solving our succession problem, and it is open to question whether it has done even that well enough. The vice-presidency in presidential government makes the presidency neither more manageable nor more democratic and accountable. Earl Warren cautioned that "alternatives proposed in times of distrust and confusion are likely to develop more problems than they wish to solve." [42] But the distrust and confusion caused by the vice-presidency in our form of government has been endured for too long. Hence, as we move into our third century one structural reform we should consider is that of eliminating the "elected" vice-presidency. As one of the growing number of adherents of this point of view put it: "Let us get rid of the office before it sinks us. With electronics and television to help us, we certainly can manage a special election for the President. The Constitution was designed for amendment. Only decadent societies cling desperately to methods that practice has proved faulty and common sense rejects." [43] One side benefit of this reform might be an increased incentive for the opposition party to form some kind of

TABLE 8–1 *(Continued)*

Vice President	Term	President
22. Levi P. Morton	1889–93	B. Harrison
23. Adlai E. Stevenson	1893–97	Cleveland
24. Garret A. Hobart[a]	1897–99	McKinley
25. Theodore Roosevelt[c]	1901	McKinley
26. Charles W. Fairbanks	1905–09	T. Roosevelt
27. James S. Sherman[a]	1909–12	Taft
28. Thomas R. Marshall	1913–21	Wilson
29. Calvin Coolidge[c]	1921–23	Harding
30. Charles G. Dawes	1925–29	Coolidge
31. Charles Curtis	1929–33	Hoover
32. John N. Garner	1933–41	F. Roosevelt
33. Henry A. Wallace	1941–45	F. Roosevelt
34. Harry S Truman[c]	1945	F. Roosevelt
35. Alben W. Barkley	1949–53	Truman
36. Richard M. Nixon	1953–61	Eisenhower
37. Lyndon B. Johnson[c]	1961–63	Kennedy
38. Hubert H. Humphrey	1965–69	Johnson
39. Spiro T. Agnew[b]	1969–73	Nixon
40. Gerald R. Ford[c]	1973–74	Nixon
41. Nelson A. Rockefeller	1974–	Ford

[a] Died in office (total number to date = 7).
[b] Resigned office (total number to date = 2).
[c] Succeeded directly to the presidency (total number to date = 9).

shadow government, for under this new arrangement the opposition party (or parties) would have to be prepared to mount a national campaign at almost any time, subject to merely a few weeks notice.

A reform of the vice-presidency is not likely to alter the policy outcomes of our political system. The issues at stake here are ones of democratic procedure and political legitimacy. But these are very important concerns and should not be ignored. Precisely because the vice-presidency is our major steppingstone to the presidency, it is an office and an institution that needs to be reappraised. Upon reappraisal, this writer favors abolishing the elected vice-presidency.

NOTES

1. James M. Naughton, "Above the Battle," *New York Times Magazine*, 24 June 1973, p. 49.
2. Quoted in Leonard Baker, *The Johnson Eclipse: A President's Vice Presidency* (Macmillan, 1966), p. 27.

3. Roland Evans and Robert Novak, *Lyndon B. Johnson: The Exercise of Power* (New American Library, 1966), p. 307.
4. Baker, *The Johnson Eclipse*, p. 28.
5. Sam Houston Johnson, *My Brother Lyndon* (Cowles, 1970), p. 109.
6. Donald Young, *American Roulette: The History and Dilemma of the Vice Presidency* (Holt, Rinehart & Winston, 1972), p. 353–54.
7. Hubert H. Humphrey, "A Conversation with Hubert H. Humphrey," National Educational Television, April 1965.
8. Paul T. David, "The Vice Presidency: Its Institutional Evolution and Contemporary Status," *Journal of Politics,* November 1967, p. 733.
9. James F. Byrnes, *All In One Lifetime* (Harper & Bros., 1958), p. 233.
10. Joseph E. Kallenbach, *The American Chief Executive* (Harper & Row, 1966), pp. 234–35.
11. Byrnes, *All in One Lifetime,* p. 235.
12. James MacGregor Burns, *The Lion and The Fox* (Harcourt, Brace, 1956), p. 414.
13. Johnson, *My Brother Lyndon,* p. 108.
14. Naughton, "Above the Battle," p. 43.
15. Naughton, "Above the Battle," p. 11.
16. Arthur Schlesinger, Jr., "Is the Vice Presidency Necessary?," *Atlantic,* May 1974, p. 37.
17. Alan L. Otten, "Sorting Out a Role For the Veep," *Wall Street Journal,* 17 August 1972, p. 10.
18. Richard M. Nixon, quoted in Theodore White, *The Making of the President 1972* (Atheneum, 1973), p. 300.
19. "A Conversation with Hubert H. Humphrey," National Educational Television, April 1965.
20. David Halberstam, *The Best and the Brightest* (Random House, 1972), p. 535.
21. Irving G. Williams, "The American Vice Presidency," *Current History,* June 1974, p. 274.
22. John Morton Blum, ed., *The Price of Vision: The Diary of Henry A. Wallace 1942–1946* (Houghton Mifflin, 1973), p. 25.
23. *Ibid.,* p. 28.
24. Quoted in *Time,* 2 July 1973, p. 17.
25. Halberstam, *The Best and the Brightest,* p. 534.
26. See Peter Lyon, *Eisenhower: Portrait of the Hero* (Little, Brown, 1974), p. 823.
27. Ibid, p. 675.
28. Milton Eisenhower, *The President Is Calling* (Doubleday, 1974), pp. 540–41. In some respects, the Rockefeller vice-presidency has much in common with Milton Eisenhower's proposal and for these reasons may seem to be an exception to the pattern of vice-presidencies to which we have become accustomed.
29. Arthur Schlesinger, Jr., *The Imperial Presidency* (Popular Library, 1974), p. 481.
30. James F. Byrnes, *All In One Lifetime,* p. 237. Clark Clifford, an adviser of former presidents Truman and Johnson, also supported this constitutional change. See, House Subcommittee on Reorganization of the Committee on Government Operations Hearings, 84th Cong., 2d sess. 16–25 January 1956.
31. George H. Gallup, *The Gallup Poll, Public Opinion 1935–1971* (Random House, 1972), p. 734. Question and answer reprinted by permission.
32. Hubert Humphrey's comments are outlined in "On the Threshold of the White House," *Atlantic Monthly,* July 1974, p. 65.
33. Birch Bayh, *Atlantic Monthly,* July 1974, p. 70.
34. Michael Novak, *Choosing Our King* (Macmillan, 1974), pp. 263–64.
35. *Ibid.,* pp. 265–66.

36. Gallup, *The Gallup Poll, Public Opinion 1935–1971* (Random House, 1972), p. 1113. Question and answer reprinted by permission.
37. Aaron Wildavsky, "Presidential Succession and Disability: Policy Analysis for Unique Cases," in A. Wildavsky, ed., *The Presidency* (Little, Brown, 1969), p. 781.
38. Ibid., p. 781.
39. A. Schlesinger, *The Imperial Presidency*, p. 493.
40. A. Schlesinger, *The Imperial Presidency*, p. 494.
41. Earl Warren, "On the Threshold of the White House," *The Atlantic Monthly*, 1 July 1974, p. 68.
42. Michael Barone, "Why Not Abolish the Vice Presidency," *Washington Post*, 25 September 1972, p. A. 20.
43. Thomas B. Adams, "On the Threshold of the White House," *The Atlantic Monthly*, 1 July 1974, p. 72.

CHAPTER 9

THE SHAPING
OF THE PRESIDENCY
THE PRESIDENTIAL JOB DESCRIPTION
—A $200,000 G.S. 118?

*I do not have the overwhelming desire to be President which is
essential for the kind of campaign that is required. . . . I admire
those with the determination to do what is required to seek the
Presidency, but I have found that I am not among them.*

*[I like to] ponder issues, sit down with knowledgeable people and
talk about them, chew them over, read a book, let them rest a little,
reach a conclusion that I'm comfortable with and go to work.
All of that's out the window in a Presidential campaign, and I'd
never get a chance to think ideas over. . . .*

*Nationally, it's more theater than the politics I know. I kept getting
constant suggestions that I needed to buy different clothes and go
to speech instructors and spend two days in Hollywood with a
videotape machine. I hated that. . . .*

— *Senator Walter F. Mondale (announcing his withdrawal
from the 1976 presidential race)* New York Times,
1 December 1974, Week in Review *section.*

*And people talk about the powers of a President, all the powers
that a Chief Executive has, and what he can do. Let me tell you
something — from experience!*

*The President may have a great many powers given to him in
the Constitution and may have certain powers under certain laws
which are given to him by the Congress of the United States; but
the principal power that the President has is to bring people in
and try to persuade them to do what they ought to do without
persuasion. That's what the powers of the President amount to.*

— *Harry S Truman*, Public Papers of the President 1948,
Government Printing Office, 1949, p. 247.

Delegated responsibilities and inflated expectations so burden the modern presidency that for it to function as well as it does is a marvel. The gap between expectations and what can actually be achieved inevitably mars presidential credibility and makes the modern presidency vulnerable to the same kind of criticism that was leveled at institutions of national leadership under the Articles of Confederation in the 1780s. If it seems naive to expect presidents to solve intractable problems that we do not fully understand and cannot agree on, this is nonetheless what we continually do.

A more realistic outlook on what presidents acting alone can accomplish might help presidents concentrate on the practicable among their priorities. This would also bring out the fact that alternative strategies and even alternative institutions for leadership do exist for effecting needed innovations, and that these strategies and institutions need more support. Realistic expectations cannot by themselves strengthen the presidency, but they might relieve the load so that the president can better lead and administer in those critical areas in which the nation has little choice but to turn to him.

Exaggerated or false expectations encourage presidents and their staffs to attempt more than they can accomplish. False expectations invite presidents to overpromise and overextend themselves. False expectations also heighten the need for image-tending activities until these by themselves drain vast energies from the office. An advance-man mentality can easily capture the White House staff: nothing is too good for a president, according to this perspective; a president must be shielded from all annoyances, pampered with all conveniences, and protected from unpleasant realities. Finally, exaggerated expectations inhibit healthy public dissent and confrontation inside the executive branch over substantive matters.

A new realism about how much presidents can accomplish is badly needed. The relatively new and increasingly accentuated roles of the president as chief legislator and as national chaplain may be the undoing of the office of the president as chief executive. By directing too many aspirations at the presidency, visiting on it too many responsibilities, and turning to it as a chief source of moral inspiration, the nation risks overloading the office. We also invite a "fires-in-the-inbasket" performance where all attention goes to crises, producing a continual frenzy of new ad hoc proposals and making it difficult for presidents to admit mistakes.

What is required is far more public and congressional skepticism about plans, information, and forecasts handed out by presidents and their spokesmen. A less reverential and deferential attitude toward the presidency might put an end to the view that presidential decisions are somehow too sacrosanct for debate. One of the more salutary — and commonsense — reforms would be for presidents, presidential candidates, and writers on the presidency to admit on a regular basis that presidents are greatly dependent on a wide range of other people, among them elite interest groups as well as influential leaders in Congress, state capitals, city halls, the bureaucracy, and in the media. Such a change in attitude could result in improvement in the effectiveness of the president. Institutional myths divert public attention from the ways in which the presidency produces its failures. The imposition of more human standards would diminish the disquieting number and breadth of credibility gaps and the unseemly and damaging presidential attempts to strong-arm the press. Skepticism also might allay some of the emotional seesawing between solid support and harsh retribution.

Americans hold exaggerated expectations about the political process as a whole. They expect that a great proportion of national or local problems can somehow be alleviated through politics or government and that the right person at the right time in the right office (usually the presidency) can solve society's most complex problems. But the so-called executive virtues of unity, expertise, secrecy, and dispatch do not always characterize the contemporary presidency and most assuredly not the sprawling executive branch. On too many occasions, the executive branch is more aptly characterized as splintered, stumbling, leaky, and caught in a web of red tape and cost overruns. Many actions boldly proclaimed by a president in behalf of the public interest have an unreasonably high cost in terms of basic freedoms and civil liberties. Those persons who look to the presidency as a moral anchor or as the nation's hope for progressive, reformist breakthroughs must be mindful also of some of the more dubious presidential commitments of the recent past: the Bay of Pigs, the bombing of North Vietnam, the invasion of a handful of small nations, the spiraling arms race, the perpetuation of an unjust tax structure, Watergate, and the general permissiveness toward the white majority's reluctance to accept black and Spanish-speaking minorities on terms of equality.

The presidency is nearly always a mirror of the fundamental forces in society: the values, the myths, the quest for social control and stability, and the vast, inert, conservative forces that maintain the existing balance of interests. Needed is the practical realization that only rarely can a president succeed in bringing about large-scale innovative social changes, and that presidents who would be representatives and activists in behalf of the have-not sectors need extensive support from sizeable numbers of those in middle- and upper-income groups. We need to more fully appreciate that "the basic reason why neither Congress nor the President is truly liberal is that liberalism normally represents a minority position in the United States — a fact often obscured by the assumption that the Democratic Party is a liberal party, rather than an exceedingly broad coalition." [1]

One of the more effective ways of changing society, including the views of a president, is to work outside of the government, harnessing private resources toward specific goals. The conventional assumption that a presidential candidate possesses or embodies the solution to the most difficult national problems generally results in the dissipation of energies in last-minute campaigning that often could be put to more effective use in enlarging the coalition favorable to a desired policy change. And when necessary, such energies should be put to use devising the proper solutions, a goal that is notably ill-served both by the election process and by those hasty efforts of presidents to prove that they can get things done. More must be asked of the presidency today than it has given before, but let us not ask of it more than it can give.

The more we learn about the character and workings of the presidency, the more it appears that a president cannot act as a serious instigator of reforms in more than a few areas at a time. If a president is forced to respond to all the major issues of the day, he doubtless will be forced to respond mainly on the plane of symbolic and superficial politics. Such overloading invites a new kind of weakened presidency in an era in which many problems — such as inflation and recession — require strong longer-range measures. To insure that presidents do respond — and are to respond — to the most salient problems, to keep presidents accountable, the public should have recourse to vigorous education and political campaigns.

Simultaneously, a renewed respect for, and attention to, other institutions, in and out of government, would strengthen them as alternative sources of reform, policy experimentation, and problem-solving leadership. Congress should be encouraged to play a larger role as a forum for new policy ideas; courts should be encouraged to exercise their powers to curb the Congress and the executive from delegating away to the special interests all of their leadership discretion; states should be recognized as necessary laboratories of reform leadership and enlightened experimentation; foundations and universities should be more accountable as pedagogical and experimental research centers; and public interest lobbies and legal-aid societies should assume more of the burden of representing the unrepresented. The presidency must not be allowed to become the only, or even the primary, instrument for the realization of government of, by, and for the people.

More often than not, new issues and ideas enter the public arena from outside the political system and impose themselves on political leaders, rather than vice versa. To vest all hope in the wisdom or omniscience of one person is to ignore the vital role of persistent extragovernmental pressures, both elite and grassroots, in bringing about desirable national policies. Too much credit is bestowed on executive leadership or the political entrepreneur and too much glamorization of presidential achievements has occurred, to the neglect of how policy issues and ideas really are generated and develop a life of their own.

Nobody really voted in the New Deal, the Great Society, or the New Federalism. Presidents and Congress respond to crises and issues as they arise, and nearly always they arise between rather than during elections. Activist and effective presidential leadership (or what is often celebrated in textbooks as the promise of the presidency) has been elicited almost exclusively by war, depression, or rare periods of vastly accelerating national revenues. Hence, the frequent presidential lament, as illustrated by the comment of President Ford quoted below, that it will take a crisis to bring about change:

> *How much more can a President do than to recommend legislation, have his people do their very best to talk to committee members, to chairmen, to the leadership?*
> *I have talked to them. I have met with the leadership. There are just roadblocks up there that are apparently unbreakable until we get a real crisis.*
> *And I am being very practical now. I do not think you are going to get a break-through in legislation in the field of energy until you get a brownout or a blackout. I think it is just that pragmatic.*
> *You won't get deregulation on natural gas until the cutbacks in natural gas in Washington and New York and New England start to hurt people or hurt jobs. That is a bad commentary on our system, perhaps, but that is the way we act, right or wrong.*[2]

The yearning for a nuclear-age philosopher-king can lead only to generalized disappointment or perhaps to the end of democracy as it has been known in America. In a majoritarian democratic republic, policies will change slowly. With few exceptions, the impressive limits and constraints on presidential leadership, especially in the domestic policy area, can be removed only through undermining the processes of coalition-based government and cooperative federalism.

Policy proposals can come to the White House in dozens of ways, but policy case studies indicate that presidential commitment to a reform program is likely to develop only when (1) the program appears to be a logical extension of previous efforts, (2) the program has been incubated for a time among professional and congressional constituencies, and (3) the program seems likely to earn political credit for the president. Presidents rarely become involved before the ideas have become popular and large numbers of people agree that a particular initiative is needed. They are most dependent on their predecessors as well as their successors: An idea suggested under one president may be championed more forcefully by the next, and only then may it actually be authorized by Congress and granted its start-up authorization. The actual evaluation and corrective restructuring of a program may await yet a third or a fourth presidency. In short, the time required to educate and to marshal public support, to translate ideas effectively into programs, and finally to achieve the desired outcomes usually exceeds the political life spans of individual presidencies. Continuity, intensity, and stamina cannot be provided by a single president.

Successful implementation, however, rests upon several additional factors, each in its way a challenge to, or a test of, a program's survival. Having a clear goal and a simple mission are of the utmost importance, but many programs suffer from a debilitating Washington affliction known as "multimissionitis." Overeager to justify a program's existence to suspicious congressional committees and to capture support from other constituencies, multiple and often contradictory goals are added on by executive branch officials. Whatever is then sent by the White House to the Congress almost always is modified, sometimes drastically. And if a president is unsuccessful in gaining legislative approval of his version of new programs, he is apt also to lose substantive control over the implementation or administration of the program that does pass. The lack of clarity in the original bill, combined with changes introduced by Congress, often produces a program muddled from the outset, with no clear understanding from the president, the White House staff, or Congress as to what precisely is intended. Uncertain about what it is directed to do, even a bureaucracy having adroit managers eager to please a president cannot propel the program through the labyrinths of the complex federal system.

One Johnson aide said: "Basically, our philosophy was to get things started. The philosophy that Lyndon Johnson had was to keep a full legislative plate before the Congress. His philosophy was that if you don't keep them [Congress] busy, they would keep you busy. Johnson was really a legislator — he was never very involved in administration or even keenly aware of management implications." Other aides echoed this view. Another Johnson staffer suggested that Johnson's many years on Capitol Hill had made him accustomed to think that the pending business of government was the business pending in Congress. Structural reform never intrigued him. If solid suggestions on administration or budgeting analysis came his way, he usually would endorse them; but he never became particularly interested.

Aides under recent presidents have hoped that the Office of Management and Budget or other components of the executive office could somehow be put in charge of monitoring and evaluation. But former White House aides now admit that these capabilities were overtaxed and ineffective throughout the 1960s. Alternatives seldom were examined carefully, and effectiveness rarely was calculated accurately. Brainstorming and "adhocracy" might have been an appropriate method for attracting legislative ideas, but it was a poor substitute for systematic policy evaluation. The blatant failure of the executive office to forecast or comprehend the fuel shortage of the mid-1970s provides an unhappy illustration. The White House simply showed little or no capacity to plan, predict, or otherwise prepare for potentially disastrous emergencies. William Carey, a former assistant director of the budget, went even farther in criticizing the ability of the executive office to keep pace with the great increase in the number of domestic programs during the middle and late 1960s. He argued that a president such as Johnson, committed to the expansion of opportunities in education, health services, and employment, badly needs systematic social intelligence and analysis to provide early warning of problems in implementation so he can know when and how to intervene: "What a President does not know about the activities under way in Defense, State, and CIA, to say nothing of the Office of Education, and the Bureau of Indian Affairs, is incalculable. There he sits, overworked and making the best of a bad situation, while all around him his princes and serfs are doing and undoing in thousands of actions the work of his administration without his having a clue." [3]

Thus, the election of a person's favorite presidential candidate offers little assurance that those changes in national policy which the person champions actually will be effected. In a system decidedly weighted against radical change, a system that clearly tempts presidents to respond to the already powerful and organized interests at the expense of the unrepresented, often the most effective step that people can take to help a president is mobilizing political support for those presidential priorities with which they agree. This step is especially effective when the president in trying to push these priorities comes under heavy pressure from wealthy and powerful defenders of the existing order.

Public administrators long have maintained that the president needs help in the form of more staff support or streamlined organization of departments and independent agencies. But he also needs a different type of help: public support on issues. Incentives for such support are small on too many occasions, in part because a variation of the "you can't beat City Hall" attitude pertains, often correctly, to the White House. But writing letters and sending telegrams can on occasion reverse a presidential decision: President Nixon's retreat from Cambodia in 1970 and surrender of his tapes to Judge John Sirica in 1973 were occasioned in large part by outbursts of public dissent.

Advocacy organizations and investigative journalism have played an increasingly important and active role in recent years. Common Cause, Ralph Nader's Public Citizen, Inc., the Federation of American Scientists, the Sierra Club, the *Washington Monthly,* a legion of consumer protection organizations, public television, and a score of similar institutions, movements, and muckrakers now know more and more about blowing the whistle, as well as advocating alternative priorities. All such efforts are, of course, minority movements, and they invite condemnation for being both unrepresentative and muckraking. In this context, a remark attributed to Drew Pearson is appropriate. Verbally accosted by a middle-aged matron as "nothing but a damn muckraker," Pearson is alleged to have replied: "Madam, this town has muckmakers far in excess of its muckrakers, and until some parity comes about, I fully intend to continue my muckraking!"

RESHAPING THE PRESIDENTIAL JOB: HOW, WHERE, AND WHY?

Has the president too much power? In the post-Vietnam era there were many who answered this question with a "yes, but...." They wanted the president to be stronger in domestic and economic matters in order to advance liberal and reform measures, but they wanted him weaker in foreign affairs to restrain him from advancing imperial goals abroad. One of the great anomalies of American politics, according to one widely-held view, is that a president can embark on various adventures in foreign policy and the public either cannot or will not challenge him very much. Yet, at home, or so this view maintained, the president seems to have *too little* power. A former White House aide saw it this way: "I think the president needs to have much more policy leadership and power and authority over domestic affairs, particularly economic matters. The American chief executive is one of the weakest in the industrialized world with respect to having controls on the economy. The tax authority really lies in Congress and the monetary policy lies in the hands of the Federal Reserve. So the President of the United States, as presently constituted, has less power and influence over the economy than he clearly should have."

A person's model of the desirable presidency depends on his or her preferred mode of government. A large role for the government in the economy generally implies a large role for the presidency. A preference for delegating power to the states and private interests has traditionally implied a lesser role. Plainly, however, this is changing. Conservatives increasingly believe that to get the executive branch behind policies they deem desirable, they can succeed only by supporting a powerful and activist centrist or conservative president. Conservative distrust of the presidency is a legacy of deep-seated conservative opposition to a perceived New Deal hegemony.

These suggestions that we should strengthen the presidency at home but weaken it in national security matters pose a dilemma. Can we have it both ways? Nearly everyone agrees that curbs legislated to prevent presidential excesses in the national security area should not destroy that capacity for action which has been sometimes the very genius of the presidency during national crises.

Those who want to strengthen the presidency continue to assume that the presidency offers the best hope for furthering the public interest. Their conceptions of the public interest may differ, of course; some may prefer more social change, some more social control, and some that the government simply leave them alone. Time and time again, it is said that the president is the only elected official who represents all of the people; that congressmen, by virtue of their delimited geographical districts, have narrower, more parochial orientations. Also, it is postulated that on most significant issues the general or public interest can indeed be discerned by a reasonable president. Often, it is also assumed that presidents will be especially attuned to the otherwise unrepresented or underrepresented minorities in the nation, the have-not sectors, the ill-clad, ill-fed, and ill-housed. Strengthening the presidency, in the view of many, is regarded as a step toward assuring more liberal, progressive influence in national policy deliberations.

Plainly, however, a president arrives at his determination of what the public interest is by the inherently political means of choosing from among the demands of many conflicting interests. He decides, for example, that some parts of one or another interest constitute the real public interest, or that parts of one interest combine with parts of another interest to form the larger public interest. Thus Johnson, Nixon, and Ford often diverged sharply in their individual perceptions of the public interest. In addition, most presidential declarations of the public interest may represent less a judgment based entirely on a weighing of abstract values than a judgment based on an adroit calculation of what the majority wants or will tolerate, or of what the most vigorous or most heavily contributing pressure groups want.

In normative terms, however, most writers on the presidency equate the promise of that office with the promotion of humanitarian measures. Amid the presidential scandals of the mid-1970s, veteran liberals who were consistent in these views sought to protect the presidency precisely because their preferred policies had benefited from it in the past. They repeatedly warned against punishing the presidency for the abuses of presidential power by Johnson and Nixon. Had not history shown the presidency to be the most effective instrument of government for achieving justice and progress? Arthur M. Schlesinger, Jr., made this argument:

> It was presidential leadership, after all, that brought the country into the twentieth century, that civilized American industry, secured the rights of labor organization, defended the livelihood of the farmer. It was presidential leadership that protected the Bill of Rights against local vigilantism and natural resources against local greed. It was presidential leadership, spurred on by the Supreme Court, that sought to vindicate racial justice against local bigotry. Congress would have done few of these things on its own; local government even fewer. It would be a mistake to cripple the Presidency at home because of presidential excesses abroad.[4]

Theodore Sorensen asked:

> Why does anyone think that the Congress over the long run is going to be less hawkish than the President when it comes to questions of war and peace?
>
> Why does anyone think that Congress is going to be more resistant to the military-industrial complex than is the President?
>
> Why does anyone think that the Congress is going to be more liberal than the Presidency on questions of civil rights and civil liberties?
>
> Why do we think the Congress is going to pay less attention to the special interests, less attention to local pressures, more attention to the unorganized, the handicapped, the weak and unrepresented individuals in this country?[5]

CENTRALIZATION OR DECENTRALIZATION?

One school of thought understands the ineffectiveness of the presidential domestic performance in the 1960s as being the result of too little power rather than of too much. A second school contends that too much has been expected of the presidency and that the nation only compounds its problems by placing all of them on the presidential doorstep.

The school of thought that claims the presidency has had too little power holds that presidential government really has not been tried — at least not since Franklin D. Roosevelt. The problem is described as follows: There is an unending contest between the White House and much of the bureaucracy, in large measure because of the triangular alliances linking interest groups, Congress, and the respective departments. This school would weaken the ties between the bureaucracy and the Congress and between the bureaucracy and interest groups and strengthen the ties of loyalty from the bureaucracy to the White House, thereby creating a hierarchy in which the president would stand at the apex of power actually as well as symbolically. Centralization, they contend, should continue also because such issues as the energy crisis and environmental protection matters are clearly so national in scope and consequence that they could not be treated effectively by states or communities, acting either alone or even regionally. Substantial doubt also exists as to whether state and local governments possess the equipment and expertise to handle vastly increased responsibilities.

There are many persons, however, Nixon and Ford aides among them, who claim that visiting more money and responsibility on local authorities will provide the best remedy for upgrading the quality and effectiveness of local government. But the attractiveness of decentralization and revenue sharing rests in large part on the assumption that local governments are well run, well staffed, and, relative to other strata of government, closest to the people. Many facts contradict this belief. Watergate notwithstanding, corruption of all kinds occurs more frequently among local than among federal officials. Duplication and waste are at least as frequent, if not more so, at the local level. Local governments are notorious as well for their mazes of absurdly overlapping administrative boundaries, inadequate expertise, and impoverished structural capacities. Finally, the notion that local governments are more alert to the needs of the people, especially to the poor or to minorities, is misleading; the record of innovation and progress in America indicates that basic social reform usually has come about through the leadership of the national government, which has been far enough removed to be able to act in the face of formidable opposition from private vested interests, local governments, and local or regional traditional ways of life. The message is clear: give the president more power over his domestic bureaucracy; streamline the executive branch and make it a ready, flexible instrument that a president can use to carry out his political mandate to the people and those statutory responsibilities delegated to him by Congress.

Among the suggestions that have emerged from the advocates of a strength-

ened presidency are the following, many of which overlap or represent somewhat different perspectives toward the direction and content of change:

— an enlarged and strengthened Office of Management and Budget
— an Office of Executive Management
— an Office of Policy Planning and National Goals
— an Office of Intergovernmental Systems
— an Advisory Council on Personnel
— an Office of Policy Coordination
— a deputy president for domestic policy
— a vice president for ceremonial affairs
— an executive vice president for program implementation
— a Council of Social Advisers or a Social Indicators Office
— a presidential presence in the regions, or "little White Houses"
— better information storage and retrieval systems
— cabinet and departmental consolidation
— an expanded White House staff.

The second school of revisionist thinking holds that the success or failure of
most domestic reform initiatives in the 1960s depended on how they were
implemented in the 50 states and in the roughly 78,000 state and local units of
government. These critics feel that the presidency, along with overcentralized
government, had become an incompetent and overextended enterprise promoting public policies for a country too large and too diverse for its own well-being.
The presidency, they feel, has become more than ever dependent on its dependents. Their remedies include:

— lowering the expectations of what the presidency and a centralized government can accomplish
— debureaucratizing the federal establishment
— regionalizing federal programs whenever feasible
— returning to the private sector as many of the federal activities as possible
— making clear that the participation of interest groups in national decision
  making carries with it some high costs in terms of equity and efficiency
— beginning large-scale revenue sharing with state and local governments
— encouraging metropolitan and regional governmental units to assume more
  service responsibility for their varying areas
— getting the federal government out of social action programs by means of
  an income strategy, a family assistance program, and various tax credit
  provisions
— doing *only* what can be done well.

In reaction to the New Frontier and Great Society efforts, this second school of thought concludes that what is needed is not a more vigorous and dominant presidency, but rather a decentralization or disaggregation of political authority and a de-escalation of governmental commitments. Some, but by no means all, members of this school call also for a vigorous reassertion of congressional authority.

To judge from many analyses of the Great Society years, U. S. troubles in the foreign policy area were only contributing factors to the emerging dislike and distrust of presidents and central government. A growing list of writings offers strident critiques.[6] Absent from these critiques is the view that the American presidency is the preeminent source of wisdom and benevolence. Absent also is the assumption that a strong presidency and central government will adopt instant remedies and allocate funds for the effective resolution of major human problems in such areas as housing, education, health, and poverty. Many of these books attack the way in which the post-New Deal federal government designed and administered domestic and economic programs. Most of the authors explicitly favor alternative sets of policies and display an overt disaffection for what they regard as the Johnsonian encore to the New Deal. Several relevant propositions can be culled from the thoughts of these writers:

— Politicians have exaggerated the extent and import of real problems and have stirred up unrealistic and overaltruistic expectations of what government can do.

— Presidential advisers are guilty of not knowing what they were proposing and have misled presidents as well as the nation.

— Interest-group liberalism, as it has developed since the New Deal, inhibits governmental planning and government by-laws.

— Bureaucracy and inept governmental administrative processes make it next to impossible for presidents to execute and to achieve even the best of their policy intentions.

— The American people have become tired of an aggressive, progressive government and now reject most presidential efforts that would exact genuine personal sacrifices or increase taxes.

Subtle but important differences underlie the various reappraisals of presidential government. Whether to rely on the presidency over alternative institutions is a different question from the question of what is the proper substantive role of government. Textbooks often confuse the two issues, misleading the student into equating a strong presidency with a liberal and progressive one; in practice, the two often have gone hand in hand, but that they inevitably will do so is not rooted in principle.

Thus, as contemporary attempts at revision move away from the textbook presidency mentality, reformers must wrestle with diverse paths of reconstitution.

Some, along with traditional conservatives and to some extent with the supporters of George Wallace, will opt for weakened presidential government in order to alter the balance of power as well as to curb presidential powers that could upset the status quo. Writers like Arthur Schlesinger, Jr., and Theodore Sorensen can be classified as remaining in favor of a strong presidency both in procedural and substantive terms. That revisionists will struggle to break out of these conventional perspectives can be anticipated, but they will have trouble doing so. Their troubles will arise in large part because a presidency that is designed for strength in carrying out such worthy progressive ideals as a more equitable tax structure also can effect fundamentally reactionary measures for greater social control. Likewise, a presidency designed to preside over the effective execution of a "good" war can be goaded on by latent militaristic tendencies in society to promote malicious and immoral war as well. Garry Wills may have correctly suggested that the "imperial presidency" so criticized by Schlesinger and others arises not from unconstitutional abuses of war-making provisions, but rather from a basic conservatism or perhaps militarism in American society: "As long as the President has the people behind him, he can cater to their vices. That is because the system does work — it gives the people what they want." [7]

The debate continues: can we have a presidency that can do what we expect of it, yet be safe for democracy? Few people claim to have a clear answer. But when the heat of debate dies down, most people seem to adopt the view that the presidency is a prized and successful American invention. The job is to make it work effectively and to understand its cross-pressures, its incentives, and its temptations. It was Harold Laski, writing a generation ago, who perhaps posed best the presidential power dilemma:

> *Power, no doubt, is always a dangerous thing; and the temptation to its abuse, as no generation has learned more surely than our own, the subtlest poison to which a man may succumb. Yet power is also opportunity and to face danger with confidence is the price of its fulfillment. That is why I end with the emphasis that the president . . . must be given the power commensurate to the function he has to perform. It must be given democratically; it must be exercised democratically; but, if he is to be a great president, let us be clear that it must be given. With all its risks, its conference is the condition upon which the American adventure may continue in that form of which its supreme exponents have most greatly dreamed. To withhold it, or to frustrate its ample operation, is to jeopardize that adventure.*[8]

But if great powers are to be delegated to presidents, especially for crisis situations, and if we do allow presidents (e.g., Jackson, Lincoln, and Franklin Roosevelt) to move outside legal channels to meet emergencies, then what, as one commentator asks, "save the vigilance and courage of the people, is to prevent Presidents from seizing dictatorial power in situations that are not genuinely critical?" [9]

THE JOB DESCRIPTION OF THE MODERN PRESIDENCY

Discussions about the presidency, about whether it is too strong or too weak, healthy or diseased, accountable or irresponsible, themselves suffer from almost constant shifting about among policy areas and from disjointed leaps from one kind of decisional activity to others substantially different. Of course, a president can be imperial and nearly dictatorial in some aspects of his job, whereas in others he may be more akin to a prisoner who is hedged in on all sides. Often, too, the same act by two different incumbents evokes markedly different degrees of acceptance, because of the nature of the times or the political climate. Thus, when President Hoover suggested that what the nation really needed was a restoration of confidence, he was answered with bitter laughter. When Franklin Roosevelt, only a short time later, declared that "the only thing we have to fear is fear itself," virtually the same message, the nation was thrilled and its spirit rallied.

Until recently, it has been fashionable to say that a president wears many hats — a commander-in-chief hat, a chief-legislator hat, a chief-of-state hat, and so on. This simple metaphor of presidential hats belongs to a simpler past. Reality as well as expectations have expanded and recast the presidency in numerous ways. First, the office is now organized around three major and interrelated subpresidencies (discussed in Chapter 1): (1) foreign affairs and national security; (2) aggregate economics; and (3) domestic policy. The president's time is absorbed by one or the other of these policy spheres, and his staff and cabinet have come to be organized around these three substantive subpresidencies.

Within each of these subpresidencies a president participates in the six functional task-oriented areas depicted in Figure 9-1. These are not compartmentalized, unrelated functions, but rather a dynamic, web-like assortment of tasks and responsibilities. This job description, or GS-118 in Civil Service jargon, does not exhaust all presidential activity; rather, the examples in Figure 9-1 attempt to classify the major substantive and functional responsibilities of the office. Of course, political activity solely for personal or institutional enhancement, though not specified in the figure, clearly should be acknowledged as a presidential preoccupation.

In practice, of course, no president can divide his job into tidy compartments. Instead, he must see to it that questions are not ignored because they fall between or cut across jurisdictional lines. An exclusively domestic or national security problem rarely exists. Ultimately, all of his responsibilities interrelate. Substantive problems and their solutions in one area inevitably have impact in the other areas, often in decidedly counterproductive ways. As an act of foreign policy and international economics, for example, the United States wheat sale to Russia during the second Nixon administration had lasting, reverberating effects on the nation's domestic economy and on presidential credit with the public.

Of the functional responsibilities, symbolic leadership and priority setting can be discussed together. Each can be initiated and carried out by a president with a minimum of staff and independent of large-scale bureaucracies. Both absorb considerable amounts of time in the early months and years of an administration. The tasks of symbolic leadership of the nation — generating hope, confidence, and a sense of national purpose — are, for the most part, beyond

FIGURE 9–1 JOB DESCRIPTION OF THE MODERN PRESIDENCY

	Foreign Policy and National Security	Aggregate Economics	Domestic Policy and Problems
Symbolic Leadership	A presidential state visit to Middle East nations	"WIN" buttons	Visiting the sick and "ill-fed"
Priority Setting and Program Design	Does the U.S. compromise pro-Israel policies for oil?	Does the U.S. fight inflation or recession? And how?	Does the U.S. have the funds for a comprehensive national health care program?
Crisis Management	Confronting fuel crisis of the mid-1970s	Confronting 8% unemployment	Confronting massive rises in health care costs. Confronting nutrition needs of the poor
Legislative and Political Coalition Building	Selling weapons to the Middle Eastern states. Selling energy conservation at home	Winning congressional passage of programs	Winning public support for National Health Insurance System
Program Implementation and Evaluation "Follow-through"	Encouraging negotiations between Israel, Egypt, P.L.O., etc.	Implementing tax cuts or fuel rationing	Improving the quality of health care for all, equitably and efficiently
Oversight of Government Routines	Maintaining foreign aid. Overseeing U.S. bases abroad	Overseeing the I.R.S.	Overseeing National Institutes of Health and Health Care Delivery Systems

Shading indicates flow of incentives and influences on presidency. See discussion which begins on page 259.

partisanship and are some of the more easily performed and more pleasant presidential responsibilities. Acting in behalf of semi-sacred, traditional American beliefs and values is much more enjoyable a way to spend time than trying to win support for a party's program, cajoling reluctant senators to confirm a controversial judicial nominee, or overseeing and overhauling the nation's farm-subsidy programs.

Priority setting has become, especially since the New Deal, a major preoccupation for presidents. A presidential embrace of new ideas and a vigorous sponsorship of new programs virtually guarantees that they will receive a legislative hearing and at least some public attention. Many people assume that presidents come into office knowing what they want to accomplish. Such, however, is seldom the case. Campaigns commonly offer little more than a chance to trace out broad policy directions. And, as noted earlier, thinking clearly about national goals is a most demanding task in the context of a system that so often is held together by bargaining and compromising over incompatible objectives. Agreements, especially on domestic objectives, are difficult to achieve; and once reached, they often are imposed on a decidedly recalcitrant nation.

To some degree, a president can control the extent of his involvement in both symbolic leadership and priority-setting activities. He can be assured at least of the general content or style of his participation. In crisis management, however, he is often little more than the victim of the interplay of events and institutions. His major tests in any given year often arise from events over which he is nearly powerless. Examples of such crises include the Japanese bombing of Pearl Harbor in 1941; the North Korean invasion of South Korea in 1950; the Supreme Court decision in *Brown* vs. *Board of Education* in 1953; the Russian launching of Sputnik in 1957; the offensive missiles placed in Cuba by the Russians in 1962; James Meredith's entry into the University of Mississippi in 1962; riots in Harlem, Watts, Newark, and Detroit from 1964 to 1967; the Viet Cong Tet offensive in 1968; the devaluations of the dollar in 1971 and 1973; and the fuel shortage crisis of 1973–74. What is required of a president during times of crisis is not only political and executive leadership but also the appearance of confident, responsible control, the show of a steady hand at the helm.

A greater share of crises in the past few decades may seem to have fallen within the national security or macroeconomic subpresidencies than within the domestic policy subpresidency. An almost permanent crisis in national security has dominated American thinking since 1940. But it may be subtly deceiving to think that most crises occur in foreign policy or macroeconomics, for the cult of the textbook presidency built up in recent decades seems to encourage the notion that where presidents should be involved is where they can make global and dramatic choices. Kennedy's Cuban missile blockade and Nixon's "historic journey for peace" to China splendidly suited the public's expectation and the presidential image.

The phrase "overtaken by events" describes much of the presidential position when he is required to respond to crises, and often he really is surprised and truly placed on the defensive. He cannot enjoy the luxury of time to plan carefully and to initiate new departures in public policy; he must react to public and congressional demands for action, to journalistic and academic analyses, and to criticism from opposition party leaders. The 1962 episode involving James Meredith and Mississippi Governor Ross Barnett illustrates an issue that had to be confronted despite the deep reluctance of modern presidents to exercise federal police power against other levels of government, even in the face of blatant violation of federal law. Certainly, President Kennedy did not encourage Meredith to enroll in the University of Mississippi. Meredith and his supporters chose an approach that was delicate and that carried high risks, both to him personally and to a president already in an awkward situation. Kennedy, through his brother and attorney general, Robert, tried desperately to avoid dramatic intervention and to compromise with Barnett. Only when these efforts failed did Kennedy finally send the 23,000 federal marshals into Mississippi. Robert Kennedy's book *Thirteen Days* also demonstrates most effectively, in the context of the Cuban missile crisis, how a crisis can cast aside nearly all other presidential responsibilities.

The fourth of the major presidential tasks consists of educational leadership and the building of legislative and political support. The building of political support, of course, goes on constantly. (Administration and implementation are highly political tasks as well, but to revive the stereotyped dichotomy between "administrative" and "political" is not the intention here.) A president must forge majoritarian coalitions, at least temporarily, if he is to move his priorities forward. Presidents Kennedy and Nixon time and again proposed new directions in various policy areas but were unable to secure congressional approval. So little was passed by the Kennedy administration that some critics sarcastically accused it of being a third Eisenhower administration. Nixon sent Congress idealistic reform messages on Indian affairs as well as on family assistance measures, but no significant changes resulted. Messages were not enough. Nixon apparently chose not to provide, or lacked the time or the political capital, partisan and educational leadership in these important areas. His family assistance program died as a result of not only the Cambodian incursion but also inadequate political leadership. The president was unable to win majority support even in his own cabinet and among his own White House staff. Division in his own household seriously weakened his campaign to persuade Congress and the nation that this was his number-one domestic initiative.

Perhaps the rarest of presidential talents in this century has been the capacity to galvanize and sustain a political party in order to realize program objectives. An effective president is of necessity an effective politician; the office does not guarantee political leadership, it merely offers its incumbents an invitation to lead politically. It is in this sense that those best suited to the job are those who can creatively shape their political environment and savor the rough-and-tumble give-and-take of political life.

Many presidents become timid about using the resources of the presidency for partisan leadership. The reason for this, of course, is that a president wants above all to be president of all the people, and yet even an outstanding performance as a symbolic chief of state cannot relieve a president from the responsibility of educating his party about his objectives. A president is also obliged to respond to the interests and expectations of the party that nominated and elected him. Having made pledges for which both he and his party will be held to account in future elections, a president must try to win support for his definition of what must be done. As James M. Burns wrote, "The crowning paradox is an old one for the American President. . . . He has had to be both a unifier and a divider of the people." [10]

Implementation, the carrying out and realization of presidential goals, is a paramount problem. The provisions made within the executive office to insure presidential control over implementation simply do not guarantee that this happens. Repeatedly, what appears to be a neat hierarchy turns out to be a confused array of shared prerogatives and reciprocal influences. The very instruments intended to increase presidential control have engendered in and of themselves new problems. The swelling of the presidency has brought about staff differentiation, overspecialization, compartmentalization, internal conflicts, and considerable conflict with the cabinet and other executive departments. The advent of the new federalism and the vast growth in the number and scope of federal grant-in-aid programs have exacerbated the problem of implementation. Confusion over goals and inadequate planning and program evaluation have added to the problem.

A case study of LBJ's and Nixon's war on crime, illuminates some of the more common problems of the new federalism.[11] The effort to strengthen the states and, in effect, to transfer power to them undermined other administration priorities. To transfer authority and vast sums of money to the states was to impose on them value choices that many states were not willing to accept. If Congress, to avoid conflict and enhance support for passage, studiously avoided a clear definition of the goals of the federal crime-prevention effort, was it not reasonable to suppose that many states would do likewise with their state plans, leaving the resulting program so blurred as to defy evaluation? What frequently happened was that states sought to please as many factions or special interests as were aware of the availability of new money. Once a program becomes distributive, and only secondarily reformist, concentrating sufficient funds to demonstrate impact is often nearly impossible.

For three years the Law Enforcement Assistance Administration enjoyed popularity without feeling pressure to show results. Two factors explain this. First, the appearance of action, the flow of substantial new money, and the establishment of a visible new Washington administration bought time. Second,

President Nixon displayed an impressive, personalized aspiration, both symbolically and in his setting of priorities, of trying to stop increases in crime. People often judge a president more on his goals than on his success in achieving them, and Nixon appeared committed. He and his top aides in the Justice Department were able to console the public with the assurance that although the number of crimes still might be rising, the rate of increase was slower. He also spoke with pride about a substantial decrease in reported crime in Washington, D. C. But after more than four years, influential congressmen, the attentive public, and even members of the administration became anxious for results. Although the rise in the crime rate had been slowed in several dozen major cities, other cities had experienced accelerations and suburban and rural crime rates had risen sharply.

The often unclear federal objectives in the war against crime were almost always subject to competing interpretations. Not only were presidential and congressional intents often at odds but local views about what needed to be done often differed from both. High-minded expressions of sentiment had been substituted for guidelines and sanctions, as both Congress and the White House delegated, sometimes deliberately but often unwittingly, more and more authority to local elites. These local elites, more often than not, represented highly traditional values and practical, established — as opposed to innovative — policies. The failure to resolve these conflicts in values continued to restrict greatly presidential attempts to move swiftly from the task of problem definition to concrete programs, and from programs to impact. The diversity of values and emotions became abundantly reflected in the legislative and administrative processes involved with this policy area and through them served to brake any decisive presidential intervention.

Greater state discretion meant a blurred focus for federal funding efforts. The federal objective of reducing crime rapidly, especially if it is to be achieved by dispersing greater political authority to the states, will require much longer than originally expected. Although having the states primarily responsible for implementing the Crime Control Act solved some problems, in practice few state governments were models of effectiveness and honesty. Some states, of course, did an admirable job; but others, including some of the wealthier northern states, have neither understood, not to mention shared, the federal objectives, nor have they been able to establish acceptable substitutes. In retrospect, the White House and the top Justice Department officials failed to appreciate sufficiently the vast variation in state problems and capabilities. Evidently, the states needed outside guidance and controls and closer White House-State House communications. The White House also did not sufficiently appreciate that the politics of the war on crime would not end with the bill signing. Enactment was not achievement.

Priority setting and budgetary planning are fundamental antecedents to implementation; instrumental leadership involves sustaining support for programs and checking to make sure that these programs work as intended. Even long after the bill-signing ceremony, presidents must work to assure the continued clarity of objectives, to help correct abuses, and to see that proper monitoring and evaluation processes are being used.

Little presidential time or stamina remains for inquiring into those routine activities that make up the great bulk of federal governmental work. Unfortunately, routine activities that are neglected or improperly monitored and evaluated can escalate to crisis proportion. But, for the most part, a president must delegate large amounts of discretion to political subordinates and career professionals, and his influence over routine activities is indirect: through appointees, budgetary examinations, or legislative clearance. A president may view these activities as self-executing, or he may even attempt to dissociate himself from them, but much of the administrative and executive burden of the presidency consists of imaginative supervision of program implementation. In many respects, the management of routine is "between-election politics." The functional task of a president in the leadership of federal implementation activities is much more than merely issuing directives to the cabinet. It entails compromise, coalition building, education, and political leadership just as much as does the winning of congressional or public support. The quality of these bread-and-butter service and assistance programs is important to the average American; and a president, like it or not, is held responsible for the general quality of governmental performance.

FEEDBACK AND PRESIDENTIAL PERFORMANCE. Only through skillful monitoring of routine governmental activities can a president know whether citizens are getting a fair return on their taxes. Only by more imaginative use of presidential resources in overseeing these activities can they be prevented from becoming sources of crises themselves. To be sure, supervision and reform must come not only from presidents but also from other quarters as well. But how effective a president is in fashioning an executive management system is crucial. On the one hand, he must be able to delegate vast responsibilities to talented managers, and, on the other hand, he must have an early-warning system that alerts him through, among other means, his managers about inadequate government performance, about experimentation that yields negative results, and about progress in research and development that could provide corrective feedback. Several other monitoring devices are discussed in the next chapter.

In short, a proper management system would insure that governmental activities concerned with implementation and routine would be brought to a president's attention when necessary and as they affected priority-setting and political-leadership tasks instead of only when they become matters of crisis management. Interior and transportation officials, for example, should detect evidence of impending fuel shortages sufficiently in advance to permit a president to commission studies and devise remedial strategies before the crisis occurs. Routine White House supervision should have uncovered the extent and scope of illegal CIA domestic spying long before it was discovered by the press. Similarly, data from government-run or funded experiments or from program evaluations should be processed by the White House in order to find more desirable or workable priorities. If the purpose of presidential power is to execute federal laws faithfully and to help avert costly crises, the presidency must be organized systematically as a learning agency, capable of anticipating and preventing system overload, communications failures, and corruption or ineptness in the operations of the executive branch.

ACCEPTANCE AND AVOIDANCE OF RESPONSIBILITY. Several underlying incentives help shape how the presidential job is performed. As they have operated in the recent past, these incentives insure that certain responsibilities get special attention whereas others become neglected. Preoccupation with problems of national security and aggregate economics leaves too little time for leadership in the area of domestic policy. Symbolic leadership, priority setting, and crisis management also crowd out the tasks of instrumental political leadership and program implementation and supervision. Creative follow-through seldom is adequate; routines often go neglected. Program evaluation and imaginative recruitment of program managers for appropriate tasks never receive the sustained attention they merit. On balance, the White House is caught running around doing either what is easy to do or what it perceives as urgent, often to the neglect of doing what is important.

The "flow" of these incentives is depicted in Figure 9-1 on p. 251. Doing what is easy or what appears to be more "presidential" seems to be rewarded. These incentives accentuate certain responsibilities over others and have consequences for the balance and quality of national policy making. Presidents have tended to assert themselves aggressively in those tasks and functions in the upper left-hand portions of Figure 9-1. In these areas the sharing and the restraint — or put differently, the cooperation and consultation — of a three-branch governmental system seldom occur. Political parties, too, are largely irrelevant in this regard, especially on questions of national security and international economic policy. Few domestic cabinet members are involved systematically in tasks of priority setting and crisis management. These tasks get pulled into the White House and treated as personal responsibilities of the president and his senior lieutenants.

Presidents, then, have concentrated in recent years on only selected areas of the presidential job. In part, this is doubtless because we have created a nearly impossible presidential job description. Plainly we expect too much. In part, however, recent presidents have also been, or so it would appear, lulled into responding to that part of their job which is more glamorous, more prominent. By concerning itself only with symbolic, priority-setting, and crisis management tasks, the presidency has acquired an empty, self-serving, swollen character.

Moreover, presidential activity in symbolic, priority-setting, and crisis contexts often conveys an image of strength, vigor, and rigor. Presidents often do appear virile and effective in these areas of the presidential job. But measuring presidential strength or evaluating presidential leadership requires a more comprehensive look at what a president is doing and what he can achieve, not only in the three substantive subpresidencies but also in the six functional leadership categories outlined in Figure 9-1. Also, as noted earlier, the true measure of presidential effectiveness is the capacity of a president to integrate where necessary his multiple responsibilities in order to avoid having initiatives in one area compound problems in another or having problems go unattended merely because they defy the usual organizational boundaries. In short, the essence of presidential leadership is the intricate relating of each aspect of the presidential job to the others. A close examination of presidential performance in recent years relative to the whole matrix of the job suggests that presidents are strong in some areas, weak in others, and that the overarching job of synthesis and integration is extraordinarily exacting and seldom performed adequately.

We are not likely to reformulate or redefine in any measurable way the presidential job description. Altering our expectations of the office can help. Strengthening other centers of political and societal leadership can help. But neither of these will be enough. Nor will structural, institutional reforms that seek to make the presidency more efficient and manageable be able to resolve entirely the paradoxes and dilemmas compounding the job of the presidency, for almost all of the complexities of the presidential condition in America revolve around political problems and American values. Those who devise structural solutions to what are essentially political questions are likely to be disappointed. In the end, we shall get improved presidential performances when we have a clearer idea of what we want to do as a nation and when we understand better the mix of incentives that now shape the way presidents respond to their political and executive duties. New and different incentives, rewards, and sanctions may be needed. New and different kinds of pressure politics will be needed as well.

For the present, however, a marked imbalance characterizes how presidents perform their jobs. Existing incentives would doubtless lead almost anyone put in that job to credibility gaps and exaggerated notions of prerogatives and salesmanship. What can be done? What might be done to fashion a presidency that could realistically perform those tasks assigned it and still, as an institution, enhance our democratic system? We now turn to these questions in the last two chapters.

NOTES

1. Gary Orfield, *Congressional Power: Congress and Social Change* (Harcourt, Brace, Jovanovich, 1975), p. 323.
2. Gerald R. Ford, *Newsweek*, 9 December 1974, pp. 33–34.
3. William Carey, "Presidential Staffing in the Sixties and Seventies," *Public Administration Review*, September–October 1969, p. 453.
4. Arthur M. Schlesinger, Jr., *The Imperial Presidency* (Popular Library, 1974), p. 404.
5. Theodore C. Sorensen, "The Case for the Strong Presidency," in C. Roberts, ed., *Has the President Too Much Power?* (Harper's Press, 1974), pp. 29–30.
6. Representative of this newly critical orthodoxy are such works as Edward C. Banfield, *The Unheavenly City* (Little, Brown, 1970); Peter F. Drucker, *The Age of Discontinuity* (Harper and Row, 1969); Andrew Hacker, *The End of the American Era* (Atheneum, 1970); Theodore J. Lowi, *The End of Liberalism* (Norton, 1969); and Daniel P. Moynihan, *Maximum Feasible Misunderstanding* (Macmillan, 1969).
7. Garry Wills, *New York Times Book Review*, 18 Nov. 1973, p. 22. For a related yet different view, which advocates that conservatives should at long last give up their distrustful view of executive power, see Jeffrey Hart, "The Presidency: Shifting Conservative Perspectives?" *National Review*, 22 November 1974, pp. 1351–1355.
8. Harold Laski, *The American Presidency* (Grosset and Dunlap, 1940), pp. 277–78.
9. See Donald L. Robinson, "The Routinization of Crisis Government," *Yale Review*, Winter 1974, p. 165.
10. James M. Burns, *Presidential Government* (Houghton Mifflin, 1966), p. 235.
11. Thomas E. Cronin, "The President, The Crime Issue, and The War on Crime" (Paper presented for the Conference on Criminal Justice, University of Chicago Law School, Chicago, Ill., June 1973; processed).

CHAPTER 10

MAKING THE PRESIDENT AN EFFECTIVE EXECUTIVE
SEPARATING POSSIBILITIES FROM PANACEAS

*The management of a bureaucracy comprising perhaps thousands of
careerists will be, at best, nominal; the agency heads will inevitably
outmaneuver a politician-secretary. Presidential orders transmitted
through such channels become more mysteriously changed to
suit the bureaucracy's preferences. Policies persist from one
Administration to another remarkably unchanged. Resistance to
change is also reinforced by the alliances between bureaucrats
and the appropriate congressmen. Altogether, it requires a most
sophisticated and determined President to effect any changes at all.*

— *Rexford G. Tugwell,*
    in The Presidency Reappraised *(Praeger, 1974), p. 290.*

*Moreover, executives are not what people seek in a President.
... Our Presidents more often than not have been atrocious
administrators. They often come from an occupation (legislator)
and a profession (law) that ill prepares them for management.*

— *Stephen Hess, former Eisenhower and Nixon aide,*
    in The Presidential Campaign *(Brookings Institution, 1974),*
    p. 21.

This chapter assesses five frequently mentioned structural reforms that purport to make the presidency more manageable and presidential leadership more effective. The central challenge here is to separate panaceas from possibilities and to identify what would consequently strengthen or weaken the larger political system. We must ask whether or not these structural alterations would in fact help a president win control over the executive establishment and permit him to fulfill more effectively his executive responsibilities. Further, we must ask at what price and at whose expense would these suggested changes be put into effect.

The proposals fall into two categories, those that would increase presidential resources (1, 2, 3) and those that would decrease the autonomy of bureaucracies (4 and 5):

1. a collegial or plural presidency
2. cabinet consolidation
3. presidential planning and evaluation staffs
4. regionalization of the presidency
5. incentive systems for a more responsive bureaucracy.

The two kinds of proposals are related but not identical; lifting one end of a seesaw is like pressing down the other, but they each take different muscles. Which strategy is favored depends on where the frustrations of a president seem to be concentrated at the moment and which methods seem to have the greatest promise.

The assessment of these reorganizational proposals is guided by three questions: To what extent are they politically possible? Who favors them? And to what extent, if instituted, would they achieve the desired results? This chapter takes as a basic premise that most presidents, by reason of background, habit, and incentives, do not savor the administrative part of the presidential job. Planning, evaluation, and managerial tasks in general are unpleasant to them. They could do them, but they seldom have been rewarded for doing so. Some presidents may be wholly inept at such tasks. More likely, however, they become bored with them, do not have adequate time, and perhaps most likely, they become apprehensive about retrospective activities, preferring always to begin some new and even more exciting venture. Here again, the curse of activism and the politics of motion are at work. To protect his personal power stakes, a president's intuition tells him it is better to take on new action and promote still newer programs. When tackling new problems he is overtly manifesting his concern, he cannot be blamed for inactivity, and he is communicating to would-be rivals that he is not about to yield his office.

For presidents, more than for other persons, the job of the presidency still looms large as the custodian of national hopes and as the cutting edge to new frontiers, and any failure in these areas is, to them, at least as grievous as neglect of managerial or executive chores. All the more reason, then, for evaluating compensatory measures that might better adapt the presidency to its executive responsibilities.

A COLLEGIAL, OR PLURAL, PRESIDENCY

Proposals to establish a system of two or more presidents have surfaced frequently since the constitutional convention of 1787. The several variations on this theme include having one presidency for foreign policy and another for domestic policy; having one for ceremonial and symbolic duties and one for policy matters; or having one for policy planning and formulation, and one for policy management and implementation. Frequently stressed is the view that the office has become too complex and its reach too extended to be entrusted to one individual's fallible judgment. What is needed, advocates of this plan urge, is not the abolition of executive power as such but rather a reconstituting of this power so that it is shared among several highly qualified individuals. This was the view of Herman Finer: "The burdens . . . are necessarily so multifarious that to avoid a fatal collapse of efficiency and responsibility the President would have to be a titan and a genius. A collective Presidency might have these qualities, but not a solitary man. A solitary President is a gamble this nation cannot afford." [1]

Other observers point out that for one person to deal with all the presidential assistants, let alone all the executive agencies, is physically impossible; the president cannot stretch time or space and cannot be more competent than the natural limit of man's energy and intelligence. Rexford Tugwell, for example, noted that, except for dictatorships, the United States is nearly alone in having a singular executive: "The vast responsibilities of the Executive who is also Chief of State and of party are nowhere expected to be assumed by a single individual except in the United States. This peculiarity of holding to a presidential form adopted in simpler circumstances than now prevail may be less a mark of virtue than of inertia, pride, or conservatism." [2]

Students of constitutional government have argued persuasively that the executive leadership essential to the success of government can be vested in a single individual (as in the United States), or in a group of elected or appointed officials (as in Switzerland), or somewhere in between (as in Canada and Great Britain). Suggestions include a three-part presidency, a five-person presidential council, a six-member cabinet directorate, a commission form of government, or a cabinet system like that of Britain. One proposal, put forward by news analyst Eric Sevareid when Lyndon Johnson was dominating the legislative process in 1965, went as follows: the number-one president would think up new legislation, help prepare bills, and oversee the passage of important and major legislation. The number-two president would be responsible for coordination and administration, for analyzing programs to see whether they worked, and for long-range planning.[3] Herman Finer suggested having one president and eleven vice-presidents. More modest proposals would appoint or elect one other vice-president. Here again are variations: two vice-presidents might handle domestic and foreign policy; or one might be a ceremonial and political vice president, such as we have now, and the other might be an executive vice-president for management and intergovernmental relations. The latter office is seen as a deputy president "with clout."

Republican U. S. Senator Mark Hatfield urges yet another form of plural executive. He suggests that a unitary executive is indeed advisable in the areas of foreign and defense policy, and hence a president should continue to nominate, and the Senate confirm, the secretaries of state, defense, and treasury. Yet, he claims that the need for coherence in foreign and defense policy does not carry over to domestic policy. Hatfield suggests that it would be better instead to disperse power over domestic policy to several national officials, each directly accountable to the electorate:

> Today, as a practical matter, the time of the President is largely devoted to foreign affairs, defense policy, and international economics. Meanwhile, domestic policy is increasingly handled by relatively unknown White House staffers often chosen for their single-minded devotion to the President and his interests. Cabinet members seem more and more to be ornaments useful primarily as public relations spokesmen rather than policymakers.

> I believe that the American people would be much better served by their federal government were it to have a plural executive like most states. The President, the Vice President, the attorney general, and the heads of the new domestic departments . . . should be elected. This would parallel the situation in many states in which candidates for such offices as governor, lieutenant governor, attorney general, treasurer, comptroller, secretary of state, and superintendent of education are separately elected.

> As a former governor, I recognize the occasional friction and frustration which such a system can produce for a chief executive. Yet, is it our concern to make life comfortable for the chief executive or to make it freer for the American people?[4]

Thus, Senator Hatfield urges adoption of a constitutional amendment requiring separate election of the president, vice-president, and various heads of cabinet departments.

Under the existing system, a president has substantial leeway in establishing subordinate positions for sharing his heavy burden. If he so desires, he can appoint a chief of staff, who is in effect an assistant president, to assume major presidential managerial or ceremonial responsibilities. James Byrnes, Averell Harriman, Sherman Adams, and Henry Kissinger all performed significant deputy-president roles at one time or another. The case of Byrnes's serving of

Franklin Roosevelt while he was director of the Office of War Mobilization and Reconversion perhaps comes closest to the notion of an assistant president, but even this relationship had its share of problems.[5]

From a president's point of view, one of the advantages of the current system is that all such assistant presidents are on temporary assignment and serve at the pleasure of the president. They can leave once a major assignment is completed, as in the case of Byrnes; they are expendable, as in the case of Adams; they can even be used as scapegoats; or they can be shifted to a more operationally independent agency, as in the case of Harriman and Kissinger. Under the existing system, a new president need not be saddled with permanent deputies. Admittedly, to establish quasi-vice-presidents or acting assistant presidents with assigned operational responsibilities, as opposed to staff functions, is to violate the original intent in creating the executive office and to invite congressional suspicion and intervention. To protect the flexibility and autonomy of the executive office, a select few of the most important presidential deputies with such operational mandates might be made subject to congressional confirmation.

A plural presidency might encourage excessive internal competition and conflict among the leaders of the executive branch. A proposal once was made, during the period immediately before the Civil War, to elect three coequal presidents, each of whom would represent a distinctive geographical region of the country. Plainly an attempt at simple structural remedy, such an arrangement would have pitted region against region even more than was already the case and might have invited the immobility that characterized France's Fourth Republic. An intraexecutive veto process might also have emerged that would have weakened executive unity, energy, and dispatch. Indeed, our current practice of nominating a vice-president to complement the political appeal of the presidential nominee means that individuals more experienced administratively or substantively often are bypassed on such grounds as geography or ethnicity. Having two or three elected vice-presidents would invite infighting and on-the-job political campaigning, with the possibility that one might break with the president or work to undercut presidential measures which might interfere with his own chances at the next election.

A president who delegates most of his ceremonial duties to a second president or to a vice-president might experience a faster decline in public support than an incumbent usually experiences over the course of his term. The pomp of ceremonial duties lends a prestige that is valuable politically. Ceremonial exercises, although they do contribute to the burdensome job of the office, are also among the more pleasant of presidential tasks. To be sure, this is not necessarily a logical reason to avoid a plural presidency, but it is an obvious reason why presidents and their loyalists will oppose this suggested reform. And if the presidency is as fragile and as vulnerable an institution as many believe, the separation of the managerial from the ceremonial may make it more not less so. A fragile and vulnerable presidency, so many observers argue, is hardly what is needed. What we want, on the contrary, is a strong, effective, and accountable presidency.

A plural presidency would also doubtless exacerbate the problems of the already swollen executive establishment. Conceivably, for example, each president, or each vice-president, would want to have his or her own staff, his or her own legislative liaison operation, public relations staff, press secretary. Soon, every major interest group would want access to or even representation in each of the various executive staffs. Presidential bureaucratization might become rampant as each of the executives vies for credit, publicity, loyalty, and success, variously defined.

Plainly, a pluralized presidency would have more difficulty in establishing priorities for the nation. For better or worse, the nation and especially the Congress look to the White House for its public policy agenda. The presidency must possess the ability to integrate, synthesize, and especially assess the relative merits of one policy with respect to others. How well can this be performed by a collective presidency, where each executive is in charge of merely a fraction of the whole?

Alexander Hamilton's brief against a plural executive remains compelling today. He argued that the restraints of public opinion would lose their efficacy if there were several executives rather than one. Whom should the people blame? Which one or set of executives should be removed from office? Hamilton believed that trust, accountability, and responsibility might be severely impaired with a plural executive. The people needed, he said (in *The Federalist Papers,* No. 70), "the opportunity of discovering with facility and clearness the misconduct" of the responsible official. But perhaps the most unappealing aspect of an elected plural presidency stems precisely from the difficulty of devising practical and democratic means of selection. As discussed in Chapter 8, the situation of "electing" a single vice-president is already an embarrassing one. Also, the history of the vice-presidency we now have most assuredly does not encourage extension and duplication.

In times of crisis the members of a truly collegial or collective presidency would be expected to show unanimity. Accordingly, the public might have less confidence in policies or strategic decisions arrived at by a 3-to-2 or 4-to-2 vote. Surely the bureaucracy might heed such decisions less assiduously. Might not a collectivized presidency court paralysis or indecision, or both, in a nuclear attack or in an international monetary crisis, when swiftness and decisiveness are often most needed? Or would we really want, for example, a president of foreign affairs to act without knowing about, or without being responsible for, domestic affairs of the nation? Obviously, a plural presidency could invite further compartmentalization of an already compartmentalized institution. Proponents of a plural presidency seldom adequately treat these questions. Moreover, it is difficult enough today to find out where a particular president stands on many issues, and it is always difficult for a president to communicate clearly and effectively. These problems doubtless would be compounded by adopting a collegial presidency.

In general, then, suggestions for institutionalizing more help for presidents by fixing into law or grafting onto the Constitution any plan for a pluralization of the presidency should be considered rather skeptically and cautiously. The presidency, as opposed to the president, is already a collective entity, and individual presidents usually have ample discretion to organize their own office pretty much as they please. Thus, Franklin Roosevelt during World War II shared substantial presidential authority with eminent leaders such as James Byrnes, Harry Stimson, Cordell Hull, Harold Ickes, Henry Wallace, and Harry Hopkins. In short, the presidency now involves a number of related political leaders, of whom the nominal chief executive is just one, even if inevitably the most important one.[6]

Still, we can hardly afford to dismiss all proposals for lessening our excessive dependence on the accident of presidential personalities. Proposals for a council of state or a joint legislative-executive cabinet have often been made but have never been given serious attention, and usually for good reason.[7] First, ours is still a system of relatively separate branches even if powers are widely shared. Second, few members of Congress who are doing their jobs well would have the time to do meaningful work as executive advisers to a president. Taking these realities into account, Benjamin V. Cohen has devised a compromise proposal that seeks to achieve some of the aims of a plural presidency yet leaves our existing singular presidency pretty much intact. His idea is to establish a small executive council of not less than five or more than eight distinguished citizens. They would be nominated by a president but subject to confirmation by the Senate. Cohen would keep the council small but insists that its members should be persons of independent political position, widely respected in and out of Congress.

Membership in this executive council would be a full-time job, according to Cohen. The idea is to oblige a president to consult this group of eminent persons *before* he acts on crucial national security matters, although he and he alone would have the ultimate power of decision and the last word. Cohen explains:

> *The Executive Council should constitute a small super-cabinet with authority to participate in the decision-making process before important or potentially important Presidential plans, programs and policies are finalized. Its members should have access to reports, memoranda, and other information on any matter within the purview of the Council. They should have authority to request additional information regarding any such matter from responsible sources in the executive establishment, in the Congress or elsewhere. . . .*
>
> *The members of the Executive Council, individually or collectively, should also have adequate authority within the limits prescribed and guidelines set by the President to*

act for him in monitoring, approving, and in coordinating the policies and programs of various departments and agencies in order to keep them within and abreast of the Presidential guidelines. But the members of the Executive Council should scrupulously avoid involvement in the minutia of departmental or agency operations. They should operate with very limited staffs of their own and avoid duplicating the staffs of the departments and agencies, although they should have authority to request permission of the heads of departments and agencies to borrow qualified persons for work on particular assignments. . . .[8]

Cohen emphasizes, as have George Reedy and others, that the real danger to presidential leadership comes from isolation from peers. Presidents are human beings subject to human frailties. "They have their off days, their blind spots, their periods of sickness and anxiety. . . . Quiet consultation by our Presidents before they make their momentous decisions with a small Council of wise and respected persons may protect our Presidents, our nation and our world from much of the hazards of fateful decisions which ultimately must be made by one man." [9]

The Cohen proposal merits consideration. His executive council could be created through legislation rather than constitutional amendment. And it might yield some of the benefits of the plural presidency without inviting most of its liabilities. To be sure, it might lessen the prestige of the existing cabinet and it could confuse the job of the vice-president. Moreover, it would require gifted, diplomatic persons possessed of shrewd political temperament. Doubtless some in the Congress would contend that such an executive council would be a further aggrandisement by the executive of legislative and policy-making powers that rightly belong to Congress. This contention has some merit. Still, many of these obstacles could be overcome. The Cohen proposal is one of the more perceptive reforms to be suggested in the post-Vietnam, post-Watergate era.

CABINET CONSOLIDATION

An increasing number of observers, among them many former White House aides and cabinet officials, believe that White House efforts to bypass the bureaucracy and to achieve faster departmental response to presidential initiatives have been institutionalized only at the high cost of diminishing self-confidence, morale, and initiative within the departments. The State Department, which several presidents virtually gave up on in attempting to make it more viable, is cited as a particularly salient case. Under Kennedy and Nixon, in particular, the presidential assistant for national security became an oversecretary of state, and a staff of between twenty to sixty foreign-policy professionals and numerous outside consultants grew up within the White House. The State

Department atrophied, its ambassadors became messenger boys, and its capacity to play any effective role in developing foreign policy deteriorated — some say, beyond repair. If the plight of the State Department often receives special attention, it is in part because during the cold war of the 1950s the secretary (e.g., Marshall, Acheson, and Dulles) and the department enjoyed an unusual preeminence and a close association with presidents and White House aides. But other departments and cabinet officers have experienced similar problems.

One of the strengths of the cabinet members — their capacity to make the strongest possible case for their programs and for departmental expansion — has proved to be their chief liability as well. Presidents need this type of advocacy, but they tire of it rapidly, as pointed out in Chapter 7, particularly as their fiscal resources and time run out and as they see programs failing to accomplish their objectives. Hence, presidents develop an increased reliance on White House staff assistants and staff policy-review committees. The same phenomenon also explains, at least in part, the importance of the recent directors of the Office of Management and Budget. Presidents want the advocacy they get from their cabinet members, but they also want the balanced technical and relatively neutral advice they feel can only come from trusted people who are removed from the firing lines of program implementation, people who can analyze problems from the point of view of multiple interests rather than from that of the narrower interest represented in and by the individual departments.

Three alternative methods of collapsing the outer domestic cabinet departments into broader-purpose departments were shown in Table 7-1. As indicated, these plausible options include reducing the number of departments from the present eleven to Nixon's proposed seven, or five, or even to a basic core of three: national security, economic affairs, and domestic policy. As is often the case, talk about the need for reform and any beginning moves in that direction, however gradual, have been preceded by practices that implicitly recognize the existence of an already distinctively differentiated cabinet. That is to say, in several aspects our recent presidents have increasingly treated the cabinet as if it were really three or four distinct cabinets — for national security, economic matters, domestic policy, and general politics, respectively.

A major assumption behind these proposals for cabinet consolidation is that large vacuums exist in the present cabinet organization, that too many new federal responsibilities, especially in the area of domestic policy, fall outside of the present departmental structure or between the established jurisdictional lines. The White House too often must fill those vacuums. A president, of course, should have the opportunity to set up an occasional new agency, to run an occasional high-priority program from directly within the executive office, or to put a beleaguered operation under extradepartmental control. Justification varies depending on the purpose at hand, although the need for flexibility, experimentation, and less legislative supervision normally is cited.

These would be more realistic options for the White House if there were not already a large number of existing and competing quasi-operational and interest-group brokerage activities going on in the presidential establishment.

President Nixon's cabinet reorganization proposals, illustrated in greater detail in Figure 10-1, would have established outside of the White House a number of important leadership centers through which presidential policies could be transmitted and delegated. This now-defunct plan was premised on the need to reduce the White House role in coordinating programs; to delegate the resolution of substantive and jurisdictional conflicts to a few strengthened cabinet offices; and to bring together similar or related programs so that wherever possible, governmental officials working on common problems could work together under a single chain of command. These changes would in turn reduce the number of people reporting to the president on related policies and programs.

These proposals presuppose also that the central conflict in White House-department relations does not lie between the president and his cabinet heads so much as between general and special interests. White House task-force studies have often advised presidents that weak, narrowly defined cabinet positions are a liability and a threat to the presidency. However loyal their occupants may want to be, they become so dependent on parochial bureaus and outside clientele that they cannot serve as counselors and representatives of presidential interests. The greatest strains occur between those devoted to specific functional programs championed by particularistic clienteles and elites and those who seek to manage and coordinate a range of particular policies.

Reducing the present number of eleven departments and a larger number of independent (nonregulatory) agencies to a few broad-ranging departments would not only enable more jurisdictional conflicts to be resolved within departments, it could also strengthen the hand of domestic cabinet members in resisting narrow special interests, thereby enabling them to serve as counselors as well as advocates. Cabinet consolidation could also have another desirable effect: it might be a step toward reducing the accumulation of power within the presidential establishment. Much of the power of budget directors and other senior White House aides lies in their role as penultimate referees of interdepartmental jurisdictional disputes. Under consolidated departments, however, a small number of strengthened cabinet officers with more access to a president might resolve these conflicts. And with fewer but broader cabinet departments, less need would exist for many of the interest-group brokers and special councils that now constitute so much of the excess baggage in the overstuffed executive office.

Support for cabinet consolidation and greater delegation of presidential authority to strong and more independent-minded cabinet members comes from dozens of former White House aides. They suggest that such developments could help arrest the tendency to concentrate too much decision making

FIGURE 10–1 EXECUTIVE DEPARTMENTS UNDER PRESIDENT NIXON'S DEPARTMENTAL REORGANIZATION PROGRAM, FEBRUARY, 1972

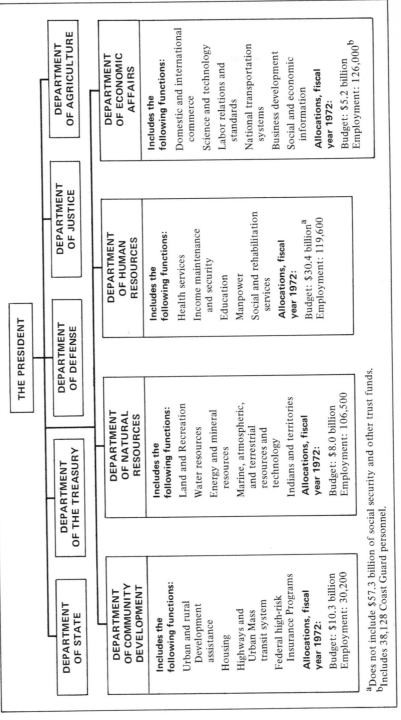

U.S. Office of Management and Budget

in the executive office of the president. To the extent that numerous agencies are involved in such matters as the energy and inflation problems, which plainly cannot be dealt with in isolation, the tasks of developing overall policy and reconciling disagreements necessarily are visited on the White House. In the absence of consolidated, broad-gauged departments, such tasks either are done there or are not done at all.

Fewer, better-organized, and better-led departments could and would leave a president more time to devote to his executive responsibilities — the recruitment and motivation of able administrators, the design of effective systems for feedback and planning, and the sorting out of what is important from what is not — and avoid miring him down in administering programs. One school of thought, however, doubts the efficacy of cabinet consolidation in light of recent experiences with HEW and Defense, the two cabinet departments that now best exemplify multiple-interest departments. Pointing out that these two superdepartments have been among the most unmanageable and difficult to monitor, the opponents of consolidation argue that consolidation should be avoided until a better administrative capability exists to make these monster entities, especially HEW, more effective in achieving their goals. One skeptic argues that the planning-programming-budgeting system (PPBS) did not make domestic programs more effective and that until something — a set of analytical tools, structural arrangements, better trained staff — comes into existence and is proven effective over time, consolidation would create greater liabilities than benefits. Students of reorganization also point out that although the Nixon administration's proposals cited the clientele-oriented cabinet departments as major obstacles to program coordination, the proposed remedy called for lumping together agencies with disparate clienteles in a way that was more likely to weaken than to strengthen the managerial capabilities of the new supersecretaries.[10]

By itself, cabinet revitalization, that is, consolidating and then attracting highly talented cabinet officers, would change little. Domestic cabinet heads have not enjoyed close working relations with the president. They have been forced into behaving not as presidential allies but as advocates, in the worst sense of that term, to the White House; and they often have been unable to bring their departments into cooperative arrangements with related departments with which they must interact functionally. Thus, submerging narrowly defined departments into broad superdepartments will make sense only if the position of departmental secretary is strengthened institutionally. These positions need competent staffs and authority and leverage to influence policy in presidentially preferred directions.

There is a need, also, for an innovative management-consultant organization within the executive office. Many of the time-consuming problems visited on the White House or faced by domestic department heads emerge from complex jurisdictional questions of overlap and coordination. During the 1960s the

White House and the Bureau of the Budget had insufficient capacity to offer sustained professional management advice to the president or to his cabinet members. As one Johnson cabinet member remarked, "If there had been a high-level and competent consulting agency available to me, I would have had it in use every day, full time!" Any cabinet official who is asked to preside over a huge superdepartment will need such assistance just as much or more.

An extended, professionalized management group to serve not only the president but also cabinet heads should draw upon personnel from within as well as from outside the government. This staff would be charged with conducting controlled experiments on different managerial strategies; with accelerating grant-consolidation programs throughout the government; and with examining when to contract out, when to centralize, and when to build more competition among existing government operations. These management specialists also should be available to a president for short-term assignments as troubleshooters or expediters in intradepartmental or intergovernmental controversies. The most important contribution of such a management-consultant organization could be to develop an increasingly professionalized career service, one that appears to work less and less according to traditional notions of organizational hierarchy.

PLANNING AND PROGRAM EVALUATION STAFFS

The 1960s was supposed to be the era of the action-intellectuals. Certainly an aura of academic vigor, if not rigor, surrounded the presidential establishment then. Considerable legislation was passed that set in motion hundreds of experimental programs. These federal initiatives, often conceived in haste and secrecy and with few precedents, were seldom subjected to systematic evaluation. Only in the late 1960s did the federal government begin medium-scale program experiments in social policy that had evaluation built in from the beginning, for example, performance-contracting in public schools and income-maintenance schemes. In large measure, what evaluation is done today is a vestige of the early sixties romance with program budgeting and rational analysis, which few take seriously but use when convenient to create an appearance of responsibility.

Learning what works and who pays and estimating what alternative approaches cost, or what their consequences would be, are not simple goals. Yet real progress without planning and evaluation is doubtful, as two Harvard scholars, commenting on the evaluation of educational policy during the 1960s, argued:

A great many innovations will be tried in one or two places each, and each will be declared the solution to our educational problems. Then as others try them, they will usually fail. . . . But unless studies are carried out in a systematic way, we will not have learned about conditions when a method may be of use and when it may not, or what features of the program still show promise in spite of general failure. These are the losses that matter, for without systematic effort, we stumble on generation after generation, learning little and fooling ourselves that we are learning something about the process because we are busy doing new things. Thus, by never getting firm facts, we are in the position of believing that "the" solution is contained in the new program just being tried.[11]

Too often, the prevailing attitude toward carefully controlled experiments, both in the White House and in Congress, has ranged from casual indifference to hostility. Whether a program is evaluated as a success or failure, those who would be disadvantaged by it, or who would profit from it, are put on the defensive. Reformers often block evaluation on grounds that it would be premature or that their proposed innovations have not yet yielded the promised investment. Congressmen from districts having federal installations may oppose studies likely to show that such installations are obsolete or blatantly inefficient. Civil servants have been known to oppose studies that would examine the possibility of abolishing their jobs or of contracting out some of their responsibilities. An administration that truly encourages a dispassionate and objective evaluation organization in its midst will probably find that its evaluation advisers indict the very administration they serve.

Where do planning and evaluation best fit into ongoing governmental operations? Should they be integrated with the budgeting process, the legislative process, the management process, or all of these? Should evaluation be based in the executive office of the president; in the departments, bureaus, regional offices, state and local governments; or in some combination of these? At what point in the unfolding of new programs should special attention be paid to evaluation? Is there a risk in evaluating a program too soon? Should planning units and evaluation units be wholly independent of those units responsible for implementing programs? When should planning and evaluation be contracted outside of the government? What kinds of competition or multiple-advocacy procedures would prevent the possibility that one set of planners would come to dominate the making of broad-range policy and political decisions? Aaron Wildavsky has dramatized some of the difficulties:

Evaluative man must learn to live with contradictions. He must reduce his commitments to the organizations in which he works, the programs he carries out, and the clientele he serves. Evaluators must become agents of change acting in favor of programs as yet unborn and clienteles that are unknown. Prepared to impose change on others, evaluators must have sufficient stability to carry out their own work. They must maintain their own organization while simultaneously preparing to abandon it. They must obtain the support of existing bureaucracies while pursuing antibureaucratic policies. They must combine political feasibility with analytical purity. Only a brave man would predict that these combinations of qualities can be found in one and the same person and organization.[12]

Not surprisingly, then, evaluators and planners are nearly always politically threatening to chief executives and administrators. Evaluators customarily are ignored by administrators, save when they can be used to validate the status quo.

While some reformers question the value of adding more staff — for whatever purpose — to the executive office, it is important to remember that staffs are necessary: to digest and distill ideas and facts that come percolating up through advisory processes and to reach out to interest groups and research institutions to elicit policy appraisals and alternatives. No one department or professional group should dominate these fact-gathering and program-developing staffs. Building-in competition is one way of inhibiting the ever-present temptation for policy advocates to skew their advice in favor of self-serving policies.[13]

Suggestions from Alexander L. George and Irving L. Janis form the kinds of thoughtful guidelines a president needs constantly to keep in mind. George calls for establishing within the White House staff a nonadvocate, neutral, objective guardian of a multiple-advocacy process. This aide or set of aides would be charged with balancing advisory resources when necessary, strengthening weaker advocates, bringing in new advisers to argue for unpopular options, setting up new channels of information, and arranging for independent evaluations of options. This function is premised on the following values: "First, the chief executive may have to take steps if not to equalize resources among the advocates, then to avoid gross disparities in them. Second, the chief executive must be alert to the danger that a sufficient range of policy alternatives may not be encompassed by the advocates available for participating in the resolution of a particular policy issue. Third, he may have to develop certain rules of the game to maintain fair competition and to avoid 'restraint of trade' among the advocates." [14]

Professor Janis writes about national policy-making groups that succumb to what he calls the problem of "groupthink." He is concerned with the tendency of like-minded advisers to develop stereotyped images that dehumanize competing out-groups and with the tendency for their collective judgment to shift toward courses of action riskier than those which any individual member would otherwise adopt. His provocative and rather frightening case analyses should be read carefully by any prospective adviser to a president. Janis not only isolates a number of factors that tempt advisers toward this groupthink mentality but also, like George, posits a number of strategies that might prevent its occurrence:

The leaders in an organization's hierarchy, when assigning a policy-planning mission to a group, should be impartial instead of stating preferences and expectations at the outset. This practice requires each leader to limit his briefings to unbiased statements about the scope of the problem and the limitations of available resources, without advocating specific proposals he would like to see adopted. . . .

The organization should routinely follow the administrative practice of setting up several independent policy-planning and evaluation groups to work on the same policy question, each carrying out its deliberations under a different leader. . . .

At every meeting devoted to evaluating policy alternatives, at least one member should be assigned the role of devil's advocate. . . .

After reaching a preliminary consensus about what seems to be the best policy alternative, the policy-making group should hold a "second chance" meeting at which every member is expected to express as vividly as he can all his residual doubts and to rethink the entire issue before making a definitive choice.[15]

Sometimes, of course, a president does not want to hear objective, balanced advice; he may have his own policy preferences and he may be more worried about gaining the cooperation of various agencies than about giving all advocates an equal hearing. Does a president want to strengthen the hand of the Office of Education or the Central Intelligence Agency even in those instances in which he disagrees with their long-standing points of view?

The recommendations of both George and Janis accentuate collegial and collective decision-making processes, processes having costs that may not be readily apparent. Increasing the number of participants in advisory processes and equalizing their resources may insure only that vested interests and seasoned bureaucrats have more chances to cast their own two cents' worth into the deliberations. Cast as advocates, certain elites whose points of view are not accepted may go outside and take their case to Congress, to the press, or to the public. Larger advisory bodies also tend to place a premium on permitting more people to exercise a veto, and a multiple-veto process might favor the status quo rather than expand alternatives.

Can White House aides be assigned to a nonadvocate, neutral guardianship of the multiple-advocacy process, while at the same time serving a president as a communications channel and monitor of program implementation? Aides who might have been fairly objective on questions of policy formulation often become unrelenting advocates and lieutenants for fixed presidential policy views in the implementation stages, especially after substantial amounts of their time have been committed to bureaucratic combat work or when the president desperately wants to accomplish at least a few of his promised objectives before the next election. In short, can persons assigned to guard and advance the president's policy interests also preserve the neutrality of the multiple-advocacy process? Would it be realistic to divorce these two sets of functions by assigning them to different people? Even then, would not advocacy be sacrificed in practice whenever it came into serious conflict with already set policy interests?

As a beginning, a revitalized Domestic Council makes sense. Plainly, however, the Domestic Council especially needs an effective Office of Planning and Program Evaluation. This staff would be particularly concerned with identifying problems within existing programs and with new problems needing national policy response. Such a staff might experiment also with developing better indicators of social policy success. Serving as an in-house center for experimentation, usually in concert with departmental or outside research centers, it could test alternative policy or program options before implementing federal programs on a nationwide scale. It might help prevent embryo programs from being battered around in Congress, exaggerated by administration spokesmen, used as political footballs, and criticized for not meeting broadscale goals when they are intended only as small-scale programs. Despite some efforts along these lines in recent years, presidents and presidential aides seem to remain indifferent to the way programs are managed and evaluated, so long as they get the political credit and little or no backfire occurs over program management.

Congress, too, needs beefed-up evaluation and supervisory staffs. The benefits of competition between evaluation in the White House and in congressional offices could well outweigh the incidental overlap or extra expenditures. Both branches need improved information and evaluation of policy. At both ends of Pennsylvania Avenue political leaders have permitted policy research and program assessments to be carried out by the same people who administer the programs or by departmentally appointed advisory panels that are tied closely, even symbiotically, to the interests of the bureau officials. To give these resources only to the executive branch may be to erode the basis necessary to maintaining a separate but significant partnership for the Congress in the national policymaking enterprise. To avoid creating wholly new structures on Capitol Hill, these tasks and functions could well be absorbed by a redesigned and expanded Congressional Research Service and by certain of the existing committee staffs, such as the joint budget committee staff and the staff of the Office of Technology Assessment. Congress, of course, cannot and should not duplicate the evaluation facilities of the executive branch, but it has a special obligation to keep informed and insure ready access to executive branch research and evaluation studies, executive privilege notwithstanding.[16]

One objection to expanding the White House planning and evaluation staffs comes from persons who believe that they should rather be located within the individual departments. They suggest that research, planning, and evaluation staffs should be centralized in the office of a department secretary but sufficiently removed from program operations in the line bureaus. Until very recently, however, Congress has been cautious about requests and appropriations that would strengthen presidentially appointed departmental leadership at the expense of the career bureau chiefs with whom congressmen often prefer to deal. Several departments are now developing stronger capabilities for program planning and evaluation. This trend should be vigorously supported, but it does not negate the need for a similar and competing capability at the White

House. A Planning and Program Evaluation Office staff would help a president set priorities by presenting results of experimentation and evaluation. Such an office, properly designed, also could help a president oversee the quality and the problems of planning and evaluation thoughout the government. Finally, just as a president needs his own budget bureau and legislative liaison staff, so now he has an inescapable need to institutionalize the functions of foresight, national planning, and evaluation, which would help clarify his goals in relation to his departments and serve as a clearing-house and synthesizer of diverse experiments, research investigations, and critical program evaluations that cut across the domains of departments and subpresidencies.

Establishing a genuine planning operation in or even near the presidential establishment will prove to be a difficult, if not impossible, challenge. Franklin Roosevelt's attempts at planning were largely defeated. Looking back at that period, some people, like Rexford Tugwell, conclude it was not yet time for it. Others suggest the thrust toward comprehensive planning was captured, subdivided, and subdued by the very interests who shared the collectivist social-management impulse but who wanted control of a very different kind. Historian Otis L. Graham, Jr., put it this way:

The perversion of the national planning ideal stemmed from no direct decision of New Dealers. In the beginning, especially, the administration seemed committed to co-ordinated national planning. But the rush of events smothered even these inclinations. Both Congress and the administration, responding to clamorous demands for public intervention by various groups, multiplied new agencies to cope with problems as they arose. Hopefully, there would be time to rationalize the government's impact, to mesh its many programs in a harmonious whole. Toward this end a harried President supported a small planning board, established two Cabinet-level coordinating committees which collapsed by 1935, and appointed in 1938 a Fiscal and Monetary Advisory Board of appropriate heads which became at once deadlocked in intergovernmental rivalries and failed to last out the year. These institutions, like the grander NRA, did not evolve into coordinating machinery suitable to the need. The NRA experiment, in particular, wasted time and shattered enthusiasm for central direction. While the President in his second term groped for control of his party and the Court, and for the right to reorganize the executive branch and the independent regulatory commissions, events made the decision about the nature and extent of management. Alliances were struck between private interests, bureaucrats, and interested politicians; the legislative mill ground forward, giving old agencies broader mandates or creating new agencies for specialized tasks. Control expanded by sectors. The advance toward social management went on, but by a hundred separate paths.[17]

What happened during the 1930s has been repeated in each subsequent decade. Presidential centralization and guidance efforts such as the Planning, Programming and Budget System of the late 1960s and the Management By Objective scheme tried during the Nixon-Ford administration faltered, usually for the familiar reasons.

Veteran critics of executive office planning also question whether presidents and their chief lieutenants can ever really engage in long-term planning and reflection. Short-range thinking and planning is difficult enough for most White House occupants. Time is not the only reason for this. Proper incentives to plan for the long range seem absent, if not wholly nonexistent. History is plainly on the side of the critics. Even minor attempts at national planning such as those undertaken by Nixon's National Goals staff proved highly unsuccessful. Hence, advocates sometimes urge that a powerful public organization for national planning be established separate from both the Congress and the White House. Such is the proposed solution of former New Dealer Rexford G. Tugwell. He has long since given up on the idea of trying to interest presidents in the formidable tasks of national planning. Tugwell, in the end, may be right, but since his dream of a visionary new branch of government — set up solely to prepare five- and ten-year national plans — is politically unacceptable to most people today, we have little choice but to try to refashion both the executive and legislative branches to do what they can to upgrade the crafts of planning and evaluation.

REGIONALIZATION OF THE PRESIDENCY

One intriguing idea is that a president needs a mediating and coordinating presence at the state or regional level. Little agreement exists to date, however, about what functions would be given over to regional White House agents. These local agents might insure that the federal departments are coordinated at the regional level to effect ambitious environmental and human-resource development programs; they might assist mayors and governors in carrying out joint local-state-federal enterprises; or they might serve as emissaries to governors and other local leaders, interpreting federal objectives and listening attentively to their problems. The rationale for a rather bold version of the federal presence was suggested by James MacGregor Burns:

> The federal government would establish "presidential" agencies in several hundred regions throughout the country. These agencies would work directly under the supervision of the president and his executive office, bypassing departmental and bureau levels if necessary. Their jobs would be to integrate all governmental policies, federal, state, and local, that related to the priority areas. In the program to eradicate poverty, for example, they would administer — or supervise the administration of — those aspects of welfare, employment, job training, education, industry and manpower relocation, health, housing, urban renewal, school lunches, child nurseries, literacy programs, local transportation, and other activities or programs that relate to poverty.[18]

What presidents and their counselors have found impossible to achieve from Washington by means of interdepartmental committees, "lead agencies" (that

is, a specified department responsible for coordination across several agencies),
or expanded White House staffs would now be attempted at the regional level.
But can the resources of the presidency be extended or transplanted to St.
Louis, Seattle, and El Paso?

Proponents of a presidential presence claim that no amount of coordination
in the executive office of the president can overcome rigid organizational operations in the field. Former budget director Charles Schultze put it this way:
"Outside of Washington there is no federal government. There are only a series
of bureaucratic fiefdoms. Even within single departments, the regional directors
often have little authority over the field operations of the particular line
bureaus. Governors and mayors, wishing to plan a coordinated attack on some
particular problem involving a number of different grant programs, have no
place to go except directly to Washington." [19] Schultze cited an example of
what happens without a regional presidential presence:

> In 1967 it was decided to establish fourteen neighborhood centers on a pilot basis, to
> provide in a single location the delivery of federally sponsored services — manpower
> counseling and training, health clinics, welfare and family planning services and the
> like. Agreement on a plan of approach and a timetable was secured from the relevant
> Cabinet officers. Direct White House participation on a continuing basis was estab-
> lished. . . . It then turned out that some field representatives had the authority to com-
> mit funds and make decisions, while others did not. . . . In some activities an agency of
> the state was the primary program operator receiving federal grants, while for other
> activities it was a city agency and in still others a nonprofit agency. Given the wide
> variety of circumstances among different communities, no central agreement among
> department heads in Washington could provide detailed enough instructions to the field
> to avoid the necessity for on-the-spot decisions. But with no central authority within
> each department in the field, painfully reached agreements in Washington became
> meaningless in the face of inertia, timidity, and protection of bureaucratic empires.[20]

A presidential presence in the field would be intended to insure that increasing departmental decentralization and increasing grants to state and local governments actually do maximize the national objectives. Loyal and neutral agents
of the president would see to it that presidential objectives are realized and
would strike the proper balance among squabbling federal departments. Presidential influence from Washington would extend into the regions under this
plan, even though cabinet members already have a semblance of, if narrower,
presence of their own in the same localities through their departmental offices
or departmental presence. The quest for presidentially directed coordination
efforts also takes into consideration the past failures when such responsibilities
were delegated to a single cabinet officer. As James Sundquist pointed out, "no
cabinet department has ever been able to act effectively, for long, as a central
coordinator of other departments of equal rank that are its competitors for
authority and funds." [21]

The chief difficulties with this idea arise from political considerations. Many members of Congress have a not unsubstantiated belief that they now exercise considerable control over certain federal bureau officials in Washington and over regional departmental civil servants located in their states or districts. Why should they look kindly on proposals that would place White House-appointed political officials in their regions? Undoubtedly, many of them would feel threatened by presidential districts being visited on their own congressional districts. Congressmen are joined in this view by nationwide interest groups, which typically prefer to have the control of departmental programs located in Washington so they need not compete with mayors or governors for influence or control over programs. Also, the activities of these presidential agents might be regarded as an encroachment on the prerogatives of Congress. And, of course, local interests might contend that the activities of these presidential agents weaken states' rights and the intent of revenue sharing.

Recent administrations have attempted to transfer more authority to the regional and field offices of domestic departments. In contrast to a regional presidential presence, this may be viewed as a regional departmental presence; the distinction is not a minor one. But departmental regionalization is often subject to politicization. Powerful local officials and congressmen have successfully secured these jobs for political appointees, and presidential counselors rightly worry that these regional departmental officials are captives of the local political elite or of narrow functional specialists, or both.

If regionalized presidential agencies do come into being, these offices could also be politicized. Such agents might not long remain aloof from partisan and regional politics. How soon would come the day when a Mayor Richard Daley, a Governor Hugh Carey, or a Governor George Wallace is promised his choice of the regional assistant president in advance of presidential nominating conventions? To local leaders, who would become the regional presidential agent could be much more important than who becomes vice-president. The stakes can be counted in terms of billions of dollars, the kind and extent of federal controls, and the leeway for bargaining, accommodation, and delay. In addition, the performance of cabinet members and even executive office personnel suggests loyalty develops to professional standards, to Congress, to political ideology, and to the constituency of a program, often in competition with loyalty to the man in the White House. Is it likely that presidential agents located 900 or 3,500 miles away will suffer any less from these centrifugal forces?

Another problem involves the none-too-cordial relations between recent White House staffs and state houses. Much of the Great Society legislation in seeking to bypass southern governors also bypassed relatively more progressive governors. Federal grant-in-aid formulas often limited a governor's discretion in responding to the peculiar problems of his own state. As a result, the traditionally weak role of governor in most states was weakened further. Placing assistant presidents in their territories invites the analogy that states are being treated like banana republics, dependent on the U. S. government for aid, trade, and now even for the supervision of their own internal affairs.

Ironically, the proliferation of intergovernmental grants-in-aid has come during a period in which no president since FDR has served in any capacity in state government. Appointing defeated or retired governors, usually from small states, to minor positions within the executive office is hardly a solution to the strained White House-state house relations, yet this has been a standard White House remedy. (Former governor Nelson Rockefeller's appointment as vice-president is an exception to the general pattern.) Regardless of the party in the White House, most governors have come there with hat in hand and have been treated as dependents. Not uncommonly, they complain of White House arrogance. A move toward a presidential management presence around the country could signify two things to governors: first, that these aides are being sent to undercut them; and, second, that presidents no longer have time to deal personally with them.

As Ira Sharkansky pointed out, however, certain states have been creative and responsible across a wide range of public services, even if others have not. The federal government should develop a more refined and differentiated view of (1) what states, generically, do well and poorly and (2) what each state does well and poorly. It should then design its technical assistance strategies accordingly. "What is preferred to the present informality of state discretion — or to the wholesale devolution of autonomy represented by some proposals for revenue sharing — is a more systematic arrangement that seeks to identify the areas of strength and weakness, then rewards strength and induces improvement in weakness." [22] For example, in the federal war on crime the Nixon administration failed to communicate to the governors a sense of accountability for the large block grants that came cascading down upon newly organized law-enforcement-assistance agencies in their states. The result: too many states experienced inadequate planning, inefficient allocation of funds, lumpy performance, and conflict of interest. Most governors assumed little responsibility for the expenditure of these funds, treating them as "soft money," a veritable giveaway program. Presidential agents in the field could have detected such state and local problems.

A president does delegate, of course, vast authority to able cabinet officers and their subordinates for overseeing the integration of federal programs with state and local programs. Although the problem of poor program coordination at the local level cannot be alleviated greatly by institutionalizing the regional representation of the presidency, some innovation in this area surely is warranted. Coordination at the local level must be done primarily, though not exclusively, by general governmental institutions based there, not in Washington. At the same time, existing presidential staffs and cabinet officials, as they are working out substantive plans for new legislation and as they are dividing up new discretionary funds, need to be concerned about managerial strategies in the field. Improving relations with governors and mayors is also a part of the problem. Governors and local officials complain constantly that they cannot get things settled at a regional level. Some of them feel that they could cultivate and win the understanding and cooperation of well-informed federal agents stationed in their territory, whereas Washington is remote, distant, cold, and unfeeling.

The assumption that governors of large states or mayors of strategic cities would resent presidential representatives in their area remains untested. Much obviously depends on the character and competence of the "Little White Houses" and their officers. If an assistant president is given that title but is chosen from among "good old boys," such as recently defeated U. S. senators who are merely looking for a political base from which to run again, and the like, the concept certainly would fail. But such a post would provide a most excellent reward for ourstanding career public servants with at least a semblance of a passion for anonymity, who know how to get things done, who can avoid unreasonable partisan politics as much as possible, and who are expert at making intergovernmental relations more effective. The career person concept, if embodied from the beginning, would be less of a threat to local leaders and would help avoid the claims of a Daley or a Wallace.

Governors and big-city mayors may indeed benefit from recent presidential efforts to rationalize the activities of federal field personnel through more effective regional coordination. A president would derive political advantage, too, by joining in a coalition with governors and mayors. Herbert Kaufman reasoned that "Congress would find it more uncomfortable to resist presidential demands for creation of strong field representatives with jurisdiction over bureau field personnel if state and local officials in their own home areas support the demands than if the President alone advances them. And these states and local officials may be receptive to such an association because [the fragmentation and competition of federal and local programs] is as vexing to them as it is to the President himself." [23]

However, the design of regional presidential influence and the filling of offices at the regional level to effect this aim require much more political energy and sophistication than presidents either have or are willing to give it. The Office of Management and Budget backed with various executive orders has attempted through the creation of federal regional councils to effect such a presidential presence in the field, but its numerous unsuccessful efforts to induce these councils to resolve issues and enhance decentralization suggest its severe limitations as a presidentially designated field coordinator.[24] Plainly, however, effective presidential leadership, especially in implementing certain redistributive domestic policies, will require substantial attention to this subject.

INCENTIVE SYSTEMS FOR THE BUREAUCRACY

Ultimately, people, rather than structure, are the source of strength and renewal in any organization. The battle to win cooperation from the bureaucracy begins far in advance of the day on which a president assumes office. Presidents in recent years have experienced major problems in acting as the government's talent scout and as the catalyst for imaginative personnel policy. Part of the problem stems from the fact that Congress, interest groups, and diverse clientele have been wooing bureaucratic loyalties for decades. Also, with all his other burdens, a president easily can allow personnel responsibilities to drift to the Civil Service Commission or to a small band of patronage advisers. During the first year of the Ford administration it seemed that this responsibility was assigned or accepted by virtually no one. But if the struggle to control the bureaucracy is a far less glamorous venture than that of winning the election of a president, it is fully as important to the success of his leadership.

White House aides often develop a simplistic and misleading view that political appointments controlled by the White House insure responsiveness, whereas the presence of career civil servants, military people, or foreign service officers leads to an indifferent performance or even sabotage. Yet many political appointees are plainly motivated by more materialistic and selfish aims than most career public servants. Often, the former are fatcat donors in search of an ambassadorship, young lawyers in search of Justice Department or regulatory commission experience and contacts with which to enhance and enrich their future private practice, and so on. Moreover, political appointees often remain more responsive to their home-state political organizations, professional or interest associations, or sponsoring congressmen than to the White House. In short, "loyalty" and "competence" are terms that are too simplistic to differentiate outside appointments from those made inside the government.

The more we recognize the nonhierarchical aspects of modern government and the more we understand the major changes brought about by professionalism, decentralization, and the increasing use of temporary organization, the more apparent the need becomes for better and more innovative incentive systems. Numerous difficulties exist. Top professionals and expert managers are lured away from private enterprise or nongovernmental research institutions only with difficulty. Large numbers of competent government workers are frustrated by the layering and rigidity that set in with highly differentiated and specialized bureaucratic organizations. Too few of the best-qualified younger civil servants now complete their careers within the government. Finding top positions, the political ones, closed to them and lateral shifts within the government widely discouraged, they have nowhere to go but out.

One tempting proposal was put forth many times by White House aides from recent administrations, who have become antagonistic to career public servants:

that the time has come to edge back toward a spoils system, that is, to the practice of more patronage and fewer civil service jobs. The pendulum, they say, has swung too far in the direction of job security and the protection of a paternalistic civil service, which permits career officials to do more or less what they please. For the White House aides as well as for many of the cabinet members, a major problem is getting career personnel to accept an enlarged personal responsibility. In addition, there is the natural frustration of not being able to discuss the political ramifications of a decision with career civil servants. In any showdown, the aides believe, the people in the departments tend to be loyal to the clientele of their departments, or to past administrations, or to previous priorities rather than to the White House.

Another modest piece of reform legislation, one endorsed by the Nixon administration, would establish an executive-service manpower pool into which career public servants can be promoted for a temporary, three-year tour of duty, or to which outside political appointments can be made. The plan is premised on the need for more flexibility in senior administrative appointments. The Nixon White House doubtless felt that it would insure more of that elusive quality known as "responsiveness to the White House." This plan also recognizes that career officials have their share of complaints about the immobilizing labyrinth of the Civil Service Commission's regulations, especially that, to date, the positions with the highest administrative authority and responsibility have been labeled "noncareer," which puts a ceiling on how far the career executive can advance. A Civil Service Commission official adds: "It has long been apparent that the present rigid distinction between 'career' and 'noncareer' positions in the Government lies along a continuum in respect to policy involvement, with only a comparative handful at either extreme which can be reliably classified into these categories. [The tendency] ... to categorize positions of highest responsibilities as noncareer ... has resulted in a limitation of opportunity for those in the career service, since a career executive who elects to move into one of these top positions forfeits the career rights he has built up over the years." [25] These are valid frustrations, and this suggestion for reform might go part of the way toward overcoming them. In any event, the proposition at the core of this reform deserves testing: would officials without job security be more responsive or simply more cautious and timid?

More lateral entry of outside professionals and business executives into government service is needed, but not at the expense of increased professional and executive in-service training and development programs for personnel already within the career services. Neither should career protection be given to persons whose blatant partisanship might work to defeat programs of future administrations. Means also must be designed to improve the mobility of bright younger members in the career services. These reforms are easier said than done, however, because of the substantial norms for seniority and against organizational change. [26]

Skepticism is warranted, moreover, toward any sweeping proposals that would greatly expand the number of political appointments. Already, political clearance for so-called nonpolitical posts has become more frequent, often in disregard of civil service statutes as well as past precedent. There is some question as well about whether the appointment prerogative should be expanded, for recent administrations have not filled existing places thoughtfully, imaginatively, or, in some cases, honestly. Vacancies and ill-considered appointments are not unusual.

Except for a few posts, presidents rely on others to tell them whom to appoint. They also use some posts and appointments as leverage in bargaining. But, on balance, the costs of exercising the appointment prerogative rigorously seem high: the more jobs to fill, the more pressures on a president and the less time he has for other facets of his position. Assuming responsibility for personnel matters in government is essential, however, if the government is to be won over to a president's program. Just as this problem can be underestimated at the outset of an administration, so it can be exacerbated when placed in less than professional hands. Caution is needed not to breed hostility and disloyalty where none now exists. White House impatience to get things moving invites resentment and hardly can help to create an objective, cooperative mood among civil servants. The we/they attitude developed, usually out of ignorance, by many White House aides toward members of the permanent government often is accompanied by feelings that career service people are untouchables and that nothing can be done to improve the situation. In fact, wide latitude exists for administrative appointments through promotion, transfer, reassignment, and various forms of lateral entry. Shrewd White House aides also learn that the perspectives of government officials who are two, three, and more levels removed from the White House are shaped by types of information, pressures, loyalties, and peer relations substantially different from those that shape White House work norms.

If, as President Nixon claimed, the bureaucracy as now organized inhibits the delivery of a dollar's worth of service for a dollar's taxes, this is so, in part, because presidents and their cabinet members have not devised open and flexible organizations in which employees will take risks, assume more initiative, and pay more attention to White House priorities.[27] Better press coverage of presidential performance in personnel recruitment and protection might encourage more presidential attention to this aspect of national government. Presidential candidates could be pressed on such issues as how they plan to improve the accountability of the federal career service not only to the White House but also to the public interests.

In sum, strengthening the presidency is never a neutral enterprise. In one sense, most institutional reforms are as deceptive as they are beguiling. Those who would substantially alter the institution of the presidency nearly always have in mind certain goals. More often than not, to change the rules by which institutions operate means that the advantages that have accrued to one elite are transferred to another.

Too often, the White House accepts the size and complexity of the large bureaucracies of the permanent government as insuperable and nonadaptive problems. What is needed is a policy that consciously recognizes presidential dependency on the federal bureaus and field operations and that takes into account the fact that presidential policy objectives will continue to lose clarity between stages of legislation and implementation. What is needed are innovative outreach and feedback strategies designed to keep organizations well informed of presidential intent, motivated to carry out such intent, and accountable for performance.

The range of reform possibilities surely has not been exhausted here; many others have been suggested. How the government is organized may often determine the degree to which a president can fulfill his responsibilities. If some progress has been made in improved information-gathering processes, further improvements now are needed in the area of program implementation and policy evaluation. A particularly important area for reform is the invention of better strategies to recruit and properly use professionals in the public service.

NOTES

1. Herman Finer, *The Presidency: Crisis and Regeneration* (University of Chicago Press, 1960), p. viii. See also a more recent plea for a more collective presidency: Milton Eisenhower, *The President Is Calling* (Doubleday, 1974).
2. Rexford G. Tugwell, *The Enlargement of the Presidency* (Doubleday, 1960), p. 493. Tugwell goes measurably beyond these thoughts in his proposed model constitution; see *The Emerging Constitution* (Harpers Magazine Press, 1974).
3. Eric Sevareid, "Time for a Pause to Reflect," reprinted in the *Congressional Record,* 87th Cong., 2d sess., 15 Sept. 1962, daily ed., App.: A5191.
4. See Mark O. Hatfield, "Resurrecting Political Life in America . . . ," *Congressional Record,* 93d Cong., 1st sess., 12 Oct. 1973, vol. 119, no. 153, pp. S. 19104–107.
5. See Herman Somers, *Presidential Agency* (Harvard University Press, 1950).
6. See Murray C. Havens, "Presidents, Subordinates and Political Responsibility" (Paper delivered at the Annual Meeting of the Southern Political Science Association, New Orleans, La., 7–9 Nov. 1974; processed).
7. See, for example, Edward Corwin, *The President: Office and Powers,* 4th ed. (New York University Press, 1957); and Thomas K. Finletter, *Can Representative Government Do The Job?* (Reynal & Hitchcock, 1945).
8. Benjamin V. Cohen, "Presidential Responsibility and American Democracy" (1974 Royer Lecture, University of California, Berkeley, 23 May 1974; processed), pp. 24–25.
9. *Ibid.,* p. 29. See also George Reedy, *The Twilight of the Presidency* (World, 1970).
10. On this last point, see Douglas M. Fox, "The President's Proposals for Executive Reorganization: A Critique" (processed; n.d.), p. 3.
11. John Gilbert and Frederick Mosteller, "The Urgent Need for Experimentation," in Frederick Mosteller and Daniel P. Moynihan, eds., *On Equality of Educational Opportunity* (Vintage, 1972), p. 378.

12. Aaron Wildavsky, "Evaluation as an Organizational Problem" (Paper delivered before the American Society of Public Administration, New York, March 1972; processed), p. 11.
13. See, for example, T. E. Cronin and N. C. Thomas, "Federal Advisory Processes: Advice & Discontent," *Science,* 26 February 1971; and Joel Primack and Frank von Hippel, *Advice and Dissent: Scientists in the Political Arena* (Basic Books, 1974).
14. Alexander L. George, "Stress in Political Decision-Making," February 1971; processed, p. 82. Many of these ideas are contained in his "The Case for Multiple Advocacy in Making Foreign Policy," *American Political Science Review,* September 1972, pp. 751–85.
15. Irving L. Janis, *Victims of Groupthink* (Houghton Mifflin, 1972), pp. 210–18.
16. See Raoul Berger, *Executive Privilege* (Harvard University Press, 1974), chs. 8 and 9.
17. Otis L. Graham, Jr., "The Planning Ideal and the American Reality: The 1930's," in Stanley Elkins and Eric McKitrick, eds., *Hofstadter Aegis: A Memorial to Richard Hofstadter* (Knopf, 1974), pp. 281–82.
18. James M. Burns, *Uncommon Sense* (Harper and Row, 1972), p. 132.
19. Charles L. Schultze, *Statement* before the Senate Committee on Government Operations, 92d Cong., 1st sess., 1971 (processed), p. 8. See also James L. Sundquist, *Making Federalism Work* (The Brookings Institution, 1969).
20. Schultze, *Statement,* p. 9.
21. James L. Sundquist, *Making Federalism Work* (The Brookings Institution, 1969), p. 244.
22. Ira Sharkansky, *The Maligned States* (McGraw-Hill, 1972), p. 163.
23. Herbert Kaufman, "Administrative Decentralization and Political Power," *Public Administration Review,* Jan.–Feb. 1969, pp. 9–10.
24. See Martha Derthick, with Gary Bombardier, *Between Nation and State* (The Brookings Institution, 1974), chap. 7.
25. Seymour S. Berlin, "The Federal Executive Service," *Civil Service Journal,* April–June 1971, p. 10.
26. See Chris Argyris, *Some Causes of Organizational Ineffectiveness within the State Department* (Department of State, 1967); and *Integrating the Individual and the Organization* (Wiley, 1964).
27. For a useful discussion of existing incentives and suggestions for improvements, see John Macy, *Public Service* (Harper and Row, 1971), chap. 20.

CHAPTER 11

MAKING THE PRESIDENCY SAFE FOR DEMOCRACY

*The curious fact about the American government recently has been
its distance from, its slow reaction to, massive movements of
sentiment and opinion. It seems to be listening mainly to itself.*

— *Ex-assistant secretary of state Charles Frankel,*
    High on Foggy Bottom *(Harper & Row, 1969), p. 234.*

*People with vast power at their disposal get cut off from reality,
and their power is inevitably misused. One Administration will have
its Watergate, another its Vietnam. Clearly, there is a need for
Congress, the courts, the media and the general public, each in its
own way to work to lessen both the power and the aura of divine
right that now surround our President.*

— *Jeb S. Magruder, convicted Nixon aide,*
    Los Angeles Times, *22 May 1974, section II, p. 7.*

*Of the many consequences of Watergate, one of the worst will be
the panaceas it puts into circulation. Generals fight the last war,
reformers the last scandal. . . . There is no failsafe mechanism
guaranteed to contain presidential power; and the effort to devise
such a mechanism may lead to forms of constitutional or statutory
overkill damaging to other national interests such as efficiency or
even liberty.*

— *Arthur M. Schlesinger,*
    The Imperial Presidency *(Popular Library, 1974), p. 464.*

Having discussed the powers and the limits on the powers of the presidency, what judgment must be reached about the accountability of the office? Presidential powers are not likely to be much reduced in the future. Thus, the problem becomes one of controlling the great power that has been vested in a single institution. Accountability implies not only responsiveness to majority desires and answerability for actions but also taking into account the people. Accountability also implies that the important decisions of leaders should be publicly intelligible and that the common sense of the common person should be adequate appraisal of how well a president is handling his responsibilities.

This is a large order in a nation of 220 million people. No president, it would seem, can be more than partially accountable to the people, for each will listen to some people and some points of view more than to others. But if this country still aspires to be an experiment in which arbitrary rule by powerful executives is anathema, certain fundamental questions must be continuously asked and the answers continuously appraised. How can the people hold incumbent leaders answerable and responsive between elections? What are the means and sanctions by which to influence, control, overrule, or even remove a president?

Other basic questions must be raised as well: to whom is accountability owed? Can accountability be made to mean the same thing to all people on all issues? Will greater accountability contribute to solutions of the complex and often technological problems that beset the nation? What should be done when there are sharp differences between experts or when expert opinion differs sharply from the preponderance of public opinion? How much accountability is desirable? Is it not possible that the quest for ultimate accountability will result in a presidency without the prerogatives and independent discretion necessary for creative leadership? Will making the presidency more accountable to the majority make it any more responsible in dealing with problems originating in the preferences, fears, or thoughtlessness of majorities, such as issues of racial injustice, capital punishment, and poverty?

The modern presidency, in fact, may be unaccountable because it is too strong and independent in certain areas and too weak and dependent in others. One of the most troublesome circumstances characterizing the state of the modern presidency is that awesome restraints often exist where restraints are undesirable and only inadequate restraints are available where they are most needed. Presidential weakness often results in an inability to respond. On the other hand, presidential strength is no guarantee that a president will be responsive, or answerable. Indeed, significant independent strength may encourage low answerability when it suits a president's short-term personal power goals. A strong presidency may also respond most dutifully to majoritarian desires — some of which may have been created, as in the case of the Vietnam

War or the law-and-order crusade — but remain largely unanswerable for the actions taken in responding to these desires.

Complicating any discussion of presidential accountability is the fact that public expectations about the strength and powers of the presidency may not correspond to reality, which is by now a familiar argument. Expectations in excess of actual power surely promote, if not invite, the reality of unaccountability, a fact of life with which presidents are plagued constantly. Demands in excess of the president's capacity to respond often weaken his position; they certainly do not increase his answerability to the people. On the other hand, they can as easily prompt a president to take ill-planned and even irrational action in those areas in which restraints on him are either weak or altogether nonexistent.

The very fact that the expectations of, and demands on, presidents so often far exceed their capacity to respond may account for a marked tendency in recent presidencies toward greater secretiveness and less answerability. Surrounded by limitations, especially in the field of domestic activity, a president is tempted, understandably, to move or to redefine problems into areas in which accountability always is less. Such strategies place an increasing proportion of his performance behind veils of secrecy that then can be justified, even exalted, in the name of national security.

THE PROBLEM AND THE POSSIBILITIES

In a strict sense, of course, government is always government by the few; the salient concern is whether government operates in the name of the few, the one, or the many, and whether it is alert and responsive to the views of the many. The ideal conditions for presidential accountability are difficult to spell out, but the public should know what presidential priorities are and what alternative policy choices might bring about, how they will be financed, and who will gain and who will lose. The public should be given a chance to react. Substantial controversy exists, however, over the extent to which public opinion should shape or dictate presidential choices. Government by public opinion, however it is devised, can never guarantee justice or wisdom.

It is valid, on the one hand, to complain about the paucity of formal means and the decline in the effectiveness of informal checks for making a president accountable. It is also valid, on the other hand, to appreciate that presidents need flexibility — perhaps today more than ever. No one seriously proposes that a president's decisions should merely reflect majority opinion. The structure of the office in part reflects the desire of its designers to prevent presidents from being threatened or rushed into action by the shifting gusts of public passion. In practice, the definition of acceptable limits for presidential accountability will vary over time. If the standards for presidential accountability tilt too far in the direction either of public opinion or of independence and isolation, a president is less able to provide those subtle accommodating and mediating elements of leadership that are essential for effective democratic government. No task defines the essence of presidential leadership in a pluralistic society better than that of devising a workable and purposeful adjustment of the conflicting views of experts, elite groups, and the people as a whole.

Although certain presidents have tried on occasion to govern without the benefit of considerable public and partisan support, they seldom have succeeded. A president usually can act as he thinks best, but presidents often are heavily influenced by their anticipation not only of the next election but also of tomorrow's headlines and editorials, next week's Gallup poll, next month's congressional hearings, and possible reprisals against their programs by Congress, the Supreme Court, the opposition party, and other institutions. The U. S. government compared with other major governments probably is reviewed, exposed, and held to account more explicitly and by more institutions than any other. Where else can a chief executive be overruled in the courts? A judicial check on a chief executive seldom exists in parliamentary systems if the leader retains his party's backing. Where else do the Jack Andersons and legions of underground newspapers and pamphleteers flourish with such tolerance and even encouragement?

Higher literacy rates and growing attention to public events increase the opportunities for the public to comprehend what is going on and to react accordingly. As voter knowledge and attention is improving, so also public opinion polls are beginning to weigh levels of intensity and information. Today, a presidential candidate who campaigns in most of the fifty states and enters dozens of state primaries is forced to learn the major complaints people have about the performance of their government, which is a vast improvement over the days when presidential candidates conducted national campaigns from their front porches. Although the modern candidate has more opportunities to educate and shape public opinion, it is nearly impossible for him not to learn in turn as he watches the faces of his audiences and gauges the manner in which people respond to what he is saying. Washington reporters may only count the number of times his speech is interrupted by applause, but his staff is more keenly sensitive to what it is that evokes applause or silence.

Yet the recurring charge that presidents on occasion have been arbitrary, devious, or isolated obviously is valid. These are problems central to the American presidency. How best to hold presidents accountable, honest, and within the Constitution are problems that will endure. Making the presidency safe from presidents and making the presidency safe for democracy — as well as the other way around — are also concerns that will and should command the most thoughtful attention from everyone who wants not to idealize but to realize a government for and by the people. Those who propose new structural remedies for enhancing accountability have the obligation to assess the kind of leadership and government their proposals would effect and to determine what costs and side effects might accrue. The remainder of this chapter will assess some of the more frequently suggested institutional and political remedies for keeping presidents in line.

INSURING ACCOUNTABILITY

IMPEACHMENT. Persons who believe that the traditional means are inadequate to keep presidents responsive to the mood of the people search vainly for alternative means to insure presidential accountability. Their central concern is how to insure responsiveness and responsibility between elections. The constitutional provision for impeachment is, of course, the most familiar of the traditional means of ultimate reprisal. But as we all know now, impeachment is a much misunderstood and an exceedingly cumbersome procedure. Its use is fraught with emotion and hazardous side effects, and it necessarily remains a technical device to be used only as a last resort.

The very existence of the impeachment provision is an effective deterrent, even though no president has ever been removed from office as a result of impeachment. The power to impeach remains an ultimate guarantee against executive abuse of power. How else to deal with the problem of a president who has become corrupt, who has committed "high crimes and misdemeanors" — however these words may be defined? When the president refuses to comply with his constitutionally defined duties, then impeachment, the ultimate political as well as legal recourse, must be used.[1] On such occasions, the high cost of its use surely is outweighed by the potentially more extraordinary cost of destroying or severely damaging the presidency itself. Congress in 1974 clearly gave assurance that the power of impeachment, albeit a slow process, was a constitutional and usable method of enforcing a president's constitutional obligations, and that a president is not above the law. Still, as the cases of both Andrew Johnson and Richard Nixon attest, impeachment is an elaborate, difficult-to-use means to hold presidents to account.

Brief mention should also be made here of the Twenty-fifth Amendment, which can be used against a psychologically disabled president. "Whenever the Vice President and a majority of either the principal officers of the executive departments or of such other body as Congress may by law provide, transmit to the President pro tempore of the Senate and the Speaker of the House of Representatives their written declaration that the President is unable to discharge the powers and duties of his office, the Vice President shall immediately assume the powers and duties of the office as Acting President." However, the conditions under which the amendment allows a president to resume his powers are ambiguous. It suggests that he can resume the powers and duties of the office merely by declaring that his disability no longer exists and by somehow preventing a majority of his cabinet from stating otherwise. Still, with all its uncertainties and potential pitfalls, the Twenty-fifth safeguards us against the disabled president about as much as is possible, for there is probably no way to write a completely sufficient safeguard into the Constitution against a president who suddenly becomes a madman.

The Twenty-fifth Amendment (ratified February 10, 1967) may now protect us against the disabled person in the White House, but what save impeachment protects us against the able-bodied president? The abuses of power by the able-bodied presidents, not the disabled, have been the cause of anger at the presidency in America. But as James Sundquist contends, "Impeachment can be seen as an extreme form of judicial process; as such, it has at least as many limitations as court proceedings. High crimes and misdemeanors must be proved. In today's meanings of those words, a president who has simply lost his capacity to lead and govern because of bungling, betrayal by ill-chosen subordinates, or any of the other weaknesses that can lead to misuse of presidential power, cannot for that reason be relieved of power." [2] Thus Sundquist and others have tried to come up with a workable check on the presidency. However, what is workable to some is unacceptable and even frightening to many others. The idea of a vote of no confidence has attracted little consensus, but it must be considered as an earnest proposal with a growing list of supporters.

Still, following the massive deceptions of Vietnam and Watergate, the idea of a vote of no confidence has gained support. The idea of either a public referendum or even of a congressional vote of no confidence has a long and rich history in America, especially dating from the Progressive Era of the early twentieth century.

REFERENDA: THE UNCERTAINTIES AND THE IMPRECISIONS. The idea persists, reasonably enough, that some between-elections sanction short of impeachment should be available when a substantial majority believes a president must be overruled. The idea of impeaching specific presidential policies suggests itself. Elections, it is argued, are a highly imperfect means of accountability, especially when the issues raised during a campaign are not necessarily those that will become of fundamental importance later during the president's term of office. Once elected, a president may alter relations with other nations and commit the nation to war; and his fiscal policies, which may be quite unrelated to anything he may have said in the campaign, can have extraordinary consequences.

Occasional proposals have been made, often in the form of suggested constitutional amendments, to have declarations of war submitted to a popular vote or to have a president step down should his party lose the mid-term congressional elections. The technology exists to make possible the extensive and regular use of referenda. For example, computerized ballots easily could be sent to all registered voters with free return postage. In the future cable television could provide for instant two-way, question-and-response communication. Government by referendum would extend the concept of citizen participation in national government above and beyond traditional electoral devices. It could become a means by which the people could exercise a popular veto on measures passed by Congress or on military or diplomatic actions undertaken by a president.

A California-based populist organization, the People's Lobby, is actively campaigning for the adoption of a new constitutional amendment that would bring the initiative and recall procedures to the national level. Twenty-two states provide for a statewide *initiative,* a petition process by which people may write laws for submission to the voters. Twenty-five states currently allow for *referendum* at the state level, a process that permits voters to submit measures passed by their legislatures to a popular vote. Fourteen state constitutions provide for *recall,* the process by which voters may submit to a popular vote the question of whether to remove or retain an elected official.

The People's Lobby contends that the people of the United States should revive these cherished tools of self-government, which were so widely supported by Populists and Progressives at the turn of the century. The Lobby argues that Americans should reserve to themselves the power of the initiative and recall and should establish the right to vote directly on whether or not any elected officials should be removed from office. Initiative and recall are viewed as tools of popular control, and the practical implementation of the ideal of government by the people, to be used whenever public officials violate the public trust. Initiatives could be placed on the next regularly scheduled election ballot; recall or a vote of no confidence would have to be conducted by a special election, save when regular national elections would soon take place. The formal amendment proposed by the People's Lobby reads as follows:

National Initiative: *The people of the United States of America reserve to themselves the power of the initiative. The initiative is the power of the electors to propose laws and to adopt or reject them. An initiative measure may not be submitted to alter or amend the Constitution of the United States.*

Vote of Confidence (Recall): *Every elected officer of the United States may be removed from office at any time by the electors meeting the qualification to vote in his state through the procedure and in the manner herein provided for, which provisions shall be known as a vote of confidence, and is in addition to any other method of removal provided by law.*[3]

Beguiling though these possibilities are, other considerations persuasively suggest that they are neither as practical nor as desirable as their proponents claim. Who would decide which issues to submit? European governments have been known to select issues for national referenda with the deliberate intent of dividing and weakening an opposition party. Would only certain kinds of issues be submitted or would all legislation? Where should the line be drawn? To involve the public only in such major issues as a declaration of war would constitute a doctrine of selective accountability. Most such critical issues generally represent the accumulation of earlier, lesser issues that, from a rational point of view, should have been considered and resolved earlier, which might either prevent the major issue from arising at all or place it within a much different framework.

National referendum processes would have other liabilities and a number of political implications. Faced with the prospect of war and a consequent referendum, a president might resort to a purposeful build-up in martial spirit. Carl Friedrich described one set of disconcerting possibilities:

> *The public will be exposed to most of the pressures of war propaganda, even before there is a war. This will greatly heighten the danger of its coming about. In fact, from this standpoint such a referendum is about the most dangerous thing imaginable; it would turn every chance of war into a probability. . . .*
>
> *It is hard to see how constitutional democracies can afford to cripple themselves in the face of totalitarian dictatorships by providing for a popular referendum on the question of war. . . .*
>
> *Even a radical democrat like Rousseau would reject this proposal; for a declaration of war is not a law but an executive decision. Its tremendous importance does not alter the fact that it is beyond the knowledge of the electorate.*[4]

Furthermore, a national referendum would increase the likelihood of dividing or possibly polarizing the country at a time requiring national unity: consider the possibilities of, for example, a proposition to go to war in the Middle East passed by 53 to 47 percent in a national plebiscite.

Certain kinds of emergency situations — for example, some of those faced by Lincoln in the Civil War and by Wilson and Roosevelt in World Wars I and II — have required unusual departures from strict constitutional procedures. Just as war cannot be waged by debating societies, a democratic constitutional process, as Clinton Rossiter argued, must be altered temporarily to whatever degree is necessary in times of external threats to its survival. Antidemocratic and unconstitutional as this may appear, Americans apparently approve, and so, for that matter, has the Supreme Court, at least most of the time. Rossiter suggested, "We must cease wasting our energies in discussing whether the government of the United States is to be powerful or not. It is going to be powerful or we are going to be obliterated."[5] The impeachment of a policy or any process of referendum could hardly take place during periods of extreme emergency. Thus, the problem becomes one of trying to restore normal procedures and routine checks and balances immediately on the cessation of the emergency. However, were despotism to emerge on the heels of such an emergency, or even to bring on the emergency itself, the recourse of referendum would be precisely what was most desperately required.

Past uses of the referendum at the state and local levels warn of further difficulties. A lower turnout of voters consistently occurs for referenda than for the election of candidates to national and state offices. Furthermore, the correlation of those who do vote to those in the upper socioeconomic class is nearly always high. Contrary to the expectation of its proponents, therefore, the referendum in practice has generally been a tool of the stalwarts supporting the status quo. Issues of metropolitan reorganization, civil liberties, and civil rights customarily have suffered setbacks in the marketplace of public referenda. Referenda are used regularly for school bond issues and property-tax increases to support education, and the results have been increasingly conservative and negative.

Referenda also are imperfect at weighing the intensity of people's views. How is it possible to weigh the fact that some people care more intensely about certain issues than others? Once an issue has been posed in a referendum that has binding force, the possibility of any compromise between a lukewarm majority and an intense minority virtually disappears. The notion that a majority is never enough for proper public legitimacy remains basic to democratic theory; minority rights constantly must be taken into account. Processes leaving room for subtle compromise often may be preferable to plebiscitary or referenda techniques. Political scientists Raymond Wolfinger and Fred Greenstein argue, for example, that "while politicians inevitably are imperfect in their calculations about intensity, voters are unlikely to make such judgments at all, particularly when their views are channeled through the referenda process." [6] Frequently, no clearly defined set of public attitudes exists at all; the will of the people often is divided, if not confused. For example, in foreign policy, precisely the area in which criticism of an imperial presidency is so great, Gabriel Almond's caution is appropriate:

> Where public policy impinges directly on their interest, as in questions of local improvements, taxation, or social security policy, there are more likely to develop views and opinions resting on some kind of intellectual structure. But on the questions of a more remote nature, such as foreign policy, they tend to react in more undifferentiated ways, with formless and plastic moods which undergo frequent alteration in response to changes in events. The characteristic response to questions of foreign policy is one of indifference. A foreign policy crisis, short of the immediate threat of war, may transform indifference to vague apprehension, to fatalism, to anger; but the reaction is still a mood, a superficial and fluctuating response.[7]

Other deficiencies of the referendum approach lie in its cumbersome, after-the-fact, and often irrelevant character. For the public ire to become sufficiently aroused to mobilize and focus on specific issues takes a long time. John Kennedy and Lyndon Johnson should not have been able to get the country into Vietnam without the knowledge or consent of anybody else, including Congress, but they did. Debates came only years later. In an age of instant decisions — to drop bombs, to send federal troops to a city, or to make crucial calculations about the gold standard — much of what the public might want to object to is already past history, presumably irreversible. Even if a policy is impeached before the fact, this may be insufficient to solve the problem at hand; merely nullifying or curbing the specific acts of the presidency seldom suggests or supplies the alternative policy that might be needed.

Further, there is the classic question of how much a nation wants or can afford to permit public opinion to guide its national leadership. In the yearning for high levels of accountability, a presidency could be devised which would register only the demands of the most boisterous elements in the constituency, perhaps the worst passions and prejudices of a majority. The old political saw — "There go my people. I must follow them, for I am their leader." — could well become strictly true of the presidency. Walter Lippmann argued that to adhere too closely to listening to the people would constitute a devitalization of governmental power and a malady that could be fatal; that is, when leaders become preoccupied with whether a decision is popular rather than whether it is good, they have, in effect, lost their power to decide, a condition deadly to the survival of a nation as a free society.

In one sense, the issue boils down to this: does power, properly won, tend to ennoble? Woodrow Wilson thought so: "The best rulers are always those to whom great power is entrusted in such a manner as to make them feel that they will surely be abundantly honored and recompensed for a just and patriotic use of it, and to make them know that nothing can shield them from full retribution for every abuse of it." [8] One may agree with Wilson in most cases, most of the time, but the rare exceptions could prove fatal. Even so, direct government is not the same as self-government. In all probability, to require total accountability to the people would paralyze the presidency and leave it even more impotent than it already is, at least in many areas. Presidential power, properly defined, must consist not merely of the power to persuade; it must consist as well of the power to achieve results. These results, in turn, must be arrived at in ways sufficiently open to permit a public accounting of means as well as ends.

ALTERING THE TERM OF OFFICE: THE SIX-YEAR SINGLE-TERM PROPOSAL.
One of the curious remedies persistently suggested in recent discussions of reforming the presidency is the idea of a single six-year presidential term. A number of influential advocates have endorsed this proposal, among them Senator Mike Mansfield, the majority leader; Dr. Milton Eisenhower; and former President Lyndon Johnson; and no less than ten other former presidents. The Gallup Opinion Index in 1973 revealed that nearly one-third of those polled favored changing to a six-year single-term presidency.

Why a six-year term? Proponents contend it would remove a president from the negative kind of partisan politics. The assumption is that once elected to such a term, with no possibility of reelection, presidents would cast aside partisan calculations and provide leadership for all of the people. He would do what is right even if this meant that his party would lose votes, his friends suffer financial losses, or his own political future be damaged. Former Johnson aide Jack Valenti writes that "If the Watergate mess tells us anything it is that the reelection of a President is the most nagging concern in the White House. . . ." Further, he asserts that "Watergate would never have occurred if Presidential aides were not obsessed with reelection. If they had been comfortable in tenure, knowing that in six years they would lose their lease — and in that short time they must write their record as bravely and wisely as possible — is it not possible that their arrogance might have softened and their reach for power might have shortened?" [9]

Advocates of the single six-year term see it as a means of making the presidency more nonpartisan, that is, more objective, neutral, and reasonable. They want to take the politics out of the presidency, to de-emphasize the divisive aspects of electoral and partisan politics, to elevate the presidency above selfish or factional ambitions. Some of those who favor this idea see it also as a means of making sure that no president succeeds himself. They prize the concept of citizen-politicians assuming the office of president for a fixed term and then retiring. Some say, too, that a term of six years would strengthen a president's hand in recruiting top managers to the executive departments. Implicit in all these arguments is the hope that the dignity of the office can be enhanced by encouraging presidents to act so as never to favor one party over another, one region over another, or one class over another. Also implicit is the verdict that the roles of politician and statesman are incompatible. Presidents look unstatesmanlike to some people when they appear at party fund-raising dinners or intervene in state and congressional elections.

A proposed constitutional amendment championed by Mike Mansfield and George Aiken in the Senate and several members in the House of Representatives would create such a six-year, single-term presidency. This change, they assume, might give a president greater courage and freedom in the exercise of his responsibilities. Arguing that we must liberate the presidency from "unnecessary political burdens," Mansfield says that it is intolerable that a president "is compelled to devote his time, energy and talents to what can be termed only as purely political tasks. . . . A president facing reelection faces . . . a host of demands that range from attending the needs of political office holders, office seekers, financial backers and all the rest to riding herd on the day-to-day developments within the pedestrian partisan arena." [10] Others also feel that the country's chief executive should be more businesslike and that reducing his reelection activities would assure more time and energy for substantive planning and systematic program implementation. Some hope, moreover, that the six-year term would enable a president to overcome both his deference to special interests and the timidity that results from having to keep his eye on the forthcoming election.

Several former White House aides have given support to the concept of a six-year term. A former administrative aide to Lyndon Johnson offered this rationale: "I would favor one six-year term for the presidency. I don't think the president should be concerned and involved with politics and the considerations of becoming elected for another term. The president's obligations should be devoted to a whole nation and not to any one section of it." A Nixon foreign policy aide provided this view: "I am in favor of a six-year term because we frankly don't have enough time to get going as it is. We are working on several things now that are just developing and will have to be dropped this year or next because of the political restraints involved in the 1972 election. . . . There can be some excellent results if we keep pushing. But we are being held back — some of the president's political aides are already sending us memos to that effect." And a former national security counselor to President Johnson wrote: "The four year presidential term with its tremendous pressures on the incumbent to lay the groundwork for his reelection inhibits . . . long-range non-partisan political thinking. . . . We have seen all too much of White House pressures for dramatic quick fixes on the grounds that 'the president needs something fast before he comes up for reelection.' The single six-year term would seem to provide an atmosphere in which . . . long-term planning and less partisan solutions might have a chance to flourish." [11]

Support for a six-year term without reelection also came from President Johnson himself, who felt that the most needed reforms take more than four years to formulate, pass, fund, and implement. From the day a new president assumes office, he feels he is racing against an almost impossible time schedule. National budgets are made a year-and-a-half or two years in advance; and, in addition, uncontrollable fiscal and political factors make it difficult for a new president to reorder national priorities significantly. The case for this reform, said Johnson in 1971, is stronger now than ever before: "The growing burdens of the office exact an enormous physical toll on the man himself and place incredible demands on his time. Under these circumstances the old belief that a President can carry out the responsibilities of the office and at the same time undergo the rigors of campaigning is, in my opinion, no longer valid." [12]

In short, the case in favor of the single six-year term is based on several expectations. Namely, that it would:

— Reduce the role of *politics* in the White House;
— Liberate a president from the worries and indignities of a reelection effort;
— Allow more time to concentrate on policy planning and program implementation;

— Eliminate the advantages of incumbency from presidential elections;
— Allow a president to make decisions free from the temptation of political expediency;
— Enforce the common sense idea that a period of six years is enough even for the most robust individual.

The Case Against the Six-Year Term. Despite some attractive features, the six-year term would probably cause more problems than it would solve. The required reelection after four years is one of the most democratic aspects of the presidency. It affords an opportunity for assessment. It enhances the likelihood that a president will carefully weigh the effects of whatever he does on his reelection chances. At the core of our system is the belief that our president should have to worry about reelection and be subject to all the same vicissitudes of politics as other elected officials.

When the U. S. Senate in 1913 passed a resolution in favor of the single six-year term, Woodrow Wilson argued against it and his reasoning still seems valid to many: "The argument is not that it is clearly known now just how long each President should remain in office. Four years is too long a term for a President who is not the true spokesman of the people, who is imposed upon and does not lead. It is too short a term for a President who is doing, or attempting a great work of reform, and who has not had a time to finish it." Wilson also contended that "to change the term to six years would be to increase the likelihood of its being too long without any assurance that it would in happy cases, be long enough. A fixed constitutional limitation to a single term of office is highly arbitrary and unsatisfactory from any point of view." [13]

The proposed divorce between the presidency and politics presupposes a significantly different kind of political system from that of the United States, which is glued together largely by ambiguity, compromise, and the extensive sharing of powers. In light of the requisites of democracy, the presidency must be a highly political office, and the president an expert practitioner of the art of politics. Quite simply, there is no other way for presidents to negotiate favorable coalitions within the country, Congress, and the executive branch and to gather the authority needed to translate ideas into accomplishments. A president who remains aloof from politics, campaigns, and partisan alliances does so at the risk of becoming the prisoner of events, special interests, or his own whims.

The Need for a Political Presidency. The very means for bringing a president in touch with reality is the process of political debate and political bargaining, with all of the necessary changes of course, arguments, and listening to other points of view. What makes domestic politics so distasteful to presidents, that it is full of groups to persuade and committees to inform, is precisely its virtue; indeed, it is the major hope for maintaining an open presidency, one neither bound by its own sources of information nor aloof to the point it will no longer listen.

By calling the president "more presidential" whenever he ignores partisan politics, citizens encourage him to even greater isolation. By turning up their noses at politics in the White House and urging the president to get on with his real business of guiding the nation, they also help to establish the two important conditions for secrecy and duplicity, with which the nation has become so familiar. First, with all the apparatus and technology for secret statesmanship at hand, a president can more easily call upon aides when something needs fixing than to persuade the public or Congress to his point of view. Second, because the president will look unpresidential if he participates in normal party politics, his aides must go through grotesque contortions to prove that their boss has never thought about anything except being president of all the people. The tactic of secrecy, so tempting to those who have it within their grasp, amounts to insulating the president from the normal checks and balances of the political system. New bait will be needed to lure presidents out of this comfortable sanctuary and into the morass of open politics, for the present enticements are small.

The premise that politics stops at the water's edge must also be rejected. To bring too little politics and partisanship to bear on foreign policy matters often means that political parties are not responding to critical issues or are not debating worthwhile alternative policies and deep-seated differences of opinion. Neither of the major American political parties is constituted along neat liberal and conservative lines. A realignment, even a moderate realignment, surely would help to create more effective opposition parties and, hence, the politics of opposition that is so vital on occasion.

One way to prevent future abuses of presidential power, as others have noted, is to make the White House more open; and one way to do that, as has not been suggested so often, is to begin regarding a president as a politician once again. Politics, in the best sense of that term, is the art of making decisions in the context of debate, dialogue, and open two-way conversations, the art of making the difficult and desirable possible. This kind of politics at the White House should not be diminished. Indeed, as pointed out above, it is highly desirable that presidents be great practitioners of the craft of politics. They, as well as Congress and our parties, would profit from more politics, not less.

Most of the effective presidents have also been highly political. They knew how to stretch the limited resources of the office, and they loved politics and enjoyed the responsibilities of party leadership. The nation has been well served by sensitive politicians disciplined by the general thrust of partisan and public thinking. Many of the least political presidents were also the least successful and seemingly the least suited temperamentally to the rigors of the office. The best have been those who listened to people, who responded to majority as well as to intense minority sentiment, who saw that political parties are often the most important vehicle for communicating voter preferences to those in public office, and who were attentive to the diversity and intensity of public attitudes even as they attempted to educate and to influence the direction of opinion.

President Nixon told the nation during his Watergate crisis that the presidency had to come first and politics second. This, he said, is why he did not involve himself in the 1972 election campaign. So too, Presidents Kennedy and Ford tried on occasion to argue that the problems facing the nation were so technical and administrative in character that they did not lend themselves to the clash of partisan and ideological debate. In essence, they appealed to the belief that highly political decisions must now be placed in the hands of dispassionate bipartisan experts, a notion that is certainly as dangerous as it is blatantly undemocratic.

Everything a president does has political consequences, and every political act by a president has implications for the state of the presidency. The nation must fully recognize that presidents will and must be political, that they ought to be vigorous partisan leaders. Bipartisanship rarely has served the nation well. James MacGregor Burns aptly noted that "almost as many crimes have been committed in the name of mindless bipartisanship as in the name of mindless patriotism." [14] If patriotism in an autocratic system implies blind loyalty to the regime, then patriotism in a democracy must include a responsibility and even obligation to speak out as a citizen whenever one believes that the government is following an unjust or misguided course of action. (Recognizing presidents as partisan political leaders also underscores our lack of an opposition party. Such a party could challenge a president's program and the presidential establishment and would be eager and able to proclaim alternative national priorities.) Decision-making processes in a democracy will be messier and often more confusing than in alternative systems, but if the dreams of Jefferson and Jackson are to be taken seriously, then the real secret and strength of democracy rests in encouraging regular elections and vigorous opposition politics.

If national leaders do become isolated or insulated from the mood of the public, then electing presidents for longer terms would only encourage this tendency.[15] Frequent elections necessarily remain a major means of motivating responsive and responsible behavior. An apolitical president, disinterested in reelection, motivated by personal principle or moralistic abstractions, and aloof from the concerns of our political parties, could become a highly irresponsible president. Elections customarily force an assessment of presidential performance. They are welcomed when promises have been kept and feared when performance has been unsatisfactory. Was it, for example, a mere coincidence, or were President Nixon's troop-withdrawal rates calculated with the election of 1972 in mind? Was the Johnson-Humphrey bombing halt of

1968 aimed toward that year's election? Nixon's economic game-plan reversal in 1971 and Johnson's vain efforts at peace negotiations in 1967 and 1968 were unmistakably related to the positive, constructive, and dynamic character of American elections.

The Fallacy of Increased Accomplishment. Although change in important national policy is a slow process, a six-year term is not necessarily an appropriate remedy for this. Frequently, policy changes whose pace has frustrated the White House have come slowly because they have been highly controversial and adequate support had not yet been assembled. Mobilizing support is just as much a presidential responsibility as proclaiming the need, and support would be no less crucial with a seven-year or a seventeen-year term. Only a shrewdly political president who is also his party's leader, who is sensitive to political moods, and who is allied with dozens of the political and party elite, can build those coalitions able to bridge the separation of powers in Washington and to offset the strong forces bent on thwarting progress.

Often, when the White House is frustrated in attempting reform, the proposed changes have not been adequately planned or tested. In the case of the Johnson administration, as has been noted earlier, too many policies were pronounced prematurely — sometimes policy was "made" by press release — and the administration acted as though bill-signing ceremonies were the culmination of the policy-making process. The administration also was frustrated in its attempt to implement sweeping domestic policy changes precisely because too much emphasis was placed on getting the laws on the books, to the neglect of developing the managerial and bureaucratic organizations necessary for imaginative administration of these laws. A White House that becomes overly transfixed with a legislative box score, or that succumbs to the unquenchable thirst for quick political credit, may appear, at least for a while, to be accomplishing great innovations. But translating paper victories into genuine policy accomplishments requires far more than monopolizing of the legislative process.

George Reedy argues that the president who cannot be reelected after four years is unlikely to accomplish anything of value if he is given a free ride for another two. What was true in the past remains true today: effective national leadership requires what the Constitution actually tried to discourage, that a party or faction disperse its members or its influence across the branches of government. Under normal circumstances, a president who ignores this maxim or retreats from these partisan and political responsibilities is unlikely to achieve much in the way of substantive policy innovation. Furthermore, as one former counselor to three presidents put it: "A President who can never again be a candidate is a president whose coattails are permanently in mothballs." [16] A president elected to a single six-year term would be a president inescapably confronted with a bureaucracy as well as senior political appointees even less responsive to him than now. Even when presidents are both popular and eligible for reelection, they depend on senior and mid-career civil servants, a situation summed up in the wry Washington saying that "the bureaucracy eats presidents for lunch." When it is known that a chief executive is to leave by a certain date, bureaucratic entrepreneurs suddenly enjoy wider degrees of discretion and independence. Re-eligibility, used or not, is a potentially significant political resource in the hands of a president; and denying that resource, even in the more limited way the Twenty-second Amendment has done, will diminish the leadership discretion of future presidents who desire to be activist initiators of policy. Former President Truman has spoken to this point:

> You do not have to be very smart to know that an officeholder who is not eligible for reelection loses a lot of influence. So what have you done? You have [by passing the Twenty-second Amendment] taken a man and put him in the hardest job in the world, and sent him out to fight our battles in a life-and-death struggle — and you have sent him out to fight with one hand tied behind his back, because everyone knows he cannot run for reelection.
>
> It makes no sense to treat a President this way — no matter who he is — Republican or Democrat. He is still President of the whole country and all of us are dependent on him; and we ought to give him the tools to do his job.[17]

(It might be added, while speaking of the Twenty-second Amendment, that it was a vote of no confidence in the political judgment of future generations; for on the rather critical matter of selecting a future president, our elders in effect substituted their judgment for that of future generations.)

President Johnson's predicament in 1968 arouses sympathy. He was losing popularity with an American public disillusioned with his war policies, and his domestic programs were running into a myriad of difficulties in implementation. Many of his domestic efforts had become controversial, many were underfunded or not funded at all. Those that received funding often foundered on the shoals of Johnson's Vietnam-generated inflation or met up with intergovernmental obstacles that had not been anticipated by White House architects of the domestic program. It is doubtful, however, that the situation would have been much different under a constitutional six-year term.

A six-year term might induce some otherwise timid president to propose more courageous and far-reaching policies, but timidity was hardly a Johnson characteristic. A six-year term might reform presidents who otherwise would become too involved with party patronage and party machinery, but this was clearly not a Johnson preoccupation. A six-year term might permit a greater degree of program follow-through, monitoring, and evaluation; but this apparently would never have become a personal interest of Johnson's. Nor would a six-year term have been any guarantee that much of what transpired in connection with the Watergate scandals would not have occurred anyway. Presidents, like Nixon, can become just as obsessed with their place in history as with winning reelection.

The single-term proposal has a comforting ring of good, old-time govern-ment and nonpartisanship to it. Yet it represents the last gasp of those who cling to the hope that we can separate national leadership from the crucible of politics and of those who contend that our presidency is too beholden to the workings of a patronage or spoils system. Neither is the case: the former remains an impossibility — it is impossible to take the politics out of public leadership in a democracy — whereas the latter is a problem whose time largely has passed. Equally undesirable is the notion that intense conflict over policy choices, that is, intense political activity, somehow can be removed from the presidency. The conflicts that surround the presidency and require a presi-dent to act as public mediator mirror those existing and potential conflicts over values that exist within the American society at large. If presidents were not required to resolve political conflicts by making political choices, they would not be fulfilling those responsibilities we rightly associate with democratic leadership.

WHAT CAN CONGRESS DO? As an institution of national leadership, Con-gress has severe limitations. Too many people feel that a revitalized Congress would be a progressive Congress. Too many people also expect Congress to be able to direct national security matters or to solve complex economic problems and a myriad of others, activities that it is ill-equipped to do and that it seems incapable even of trying to do. However, Congress, properly rejuvenated and with a large influx of more progressive members (as in the 94th Congress), doubtless could do a better job of keeping presidents answerable and thereby enhancing popular control. The devices available to it for insuring presidential accountability are numerous: rejection of his legislative programs, refusal to confirm his nominees, well-run and publicized investigative hearings, indepen-dent G.A.O. audits, indifference to his appropriation requests, riders to ap-propriation legislation, vetoes of reorganization plans, "sense of the Congress" resolutions, and so on. Some of these devices have grown ineffective because of their misuse or nonuse; but the arsenal of congressional tools remains im-pressive, especially if the members of Congress have the courage and the will to exert themselves.

Congress, of course, has not carved out a record of performance that would justify congressional dominance as a preferable alternative to presidential domi-nance. Congress has dubious claims, despite what some critics of the presi-dency imply to the contrary, to portray itself as the branch of peace, that is, as the branch which most often promotes peace-making and which keeps the United States out of wars. Congress has sometimes been progressive, has some-times supported much-needed redistributive policies, but most of the time its orientation has been conservative or centrist.[18] Even when Congress has ap-parently had the strength, it often has not asserted itself constructively. Thus, in those decades when Congress was the dominant branch, notably in the years from 1865 to 1903, its performance was largely obstructionist and selfish. At other times, it has appeared unimaginative or even uninvolved, less because it has been a sick, sluggish institution than because it fundamentally has agreed with presidential priorities. Thus, a congressional majority supported the war in Vietnam right up until President Johnson announced his retirement. If anything, it would have been more militant than President Kennedy in the Cuban missile crisis of 1962. Congress also went along with the way the Great Society was drafted and designed; its grave reservations about intent and implementation came two, three, and four years later.

Political analyst David Broder posed the question: "Can Congress be taken seriously? That is not a facetious question. It is a question that must be asked, considering the response so far from the Congress to the problems which Watergate revealed in the executive branch." [19] The problems that need to be addressed involve executive secrecy, the runaway power of presidential staffs, the diminished role of Congress in policy determination, and the lack of effective supervision of on-going federal activities. Watergate, it should be pointed out, was not necessarily the result of a strong presidency, rather it was the result of the abuse of presidential powers and a neglect of constitutional obligations. Safeguards, reforms, and political innovations are needed, but it is increasingly clear as well that we cannot rely exclusively on any one structural or political change.

National issues seldom are debated in Congress in such a way as to educate or instruct the American people. Reports of hearings and the *Congressional Record* are organized and published in a manner almost calculated to attract dust rather than readers. In addition, Congress has tended to become dependent on the president's State of the Union, Budget, and other messages for major guidance in setting its own agenda. The executive branch, the presidency in particular, often overwhelms the Congress with its expertise, its reports, its commission studies, and, in short, its near monopoly on the resources of information and evaluation. These factors make it exceedingly unlikely that Congress will recapture for itself much of that authority and discretion which it has delegated away. Although some part of the problem lies in the way Congress is organized, another part lies in the fact that nearly all representatives and most senators tend to look after local interests first and national interests second. All of which means that it is rather impractical to keep insisting that members of Congress legislate and concentrate only on what is in the national interest when their chief incentives dictate that they first serve the immediate interests of powerful groups in their home districts.

Still, as political scientist Nelson Polsby warns, improvements must be made in congressional sources of technical knowledge. "It is romantic for Congressmen to think of themselves as not in need of expert and detailed explicit analysis because they are 'generalists.' Generalism is too often a genteel name

for ignorance. The professionalization of economic forecasting and defense procurement in the executive branch led to tremendous increases in the power of
political decision makers to identify options and choose among them." [20] Congress
must strengthen itself in this regard if it is to produce new policy directions,
and if it is to know when and how to oppose a president effectively, especially
when such opposition is urgently needed.

The remedy frequently proposed is that Congress itself go into the business
of countervailing expertise, that it set up its own think tanks and study commissions, hire more experts and staffs — in short, make itself more like the
presidency and the executive office. This could, however, make it even more
remote from that man-in-the-street contact which always was supposed to be
its major strength and virtue. Also, as Theodore Roszak cautioned, would not
this trend merely "further enforce the public's reliance on expertise?" Roszak's
fears of society's increasing reliance on a technocracy of experts are worth
bearing in mind, especially in an era in which many a status- or power-seeking
expert is always available for the right price: "Does it not ultimately leave
the citizen still in the hands of experts whose words he must take on faith,
trusting that they have his best interests at heart and provide the wisest counsel? Does our democracy not continue to be a spectator sport in which the
general public chooses up sides among contending groups of experts, looking on
stupidly as the specialists exchange the facts and figures, debate the esoteric
details, challenge one another's statistics, and question one another's prognos-
tications? It is difficult to see that in the long run, such a counterbalancing of
expertise can be a real victory for the democratic autonomy of ordinary citizens. They remain expert-dependent." [21] The cardinal aim of whatever is proposed to strengthen the Congress should be to assure that, in a period in which
the presidency often seems isolated and remote, the same condition is not allowed to befall Congress.

The Agenda for Congress. Congress and those who champion its status as a
coequal branch and claim that it has not asserted itself adequately in recent
years, sometimes overlook the fact that Congress itself has been an eager participant in the surrender of more and more of its powers to the executive. If
Congress genuinely wants a leaner presidency, it should ask more of itself
and be willing to make some of those tough decisions about priorities and
budgetary questions that all too often it passes along to the presidential establishment. In the matter of the impoundment of authorized funds by the
executive, for example, critics have time and again charged that the president
deliberately and arbitrarily thwarts the will of Congress. Often, however, Congress acquiesces. Sometimes it does so because it agrees with the presidential
intentions behind the impoundment. Sometimes it simply does not want to
accept the blame from the public, on the one hand, or from high-powered

special interests, on the other, if instead of delegating the job to the White House, it were to insist on its rights to reorder fiscal priorities. Moreover, Congress yields easily to requests for new national debt ceilings. Under the Budget Reform Act of 1974, Congress may be able to set overall fiscal spending limits, the net effect of which may be to encourage an administration to slow down some government programs, defer some, and freeze still others — but on the administration's own terms. Deciding policy by impounding funds to the extent that it was done by the Nixon administration is certainly not desirable. The courts and the Congress were finally moved to circumscribe this expansion of presidential discretion. In the end, however, if these decisions are to be made outside of the presidency, Congress must reorganize itself and tackle the organization of the priority-setting and appropriations processes so that its members, rather than unelected presidential aides, may serve as the national legislators.

More refined and modernized versions of the notions of executive agreement and executive privilege are needed as well. Both notions constitute escapes for Congress from its responsibility to set overall national priorities. As numerous people have pointed out, most U. S. foreign policy is determined in secret by presidents and their aides by treaties and executive agreements that are virtually immune from congressional scrutiny. The worst features of U. S. foreign policy and diplomacy since World War II have arisen out of the concepts of executive agreement. The Senate, which once played a vital part in foreign policy matters, today serves largely as an echo of the Pentagon and the White House. Congress, at the very least, should instruct its foreign relations committees to develop new guidelines for what is an appropriate agreement. Congress, not the executive, should determine what qualifies as an executive agreement.[22]

Executive agreements, executive orders, and emergency powers have become the order of the day.[23] With every expansion of U. S. interests abroad has come the direct or indirect establishment of a military base or a military-aid mission, thereby conferring upon the president the wide discretionary powers inherent in his prerogatives as commander-in-chief. The failures of Congress in Vietnam have become legendary. Civilian leaders did not do their part in giving direction, determining policy, and taking diplomatic action to end the war. We should repeal, wherever possible, the large catalogue of emergency powers and executive agreements that permit such extensive commitment — what is, in effect, private diplomacy — by the executive branch abroad. Congress has the powers at its disposal to reassert itself in treaty commitment, war-making, and the conduct of war. Political scientist Theodore Lowi has noted also that many of Congress' most effective war powers derive from domestic powers: "If total war means total involvement of resources and population, then limited war means limited involvement of resources and population. Congress has the power to limit or expand war and other international involvements by setting limits on the amount of domestic involvement. Such limits are directly effective in the degree to which they put resources in the hands of the President and the military. Such actions are also effective in symbolizing to the Executive and to the world the extent to which the country intends to be involved." [24] As examples of domestic powers that can be used to affect executive war powers, he cites conscription and civil liberties.

Congress also should narrow the conditions under which claims of executive privilege will be allowed. Freedom of information and the right to know are essential if Congress is to act in the national interest. On proper occasions, of course, a presidential counselor should be able to preserve a confidential relation in his communications with a president; and on matters of truly sensitive economic and foreign policy, a president should be able to explore policy options fully and candidly with his senior staff with the confidence that such conversations are immune from external interrogation. But Congress, either on its own or by taking the issue to the courts, must specify as best it possibly can the purpose and the limits of the doctrine of executive privilege. Large numbers of unelected, unconfirmed, and unknown White House aides should not be allowed to hide behind the shield of executive privilege. More important, partisan and political campaign strategies should be specifically excluded as topics that can be concealed on the grounds of executive privilege. The claims for executive privilege made prior to the Supreme Court verdict in *United States* v. *Richard M. Nixon* (July 1974) egregiously broadened the doctrine of executive privilege, even permitting it to shield alleged criminal activity.

Senator Sam Ervin's subcommittee on separation of powers discovered, by means of a survey of congressional committees in both houses, nearly three hundred reported instances in which the executive branch had refused to provide information that had been requested by Congress from 1964 to 1973. Ervin is correct when he contends that the executive's evasiveness and outright denial to the Congress of information it requires in its legislative functions, or the executive's unilateral assumption of authority to decide what information will be provided or which witnesses will appear, are clear encroachments by the executive establishment upon the powers of Congress. Ervin's proposed remedies appear too gentle and incremental, but they provide at least a starting point: "It might be productive and necessary for the Congress to take special and innovative measures to be more watchful over refusals of information. It has been suggested that procedures be devised whereby committee chairmen could report to a central office, on a continuing basis, instances of refusals of information. A similar suggested remedy is the proposal that in each House of the Congress there be established an office which would specialize in following up on requested information that had been denied, and in assisting individual members in enforcing the processes available to the Congress." [25] The magnitude and scope of the information and secrecy problems suggest that legislative and court remedies may be needed as well.

We may want a strong presidency, but a strong presidency does not require secrecy, seclusion, and preposterous subterfuges. Executive privilege as defined by Nixon's acting attorney general, Richard Kleindienst, provided that the White House could prevent testimony from any individual employed by the executive branch and, further, that it applied to past presidential aides as well as present aides for all time. If what Kleindienst claimed had ever held up, Congress might just as well have gone out of business. In fact, however, executive privilege is, as Raoul Berger points out, a myth, without constitutional foundation.[26]

In the past, Congress has been too willing a partner in the enlargement of the presidency and it must now curb its impulse to establish new presidential agencies and to ask for yet additional reports and studies from the president. If Congress genuinely wants to reassert itself as both a priority setter and a sentry, it should make much better use of its own General Accounting Office and Congressional Research Service for chores that now are often assigned to the Executive Office of the President. Congress also needs to reappraise its capacity and willingness to oversee and hold to account the Executive Office of the President. The power of the inner circles of the executive establishment is now too great to be neglected. The government operations committees in both houses of Congress should be mandated to keep close watch over the purposes, powers, and payrolls of all staff units in the now huge executive office. Congress should be willing to evaluate closely the White House budget and be willing to cut budgets when White House activities seem unwarranted.

Should appointed senior White House and executive office officials be confirmed and subject to congressional testimony? Congress has already acted to insure that future directors and deputy directors of the OMB must be confirmed. Others in the Congress, like Senator Walter Mondale, feel strongly that the future John Ehrlichmans and Henry Kissingers — the senior domestic, national security, and economic advisers to a president — should be confirmed. Mondale admits that confirmation itself may not be all that important, but he believes it may have a sobering effect on appointees. Further, he argues that both the Congress and the top White House aides can learn a lot when these officials have to testify at congressional hearings and answer questions on a regular basis.

Congress doubtless should have the right to confirm those in the White House who are acting as virtual cabinet members or who are operating little administrative empires of their own. But another way for Congress to approach this problem is to insist that empire building and government by a palace guard be halted. Those in the White House should be personal advisers and general assistants to a president, not the functional equivalent of department heads. Congress should do everything it can to transfer to the appropriate departments (and to appropriate cabinet officers) those activities and operations now in the executive office that don't belong there. If this cannot be achieved, Congress perhaps should establish standing committees on executive office operations designed explicitly to monitor and oversee the White House bureaucracy itself. No longer can the task of overseeing presidential operations be conducted so haphazardly and be dispersed among dozens of committees and subcommittees, each of which is more or less parallel to cabinet departments and can, therefore, look at only small segments of the presidential establishment.

Such a committee or committees might also have responsibility for reining in our penchant to royalize the presidency. They should, for example, curb the tendency toward a lavish empire of homes, yachts, jets, helicopters, presidential anthems ("Hail to the Chief"), and so on. They should bring a halt to the needless building of presidential pyramids to house the personal papers of ex-presidents. These library temples are all maintained and staffed by the government at extravagant expense to the taxpayer. The committees should also establish guidelines that prevent ex-presidents from treating all their personal papers as private property. Presidential pensions and retirement slush funds also need to be reexamined. Can a democracy really justify paying $500,000 or more for ex-presidents to use at their discretion? One acquaintance suggested to this writer the novel idea of gearing a president's pension to the national average income of persons the president's age at the time of his leaving the White House. Although hardly likely to be adopted, this might encourage a president to have greater concern for the material quality of life of people in the upper age brackets, since he himself would be directly affected.

Adding yet another committee to the already overburdened congressional system may seem like adding another council to the overstuffed presidential establishment. But the central importance of what the presidency does (and does not do) must rank among the most critical of the oversight tasks for the contemporary Congress. As things are organized now, the presidency escapes adequate scrutiny. Equally important, Congress needs these committees to help protect itself from its own tendency to relinquish more of its diminishing resources and prerogatives to the presidency. Since Truman, presidents have had staffs to oversee and lobby the Congress; it is time for Congress to reciprocate.

Congress also needs to establish some kind of joint committee to oversee the intelligence operations of the CIA and FBI. Revelations during Watergate and again in 1974 and 1975 suggest convincingly that existing supervision in this area has been inadequate. This committee should be designed to be representative of Congress as a whole, and perhaps would be most effective by having its members serve only for four or six years to insure rotation.

The establishment of an Office of Counsel General with a small staff comparable to that of the comptroller general of the G.A.O. is also an idea whose time has come. Such an office could serve Congress in its investigations of, and in any necessary legal action against, illegal executive branch activities. The related suggestion that a permanent special prosecutor be created also holds some appeal. This proposed investigatory and prosecutory ombudsman would look into those conflicts of interest that cannot reasonably be handed over to an often politicized Department of Justice. In addition it might litigate alleged abuses of executive privilege or executive agreement and other denials of information to the Congress.

The recommendation of the Ervin Watergate committee deserves careful consideration. It recommended that Congress enact legislation "to establish a permanent Office of Public Attorney which would have jurisdiction to prosecute criminal cases in which there is a real or apparent conflict of interest within the executive branch. The Public Attorney would also have jurisdiction to inquire into (with power to gain access to executive records) the status and progress of complaints and criminal charges concerning matters pending in or involving the conduct of Federal departments and regulatory agencies. The Public Attorney would be appointed for a fixed term (e.g., 5 years), be subject to Senate confirmation and be chosen by members of the judicial branch to ensure his independence from executive control or influence." [27] The intent here is not just to create a constant reminder that the president, too, is subject to the law but also to assure the availability of prosecutors, independent of White House direction, who would investigate and prosecute violations of federal election laws and federal crimes committed by government officials. Some suggest, too, that the officials of the national political parties should also come under their purview.

Nearly everyone agrees that excessive partisan politics should be removed from the administration of justice. People differ greatly as to how this could be achieved.[28] Former senator Sam Ervin once proposed that the Department of Justice become a separate establishment in the national government, independent of the president. Other persons suggest that through legislation the attorney general should be a lawyer who has no place in party machinery and who has not recently participated in the direction of political campaigns. Still others think it is nearly impossible to legislate a divorce between politics and the Department of Justice; they think the chief safeguard should be the Senate's exercise of maximum care in scrutinizing nominees for the top ranks of the Justice Department.

Several sensible objections have been made to the idea of establishing a counsel general or permanent special prosecutor. A former White House aide to Lyndon Johnson notes, for example, that "it is all very well to imagine an Archibald Cox, or a Leon Jaworski, fearlessly prosecuting scoundrels whom John Mitchell sought to protect. But what if the special prosecutor were a Joe McCarthy, vested with wide investigative and prosecutorial powers, and protected from removal during a fixed term?" [29] Archibald Cox himself opposes the idea of creating a permanent office of special prosecutor. His chief reasons are:

The primary responsibility for preventing wrongdoing high in the executive branch, for exposing it promptly and dealing vigorously with wrongdoers, lies with the President. There is no substitute for that responsibility and no President should be relieved of it or of the consequences if he does not deal with it. Setting up a separate organization would dilute the President's responsibility and the responsibility of those under him. That would be a grave mistake.

Second, I doubt the need for such an office. I think that we have been able to trust in most of our Presidents. I pray that we will be able to trust in the integrity of future Presidents. I do not think the volume of business, likely business, would support such an office, and that this would result in the people in the office running around looking for something to do. [30]

Congress needs to give critical considerations to remedial action in this area and also due consideration to these sober objections.

Finally, there have been repeated suggestions that Congress reassert itself by grafting onto its charter some of the more attractive features of the parliamentary system. Those who feel Congress is the broken branch and that it has permitted itself to become somewhat a marginal institution of government say that Congress would truly be a coequal branch only if it had the power of dissolving government by means of a vote of no confidence. Advocates of this substantial departure from current practice argue that our checks and balances are inadequate. They say that most of the checks and balances (e.g., impeachment, power of the purse, investigations) operate after the fact, usually long after the abuse of power. They also note that informal checks, such as the cabinet and the political parties, have also operated ineffectively. Thus, they argue the need for the device of dismissing government through a parliamentary vote of no confidence, a measure that would, of course, require a constitutional amendment.

James Sundquist, an advocate of the no-confidence reform, says that no other democratic government leaves itself so vulnerable. He sees this parliamentary feature as a means of keeping presidents in touch with reality and enhancing plural decision-making at the presidential level.

If the "no confidence" procedure were introduced into our Constitution, a President to keep his office would have to do more than keep himself free of indictable crime. He would have to satisfy the Congress — and therefore the people....

A President who was forced, under the Constitution, to maintain the confidence of the country and of the Congress would find it necessary to consult with congressional leaders in the exercise of his executive powers. He would not dare to do otherwise: it would be dangerous to flout them and risky to keep secrets from them. To retain their confidence, he would have to take them into his. [31]

Some members of Congress have urged that Congress should have the right, via a two-thirds or perhaps 60 percent vote in both houses, to call for a new presidential election after such a vote of no confidence while remaining in office itself. However, under Sundquist's no-confidence arrangement, Congress would also be forced to face a new election if and when it exercised its no-confidence privilege. It would have to take its decision, in effect, to a referendum.

The objections to the vote of no confidence reform are many and, on balance, persuasive. Perhaps the chief argument is that impeachment does exist and it can be made to work. If the Andrew Johnson case gave impeachment a bad name, the virtual impeachment of Richard Nixon has redeemed this wholly appropriate constitutional safeguard. Further, actions by the 93rd and 94th Congresses suggest that other checks and balances can be made to work. For example, funds were eliminated for military land actions by our troops in Indochina. Presidential authority to commit troops to extended combat overseas has also been challenged and made subject to congressional veto (although this so-called advance has some questionable aspects).[32] The Budget Reform Act of 1974 and the Impoundment Control Act of 1974 also reaffirmed Congress' willingness to respond to executive incursions on legislative powers. Lastly, the internal machinery of the House has been revitalized.

If Congress too often has failed to check presidential war making and fiscal policy actions, this is due less to the lack of an available formal mechanism, such as a vote of no confidence, than to the lack of will or creative partisan opposition. Moreover, as James MacGregor Burns points out, "the loyal party opposition has failed to oppose, largely because of bipartisan understandings about 'adjourning politics in time of national crisis.' The checks and balances do not operate because crisis usually produces a sharp if fleeting solidarity in the otherwise divided political system." [33]

The day may come when we could use a vote of no confidence procedure. Various proposals to institutionalize such an arrangement should be fully explored in the meantime, just in case. On balance, however, it would seem best to revivify existing checks and balances, encourage the development of a vigorous loyal opposition, and promote more vital political parties whose leaders would stand up to any president who violates the constitutional duties of the office. The better way to inject a sense of collective responsibility into the presidency would be to bind a president somewhat more to the platforms, principles, and political judgment of a large political party. Separation of powers can be restored by existing constitutional and political means. The key is to make sure that every president is a part of the larger political system. Congress and the parties can and must see that this is done, for how a president acts is a function not only of his personality and character but also of what others expect of him.

PRESIDENTIAL LEADERSHIP AND THE AMERICAN PEOPLE

The assertion that the ills of democracy could best be cured by more democracy was long fashionable. There is much that is profound in that insight, for American voters are far wiser than is generally acknowledged. Voters are, as V. O. Key, Jr., has said, a good deal less irrational, ill-informed, or sheeplike than is sometimes supposed. Few of the answers to the always unfinished task of fashioning an even more perfect union and a more respectable democracy in this nation will be brought about by structural reforms. The basic question here and throughout this book is not whether government by the people is possible or even desirable in the modern world, but rather how the political system and the relationship between the leadership and the citizens can be transformed so they will approach more closely the ideals of democracy. This argument has explicitly rejected the view that things must remain as they are because that is the way underlying forces make them. These pages often have emphasized the need for a strong but also a lean and accountable presidency, a presidency that could achieve the reforms and innovative changes that would broaden the economic and political share of the common person in the polity and in the socioeconomic system. In short, the problem is not that the presidency has become too strong; the problem is, fundamentally, the emergence of a secretive, personalized, and antipolitical presidency.

The simplistic notion that returning to the drawing boards and coming up with a new charter or a new constitution will provide the needed solutions must be rejected. The tendency toward a constitutional convention must be watched with care. The means of improving the setting and fulfilling of national priorities and of better controlling the presidency are likely to be political rather than constitutional avenues. No single institutional innovation that this writer has ever heard of could guarantee a commitment to truth, compassion, and justice. Formal constitutional provisions to guard against presidential isolation, such as the institutionalization of government-sponsored votes of confidence or a lengthened presidential term, are not the most sensible way to increase accountability. When people complain that it is the constitutional system that is obsolete, the warning once offered by Judge Learned Hand is apt: that freedom would not survive in the Constitution if it had already died in the hearts of the people. And he added that we would not realize a free society unless we have a free people.

The fact that the American political system and leaders are asked to undertake much of what the rest of society refuses to do is a continual problem in this nation. The promise of the presidency symbolizes the hopes of the people, and certainly there is nothing wrong in calling on our president to summon up exalted national instincts and commitments. But the attempt to reconstitute any single institution in a large, complex society may be rather futile if the fundamental purpose of that institution is to represent and respond to the dominant values of the society. There is little doubt that this society's values are rooted in a strong faith in political and social gradualism, in a deep fear of revolutionary change, and in a steadfast devotion to most of what constitutes the existing order and the existing distribution of wealth and advantages. This is what leads many people to the view that the country by and large gets the kind of leadership it deserves — and that it wants.

Political controls, however, do need to be sharpened and strengthened to insure a continual public and congressional scrutiny of presidential activity. Impeachment, even impeachment of particular policies or votes of no confidence, are by themselves incomplete solutions; they are merely temporary palliatives, even if practical use could be made of them. To describe fully all of the potentially available mechanisms would require another book. But it is clear that openness and candor have been lacking. Presidents and their aides supply disappointingly little information to the press, to Congress, or to the public on matters of impoundment, executive agreements, vetoes, executive orders, and a vast list of other subtle shifts in administrative emphasis. In the seemingly endless attempt to accentuate the positive, White House image-makers too often have distorted news and thereby aggravated difficulties in credibility by claiming too much credit for fortuitous events or for policy initiatives that may or may not achieve sustained or desirable ends, and by projecting the appearance of novelty and boldness usually at the expense of candid discussions of the complexity of problems, the modesty of proposed solutions, and the realities of who must pay and how much.

A free society must mean a society based explicitly on free competition, most particularly competition in ideas and opinions, and by frank discussions of alternative national purposes and goals. Elected leaders and a vigorous press must ceaselessly attack ignorance, apathy, and mindless nationalism — the classic enemies of democracy. The citizen must ceaselessly resist sentimental and unctuously rhetorical patriotism that espouses everything as a matter for top priority but in practice eschews the tough political reforms that must be begun and implemented. What is needed is a far more thoughtful way of looking at the presidency and at citizen responsibilities in this complex age. Both sides require political reappraisal and a better determination of who should do what, when, and how.

In addition, Congress, the press, and the public must use all existing political controls as a means to inspire as well as to check their presidents. Citizens must insist that their president lend his voice and energies to the weak and the have-not sectors of society. Strengthening the have-not sectors of society and giving a fair hearing to minorities will always remain major presidential responsibilities and an essential part of the legitimacy of the modern presidency. Yet it is well to remember, as most authorities on political change constantly warn, that the way of the reformer, of the catalyst of creative political change, is always hard: he necessarily fights a two-front war against reactionaries on the one hand and impractical revolutionaries on the other.

NEEDED: A REGENERATION OF THE PARTIES.

A president attempting noble innovations thus stands in great need of public support and, especially, of strong partisan backing. A partyless government is almost invariably an arbitrary and reactionary regime. This country has an extraordinary need for revitalized parties: first, to serve as instruments of support for, and to discipline the whims of, elected leaders; and, second, to serve as vehicles for the two-way communication of voter preferences on policy. Too many presidents have looked upon their own party as an uninvited guest within the walls of their special brand of personalized or consensus government.[34]

There is a great need as well for a true opposition party, a competitive shadow government, that will contribute to a dialogue on issues and priorities. Short of adopting a parliamentary form of government, cannot opposition parties formulate alternative proposals and engage in deep discussions to clarify the meaning of the great public issues of the day? In the recent past, American parties out of power seldom have functioned well as an opposition. The opposition party usually is financially strapped and is almost entirely caught up with fund raising and finding someone who may be able to win the presidency next time. The meaning of "opposition" is further emasculated when, as so often is the case, the two dominant parties agree on far more than they disagree and when, as a practical matter, both must appeal to the growing ranks of independent voters.

Americans have never been completely clear on what they wanted their parties to do, whether they wanted the parties to sharpen issues or to defuse them, to serve as mechanisms for choice or for consensus. At the very least, the nation now needs a major clarification of party alliances. Despite, and perhaps even because of, the increase of ticket splitting and in the number of independent voters, the Democratic party has been undergoing at least a modest transformation since the 1950s. With this has come a modest increase in party control. Still, party reform on a major scale has never really been tried. Television, as used to date, encourages presidential candidates to display themselves as nonpartisan individuals devoid of a party banner or a party program. New incentives are needed to counteract these antiparty and antipolitics trends. A new strengthening of party loyalties is needed.

Pressure must be put on the presidency to reverse its growing penchant for secrecy in favor of the people's right to know. To the fullest extent possible, government must be public in everything that it effects. Conclusions of government-sponsored research and evaluation should be communicated intelligibly to the general public when they are made available to public officials. Presidential claims that policies emanating from the White House are the product of the best minds in the country deserve not acquiescence but debate and scrutiny.[35] There should be increased congressional and public attention to where federal research money is invested, what the results are, and what the biases of the researchers may have been.

NEEDED: A REBIRTH OF CITIZEN-POLITICS.   Events in recent years have brought opprobrium to the term "politician." Yet these are times when so many of the nation's problems are political, so many of the remedies must be political, and so large a proportion of the crucial decisions must be political. In the absence of vigorous, competitive, goal-oriented political parties, must not pressure groups, public-interest lobbies, educators, and members of the press become the vigilant executors of the public trust? Granting the centrality of politics in the conduct of government, is it not possible for the American nation and people to begin a movement toward deprofessionalizing politics, toward placing the cloak of political man upon all persons? Robert Hutchins summed up the potential some years ago when he admonished that anybody who feels at ease in the world today is naive: "Education and communication are of prime importance, because if you can't hear what the others are saying, or can't understand it, or if they can't hear or understand you, there can't be any dialogue, and democracy becomes meaningless. The democratic faith is faith in man, faith in every man, faith that man, if he is well enough educated and well enough informed, can solve the problems raised by his own aggregation." [36]

Several concrete remedies that could help open up the presidency and make it more publicly answerable deserve mention. First, to let the salutary light of public attention shine more brightly on the presidency, the serious journals and news media of the nation should immediately upgrade coverage of the White House and the presidential establishment, this in addition to greatly increased oversight by Congress. For too long, publishers and editors have believed that covering the presidency only means assigning a reporter to the White House press corps. Unfortunately, however, those who follow a president around the country on his travels are rarely in a position to do investigative reporting on what is going on inside the presidential establishment and to unmask complicated public relations charades. Covering the Executive Office of the President requires more than a president watcher; it requires specialists who understand the arcane language and highly complicated bureaucratic politics and intrigues that have developed within the presidential establishment.

Second, the popular notion that conventional presidential campaign debates on television add much to our presidential elections would best be set aside. It goes without saying that thoughtful scrutiny of candidates could and must be vastly improved, but are presidential debates the best means? Are qualities of judgment, character, courage, compassion, and justice revealed well in debates such as those between Kennedy and Nixon in 1960? This kind of confrontation tests the ability to render off-the-cuff answers and to tolerate heat, with victory to the contestant who is most adroit at the extemporaneous. Henry Steele Commager's points are important:

> Here a Gresham's Law of politics will almost certainly operate — the glib, the evasive, the dogmatic, the melodramatic, the meretricious will drive out the sincere, the serious, the judicious, the sober, the honest in political discussion. But it is not the instrument of television itself that is at fault; it is our abuse of it. It would be imbecility not to take full advantage of television in ... campaigns. The trouble is that we are not taking advantage of it at all, but permitting it to take advantage of us.
>
> The present formula of the TV "debate" is designed to corrupt the public judgment, and, eventually the whole political process. The American Presidency is too great an office to be subjected to the indignity of this technique. What we need is ... the searching out of the meaning of the great public issues and the full revelation of the minds and characters of the candidates.[37]

Debates about national priorities should rediscover the grand manner of the Lincoln-Douglas debates or Woodrow Wilson's New Freedom addresses of 1912. Is it not possible to invent public forums in which issues are not allowed to remain beneath the dignity of the political candidate nor above the intelligence of the common person? Perhaps in certain national debates, Commager urged, the questioning newsmen should be moved out of the picture and the debaters allowed to develop the argument and define their view of a better and more desirable America.

Third, every reasonable effort should be made by the press, Congress, and the public to insist on regularly scheduled presidential press conferences.[38] Even at the risk of boring the public, these should be of the longer rather than the shorter variety. It is said often that presidents easily dominate these affairs and use them for their own purposes. Sometimes this is the case; frequently, however, presidents wish that this relatively new practice had never been devised. The regularly scheduled press conference offers the press a much needed opportunity to ask embarrassing questions, to probe arbitrary or devious presidential activities, and to hold a president answerable. These conferences are, to be sure, an imperfect device, but both sides might experiment with ways to improve them. Thus, selected members of Congress might be among the questioners. Congress could pose questions to the president and vice versa. Alternatively, or in addition, a sampling of citizens selected by lot, who would serve as semi-tribunes or ombudsmen for one-year terms, also could constitute a public forum before which presidents might come once every several weeks to answer whatever questions are important at the time. In addition to asking questions of the president, they might also pose tough questions to the leadership of both parties in the Congress. Presidents might also experiment with the idea of having several members of their cabinet join them at the presidential news conference to respond occasionally to questions.

Held regularly and conducted properly, these sessions could be one of the most useful means of keeping presidents alert to the questions that are bothering the general public. Occasionally, they can also inform a president about scandals, maladministration, or other irresponsible actions occurring within the federal government that his aides, for one reason or another, might not have brought to his attention. It is well known that President John Kennedy used his frequent presidential press conferences and the preparation that took place prior to them as one of the critical action-forcing and problem-detecting devices informing his exercise of leadership. Perhaps the greatest tribute to the utility of the press conference is that recent presidents most avoided them precisely when unsuccessful policies or grievous scandals made it embarrassing for them to face the public.

A democratic society is inconceivable without creative tension; and it is the responsibility of the press, of interest groups, and of the educator to insure continuation of productive tension and civilized dialogue. As for government officials, plainly a democratic government can exist only to the extent of the willingness of its officials to accept in the fullest sense the responsibility to explain themselves and to seek the public's consent for their policies.

CONCLUSION

In the end, presidents will be kept in line only if the people, according to their own personal views, exercise their rights and their political responsibilities. If the people insist both at and between elections that there be more respect for the doctrine of self-restraint, which all branches, especially the presidency, have been violating in recent years, it will happen. People can "vote" between elections in innumerable ways — by changing parties, by organizing protests, by civil suits and litigation, by swelling the readership ranks of the more responsible newspapers and periodicals; in short, by "sending them a message," to borrow George Wallace's phrase. Persistence and intensity will have impact, especially if the political parties can be recast as educational and communications vehicles. The best insurance system to prevent presidential autocracy, on the one hand, and presidential feebleness, on the other, lies in investment in education, dialogue, and rigorous political organizing, in the building of better parties, and in the strengthening of citizen-politics at all levels of government. As we move into the nation's third century we need especially to recast the institution of the presidency along the lines of a learning and education institution, one that accentuates the sharing of information and ideas and expands on the citizens' right to know. The presidency needs the effective mechanisms for detecting errors and providing feedback outlined in earlier chapters and also the capability for learning and foresight. All of these will aid both the president and the nation to overcome those who always oppose change because they do not truly trust progress or anything new until they have had actual experience with it.

As Associate Justice Robert Jackson once warned us: "The chief restraint upon those who command the physical forces of the country, in the future as in the past, must be their responsibility to the political judgments of their contemporaries and to the moral judgments of history." [39] Popular government demands that elected officials be accountable, but this will be achieved only to the extent that the people exercise the duty of initiative. The best guarantee for the future lies in a politically alert and discerning citizenry willing and able to make tough judgments, to back these up with appropriate sanctions, and, if necessary, to impeach or otherwise remove officials who are not equal to the demands and duties of their office.

NOTES

1. On impeachment, see Raoul Berger, *Impeachment: The Constitutional Problem* (Harvard University Press, 1973); and Irving Brant, *Impeachment* (Knopf, 1972).
2. James L. Sundquist, "Needed: A Workable Check on the Presidency," *Brookings Bulletin* 10, no. 4 (1973), p. 7.
3. People's Lobby, *National Initiative and Vote of Confidence: Tools for Self-Government* (People's Lobby Press, 1974).
4. Carl J. Friedrich, *Constitutional Government and Democracy* (Ginn, 1959), p. 559.
5. Clinton Rossiter, *Constitutional Dictatorship* (Princeton University Press, 1948), p. 314. See also Donald Robinson, "The Routinization of Crisis Government," *The Yale Review,* Winter 1974, pp. 161–74.
6. Raymond Wolfinger and Fred Greenstein, "The Repeal of Fair Housing in California: An Analysis of Referendum Voting," *American Political Science Review,* September 1968, p. 769. On the limits of referenda and initiative, see also V. O. Key, Jr., and Winston Crouch, *The Initiative and the Referendum in California* (University of California, 1939); and Lindsay Rodgers, *The Pollsters, Public Opinion, Politics and Democratic Leadership* (Knopf, 1949).
7. Gabriel Almond, *The American People and Foreign Policy* (Praeger, 1950), p. 53.
8. Woodrow Wilson, *Congressional Government* (1885; reprint ed., Meridian Books, 1936), p. 187.
9. Jack Valenti, "A Six-Year Presidency?" *Newsweek,* 4 February 1974, p. 11.
10. Mike Mansfield, *Statement in support of Senate Joint Resolution 77,* before the Subcommittee on Constitutional Amendments of the Senate, Committee on the Judiciary, 28 October 1971; processed. For his extended views and those of several other witnesses, see U.S., Congress, Senate, Committee on the Judiciary, Subcommittee on Constitutional Amendments, *Single Six-Year Term for President,* 92d Cong., 1st sess., 1972, p. 32.
11. Chester Cooper, *Perspective* 1 (March 1972):47.
12. Lyndon B. Johnson, *The Vantage Point* (Holt, Rinehart and Winston, 1971), p. 344.
13. Woodrow Wilson, letter placed in the Congressional Record, 64th Cong., 2d sess., 15 August 1916, vol. 53, pt. 13:12620.
14. James MacGregor Burns, "Keeping the President In Line," *New York Times,* 8 April 1973, p. 15E.
15. The possibility also exists that a six-year term, or "a term-and-a-half" as some call

it, with reelection precluded would intensify the presidential selection process. Certainly in such a winner-take-more situation, there is the likelihood that ideological competition would be more aggressive and perhaps more bitter than at present. Conflict would assuredly be heightened. How harmful this would be is difficult to assess, but judging from how corrupt the 1972 reelection campaign became this factor must be considered.

16. Clark Clifford, in hearings before the Subcommittee on Constitutional Amendments of the U.S. Senate, Committee on the Judiciary, October 1971; processed, 92d Cong., 1st sess.

17. Harry S Truman, testimony before the Subcommittee on Constitutional Amendments of the U.S. Senate, Committee on the Judiciary, *Hearings on S. J. Resolution 11,* "Presidential Term of Office," 86th Cong., 1st sess., 1959, Part I, p. 7.

18. For a strident critique of Congress see the report of the Ralph Nader Congress Project, Mark J. Green, James M. Fallows, and David R. Zwick, *Who Runs Congress? The President, Big Business or You?* (Bantam, 1972). For a more balanced evaluation see Gary Orfield, *Congressional Power: Congress and Social Change* (Harcourt, Brace, Jovanovich, 1975).

19. David S. Broder, "Comity, Cop-Outs and Congress," *Los Angeles Times,* 10 September 1973, pt II, p. 7.

20. Nelson W. Polsby, "Strengthening Congress in National Policy-Making," *The Yale Review,* June 1970, p. 495. See also, by the same author, *Political Promises* (Oxford University Press, 1974); and U.S., Congress, House, the Select Committee on Committees of the U.S. House of Representatives, *Hearings and Reports,* 93d Cong., 1973, 1974.

21. Theodore Roszak, *Where the Wasteland Ends* (Anchor, 1972), p. 50.

22. For a general treatment of Congress' loss of involvement and authority in foreign policy-making and what should be done about it, see Thomas F. Eagleton, *War and Presidential Power* (Liveright, 1974).

23. See the following documents for useful discussions: U.S., Congress, Senate, Committee on the Judiciary, Subcommittee on Separation of Powers of the U.S. Senate, *Executive Privilege: The Withholding of Information by the Executive,* 92d Cong., 2d sess., 1971; U.S., Congress, Senate, Special Committee on National Emergencies and Delegated Emergency Powers of the U.S. Senate, *Executive Orders in Times of War and National Emergency,* 93d Cong., 2d sess., June 1974; U.S., Congress, Senate, Special Committee on the Termination of the National Emergency of the U.S. Senate, *Emergency Power Statutes: Provisions of Federal Law Now in Effect Delegating to the Executive Extraordinary Authority in Time of National Emergency,* 93d Cong., 2d sess., 19 Nov. 1973.

24. Theodore J. Lowi, prepared testimony before Subcommittee on National Security Policy and Scientific Developments of the House Committee on Foreign Affairs, 91st Cong., 2d sess., 29 July 1970; processed, p. 6.

25. U.S., Congress, Senate, Committee on the Judiciary, Subcommittee on Separation of Powers of the U.S. Senate, *Refusals by the Executive Branch to Provide Information to the Congress,* 1964–1973, 93d Cong., 2d sess., November 1974, p. v.

26. Raoul Berger, *Executive Privilege* (Harvard University Press, 1974).

27. U.S., Congress, Senate, Select Committee on Presidential Campaign Activities of the U.S. Senate, *Final Report,* 93d Cong., 2d sess., June 1974, p. 96.

28. See the various views of witnesses and members of Congress in U.S., Congress, Senate, Committee of the Judiciary, Subcommittee on Separation of Powers of the U.S. Senate, *Removing Politics from the Administration of Justice,* 93d Cong., 2d sess., April 1974.

29. Harry C. McPherson, "The System Worked, But Can It Be Improved?" *New York Times,* 25 August 1974, p. E 3.
30. Archibald Cox, testimony, *Removing Politics From the Administration of Justice,* p. 201.
31. Sundquist, "Needed: A Workable Check on the Presidency," p. 11.
32. Thomas F. Eagleton's complaint in *War and Presidential Power* against the War Powers Act of 1973 merits due consideration.
33. James MacGregor Burns, *Uncommon Sense* (Harper & Row, 1972), pp. 169–70.
34. David S. Broder, *The Party's Over* (Harper & Row, 1972). See also a useful analysis by Donald A. Robinson, "Presidents and Party Leadership" (Paper delivered at the 1974 Annual Meeting of the American Political Science Association, Chicago, Ill., (1 September 1974; processed).
35. David Wise, *The Politics of Lying: Government Deception, Secrecy and Power* (Random House, 1973). See also, David Halberstam, *The Best and the Brightest* (Random House, 1972).
36. Robert Hutchins, "Is Democracy Possible?" *Saturday Review* (21 February 1959), p. 15.
37. Henry Steele Commager, *Freedom and Order* (Meridian Books, 1966), p. 198.
38. See the perceptive diagnosis and suggestions by Harry Kranz, "The Presidency versus the Press — Who Is Right?" *Human Rights,* March 1972, pp. 27–47. Quoting from Sigma Delta Chi, the professional journalism society, he notes that the press would like to see presidential press conferences be revised to become "monthly one-hour, on-the-record, sitdown, non-televised news conferences with no more than twenty reporters." While this is a format that should be used more regularly, it should not preempt televised conferences, but be in addition to them.
39. Robert H. Jackson, *Korematsu* v. *United States,* 323 U.S. 214 (1944), 143.

SELECTED INFORMATION ON THE PRESIDENCY

TABLE A–1   PRESIDENTS AND THEIR TERMS

| President | Term | Party | Prior Service | | | | |
			VP	Cab-inet	Cong.	Gov.	Gen.
1. George Washington	1789–97	Fed.					x
2. John Adams	1797–1801	Fed.	x				
3. Thomas Jefferson	1801–09	D/R	x	x		x	
4. James Madison	1809–17	D/R		x	x		
5. James Monroe	1817–25	D/R		x	x	x	
6. John Quincy Adams	1825–29	D/R		x	x		
7. Andrew Jackson	1829–37	Dem.			x	x^a	x
8. Martin Van Buren	1837–41	Dem.	x	x	x	x	
9. William Harrison	1841	Whig			x	x^a	x
10. John Tyler	1841–45	Whig	x		x	x	
11. James Polk	1845–49	Dem.			x	x	
12. Zachary Taylor	1849–50	Whig					x
13. Millard Fillmore	1850–53	Whig	x		x		
14. Franklin Pierce	1853–57	Dem.			x		x
15. James Buchanan	1857–61	Dem.		x	x		
16. Abraham Lincoln	1861–65	Rep.			x		
17. Andrew Johnson	1865–69	Dem.	x		x	x	
18. U. S. Grant	1869–77	Rep.		x			x
19. Rutherford Hayes	1877–81	Rep.			x	x	x
20. James Garfield	1881	Rep.			x		x
21. Chester Arthur	1881–85	Rep.	x				x
22. Grover Cleveland	1885–89	Dem.				x	

Continued

TABLE A–1 (Continued)

President	Term	Party	VP	Cab-inet	Cong.	Gov.	Gen.
23. Benjamin Harrison	1889–93	Rep.			x		x
24. Grover Cleveland	1893–97	Dem.				x	
25. William McKinley	1897–1901	Rep.			x	x	
26. Theodore Roosevelt	1901–09	Rep.	x			x	
27. William Taft	1909–13	Rep.		x		xª	
28. Woodrow Wilson	1913–21	Dem.				x	
29. Warren Harding	1921–23	Rep.			x		
30. Calvin Coolidge	1923–29	Rep.	x			x	
31. Herbert Hoover	1929–33	Rep.		x			
32. Franklin Roosevelt	1933–45	Dem.				x	
33. Harry Truman	1945–53	Dem.	x		x		
34. Dwight Eisenhower	1953–61	Rep.					x
35. John Kennedy	1961–63	Dem.			x		
36. Lyndon Johnson	1963–69	Dem.	x		x		
37. Richard Nixon	1969–74	Rep.	x		x		
38. Gerald Ford	1974–	Rep.	x		x		
Totals (to 1975)			13	9	23	16 ᵇ	11

ª Denotes territorial governorship.

ᵇ Total is less than the number of items listed because Cleveland appears twice, but served as governor only once.

TABLE A–2 EXECUTIVE OFFICE OF THE PRESIDENT UNITS SINCE 1939 ª

The White House Office, 1939–
Council on Personnel Administration, 1939–1940
Office of Government Reports, 1939–1942
Liaison Office for Personnel Management, 1939–1943
National Resources Planning Board, 1939–1943
Bureau of the Budget, 1939–1970
Office of Emergency Management, 1940–1954
Committee for Congested Production Areas, 1943–1944
War Refugee Board, 1944–1945
Council of Economic Advisers, 1946–
National Security Council, 1947–

Continued

TABLE A–2 *(Continued)*

National Security Resources Board, 1947–1953
Telecommunications Adviser to the President, 1951–1953
Office of Director of Mutual Security, 1951–1954
Office of Defense Mobilization, 1952–1959
Permanent Advisory Committee on Government Organization, 1953–1961
Operations Coordinating Board, 1953–1961
The President's Board of Consultants on Foreign Intelligence Activities, 1956–1961
Office of Civil and Defense Mobilization, 1958–1962
National Aeronautics and Space Council, 1958–1973
The President's Foreign Intelligence Advisory Board, 1961–
Office of Emergency Planning, 1962–1969
Office of Science and Technology, 1962–1973
Office of Special Representative for Trade Negotiations, 1963–
Office of Economic Opportunity, 1964–1975
Office of Emergency Preparedness, 1965–1973
National Council on Marine Resources and Engineering Development, 1966–1971
Council on Environmental Quality, 1969–
Council for Urban Affairs, 1969–1970
Office of Intergovernmental Relations, 1969–1973
Domestic Council, 1970–
Office of Telecommunications Policy, 1970–
Council on International Economic Policy, 1971–
Office of Consumer Affairs, 1971–1973
Special Action Office for Drug Abuse Prevention, 1971–1975
Federal Property Council, 1973–
Council on Economic Policy, 1973–1974
Energy Policy Office, 1973–1974
Federal Energy Office, 1973–1974
Council on Wage and Price Stability, 1974–
White House Labor–Management Committee, 1974–
Economic Policy Board, 1974–

---

[a] This listing does not include the dozens of short-term advisory commissions and study councils that often exist to help advise and guide a president and his staff.

The Central Intelligence Agency since 1947 is formally listed as part of the Executive Office of the President, although in practice it operates as an independent agency.

FIGURE A–1 RECENT PRESIDENTS AND FEDERAL EXPENDITURES

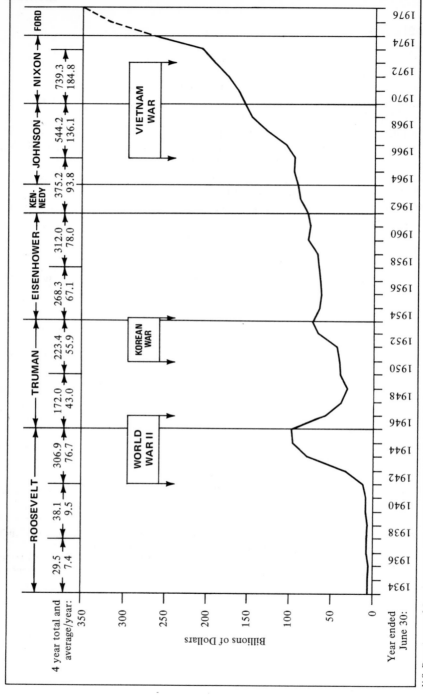

U.S. Department of Commerce and U.S. Office of Management and Budget

TABLE A–3   RELEVANT SECTIONS OF THE CONSTITUTION OF THE UNITED STATES

ARTICLE I

SECTION. 1. All legislative Powers herein granted shall be vested in a Congress of the United States, which shall consist of a Senate and House of Representatives.

SECTION. 2. The House of Representatives shall be composed of Members chosen every second Year by the People of the several States, and the Electors in each State shall have the Qualifications requisite for Electors of the most numerous Branch of the State Legislature. . . .

SECTION. 3. The Senate of the United States shall be composed of two Senators from each State, [chosen by the Legislature thereof,] for six Years; and each Senator shall have one Vote. . . .

The Vice President of the United States shall be President of the Senate, but shall have no Vote, unless they be equally divided.

The Senate shall chuse their other Officers, and also a President pro tempore, in the Absence of the Vice President, or when he shall exercise the Office of President of the United States.

The Senate shall have the sole Power to try all Impeachments. When sitting for that Purpose, they shall be on Oath or Affirmation. When the President of the United States is tried, the Chief Justice shall preside: And no Person shall be convicted without the Concurrence of two thirds of the Members present.

Judgment in Cases of Impeachment shall not extend further than to removal from Office, and disqualification to hold and enjoy any Office of honor, Trust or Profit under the United States: but the Party convicted shall nevertheless be liable and subject to Indictment, Trial, Judgment and Punishment, according to Law. . . .

SECTION. 7. All Bills for raising revenue shall originate in the House of Representatives; but the Senate may propose or concur with Amendments as on other Bills.

Every Bill which shall have passed the House of Representatives and the Senate, shall, before it become a Law, be presented to the President of the United States; If he approve he shall sign it, but if not he shall return it, with his Objections to that House in which it shall have originated, who shall enter the Objections at large on their Journal, and proceed to reconsider it. If after such Reconsideration two thirds of that House shall agree to pass the Bill, it shall be sent, together with the Objections, to the other House, by which it shall likewise be reconsidered, and if approved by two thirds of that House, it shall become a Law. But in all such Cases the Votes of both Houses shall be determined by yeas and Nays, and the Names of the Persons voting for and against the Bill shall be entered on the Journal of each House respectively. If any Bill shall not be returned by the President within ten Days (Sundays excepted) after it shall have been presented to him, the Same shall be a Law, in like Manner as if he had signed it, unless the Congress by their Adjournment prevent its Return, in which Case it shall not be a Law.

Every Order, Resolution, or Vote to which the Concurrence of the Senate and House of Representatives may be necessary (except on a question of Adjournment) shall be presented to the President of the United States; and before the Same shall take Effect, shall be approved by him, or being disapproved by him, shall be repassed by two thirds of the Senate and House of Representatives, according to the Rules and Limitations prescribed in the Case of a Bill.

SECTION. 8. The Congress shall have Power To lay and collect Taxes, Duties, Imposts and Excises, to pay the Debts and provide for the common Defence and general Welfare of the United States; but all Duties, Imposts and Excises shall be uniform throughout the United States;

To borrow Money on the credit of the United States;

To regulate Commerce with foreign Nations, and among the several States, and with the Indian Tribes;

To establish an uniform Rule of Naturalization, and uniform Laws on the subject of Bankruptcies throughout the United States;

To coin Money, regulate the Value thereof, and of foreign Coin, and fix the Standard of Weights and Measures;

To provide for the Punishment of counterfeiting the Securities and current Coin of the United States;

To establish Post Offices and post Roads;

To promote the Progress of Science and useful Arts, by securing for limited Times to Authors and Inventors the exclusive Right to their respective Writings and Discoveries;

To constitute Tribunals inferior to the supreme Court;

To define and punish Piracies and Felonies committed on the high Seas, and Offences against the Law of Nations;

To declare War, grant Letters of Marque and Reprisal, and make Rules concerning Captures on Land and Water;

To raise and support Armies, but no Appropriation of Money to that Use shall be for a longer Term than two Years;

To provide and maintain a Navy;

To make Rules for the Government and Regulation of the land and naval Forces;

To provide for calling forth the Militia to execute the Laws of the Union, suppress Insurrections and repel Invasions;

To provide for organizing, arming, and disciplining, the Militia, and for governing such Part of them as may be employed in the Service of the United States, reserving to the States respectively, the Appointment of the Officers, and the Authority of training the Militia according to the discipline prescribed by Congress;

To exercise exclusive Legislation in all Cases whatsoever, over such District (not exceeding ten Miles Square) as may, by Cession of particular States, and the Acceptance of Congress, become the Seat of the Government of the United States, and to exercise like Authority over all Places purchased by the Consent of the Legislature of the State in which the Same shall be, for the Erection of Forts, Magazines, Arsenals, dock-Yards, and other needful Buildings; — And

To make all Laws which shall be necessary and proper for carrying into Execution the foregoing Powers, and all other Powers vested by this Constitution in the Government of the United States, or in any Department or Officer thereof. . . .

ARTICLE II

SECTION. 1. The executive Power shall be vested in a President of the United States of America. He shall hold his Office during the Term of four Years, and, together with the Vice President, chosen for the same Term, be elected, as follows

Each State shall appoint, in such Manner as the Legislature thereof may direct, a Number of Electors, equal to the whole Number of Senators and Representatives to which the State may be entitled in the Congress: but no Senator or Representative, or Person holding an Office of Trust or Profit under the United States, shall be appointed an Elector.

[The Electors shall meet in their respective States, and vote by Ballot for two Persons, of whom one at least shall not be an Inhabitant of the same State with themselves. And they shall make a List of all the Persons voted for, and of the Number of Votes for each; which List they shall sign and certify, and transmit sealed to the Seat of the Government of the United States, directed to the President of the Senate. The President of the Senate shall, in the Presence of the Senate and House of Representatives, open all the Certificates, and the Votes shall then be counted. The Person having the greatest Number of Votes shall be President, if such Number be a Majority of the whole Number of Electors appointed; and if there be more than one who have such Majority, and have an equal Number of Votes, then the House of Representatives shall immediately chuse by Ballot one of them for President; and if no Person have a Majority, then from the five highest on the List the said House shall in like Manner chuse the President. But in chusing the President, the Votes shall be taken by States, the Representation from each State having one Vote; A quorum for this purpose shall consist of a Member or Members from two thirds of the States, and a Majority of all the States shall be necessary to a Choice. In every Case, after the Choice of the President, the Person having the greatest Number of Votes of the Electors shall be the Vice President. But if there should remain two or more who have equal Votes, the Senate chuse from them by Ballot the Vice President.] [1]

The Congress may determine the Time of chusing the Electors, and the Day on which they shall give their Votes; which Day shall be the same throughout the United States.

No Person except a natural born Citizen, or a Citizen of the United States, at the time of the Adoption of this Constitution, shall be eligible to the Office of President; neither shall any Person be eligible to that Office who shall not have attained to the Age of thirty five Years, and been fourteen Years a Resident within the United States.

[In Case of the Removal of the President from Office, or of his Death, Resignation, or Inability to discharge the Powers and Duties of the said Office, the Same shall devolve on the Vice President, and the Congress may by Law provide for the Case of Removal, Death, Resigation or Inability, both of the President and Vice President, declaring what Officer shall then act as President, and such Officer shall act accordingly, until the Disability be removed, or a President shall be elected.] [2]

The President shall, at stated Times, receive for his Services, a Compensation, which shall neither be encreased nor diminished during the Period for which he shall have been elected, and he shall not receive within that Period any other Emolument from the United States, or any of them.

Before he enter on the Execution of his Office, he shall take the following Oath or Affirmation: — "I do solemnly swear (or affirm) that I will faithfully execute the Office of President of the United States, and will to the best of my Ability, preserve, protect and defend the Constitution of the United States."

SECTION. 2. The President shall be Commander in Chief of the Army and Navy of the United States, and of the Militia of the several States, when called into the actual Service of the United States; he may require the Opinion, in writing, of the principal Officer in each of the executive Departments, upon any Subject relating to the Duties of their respective Offices, and he shall have Power to grant Reprieves and Pardons for Offences against the United States, except in Cases of Impeachment.

He shall have Power, by and with the Advice and Consent of the Senate, to make Treaties, provided two thirds of the Senators present concur; and he shall nominate, and by and with the Advice and Consent of the Senate, shall appoint Ambassadors, other public Ministers and Consuls, Judges of the supreme Court, and all other Officers of the United States, whose Appointments are not herein otherwise provided for, and which shall be established by Law: but the Congress may by Law vest the Appointment of such inferior Offices, as they think proper, in the President alone, in the Courts of Law, or in the Heads of Departments.

The President shall have Power to fill up all Vacancies that may happen during the Recess of the Senate, by granting Commissions which shall expire at the End of their next Session.

SECTION. 3. He shall from time to time give to the Congress Information of the State of the Union, and recommend to their Consideration such Measures as he shall judge necessary and expedient; he may, on extraordinary Occasions, convene both Houses, or either of them, and in Case of Disagreement between them, with Respect to the Time of Adjournment, he may adjourn them to such Time as he shall think proper; he shall receive Ambassadors and other public Ministers; he shall take Care that the Laws be faithfully executed, and shall Commission all the Officers of the United States.

SECTION. 4. The President, Vice President and all civil Officers of the United States, shall be removed from Office on Impeachment for, and Conviction of, Treason, Bribery, or other high Crimes and Misdemeanors.

RELEVANT AMENDMENTS TO THE CONSTITUTION

AMENDMENT XII (1804)

The Electors shall meet in their respective states, and vote by ballot for President and Vice President, one of whom, at least, shall not be an inhabitant of the same state with themselves; they shall name in their ballots the person voted for as President, and in distinct ballots the person voted for as Vice President, and they shall make distinct lists of all persons voted for as President, and of all persons voted for as Vice President, and of the number of votes for each, which lists they shall sign and certify, and transmit sealed to the seat of the government of the United States, directed to the President of the Senate; — The President of the Senate shall, in the presence of the Senate and House of Representatives, open all the certificates and the votes shall then be counted;

— The person having the greatest number of votes for President, shall be the President, if such number be a majority of the whole number of Electors appointed; and if no person have such majority, then from the persons having the highest numbers not exceeding three on the list of those voted for as President, the House of Representatives shall choose immediately, by ballot, the President. But in choosing the President, the votes shall be taken by states, the representation from each state having one vote; a quorum for this purpose shall consist of a member or members from two-thirds of the states, and a majority of all the states shall be necessary to a choice. And if the House of Representatives shall not choose a President whenever the right of choice shall devolve upon them, before the fourth day of March next following,[3] then the Vice President shall act as President, as in the case of the death or other constitutional disability of the President. — The person having the greatest number of votes as Vice President, shall be the Vice President, if such number be a majority of the whole number of Electors appointed, and if no person have a majority, then from the two highest numbers on the list, the Senate shall choose the Vice President; a quorum for the purpose shall consist of two-thirds of the whole number of Senators, and a majority of the whole number shall be necessary to a choice. But no person constitutionally ineligible to the office of President shall be eligible to that of Vice President of the United States. . . .

AMENDMENT XX (1933)

SECTION 1. The terms of the President and Vice President shall end at noon on the 20th day of January, and the terms of Senators and Representatives at noon on the 3d day of January, of the years in which such terms would have ended if this article had not been ratified; and the terms of their successors shall then begin.

SECTION 2. The Congress shall assemble at least once in every year, and such meeting shall begin at noon on the 3d day of January, unless they shall by law appoint a different day.

SECTION 3. If, at the time fixed for the beginning of the term of the President, the President elect shall have died, the Vice President elect shall become President. If a President shall not have been chosen before the time fixed for the beginning of his term, or if the President elect shall have failed to qualify, then the Vice President elect shall act as President until a President shall have qualified; and the Congress may by law provide for the case wherein neither a President elect nor a Vice President elect shall have qualified, declaring who shall then act as President, or the manner in which one who is to act shall be selected, and such person shall act accordingly until a President or Vice President shall have qualified.

SECTION 4. The Congress may by law provide for the case of the death of any of the persons from whom the House of Representatives may choose a President whenever the right of choice shall have devolved upon them, and for the case of the death of any of the persons from whom the Senate may choose a Vice President whenever the right of choice shall have devolved upon them.

SECTION 5. Sections 1 and 2 shall take effect on the 15th day of October following the ratification of this table.

SECTION 6. This article shall be inoperative unless it shall have been ratified as an amendment to the Constitution by the legislatures of three-fourths of the several States within seven years from the date of its submission.

AMENDMENT XXII (1951)

SECTION 1. No person shall be elected to the office of the President more than twice, and no person who has held the office of President, or acted as President, for more than two years of a term to which some other person was elected President shall be elected to the office of the President more than once. But this Article shall not apply to any person holding the office of President when this Article was proposed by the Congress, and shall not prevent any person who may be holding the office of President, or acting as President, during the term within which this article becomes operative from holding the office of President or acting as President during the remainder of such term.

SECTION 2. This Article shall be inoperative unless it shall have been ratified as an amendment to the Constitution by the legislatures of three-fourths of the several States within seven years from the date of its submission to the States by the Congress.

AMENDMENT XXV (1967)

SECTION 1. In case of the removal of the President from office or of his death or resignation, the Vice President shall become President.

SECTION 2. Whenever there is a vacancy in the office of the Vice President, the President shall nominate a Vice President who shall take the office upon confirmation by a majority vote of both houses of Congress.

SECTION 3. Whenever the President transmits to the President pro tempore of the Senate and the Speaker of the House of Representatives his written declaration that he is unable to discharge the powers and duties of his office, and until he transmits to them a written declaration to the contrary, such powers and duties shall be discharged by the Vice President as Acting President.

SECTION 4. Whenever the Vice President and a majority of either the principal officers of the executive departments or of such other body as Congress may by law provide, transmit to the President pro tempore of the Senate and the Speaker of the House of Representatives their written declaration that the President is unable to discharge the powers and duties of his office, the Vice President shall immediately assume the powers and duties of the office as Acting President.

Thereafter, when the President transmits to the President pro tempore of the Senate and the Speaker of the House of Representatives his written declaration that no inability exists, he shall resume the powers and duties of his office unless the Vice President and a majority of either the principal officers of the executive department or of such other body as Congress may by law provide, transmit within four days to the President pro tempore of the Senate and the Speaker of the House of Representatives their written declaration that the President is unable to discharge the powers and duties of his office. Thereupon Congress shall decide the issue, assembling within forty-eight hours for that purpose if not in session. If the Congress within twenty-one days after receipt of the latter written declaration, or, if Congress is not in session, within twenty-one days after Congress is required to assemble, determines by two-third vote of both Houses that the

President is unable to discharge the powers and duties of his office, the Vice President shall continue to discharge the same as Acting President; otherwise, the President shall resume the powers and duties of his office.

---

1. Superseded by the Twelfth Amendment.
2. Superseded by the Twenty-fifth Amendment.
3. Modified by the Twentieth Amendment.

SELECTED BIBLIOGRAPHY

*This bibliography, which is not intended to be comprehensive, includes important polit-
ical analyses of the office of the president and the people who have held it. Many of
the studies cited here treat major controversies surrounding this embattled institution. More generally, this listing permits me the chance to single out several books
that were helpful in writing about the state of the presidency.*

1. THE PRESIDENCY IN GENERAL

Anderson, Patrick. *The Presidents' Men*. Garden City, N.Y.: Doubleday, 1968.

Bailey, Thomas A. *Presidential Greatness*. New York: Appleton-Century-Crofts, 1966.

Barber, James David. *The Presidential Character*. Englewood Cliffs, N.J.: Prentice-
Hall, 1972.

Berger, Raoul. *Impeachment: The Constitutional Problems*. Cambridge, Mass.: Harvard University Press, 1973.

————. *Executive Privilege: A Constitutional Myth*. Cambridge, Mass.: Harvard University Press, 1974.

Binkley, Wilfred E. *The Man in the White House*. Baltimore: Johns Hopkins Press,
1958.

Brant, Irving. *Impeachment*. New York: Knopf, 1972.

Broder, David S. *The Party's Over*. New York: Harper and Row, 1971.

Brownlow, Louis. *The President and the Presidency*. Chicago: University of Chicago
Press, 1949.

Bundy, McGeorge. *The Strength of Government*. Cambridge, Mass.: Harvard University Press, 1968.

Burns, James M. *Presidential Government*. Boston: Houghton Mifflin, 1966.

Chamberlain, Lawrence H. *The President, Congress and Legislation*. New York: Columbia University Press, 1946.

Cornwell, Elmer E. *Presidential Leadership of Public Opinion*. Bloomington: University of Indiana Press, 1962.

Corwin, Edward S. *The President: Office and Powers*. New York: New York University Press, 1940.

Cotter, C. P., and J. M. Smith. *Powers of the President During National Crises*. Washington: Public Affairs Press, 1961.

Dunn, Delmer D. *Financing Presidential Campaigns*. Washington: The Brookings Institution, 1972.

Fenno, Richard F. *The President's Cabinet*. New York: Vintage, 1959.

Finer, Herman. *The Presidency: Crisis and Regeneration*. Chicago: University of Chicago Press, 1960.

Fisher, Louis. *President and Congress*. New York: Free Press, 1972.

Grabner, Doris. *Public Opinion, the President and Foreign Policy*. New York: Holt, Rinehart and Winston, 1968.

Hardin, Charles. *Presidential Power and Accountability*. Chicago: University of Chicago Press, 1974.

Hargrove, Erwin C. *Presidential Leadership*. New York: Macmillan, 1966.

————. *The Power of the Modern Presidency*. New York: Knopf, 1974.

Herring, Pendleton. *Presidential Leadership*. New York: Farrar and Rinehart, 1940.

Hobbs, Edward. *Behind the President: A Study of Executive Office Agencies*. Washington, D.C.: Public Affairs Press, 1954.

Hofstadter, Richard. *The American Political Tradition*. New York: Vintage, 1948.

Holtzman, Abraham. *Legislative Liaison: Executive Leadership in Congress*. Chicago: Rand McNally, 1970.

Hughes, Emmet John. *The Living Presidency*. New York: Coward, McCann & Geoghegan, 1973.

Hyman, Sidney. *The American President*. New York: Harper and Bros., 1954.

James, Dorothy B. *The Contemporary Presidency*. New York: Pegasus, 1969.

Kallenbach, Joseph E. *The American Chief Executive*. New York: Harper and Row, 1966.

Koenig, Louis. *The Chief Executive*. Rev. ed. New York: Harcourt, Brace and World, 1968.

Laski, Harold. *The American Presidency*. New York: Grosset and Dunlap, 1940.

McConnell, Grant. *The Modern Presidency*. New York: St. Martin's, 1967.

McGinniss, Joe. *The Selling of the President 1968*. New York: Trident Press, 1969.

Milton, George F. *The Use of Presidential Power*. Boston: Little, Brown, 1944.

Minow, Newton M., and others. *Presidential Television*. New York: Basic Books, 1973.

Mueller, John E. *War, Presidents and Public Opinion*. New York: Wiley, 1973.

Neustadt, Richard. *Presidential Power*. New York: Wiley, 1960.

Novak, Michael. *Choosing Our King*. New York: Macmillan, 1974.

Patterson, C. P. *Presidential Government in the United States*. Chapel Hill: University of North Carolina Press, 1947.

Pollard, James F. *The Presidents and the Press*. Washington: Public Affairs Press, 1964.

Polsby, Nelson W. *Congress and the Presidency*. Englewood Cliffs, N.J.: Prentice-Hall, 1971.

————, and Aaron Wildavsky. *Presidential Elections*. New York: Scribners, 1968.

Reedy, George E. *The Twilight of the Presidency.* New York: World, 1970.
Rossiter, Clinton. *Constitutional Dictatorship.* New York: Harcourt, Brace, 1948.
———. *The American Presidency.* Rev. ed. New York: Harcourt, Brace and World, 1960.
Schlesinger, Arthur M., Jr. *The Imperial Presidency.* Boston: Houghton Mifflin, 1973.
———, and Alfred deGrazia. *Congress and the Presidency: Their Role in Modern Times.* Washington: American Enterprise Institute for Public Policy, 1967.
Schubert, Glendon. *The Presidency in the Courts.* Minneapolis: University of Minnesota Press, 1957.
Scigliano, Robert. *The Supreme Court and the Presidency.* New York: Free Press, 1971.
Sorensen, Theodore C. *Decision-Making in the White House.* New York: Columbia University Press, 1963.
———. *Watchman in the Night: Presidential Accountability and Watergate.* Cambridge, Mass.: The MIT Press, 1975.
Strum, Philippa. *Presidential Power and American Democracy.* Pacific Palisades, Calif.: Goodyear, 1972.
Sundquist, James L. *Politics and Policy: The Eisenhower, Kennedy, and Johnson Years.* Washington: The Brookings Institution, 1968.
Tugwell, Rexford G. *How They Became President.* New York: Simon and Schuster, 1965.
———. *The Enlargement of the Presidency.* Garden City, N.Y.: Doubleday, 1960.
Vinyard, Dale. *The Presidency.* New York: Scribners, 1971.
White, Theodore H. *The Making of the President 1960; 1964; 1968; 1972.* New York: Atheneum, 1961; 1965; 1969; 1973.
Wilson, Woodrow. *Congressional Government.* 1885. Reprint. New York: Meridian Books, 1956.
Young, James S. *The Washington Community 1800–1820.* New York: Columbia University Press, 1966.

2. USEFUL ANTHOLOGIES ON THE PRESIDENCY

Bach, Stanley, and George T. Sulzner, eds. *Perspective on the Presidency.* Lexington, Mass.: D. C. Heath, 1974.
Barber, James David, ed. *Choosing the President.* Englewood Cliffs, N.J.: Prentice-Hall, 1974.
Clark, Keith, and Lawrence Legere, eds. *The President and the Management of National Security.* New York: Praeger, 1969.
Cornwell, Elmer E., ed. *The American Presidency: Vital Center.* Chicago: Scott, Foresman, 1966.
Cronin, Thomas E., and Sanford D. Greenberg, eds. *The Presidential Advisory System.* New York: Harper and Row, 1969.
Dunn, Charles, ed. *The Future of the American Presidency.* Morristown, N.J.: General Learning Press, 1975.
Haight, David E., and Larry D. Johnson, eds. *The President: Roles and Powers.* Chicago: Rand McNally, 1965.
Halpern, Paul, ed. *Why Watergate?* Pacific Palisades, Cal.: Palisades Press, 1975.
Hirschfield, Robert S., ed. *The Power of the Presidency.* New York: Atherton, 1968.

Hoxie, R. Gordon, ed. *The White House: Organization and Operation.* New York: Center for the Study of the Presidency, 1971.

————, ed. *The Presidency of the 1970s.* New York: Center for the Study of the Presidency, 1973.

Jackson, Henry M., ed. *The National Security Council.* New York: Praeger, 1965.

Johnson, Donald B., and Jack L. Walker, eds. *The Dynamics of the American Presidency.* New York: Wiley, 1964.

Moe, Ronald C., ed. *Congress and the President.* Pacific Palisades, Cal.: Goodyear, 1971.

Polsby, Nelson W., ed. *The Modern Presidency.* New York: Random House, 1973.

Roberts, Charles, ed. *Has the President Too Much Power?* New York: Harper's, 1974.

Saffell, David C., ed. *Watergate: Its Effects on the American Political System.* Cambridge, Mass.: Winthrop, 1974.

Thomas, Norman C., and Hans W. Baade, eds. *The Institutionalized Presidency.* Dobbs Ferry, N. Y.: Oceana, 1972.

————, ed. *The Presidency in Contemporary Context.* New York: Dodd, Mead, 1975.

Tugwell, Rexford G., and Thomas E. Cronin, eds. *The Presidency Reappraised.* New York: Praeger, 1974.

Wildavsky, Aaron, ed. *The Presidency.* Boston: Little, Brown, 1969.

3. SPECIFIC PRESIDENTS AND THEIR ADMINISTRATIONS

Acheson, Dean. *Present at the Creation.* New York: Norton, 1969.

Adams, Sherman. *First-Hand Report.* New York: Harper and Bros., 1961.

Albertson, Dean, ed. *Eisenhower as President.* New York: Hill and Wang, 1963.

Bernstein, Barton J., ed. *Politics and Policies of the Truman Administration.* Chicago: Quadrangle, 1970.

Burns, James M. *The Lion and the Fox.* New York: Harcourt, Brace, 1956.

————. *Roosevelt: Soldier of Freedom.* New York: Harcourt, Brace, 1971.

Cochran, Bert. *Harry Truman and the Crisis Presidency.* New York: Funk and Wagnalls, 1973.

Donald, Aida DiPace, ed. *John F. Kennedy and the New Frontier.* New York: Hill and Wang, 1966.

Donovan, Robert J. *Eisenhower, The Inside Story.* New York: Harper and Bros., 1956.

Eisenhower, Dwight D. *Mandate for Change.* Garden City, N.Y.: Doubleday, 1963.

Evans, Rowland, and Robert Novak. *Lyndon B. Johnson: The Exercise of Power.* New York: New American Library, 1966.

————. *Nixon in the White House.* New York: Random House, 1971.

Fairlie, Henry. *The Kennedy Promise.* Garden City, N.Y.: Doubleday, 1973.

Flexner, James Thomas. *Washington: The Indispensable Man.* Boston: Little, Brown, 1974.

George, Alexander L., and Juliette L. George. *Woodrow Wilson and Colonel House.* New York: Dover, 1956.

Goldman, Eric F. *The Tragedy of Lyndon Johnson.* New York: Knopf, 1969.

Hughes, Emmet John. *The Ordeal of Power.* New York: Dell, 1962.

Johnson, Lyndon B. *The Vantage Point.* New York: Holt, Rinehart and Winston, 1971.

Latham, Earl, ed. *J. F. Kennedy and Presidential Power*. Boston: D. C. Heath, 1972.

Lyon, Peter. *Eisenhower: Portrait of the Hero*. Boston: Little Brown, 1974.

McPherson, Harry C. *A Political Education*. Boston: Atlantic-Little, Brown, 1972.

Magruder, Jeb Stewart. *An American Life*. New York: Atheneum, 1974.

Miller, Merle. *Plain Speaking: An Oral Biography of Harry S Truman*. New York: Medallian, 1974.

O'Brien, Lawrence. *No Final Victories: From John F. Kennedy to Watergate*. Garden City, N.Y.: Doubleday, 1974.

Osborne, John. *The Nixon Watch*. (A series.) New York: Liveright, 1970–1975.

Phillips, Cabell. *The Truman Presidency*. New York: Macmillan, 1966.

Rather, Dan, and Gary Paul Gates. *The Palace Guard*. New York: Harper & Row, 1974.

Schlesinger, Arthur M., Jr. *A Thousand Days: John F. Kennedy in the White House*. Boston: Houghton Mifflin, 1965.

———. *The Age of Roosevelt*. 3 vols. Boston: Houghton Mifflin, 1957, 1958, 1960.

Sherwood, Robert E. *Roosevelt and Hopkins*. New York: Harper and Bros., 1948.

Sidey, Hugh. *A Very Personal Presidency: Lyndon Johnson in the White House*. New York: Atheneum, 1968.

Sorensen, Theodore. *Kennedy*. New York: Harper and Row, 1965.

Truman, Harry S *Memoires*. 2 vols. Garden City, N.Y.: Doubleday, 1955, 1956.

Tugwell, Rexford G. *In Search of Roosevelt*. Cambridge, Mass.: Harvard University Press, 1972.

———. *The Democratic Roosevelt*. Garden City, N.Y.: Doubleday, 1957.

Wills, Garry. *Nixon Agonistes*. Boston: Houghton Mifflin, 1970.

4. BUREAUCRATIC POLITICS AND PROGRAM IMPLEMENTATION

Allison, Graham T. *Essence of Decision: Explaining the Cuban Missile Crisis*. Boston: Little, Brown, 1971.

Davis, James W., Jr. *The National Executive Branch*. New York: Free Press, 1970.

Derthick, Martha. *New Towns In-Town*. Washington: Urban Institute, 1972.

Destler, I. M. *Presidents, Bureaucrats and Foreign Policy*. Princeton, N.J.: Princeton University Press, 1972.

Donovan, John C. *The Policy-Makers*. Indianapolis: Pegasus, 1970.

Downs, Anthony. *Inside Bureaucracy*. Boston: Little, Brown, 1967.

Enthovan, Alain C., and Wayne Smith. *How Much is Enough? Shaping the Defense Program, 1961–1969*. New York: Harper and Row, 1971.

Freeman, J. Leiper. *The Political Process*. Rev. ed. New York: Random House, 1965.

George, Alexander, and others. *The Limits of Coercive Diplomacy*. Boston: Little, Brown, 1971.

Halberstam, David. *The Best and the Brightest*. New York: Random House, 1972.

Halperin, Morton H. *Bureaucratic Politics and Foreign Policy*. Washington: The Brookings Institution, 1974.

Hickel, Walter J. *Who Owns America?* Englewood Cliffs, N.J.: Prentice-Hall, 1971.

Hilsman, Roger. *To Move a Nation*. Garden City, N.Y.: Doubleday, 1967.

Hoopes, Townsend. *The Limits of Intervention*. New York: McKay, 1969.

Janis, Irving L. *Victims of Groupthink.* Boston: Houghton Mifflin, 1972.

Kaufman, Herbert. *The Limits of Organizational Change.* University, Ala.: University of Alabama Press, 1971.

Kennedy, Robert F. *Thirteen Days: A Memoir of the Cuban Missile Crisis.* New York: Norton, 1969.

Kessel, John. *The Domestic Presidency.* Scituate, Mass.: The Duxbury Press, 1975.

Lowi, Theodore J. *The End of Liberalism.* New York: Norton, 1969.

McConnell, Grant. *Steel and the Presidency.* New York: Norton, 1963.

MacMahon, Arthur W. *Administering Federalism in a Democracy.* New York: Oxford University Press, 1972.

Morgan, Ruth P. *The President and Civil Rights.* New York: St. Martin's, 1970.

Moynihan, Daniel P. *Maximum Feasible Misunderstanding.* New York: Free Press, 1969.

———. *The Politics of a Guaranteed Income.* New York: Random House, 1973.

Neustadt, Richard E. *Alliance Politics.* New York: Columbia University Press, 1970.

Orfield, Gary. *The Reconstruction of Southern Education.* New York: Wiley, 1969.

Pressman, Jeffrey, and Aaron Wildavsky. *Implementation.* Berkeley: University of California Press, 1973.

Reagan, Michael. *The New Federalism.* New York: Oxford University Press, 1972.

Rivlin, Alice M. *Systematic Thinking for Social Action.* Washington: The Brookings Institution, 1971.

Rourke, Francis E. *Bureaucracy, Politics and Public Policy.* Boston: Little, Brown, 1969.

Seidman, Harold. *Politics, Position and Power.* New York: Oxford University Press, 1970.

Steiner, Gilbert Y. *The State of Welfare.* Washington: The Brookings Institution, 1971.

Sundquist, James L. *Making Federalism Work.* Washington: The Brookings Institution, 1969.

Thomas, Norman C. *Politics in National Education.* New York: David McKay, 1975.

Tobin, James. *The New Economics One Decade Older.* Princeton, N.J.: Princeton University Press, 1974.

Wann, A. J. *The President as Chief Administrator.* Washington: Public Affairs Press, 1968.

Wildavsky, Aaron. *The Politics of the Budgetary Process.* Boston: Little, Brown, 1964.

Wise, David. *The Politics of Lying.* New York: Random House, 1973.

Wolman, Harold. *Politics of Federal Housing.* New York: Dodd, Mead, 1971.

ACKNOWLEDGMENTS

This study benefitted from the assistance and criticism of a number of people over the past few years. I have profitted from conversations with colleagues at the Aspen Institute for Humanistic Studies, The Brookings Institution, and the Center for the Study of Democratic Institutions. Ideas and helpful suggestions also came from friends and associates at Stanford University, the University of North Carolina, and the University of California at Santa Barbara. Thus, two of my early advisers, Heinz Eulau and Gabriel Almond graciously introduced me to the world of empirical analysis of governmental elites. A gifted younger associate, Michael Couzens, served as an important research assistant in the early stages of this undertaking. The following people were especially kind in offering advice (not always taken) for improving portions of the manuscript: Delmer D. Dunn, John Kessel, Herbert Kaufman, James Sundquist, Harold Gosnell, Stephen Hess, Paul Halpern, Louis Fisher, William Keech, Judith Parris, I. M. Destler, Caren Dubnoff, and Norman C. Thomas. Throughout the writing of this book I profitted too from extended conversations with Dom Bonafede, James MacGregor Burns, Douglass Cater, Benjamin V. Cohen, Alexander George, Rexford G. Tugwell, and Ben J. Wattenberg. I am indebted as well to the over one hundred former White House staff members and cabinet members who permitted me to interview them. Dozens of people in the Washington press corps or in the career public service also contributed ideas, encouragement, and advice. I want to thank Goddard Winterbottom for editorial advice on an early draft. Secretarial assistance came from Irish Langton, Kathreen Breen, Susan Sterling, and Priscilla DeWolf. Rick Boyer, Lynn Lloyd, and Wayne Andrew Howitt at Little, Brown and Company helped transform a manuscript into an attractive book. Above all, however, my thanks also to Alexander (Doug), and to my wife Tania for her faith, hope, and clarity.

— TEC

ABOUT THE AUTHOR

Thomas E. Cronin is a graduate of Holy Cross College and Stanford University where he received his Ph.D. (1968) in political science. He has served as a White House Fellow on the domestic policy staff at the White House (1966–1967) and as a special consultant to a cabinet member. Dr. Cronin has also served on the staffs of a governor, a U. S. senator, and been a special adviser to several members of Congress, executive branch departments, and the U. S. Civil Service Commission. He has been in residence as a research scholar at The Brookings Institution (1970–1972), The Center for the Study of Democratic Institutions (1972–1974) and the Aspen Institute for Humanistic Studies (1974–1975).

Cronin served as a Teaching Fellow in Political Science at Stanford University and later on the faculties at the University of North Carolina (Chapel Hill) and the University of California (Santa Barbara). He is a co-author and editor of *The Presidential Advisory System* (1969), *The Presidency Reappraised* (1974), and collaborating author of *Government by the People*, 9th edition (1975). His essays and articles have appeared in *Science, Public Policy, Law and Contemporary Problems, The Saturday Review, The Washington Monthly, Commonweal, The Public Administration Review*, and many other journals. His articles on the presidency and national politics have also appeared or been reprinted in a score of anthologies or special collections. Dr. Cronin has lectured at over 75 colleges or research institutes in this country and in Europe.

INDEX

accountability, 7, 156, 257–258, 266, 290, 291–292; economy, 15, 257; insuring, 293–321
Acheson, Dean, 174, 196, 269
activism, lauded, 4, 29–30, 37–38, 43, 113, 143, 203, 240–241
Adams, John, 178–179, 216, 218, 223
Adams, Sherman, 170, 182, 196, 264, 265
administrative staff, 132–135
advisers: as advocates, 62, 197; commissions, 63–65; economics, 194–196; evaluation, 65–66, 248; inner circles, 196–197; legal, 194–196; national security, 192–194, 209 n. 27; reform and, 264–265, 267–268, 311; vice presidents as, 223–227
advocacy: advisers and, 62, 197, 269; conflicts, 198–199; interest groups, 243; merits of, 205–208
agencies, importance of some, 189
Agency for International Development (AID), 69, 131
Agnew, Spiro, 75, 148, 194, 213, 215, 219–220, 221, 222, 225, 231
Aiken, George, 299
Allen, James E., 57–61
Alliance for Progress, 41
Almond, Gabriel, 297
Alsop, Stewart, 191, 192
American Medical Association, 59, 70
American Presidency, The (Rossiter), 28–29

Anderson, Clinton, 214
Anderson, Jack, 23
Anderson, Patrick, 117
Anderson, Robert, 192, 219
appointments: Allen case, 57–61; basis for, 55–56, 108–109; dismissal power, 60–61; judicial, 56–57; patronage and, 59, 284
Armstrong, Anne, 197
Articles of Confederation, 178, 238
Ash, Roy, 79, 201
Atomic Energy Commission, 92

Ball, George, 139, 225
Barber, James David, 31
Barkley, Alben, 79–80
Barnett, Ross, 253
Bayh, Birch, 228
Berger, Raoul, 311
Bernstein, Marver, 81
bipartisanship, criticized, 303
Bishop, Jim, 106
Boyd, Alan, 159
Brennan, William J., Jr., 57
Brinkley, David, 19
Broder, David, 307
Brown vs. *Board of Education*, 104, 252
Bryan, William Jennings, 206
Buchanan, Patrick, 150
Budget Reform Act of 1974, 315

budgets: Congress and, 89; lead-time, 16; planning per, 255–256

Bundy, McGeorge, 130, 131, 156, 174, 193, 196

Bureau of the Budget, 124, 128, 194–195; increased authority, 17, 118

bureaucracy, 68; alliances, 69–70, 94–95; constraint on president, 91–99, 203, 246, 248, 304–305; of executive branch, 11, 266; incentive systems proposed, 284–287; and national interest, 92–93; staff attitude re, 131, 154, 156; veto of, 93–96

Burns, Arthur, 140, 196

Burns, James MacGregor, 254, 279, 303, 315

Burr, Aaron, 213, 220, 231

Bush, Vannevar, 62

Butz, Earl, 159

Byrnes, James F., 216, 218, 227, 264, 265, 267

cabinet, 176–208; decline of, 174; distrust, 179–180; inner, 191–192; loyalty, 168; meetings of, 183, 185; national security and, 192–194; outer, 197–198, 269; and policy differentiation, 16, 198–199, 207, 269; recruitment, 159, 179, 197; reform and, 180, 268–273; staff and, 184, 199, 202–205; strong/weak, 18–19; textbooks on, 27; unequal importance, 188–201; use of, 183–188; vice president and, 223–227

Calhoun, John C., 220

Califano, Joseph, 81, 126, 222, 223

Cambodia, invaded, 14, 58, 80, 146–147, 149, 243, 253

campaigns: financing, 7; and promises, 41, 248

Carey, Hugh, 281

Carey, William, 242-243

Central Intelligence Agency (CIA), 131, 189, 257, 312

centralization, 245–249, 278–279

Civil Service Commission, 172, 285

Clark, Ramsey, 189

Clark, Tom, 57

Cleveland, Grover, 77, 118

Clifford, Clark, 142, 159, 174

Cochran, Bert, 10, 103

Cohen, Benjamin V., 174, 180, 267–268

Cohen, Wilbur, 198

cold war, 25, 39, 121, 269

collegial presidency, proposed, 263–268; shortcomings, 266–267

Colson, Charles, 150, 184

Commager, Henry Steele, 320

Commission on Campus Unrest, 44–45

commissions, special, 27, 63–65

Common Cause, 243

conflict, staff-departments, 161–171, 202–205

Congress (see also Senate): and appointees, 56, 311; and bureaucracy, 98–99; constraints on president, 87–91, 244; and domestic policy, 16, 198, 254, 307; and executive reorganization, 68–69; and presidential abuses, 7, 114, 293; and reform, 277, 306–315; and veto power, 77, 80; and Vietnam, 113, 121, 307, 309; weaknesses of, 14, 80, 121, 138, 307; White House staff re, 135–136

Congressional Quarterly, 87–88

congressional relations staff, 135–136

Congressional Research Service, 277

Connally, John B., 100, 148, 159, 192, 195, 196

consensus leadership, 7, 9, 147; among elites, 101–102

Constitution, 7, 103, 121, 178, 316, 329–335; Twelfth Amendment, 332–333; Twentieth Amendment, 333; Twenty-second Amendment, 305, 334; Twenty-fifth Amendment, 229, 293–294, 334

Coolidge, Calvin, 26, 213, 223, 226

Corwin, Edward S., 38, 113

Coser, Lewis, 172

Council of Economic Advisers, 27, 121, 128, 195

Council on Economic Policy, 15, 121, 128, 193

Council on Environmental Quality, 27, 121

Council on International Economic Policy, 121, 128, 193

Council for Urban Affairs, 71

Council on Wage and Price Stability, 128

courts, constraints of, 103–106, 292, 296

Cox, Archibald, 7, 60, 313, 314
credibility, diminished, 4–5, 75, 150
Crime Control Act, 255
crisis, 257, 258, 266; and growth of
    presidency, 121–122; presidency
    considered during, 54, 240, 252
Cuba, 192; Bay of Pigs, 40, 61, 121, 130,
    142, 205, 239; missile crisis, 11, 39, 195,
    252, 253, 307
cynicism, idealized image and, 47–48

Daley, Richard, 281
Dawes, Charles, 184, 220, 226
Day, J. Edward, 166, 185
decentralization, 86, 245–249, 279–283,
    284
Democratic Party, 239
Department of Agriculture, 197
Department of Commerce, 197
Department of Defense, 130–131, 188,
    189, 205, 272
Department of Health, Education and
    Welfare, 70, 189, 191, 197, 272
Department of Housing and Urban
    Development, 70–72, 189, 197
Department of the Interior, 70, 197
Department of Justice, 194–196, 205,
    254–255, 313; under Kennedy, 57, 189
Department of Labor, 59, 70, 189, 197
Department of State, 132, 191; White
    House relations, 130–131, 161–162, 188,
    192–193, 268–269
Department of Transportation, 68, 197
Department of the Treasury, 205;
    secretary as counselor, 194–195
departmentalists, 155–161
departments (see also cabinet): and
    conflict, 167–171; loyalists, 157–159;
    reform and, 268–273; regionalization,
    281; self-evaluation, 65–66; special
    interests and, 19, 59, 67, 69–70, 197,
    272; unequal importance of, 188–201;
    White House staff and, 130–131,
    153–175, 199, 202–205, 270
Derthick, Martha, 18
Dewey, Thomas E., 142
Dillon, C. Douglas, 131, 159, 191, 192,
    195, 196
Domestic Council, 121, 126–128, 129, 227

domestic policy, 250; changing nature,
    18; coordinating, 282–283; presidential
    influence, 5, 244; reform and, 263; staff
    for, 124–128; subordinate role, 12–13
Douglas, Paul, 100
Downs, Anthony, 109
Drucker, Peter, 124, 206
Dulles, John Foster, 188, 193, 269
Dungan, Ralph, 203

Eagleton, Thomas, 228
economic counsel, 194–196
economic policy, aggregate, 14; im-
    portance of, 14–15, 244, 250; income
    redistribution, 15; staff for, 128–130;
    taxation and, 15
Economic Policy Board, 68, 128
Edelman, Murray, 36
Ehrlichman, John, 48, 127, 140, 153, 159,
    199, 201
Eisenhower, Dwight D., 25, 26, 30, 33, 35,
    36, 39, 57, 62, 64, 70, 78, 104, 108, 109,
    121, 143; cabinet use, 181–183, 195;
    and Nixon, 216, 219, 224, 225–226
Eisenhower, Milton, 64, 68, 85, 139, 181,
    226–227, 231, 298
elites, 47, 100, 101–102
Ellsberg break-in, 3, 14, 127
emergency powers, 8, 309
Employment Act of 1946, 15, 128
Ervin, Sam, 310, 313
evaluation: advice on, 65–66; of policy,
    242–243, 257–258; staff reform
    proposed, 273–279
Evans, Roland, 214
Ewing, Oscar, 70
executive, president as, 9, 10–11, 12,
    16–19, 118, 265–266
executive agreements, 7, 309
executive branch (see also staff, White
    House): effects of growth, 138–140;
    expansion of, 118–151; organization of,
    18–19
Executive Council, proposed, 180,
    267–268
Executive Office of the President, 118,
    155, 223, 311, 319, 326–327. See also
    staff, White House
executive orders, 118

executive privilege, 7, 309, 310–311
expectations, 41, 238–239, 248; disparity
with results, 4–5, 34–36, 106

Fairlie, Henry, 63, 73, 173, 186
Family Assistance Program, 169, 253
Federal Energy Administration, 68, 92,
189
Federal Reserve Board, 189, 195, 244
Federation of American Scientists, 243
Feldman, Meyer, 159, 203
Finch, Robert, 58, 196, 200
Finer, Herman, 263, 264
Fitzgerald, A. Ernest, 60–61
Flanigan, Peter, 56, 166
Ford, Gerald R., 4, 8, 13, 42, 43, 56, 73,
80, 127–128, 147–148, 222, 241, 245, 246,
303; appointees, 61, 68; and economic
policy, 15, 128–129; pardons Nixon,
43, 45; and reorganization, 67–68
foreign policy: aid agencies, 69;
dominance of, 12–13, 250; reform and,
263, 268–269, 309; staff for, 130–132
Forrestal, James, 132
Fowler, Henry H., 195–196
Frankel, Charles, 289
Frankel, Max, 75
Freeman, Orville, 161
Friedrich, Carl, 296
fuel crisis, 242, 252, 257

Gaither Committee, 64
Galbraith, John Kenneth, 62
Gardner, John W., 69, 159, 189, 191
Garment, Leonard, 14
Garner, John Nance, 212, 214, 222; and
FDR, 219, 225
General Accounting Office, 169, 172, 311
George, Alexander L., 31, 275–276
Goldberg, Arthur, 191
Goldwater, Barry, 147, 220
Gore, Albert, 214
government: expanded role, 18, 41,
170–171; grant programs, 101–102,
281–282; managing, 16–19
governors, 106–107, 280, 281, 283; route
to presidency, 11–12
Graham, Otis L., Jr., 278
Great Depression, 25, 121
Great Society, 4, 41, 96, 169, 240

Greenstein, Fred, 297
Griffis, Carolyn S., 78

Hacker, Andrew, 112
Hagerty, James, 138
Haig, Alexander, 7, 167, 201
Halberstam, David, 211, 225
Haldeman, H. R., 133, 142, 159, 185, 223
Halperin, Morton, 93
Hamilton, Alexander, 155–156, 178, 179,
266
Hand, Learned, 316
Harding, Warren G., 26, 223
Hargrove, Erwin, 31
Harlow, Bryce, 136, 196
Harriman, Averell, 174, 264, 265
Hatfield, Mark, 264
Heard, Alexander, 63
Heller, Walter, 197
Hendrick, Burton, 179
Herring, Pendleton, 38, 113
Hess, Stephen, 261
Hickel, Walter J., 60, 148, 176, 186, 189,
199, 200–201
Hodgson, James O., 59
Hofstadter, Richard, 38
Hollings, Ernest, 166
Holtzman, Abraham, 136
honeymoon period, 42, 108, 146, 149, 181
Hoover, Herbert, 26, 45, 188, 226, 250
Hopkins, Harry, 223, 267
Housing Act of 1958, 78
Howard, Anthony, 42
Hughes, Emmet J., 170, 191
Hull, Cordell, 224, 267
Humphrey, George M., 188, 192, 195
Humphrey, Hubert H., 122, 148, 225,
228; as vice president, 211, 215, 217,
221–222, 224
Hutchins, Robert, 319

Ickes, Harold, 267
impeachment, 293–294, 315, 317; of a
policy, 296, 317
Impoundment Control Act of 1974, 315
impoundment issue, 7, 308–309
income redistribution, 15
initiative, 295
inner cabinet, 191–192, 205; versatility
of, 196–197

interest groups, 281; as advocates, 243, 248; and competing policies, 14, 86; constraints of, 99–103; and departments, 19, 59, 67, 69–70, 71, 197, 272; and growth of presidency, 123–124

Jackson, Andrew, 48, 249, 303
Jackson, Robert, 322
Janis, Irving L., 56, 172, 275–276
Jaworski, Leon, 313
Jefferson, Thomas, 34, 43, 48, 178, 220, 223, 303
Johnson, Andrew, 293, 315
Johnson, Lyndon B., 8, 33, 36, 63, 78, 108, 109, 143–144, 145, 193, 245, 254, 263, 298, 300; activist, 4, 43, 143–144, 304; and advisers, 64, 131, 196–197; and cabinet, 60, 166, 186–187, 192, 201, 202, 207, 209 n. 19; as candidate, 31–32; and Congress, 87, 88, 107, 242; as executive, 17, 170; and foreign policy, 13; and media, 73, 75; and staff, 124–125, 126, 133, 170; as vice president, 184, 191, 211, 213–214, 219, 220–221, 225; and Vietnam, 45, 144, 165, 209 n. 19, 222, 297, 303, 305
Johnson, Sam Houston, 214
Jones, Jesse H., 224
Jordan, Len, 215

Kallenbach, Joseph, 79, 216–217
Katzenbach, Nicholas, 196
Kaufman, George S., 218
Kaufman, Herbert, 283
Kennedy, John F., 33, 53, 55, 58, 78, 143, 145, 148, 193, 214, 217, 313; activist, 4; and advisers, 61, 64, 121, 124–125, 130, 131–132, 170, 173, 196, 203; and cabinet, 166, 181, 183, 185–186, 191, 192, 194, 197, 200, 207, 268; as candidate, 31, 70–71, 79; and civil rights, 253; and Congress, 87, 89, 253; as executive, 16–17, 85; and foreign policy, 12–13, 297; and media, 72–73, 75, 320, 321; and missile crisis, 11, 39, 195, 252, 253, 307
Kennedy, Robert F., 11, 189, 191, 253
Kerr, Robert, 100
Key, V. O., Jr., 316

Kissinger, Henry, 40, 48, 148, 160–161, 193–194, 197, 264, 265
Klein, Herbert, 136, 159
Kleindienst, Richard, 311
Korean War, 39, 104, 252
Kranz, Harry, 324 n. 38
Kristol, Irving, 11
Krock, Arthur, 54
Krogh, Egil, 48–49

Laird, Melvin, 138, 196
Laski, Harold, 38, 85, 113, 182, 249
Lavelle, John D., 67
Law Enforcement Assistance Administration, 254–255
Leacacos, John, 193
leadership: and accountability, 7, 316–321; by consensus, 7, 9, 147; defined, 5; effectiveness, 5, 20, 257–258; and loyalty, 19; moral, 9–10, 18, 35, 44–45, 72, 239; in policy implementation, 5, 251–253, 254–256; political, 253–254; social reform, 109–113; symbolic, 10, 251–252, 257–258; vacuums, 104–105
legal counsel, 194–196
Liason Office for Personnel Management, 118
liberalism, 239
Liebling, A. J., 75
Lincoln, Abraham, 29, 33, 34, 43, 48, 113, 118, 150, 179, 249, 296
Lippmann, Walter, 298
Lowi, Theodore, 102, 309
loyalty, 139, 154, 155; aides, 159, 167; departmental, 157–159, 168; leadership and, 19; vice president, 221–222

MacArthur, Douglas, 60
McCarthy, Eugene, 35–36, 228
McCarthy, Joe, 313
McCormack, John, 211
McGinniss, Joe, 73
Machiavelli, Niccolo, 140, 145
Macmillan, Harold, 44
McNamara, Robert S., 130, 159, 161, 168, 188, 191, 192, 196
Magruder, Jeb Stuart, 103, 119, 126, 184, 289
Malek, Frederick, 79
Management By Objectives, 278

Mansfield, Mike, 135, 213, 298, 299
Marshall, George C., 188, 269
Marshall, Thomas R., 223
Marshall Plan, 39
Meany, George, 59, 169, 174
Meredith, James, 252, 253
Mills, C. Wright, 47
Mitchell, John M., 313
Model Cities, 41, 169
Moffett, Toby, 164
Mondale, Walter F., 180, 237, 311
monetary policy, 244
moral leadership, 9–10, 18, 35, 44–45, 72, 239
Morton, Rogers, 68
Moyers, Bill, 153, 159
Moynihan, Daniel P., 23, 62, 140, 164–165, 196

Nader, Ralph, 90, 243
National Aeronautics and Space Administration, 189
National Association of Home Builders, 71
National Commission on the Causes and Prevention of Violence, 64–65
National Resources Planning Board, 118
national security, 209 n. 27, 257; and cabinet, 192–194; Congress and, 14, 80; dominance of, 13–14, 250; staff for, 130–132
National Security Act of 1947, 224
National Security Council, 27, 121, 126, 132, 183, 193, 224
Navasky, Victor S., 66
Neighborhood Service Centers, 169
Neustadt, Richard E., 23, 29–30, 50 n. 16, 160, 174
New American Revolution, 4, 41
New Deal, 128, 240
New Federalism, 240, 254–255
New Frontier, 4, 214
New York Times, 42, 105
Nixon, Richard M., 8, 33, 44, 144, 146, 148, 176, 245, 246, 254–255, 303, 315; activist, 4, 43; advisers, 64–65, 132, 196–197; and Agnew, 219–220; appointees, 57, 61, 63; and cabinet, 17, 60, 180, 181, 187–188, 194, 199, 200–201, 253, 268, 270; and Congress, 79, 80, 87, 90, 253; and courts, 105–106; and

economic policy, 14–15, 129, 304; as executive, 17, 32, 92, 97–98, 120, 122, 193; and executive privilege, 310–311; and foreign policy, 13, 14, 40, 252; loyalty to, 56, 119, 167, 169; and media, 73, 74, 75, 137, 149, 150, 320; and reorganization, 66–67, 127, 135, 193, 206, 270, 285, 286; resignation, 7, 61, 293; and special interests, 100; staff, 125, 126, 130, 133, 137, 139, 167, 170; and veto power, 79, 80; as vice president, 219, 225–226; and Vietnam, 146–147, 243, 303
no confidence, vote of proposed, 294, 314–315, 317
Novak, Michael, 35, 228–229
Novak, Robert, 214
nuclear weapons, power re, 5, 7, 8, 25, 33

O'Brien, Lawrence, 136, 159
O'Donnell, Kenneth, 159
Office of Consumer Affairs, 121
Office of Counsel General, proposed, 312–313
Office of Economic Opportunity, 92, 105
Office of Government Reports, 118
Office of Management and Budget, 27, 129–130, 135, 169, 242, 269, 277, 283, 311
Office of Planning and Program Evaluation, proposed, 277–279
Office of Public Attorney, proposed, 313
Office of the Special Representation for Trade Negotiations, 128
Office of Technology Assessment, 277
Office of Telecommunications Policy, 137
Otten, Alan, 221
outer cabinet, 197–198, 205; isolation, 199–201, 269

patronage, 59, 285
Peabody, Endicott, 229
Peace Corps, 68
Pearson, Drew, 243
Pechman, Joseph, 77
People's Lobby, 295
Peterson, Peter, 148
planning and program evaluation staffs, reform proposed, 273–279

Planning, Programming and Budgeting System (PPBS), 188, 272, 278–279
politician, president as, 8–9, 250; campaigning, 10–11; party leader, 253–254; personalization and, 31, 43
politics: abstention from, 301–304; citizens and, 46–47, 295, 319–321; need for strong parties, 318–319; presidents and, 8–9, 10–11, 36–37, 250, 253–254, 300, 301–304
Polk, James K., 78
Polsby, Nelson, 90, 307–308
Powell, Lewis, 57
power(s): abuses of, 7, 25, 43, 157, 245, 302; appointments, 55–61; constraints on, 86–114; debate re, 6–7, 243–245, 248–249; emergency, 8, 309; expanded, 2, 24; reorganization, 66–72; textbooks on, 26–30; of veto, 76–81
presidency: analysis of, 19–21; confidence in strained, 2, 4–5, 8, 24; crisis and, 54–55, 121–122, 240, 252, 257–258, 266; decentralized, 86, 120; defining, 5, 6; growth of, 118–151; heritage esteemed, 29, 34–35, 43, 48; insuring accountability, 293–315; job description, 250–258; lavishness, 312; myths re, 42–43, 100; paradoxes, 6–10; personalized, 30–32, 41–44; reform, 243–249, 262–287, 298–306; roles, 7, 9; textbook view of, 24–41, 45–49, 88–89, 106, 248
Presidential Power (Neustadt), 29–30, 50 n. 16
presidentialists, 155–161
presidents, 325–326; advisers to, 61–66, 128–151, 264–265; appointments by, 55–61, 108–109; and bureaucracy, 91–99, 122, 246, 248; feedback, 256–257; functions, 4; idealized image, 25–33, 72, 140–151, 248; isolation, 2–3, 292, 302; as politician, 8–11, 31, 43, 250, 253–254, 292, 300, 301–304; power excess, 2, 24; and public opinion, 106–114; and public relations, 72–76, 140–151, 238; reorganization by, 66–72, 92; restrictions on, 2, 17, 54–81, 86–114; travels, 14, 42, 137, 147–148, 252; and veto, 76–81; and vice presidents, 148, 218–222
President's Committee on Administrative Management, 117

press, 41, 149; aides, 137–138; conferences, 74, 320–321, 324 n. 38; need for vigorous, 243, 292, 317, 319; and personalization of president, 32; relations with, 74–76
Price, David, 90
Pritchett, Herman, 104
professionals, government, 94–95, 284; White House staff and, 19, 154
Proxmire, William, 60
Public Citizen, Inc., 243
public opinion, 291–292, 298; constraint on president, 106–114; shaping, 140–151
public policy: competing areas, 12–16; coordinating, 282–283; defined, 5; formation of, 107, 124–126, 165–166, 195, 241–243, 251–252, 257–258
public relations, 72–76; staff for, 137–138

Rayburn, Sam, 135
recall, 295
recession, 15, 128–129
recruitment process: cabinet, 159, 179, 197; presidents, 11–12
Reedy, George E., 48, 73–74, 158, 159, 180, 268, 304
referenda, 294–298; defined, 295; shortcomings of, 296–298
reforms, proposed, 86, 156–157; cabinet, 180, 268–273; collegial presidency, 263–268; Congress, 277; presidency, 243–249, 262–287, 298–306; six-year term, 298–306; structural, 3, 206, 262–287; vice presidency, 215–218, 226–233
regionalized presidency, proposed, 279–283
reorganization power, 66–72
reprogramming, 7
Reston, James, 44
Richardson, Elliot, 61, 148, 159, 196
Rivlin, Alice, 101
Rockefeller, David, 174
Rockefeller, Nelson, 31, 56, 127–128, 194, 211, 217, 222, 282
Rogers, William, 193, 196
Romney, George, 112
Roosevelt, Franklin D., 24, 25, 33, 34, 39, 44, 73, 75, 77, 79–80, 146, 183, 214, 215, 217, 249, 250, 265, 267, 296; activism,

Roosevelt, Franklin D. (*Continued*)
38, 68, 113, 118, 173; and Congress, 87,
88, 89; as executive, 18, 198, 246, 278;
and Garner, 219, 225; and Supreme
Court, 87; and Henry Wallace, 223–
224, 225
Roosevelt, Theodore, 33, 34, 44, 147
Ross, Arthur, 66
Rossiter, Clinton, 28–29, 72, 296
Rostow, Walt, 40, 130
Roszak, Theodore, 308
Rourke, Francis, 67
Ruckelshaus, William, 60
Rumsfeld, Donald, 138, 196
Rusk, Dean, 40, 131, 159, 168, 186, 187,
191, 192, 193, 197
Ryskind, Morrie, 218

Sawhill, John, 61, 68
Schick, Allen, 81
Schlesinger, Arthur, Jr., 39, 91, 156, 168,
212, 220, 221, 227, 231, 245, 249, 289
Schultze, Charles, 280
Scigliano, Robert, 56
Scranton, William, 64
secrecy, 7, 14, 122, 149, 302, 307, 309
Senate, 106–107; route to presidency,
11–12; vice presidency and, 213–218
Sevareid, Eric, 263–264
Sharkansky, Ira, 282
Shultz, George, 128, 140, 188, 192,
201
Sidey, Hugh, 75
Sierra Club, 243
Silk, Leonard, 195
Simon, William, 192, 195
Sirica, John, 106, 243
six-year term, proposed, 298–306, 322 *n.*
15; shortcomings, 301–304
Sorenson, Theodore, 39, 59, 62, 159,
185–186, 191, 196, 197, 203, 212, 245,
249
special elections, proposed, 315
Sputnik, 121, 252
staff, White House, 40, 159; administrative, 132-135; and cabinet, 184, 199,
202–205; and conflict, 161–171, 202–205;
and Congress, 88, 135–136; and departments, 130–131, 153–175, 199, 202–205,
270; differentiated, 16, 124–138; and
government professionals, 19, 122; and

policy formation, 165–166; recruitment,
159; textbooks on, 27
Stans, Maurice, 166
State of the Union addresses, 13
Stimson, Henry, 196, 267
Sundquist, James, 89, 281, 294, 314
Supreme Court, 106–107; appointees,
56–57, 103; under Burger, 105–106;
constraint on president, 103-106, 292,
296; FDR and, 87, 104; under Warren,
104–105, 106
symbolic leadership, 10, 251–252, 257,
258; reform and, 263, 265–266

taxation policy, 15, 77, 101, 112; Congress
and, 89, 244
Teacher Corps, 169
television, 33, 41, 72–73, 150, 295;
debates criticized, 319–320; and
elections, 42; public, 243
terHorst, Jerald, 61
textbooks, view of presidency, 24–33,
49 *n.* 1, 88–89, 106, 248; authors' aims,
37–39; dimensions of exaggeration,
32–33; origins of, 33–41; sources,
39–40; and veto power, 77
Thirteen Days (Kennedy), 253
travels, foreign, 14, 42, 137, 147–148,
252
Truman, David, 157
Truman, Harry S, 10, 19, 25, 39, 57, 60,
62, 73, 75, 91, 104, 109, 142, 149, 181,
214, 237, 305, 312
Tuchman, Barbara, 43
Tugwell, Rexford G., 53, 261, 263, 278,
279

United States vs. *Richard M. Nixon*, 105,
310

Valenti, Jack, 159, 299
Vanderbilt, Arthur, 57
Veterans Administration, 189
veto power, 76–81; bureaucrats, 93–96
vice presidency, 211–233; ignominy of,
212; loyalty to president, 221–222;
president of Senate, 213–218;
president's role for, 148; proposals re,
215–218, 226–233; route to presidency,

11–12, 217, 231; "Throttlebottom complex," 218–222; travels, 224–225
vice presidents, 232–233
Vietnam, 3, 24, 45, 54, 143, 149, 165, 189, 192, 205, 290, 297, 305 (see also Cambodia); Congress and, 113, 121, 307, 309; Mylai coverup, 76; opposition to policy, 58, 209 n. 19, 222, 225; politics and, 303–304; secret bombings, 14, 40, 67, 121, 239; Tonkin resolution, 113
Vinson, Fred, 192

Wallace, George, 249, 281, 321
Wallace, Henry, 206, 223–224, 225, 267
war-making power, 7, 121, 315
Warren, Earl, 57, 104, 232
Washington, George, 34, 43, 118, 178, 192, 219, 223
Washington Monthly, 243
Watergate, 3, 7, 11, 24, 26, 41, 76, 80, 96, 105–106, 113, 119, 127, 142, 146, 149, 172, 239, 299, 307, 312

Weaver, Robert C., 71
Webster, Daniel, 212
White, Byron, 57
White, Theodore, 14, 28, 32, 212, 221
White House Labor-Management Committee, 128
Wildavsky, Aaron, 53, 143–144, 161, 230, 274–275
Williams, Irving, 222
Wills, Garry, 249
Wilson, Woodrow, 5, 33, 45, 88, 113, 118, 182, 296, 298, 301
WIN program, 4, 41, 73, 169
wiretapping, 7, 122
Wolfinger, Raymond, 297
Wood, Robert C., 158–159
World War II, 25, 38, 121, 252

Youngstown Sheet & Tube Co. vs. Sawyer, 104

Zeigler, Ronald, 159